Entering the Academic Conversation

Entering the Academic Conversation

Strategies for Research Writing

John Charles Goshert
Utah Valley University

Longman

Boston   Columbus   Indianapolis   New York   San Francisco
Upper Saddle River   Amsterdam   Cape Town   Dubai   London   Madrid   Milan
Munich   Paris   Montreal   Toronto   Delhi   Mexico City   Sao Paulo   Sydney
Hong Kong   Seoul   Singapore   Taipei   Tokyo

Senior Acquisitions Editor: Suzanne Phelps Chambers
Editorial Assistant: Laney Whitt
Development Editor: David Kear
Senior Supplements Editor: Donna Campion
Senior Marketing Manager: Sandra McGuire
Senior Media Producer: Stefanie Liebman
Project Manager: Barbara Mack
Project Coordination, Text Design, and Electronic Page Makeup:
     PreMediaGlobal
Operations Specialist: Mary Ann Gloriande
Art Director, Cover: Anne Nieglos
Cover Designer: Joseph DePinho
Cover Photos: Shutterstock Images: Monkey Business Images; michaeljung;
     Viktoriya; Kenneth V. Pilon; Onur Ersin; dslaven. Superstock: Blend
     Images; Exactostock
Printer and Binder: Courier/North Chelmsford
Cover Printer: Courier/North Chelmsford

For permission to use copyrighted material, grateful acknowledgment
is made to the copyright holders on pages 486–487, which are hereby
made part of this copyright page.

Library of Congress Cataloging-in-Publication Data

Control number is on record at the Library of Congress.

ISBN-13: 978-0-13-243597-0
ISBN-10: 0-13-243597-7

2 3 4 5 6 7 8 9 10—V092—15 14 13

Longman
Prentice Hall
are imprints of

www.pearsonhighered.com

For Numsiri, who made it possible

Contents

CHAPTER 6   Incorporate Source Material into Your Writing   120

CHAPTER 7   Prepare Bibliographies   143

PART THREE   A RESEARCH DOSSIER

CHAPTER 13   Research Dossier: Six Readings on Surveillance   352

PART FOUR   FINAL PRODUCT

CHAPTER 14   Designing, Organizing, and Editing Your Research Writing Projects   429

Preface

Entering the Academic Conversation combines instruction in rhetoric with a sequence of assignments to guide students into academic research writing. The text introduces students to academic discourse as an inquiry-guided conversation about ideas and helps them see how scholarship can touch on any issue, idea, or question they might bring to the classroom. Together, rhetorical instruction and writing assignments invite students to locate and enter into one or more academic conversations as engaged participants rather than as observers.

This text emphasizes the role and value of scholarship in the academic enterprise, explicates the skills needed for reading and responding to scholarly prose, and gives sustained attention to research technologies available to all schools today. Its sequence of assignments is clearly scaffolded—building and connecting together manageable research writing practices that culminate in a formal research argument. The book provides instructors with the tools and resources they need to engage students in academic conversations across the disciplines and introduces students to core skills and strategies to help them become more effective research writers in college and beyond.

PARTS OF THE BOOK

Rhetorical Instruction—Part One: The Academic Conversation

Part One (Chapters 1–7), "The Academic Conversation," provides rhetorical instruction designed to help students engage in academic thinking, reading, and research practices. Together, the chapters in Part One offer recursive coverage of core skills:

1. Illustrating critical thinking and inquiry as the foundations of academic work
2. Reading and responding actively to texts

3. Developing and refining research questions
4. Performing academic research with special focus on scholarship
5. Using and documenting source materials purposefully

Each chapter includes readings and brief writing assignments that help students participate in academic conversations across the disciplines.

Assignment Sequence—Part Two: Research Writing Projects

Part Two (Chapters 8–12), "Research Writing Projects," is a sequence of assignments designed to help students engage purposefully with writing practices common to academic research across the disciplines. Focusing on process, and identifying core strategies and component skills, assignments help students break large projects into manageable chunks. Each chapter in Part Two incorporates common features that guide students through their writing projects:

1. Project goals and outcomes
2. Accessible examples of student, professional, and academic writing
3. Activities that identify skills and strategies for successful drafting
4. Research pitfalls that help students avoid common mistakes
5. Detailed guidelines for peer review
6. Complete, representative student essays

The five assignments work together to give students a scaffolded approach to research writing that builds upon and integrates core skills over the course. Together, the book's two parts help students see the process of entering academic conversations as both manageable and personally rewarding.

Thematic Reader—Part Three: A Research Dossier

Part Three (Chapter 13), "Six Readings on Surveillance," is a selection of professional and academic research articles. These articles introduce students to the ways in which a question, concept, or current issue may be examined through various disciplinary perspectives. Personal reflections by authors on the inquiry and research processes that went into the finished work introduce these readings. By reflecting on strategies of developing a research question, incorporating research materials into an argument, and the value of revision and peer review, professional authors provide novice researchers with an unprecedented view behind the scenes of published research projects. Accompanying each of these readings is an introductory note that describes the academic field and major themes covered by the writers. Questions following the readings encourage students to reflect on key aspects of writers' arguments, consider the rhetorical strategies they use, and identify recurring themes to help them make connections between two or more readings.

Handbook—Part Four: Final Product

Part Four (Chapter 14), "Designing, Organizing, and Editing Your Research Writing Projects," is a brief handbook that introduces students to the conventions of design and formatting; provides sustained coverage of argument, purpose, organization, and development; and addresses challenges in voice, style, mechanics, and usage faced by many students in first-year writing courses. Illustrations and references in the handbook recall sample student and professional writing used throughout the text.

SUPPORT FOR INSTRUCTORS

An instructor's manual, *Strategies and Resources for Teaching Entering the Academic Conversation*, is available as a download from Pearson.com to help you design and teach a course using this text. The first part of the manual describes ways of planning a course with *EAC*, including:

- Anticipating ways to pace the text over terms of various lengths
- Organizing and sequencing chapters
- Using, supplementing, and replacing sample readings.

The second part of the manual is a chapter-by-chapter description of goals and teaching strategies. Based on piloting experiences, these chapter descriptions also help instructors anticipate and resolve questions students may have while working through the text.

Other instructional resources are available through Pearson.com, including access to MyCompLab.

ACKNOWLEDGMENTS

Special thanks to the first members of the team: Shannon Howard, my local sales representative for Pearson, and Paul Crockett, my acquisitions editor at Pearson. Shannon and Paul were incredibly generous with their time and support as they listened to my ideas and goals for this book. Paul's interest and confidence in the project provided it with a home at Pearson, and he helped guide me through the proposal and early stages of the manuscript. Shannon's considerable knowledge about the publishing industry and processes of development and review—coupled with her willingness to provide advice and support—helped me navigate the often baffling process of textbook writing through its many stages. Development editor Karen Mauk provided valuable insights as the first draft took shape and worked its way through the peer review and revision process. Later, Suzanne Phelps Chambers graciously took over the editorial role and continued to support the project as it took final shape. Her observations, questions, and advice—all offered with admirable patience and professionalism—made the final product possible.

Thanks to interns and teaching assistants Travis "Grabbo" Low, Joe Pritchard, Jen Allen, Jared Colton, Whitney Mower, and Whitney Nelson, who have all made profound contributions to the development of the book's activities and instructional support.

My faculty colleagues have always been willing to take the time to share ideas and strategies, offer advice and feedback on early drafts of this text, and pilot the book in their own writing courses. Specifically, I would like to acknowledge the generous support and feedback of Amy Parsons (University of Wisconsin at Platteville) and Janet Neary (Hunter College) for piloting an earlier version of the text. Thanks also to Holly Rawlings and Marcia Smith, who class tested assignment sequences in their formative stages. My colleagues in UVU's writing program administration, Grant Moss and Gae Lyn Henderson, provide ongoing energy and insight into the teaching of writing, and—just as importantly—into ways of supporting writing teachers to help all students successfully enter the academic conversation. Thanks to other faculty colleagues who have contributed their time and support to me as this book developed over the past few years: Robert Cousins, Christa Albrecht-Crane, Doug Downs, Brian Whaley, Steve Gibson, Mark Crane, and Ryan Simmons.

I also received some excellent advice and assistance from a number of colleagues at one point or another in the development of this book: Joe Carrithers, Fullerton College; Kelly Kinney, University of Notre Dame; Cheryl Wilson, Indiana University of Pennsylvania; Sharon Walsh, Loyola University Chicago; Kevin DePew, Old Dominion University; Anne Balay, University of Illinois at Chicago; Susan Miller-Cochran, North Carolina State University; Wendy Austin, Edinboro University of Pennsylvania; James Allen, College of DuPage; Anne Williams, Indiana University-Purdue University Indianapolis; Gwen Argersinger, Mesa Community College at Red Mountain; Tami Haaland, Montana State University-Billings; David Mauricio, Hawaii Pacific University; Holly Hunt, Metropolitan State College of Denver; Mark Crane, Utah Valley State College; Kristina Leonard, Metropolitan State College of Denver; and Doug Downs, Utah Valley State College.

The hard work and feedback of my Utah Valley University students ensured that this text benefitted from sustained class testing. Some have their contributions represented, in some cases pseudonymously, by sample readings and student voices that appear throughout the text. Other students contributed equally strong work and commentary that could not be included in this edition. Students at piloting institutions also provided valuable feedback about the text. Thanks to each and every one of you. Special thanks to Darryl McAllister, John Gunders, Nancy Nisbet, Chris Taylor and Annabelle James, Nick King, and Gary Marx. Their personal reflections on academic writing add valuable depth and context to their published work.

Thanks to Doug Ybarra and Anton Yakovlev at Pearson Learning Solutions for producing an earlier version of the text for class piloting. Thanks to local and regional Pearson representatives Andy Draa, Steve Foster, Amber Gardner, and Barbara McCann.

My final, and greatest, thanks to Numsiri Cindy Kunakemakorn, who listened to every idea, read every manuscript, and managed every crisis. This book wouldn't be possible without you.

Introduction

Conversations provide us with opportunities to hear others' ideas, to explain our ideas, and invent altogether new ideas. What kinds of conversations are important in your college experience? Are they formal, informal, or both? Where do they take place?

When we read, write, and work with fellow students, instructors, and others, we can use their voices to guide us in adjusting, revising, reinforcing, and even abandoning, our own ideas.

THE ACADEMIC CONVERSATION

Take a moment to imagine the work a researcher does when he or she prepares and writes a report, an article, or a book to share with colleagues and other readers. Imagine a scholar, perhaps one of your own instructors, who conducts research and makes presentations to students and colleagues, publishes papers and books, and engages in other professional activities. If you're like many students, one of the first images that comes to mind is of an isolated thinker working (and probably struggling) in solitude. This is a common assumption about academic activity especially among students

Research is a social activity.

Computers are now an essential part of our learning process and our very sense of how we interact with others. And yet, even as computers give us access to a vast world of communication and information, face-to-face interaction remains important.

beginning their academic careers. In this book, you gain a new perspective and approach on academic work as a process of research and writing, and a collaborative, social activity. This book is intended to help students like you see academic reading and writing as a conversation in which you are invited to participate. This book encourages you to think of research as a way to build deep connections with experts in an academic field and with your peers in- and outside the classroom. In other words, this book provides skills and strategies that allow you to enter the *academic conversation*. This term means the various ways that members of the academic community interact, communicate, and cooperate with each other to share information, explore ideas, test old knowledge, develop new knowledge, and build connections between fields.

Skills you learn here work together to give you a voice in the conversation.

These academic conversations take place anywhere: in formal settings between scholars and students in the classroom, in lectures, in conferences, and the like. They also take place in informal locations such as restaurants, coffee shops, and even the local bar. Most importantly, however, they take place through the *exchange of texts*, as members of the academic community share their written contributions to the conversation.

This book invites you into the academic community by letting you discover and practice the techniques of reading and writing that make up academic discourse.

FROM OBSERVATION TO ENGAGEMENT

Practice in academic research writing will help you meet the demands of your major or future profession and positively impact your college experiences. The work you do here also has the power to make all your life pursuits more rewarding. This book introduces you to *academic habits of mind* that are valuable no matter how long you pursue your academic career beyond this course. These habits of mind include a willingness to wrestle with difficult questions, an ability to weigh a variety of positions and perspectives on an issue, and a desire to participate in the construction of knowledge.

Acquire "academic habits of mind."

Thinking like an academic allows you to converse with other members of a community by listening, responding, and exchanging ideas with them. You'll no longer be a passive outsider, but instead become a contributing participant in a community of engaged thinkers.

You also learn to manage the task of academic research writing. This book is designed to develop critical decision-making skills that let you organize the research–writing process into *component parts*:

- Keeping your topics and research manageable
- Determining an appropriate scope for your project
- Gathering sources appropriate to your academic field
- Reading specialized material
- Analyzing and synthesizing multiple sources
- Incorporating sources into your writing
- Developing an argument through research

Critical decision making will help you become more comfortable with participating in the discussions and debates taking place around you, and in the academic conversations you wish to join.

Finally, this book encourages you to develop your own interests— issues important to your major or anticipated profession, or any everyday issue that makes you curious—into questions that can be explored by the academic world's discourse communities. In general, a "discourse community"

Pursue your own interests through research.

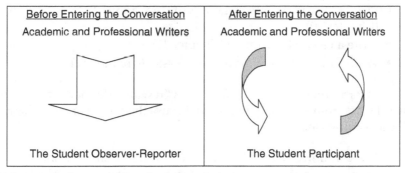

Before Entering the Conversation	After Entering the Conversation
Academic and Professional Writers	Academic and Professional Writers
The Student Observer-Reporter	The Student Participant

Before and after entering the conversation.

is made of people who share a unique way of looking at the world and a particular language for talking about it. They may be skateboarders, sports car enthusiasts, scuba divers, or elementary school teachers. Academic discourse communities develop within particular fields, such as organic chemistry, analytic philosophy, geriatric nursing, hotel management, speech pathology, and mechanical engineering, to name a few.

ORGANIZATION OF *ENTERING THE ACADEMIC CONVERSATION*

This book is divided into four parts that build skills *sequentially*. You should plan to use the parts *recursively* as well, reviewing and revising important concepts and skills as necessary.

In Part One, Chapters 1 through 7 develop academic habits to:

- Identify the important characteristics of academic conversations (Chapter 1)
- Read sources for information (Chapter 2)
- Practice reading and responding to academic texts (Chapter 3)
- Identify an issue and begin the research process (Chapter 4)
- Locate and evaluate sources for research writing projects (Chapter 5)
- Integrate sources into your research writing (Chapter 6)
- Add a bibliography and explanatory notes to your writing projects (Chapter 7)

In Part Two, Chapters 8 through 12 develop interrelated writing skills, which build toward a formal research essay. These chapters show you how to:

- Define an academic term or concept (Chapter 8)
- Summarize and engage with an academic text (Chapter 9)

- Plan a research project and write an annotated bibliography (Chapter 10)
- Write a research narrative (Chapter 11)
- Write a formal academic research essay (Chapter 12)

In Part Three, Chapter 13 features a "research dossier" of readings by scholars from six disciplines who discuss the theme of surveillance. These readings include:

- "Law Enforcement Turns to Face-Recognition Technology," in which a California police commander Darryl McAllister researches the use of face recognition technologies to solve and prevent crime
- "'Here's Lookin' at You': Video Surveillance and the Interpellated Body," in which philosopher John Gunders examines the social effects of public surveillance cameras
- "The Influence of Anxiety: September 11, Bioterrorism, and American Public Health," in which medical historian Nick King explores uses of surveillance techniques to control public health crises
- "Resisting Surveillance: Identity and Implantable Microchips," in which professional artist Nancy Nisbet increases her audience's awareness of surveillance techniques in everyday life
- "Video Games: Some Pitfalls of Video Evidence," in which legal scholars Chris Taylor and Annabelle James raise concerns about the uses of video evidence in criminal cases
- "What's New about the 'New Surveillance'," in which sociologist Gary Marx challenges old definitions of surveillance to account for recent technological developments, describes their social effects, and imagines ways to challenge them.

Each of these readings is accompanied by the authors' personal reflections on the process of invention, research, and writing that lead to the final versions included in this part. These insights into the writing process will be an inspiration and guide to as you develop your ideas and draft your research projects.

Part Four, Chapter 14, is a guide to help you write effective research papers. This part covers:

- Document design, formatting, and ways to incorporate visual elements (such as tables, graphs, and images) into your writing projects
- Elements of argument and patterns of organization to ensure well-made claims and purposeful development of your writing projects

- Strategies for writing and revising, including coverage of paragraphs, sentences, word choice, voice, style, and punctuation

The steps outlined in each of these parts work together to help you develop the moves that make participation in the academic conversation manageable and rewarding. Your participation through this course, your college career, and beyond, renews the academic conversation and prepares the ground for the participants who will follow you in courses and years to come. Finally, and perhaps most importantly, you will have the opportunity to extend the academic conversation beyond your college classrooms as a way of enlivening every facet of your life.

1

Seeing the Academic Conversation

CHAPTER OBJECTIVES

In this chapter, you'll learn to:

- See academic thinking and writing as a conversation
- Identify key traits of academic conversations
- Value process and inquiry—"making" knowledge—through research
- Relate your own personal and professional interests to an academic conversation

---

A cademic conversations emerge from an ongoing give-and-take process among people who are passionately interested in exploring ideas. Writers research in order to share their curiosity about the world and wrestle with questions raised by others. Each academic conversation involves a community, which draws members together based on shared interests—like nursing, physics, education, economics, or law—and which survives on critical questions and an exchange of ideas.

Are you feeling apprehensive about beginning a research writing course? If so, you're certainly not alone. Think for a moment about your past experiences and the kinds of preconceptions you have about research writing. How have those experiences shaped your current perceptions about the course you're beginning? You may share some of the concerns listed by students in previous classes:

- Writing with sources means writing impersonally.
- I don't have any good ideas to research and write about.
- I can't possibly fill eight to ten (or however many) pages.
- Facts are always true, and not subject to debate.
- Research writing isn't creative.
- Disagreements between experts are resolved when one side wins and the other loses.
- Research writing is most successful when it follows all the rules.

Activity 1: Identify Your Interests

Before we continue, take a few minutes to consider at least three ideas or issues that interest you. Have you read about a current event in print or online that sparks your curiosity? In a recent class, have you discussed an issue that you'd like to explore in more depth? Do you have questions about a career path you've been considering, or do you know of any important issues in your anticipated profession?

As you think about these issues, jot down some notes describing what you already know about them, where (or among whom) a discussion or debate is happening, and which issues you'd like to find out more about.

Describe three issues that interest you. These issues might be:

- **Academic:** From a recent class or related to your academic major
- **Professional:** Related to work you have done or intend to do after college
- **Personal:** Related to your cultural, social, or political interests
- Any combination of the three

For each issue you choose, clearly introduce it, and then write a couple of sentences describing what you already know about it and why it's interesting.

CHOOSING AN ACADEMIC CONVERSATION TO ENTER

This book will help you build on past experiences in order to continue your academic journey and increase your comfort with reading and writing in the academic community. You'll see how the research and writing needed to enter an academic conversation is not a single

---

Student Voice

Julia describes overcoming one of her apprehensions about beginning a research writing course.

> *In past research writing I've done, I've had a hard time "entering the conversation." I think one reason I struggled was my avoidance of writing about anything personally meaningful to me, since I was taught never to use "I" in a research paper. But now I realize that I can write about things that are important to me and assert what I believe about them because my voice matters as much as my sources. Really, learning about the research conversation helped show me ways of making issues meaningful to me also meaningful to my readers. When I do use "I" now, it refers to me speaking as a member of the conversation instead of as a lone voice.*

---

hurdle to overcome. Instead, participating in academic conversations is a process made up of interrelated parts, or skills, that together lead to enjoyable and productive work.

Some students have been convinced by previous experiences that they simply aren't "writers." You may also wonder about the relevance of research writing to your major, to your anticipated profession, and other issues of "real life." Students often come to a course sharing some or all of these concerns:

- How do I come up with a good topic for my project?
- Once I come up with a topic, how do I actually do the research?
- How do I find useful sources?
- How can I research efficiently, so I don't spend all of my time in the library?
- How will I meet requirements for length and number of sources?

Some students don't like research writing, saying simply, "I don't know how to do it." Like many of us, this kind of student connects research with report writing and is rarely committed to the topics being reported and is rarely asked to develop genuinely interesting questions from those topics.

Connect your interests to research

In contrast, the writing projects in this book are set up to help you connect your own interests to the goals of research writing. Making the process relevant to your interests and goals keeps ideas fresh and compelling; a question that genuinely interests you will help sustain your energy throughout the research and writing process. When the process is manageable it becomes more pleasurable and productive, by giving you a sense of accomplishment as you complete various parts along the way and by letting you see how those parts work together.

Even though your instructor will assist you in pursuing research questions that are close to your own interests, he or she will also shape readings and assignments to best serve your writing class. Make sure that you are aware of special requirements, and be sure to keep them in mind as you work your way through the book.

CHALLENGING FAMILIAR IDEAS THROUGH ACADEMIC CONVERSATION

The phrase "I think therefore I am" is instantly recognizable to many college students. We may hear the phrase and agree or disagree, but we rarely think about the critical questions that motivated it. We are seldom asked to reflect on its source and significance; instead, we tend to think about the claim as a self-contained and objective statement.

Academic habits of mind encourage us to question truths.

The same could be said for many ideas and claims. Because of their familiarity, we tend to simply accept them as self-evident, as obvious, or as natural. Yet, each of these ideas contains a world of questions and competing ideas that create a dialogue, a critical conversation that emerges once we scratch the surface. By learning the academic habits of mind in this text, you will begin to spark investigations beneath the surface of accepted ideas.

We want you to think in the complex ways valued in the academic community, and to engage with complexity in your own writing. The process we explore here helps you to *problematize* ideas as they work in academic conversations. To "problematize" is to accept uncertainty and seek new challenges even as we seek to answer a question or understand an issue. We want you to challenge the notions that research writing is detached and objective, or that your role is simply to discover and report facts to readers. While the kinds of writing you'll do here are intensely academic, and often quite traditional, they are also intensely personal. You'll see a role, and even a requirement, for your own creative engagement with the questions and texts on which you choose to focus your research.

Integrate the personal and academic through creative engagement.

The rhetorician Kenneth Burke describes the importance of placing familiar ideas in a new light. Academic thinkers are interested in *defamiliarizing* ideas so that they become topics for an active discussion in which we participate without having to come up with the last word.

> *Defamiliarizing is the process of making familiar ideas foreign.*

The conversation about ideas is like a gathering to which we arrive late:

> When you arrive, others have long preceded you, and they are engaged in a heated discussion, a discussion too heated for them to pause and tell you exactly what it is about. In fact, the discussion had already begun long before any of them got there, so that no one present is qualified to retrace for you all the steps that had gone before. You listen for a while, until you decide that you have caught the tenor of the argument; then you decide to put in your oar. Someone answers; you answer him; another comes to your defense; another aligns himself against you, to either the embarrassment or gratification of your opponent, depending on the quality of your ally's assistance. However, the discussion is interminable. The hour grows late, you must depart, with the discussion still vigorously in progress.[1]

Even though you may not find all of your college classrooms quite as stimulating as this gathering, we can see how each class, each idea, and each question you encounter in your academic journey leads into ongoing conversations. You are invited to build familiarity with those conversations—developing what is called *academic literacy*—and to contribute to them in turn.

For example, think about how legal scholars, legislators, and judges are constantly engaged in revisiting and reviewing ideas within their conversations. Especially in recent decades we have seen a renewed interest among many Americans in the Constitution, which has led to conversations surrounding gay marriage amendments at state and national levels, debates over the renewal of the 1965 Voting Rights Act, challenges to state referenda, and concerns about the legal standing of prisoners of war. These issues have helped sustain over two centuries of conversations among Americans and others about the Constitution and the many texts that surround it.

> *Academic knowledge is created through conversations.*

BUILDING ACADEMIC LITERACY

Research writers are critical thinkers who are committed to participating in a dialogue with fellow researchers, and who see information as the foundation for informed and credible work. Their personal

Academic literacy is the ability to read, write, and engage in a discipline.

commitments and passions provide the inspiration for much of the work they do, especially when they risk making new contributions to their conversations.

As we begin our own research journeys, it's important to see how academic literacy—the ability to read, write, and engage in a discipline—grows as much from our conversations about ideas as it does from just the memorization of facts and theories. We can also see how knowledge is *created* through the particular languages and ways of thinking valued within each conversation. The Constitutional conversations about gay marriage, for instance, will be differently "embedded" among economists, historians, legal scholars, theologians, and others. Whether we are thinking about philosophy during the 1600s, scientific examinations of global climate change, or a critical essay on *Harry Potter* books, we can see how any idea can take shape within the academic community and go on to spark further inquiry and conversation.

THINKING CRITICALLY INSIDE ACADEMIC CONVERSATIONS

Inquiry combines critical thinking and questioning.

Academic writers seek to explore questions and problems that genuinely challenge them. In this light, we see academic writing as open-ended and *process*-oriented rather than closed and focused only on the *product* of research. Because it values inquiry, academic work does not focus on generally available informational resources like newspapers and the Internet, nor does it always appeal to audiences outside the academic world. Instead, academics focus on building the *specialized knowledge* of one or more academic disciplines—scholarly conversations in the sciences, in the humanities, in medicine, and others.

Shifting focus from product to process helps us see research writing as a *step-by-step journey* that begins with an idea or question; acknowledges your own preconceptions and values; explores ideas in conversation with others; and contributes to the conversation.

Because the ways you choose to explore issues and persuade others of the value of your work are often as significant as the issues themselves, we focus not only on building the subject matter of your research, but also on its *rhetorical aspects*. These rhetorical aspects include:

- **Purpose:** Why am I writing?
- **Audience:** Who is going to read my writing?
- **Genre:** What kind of writing will present my argument most convincingly?

You may expect that research projects assigned in your courses are really reports. At first, many of us focus our energy on accumulating data and incorporating information from websites, books, and articles, with the purpose of producing the number of pages, number of sources, or number of quotations required by our instructors. This approach to projects is more concerned with meeting requirements than with creatively exploring what to say and how to say it. Although the reporting mode of research writing has an important place in the process, we go further and focus on wrestling with content through critical thinking.

It can be liberating to escape the report model because no longer are you limited to simply reproducing what has already been written or said about an issue. As the Brazilian education scholar Paulo Friere recognized, the "banking method" of education reflects that reproductive model, and asks for very little in the way of invention, engagement, or substantial contribution from writers.[2] As you make your escape from the banking method, you will be encouraged to:

Focus on content and critical thinking.

- discover what has already been written or said;
- develop ways in which information becomes uniquely significant to you; and
- shape information in response to a particular question you're interested in pursuing.

AS YOU READ:

✓ Connect ideas from research to your own interests.

✓ Question familiar ideas and claims.

✓ Engage with research as a meaningful process.

✓ Ask questions and make new connections.

As you develop an inquiry-based approach to thinking and writing, you will deepen your personal investment in your work. You will also face new rhetorical responsibilities that the report writer rarely has to think about, such as:

- Choosing from a wide range of possible approaches and genres for your writing projects
- Shaping projects according to your own purpose and the conventions of your research field
- Addressing the needs, interests, and prior knowledge of your audience

WRITING TO SEEK
"MORE INTERESTING PROBLEMS"

Academic writers are engaged in an ongoing, *recursive* process of inquiry, analysis, and critical thinking. Philosopher Karl Popper described a conversational model for scientific work that showed that as we learn more about ideas our knowledge may become less certain:

> Our ignorance is sobering and boundless. Indeed, it is precisely the staggering progress of the natural sciences . . . which constantly opens our eyes anew to our ignorance, even in the field of the natural sciences themselves . . . . With each step forward, with each problem which we solve, we not only discover new and unsolved problems, but we also discover that where we believed that we were standing on firm and safe ground, all things are, in truth, insecure and in a state of flux.[3]

Think about the ways in which new technological advances allow scientists to see parts of the world more clearly, but how they also reveal new limitations and present researchers with new blind spots to explore. This approach to knowledge focuses on asking critical questions rather than on finding answers alone, and it values exploring knowledge in conversation with others. The approach shows how critical thinkers:

- Explore new ideas and theories
- Question current claims
- Develop more interesting problems
- Renew the process of inquiry and discussion

We can visualize this approach as a recursive cycle that renews itself throughout the process of exploring ideas as shown in Figure 1.1.

Questioning current claims and exploring new ideas shows how research is a process of exploration. Researchers, whether in the sciences, arts, or medicine, are responsible for participating in informed debates with their peers, not for ending the debate altogether with the discovery of a final truth or solution. To borrow from writing scholars Robert Davis and Mark Shadle, the exploratory approach to research writing depends on "less efficiency, more mystery."[4]

Strong research writing depends more on reflection (mystery) than speed (efficiency).

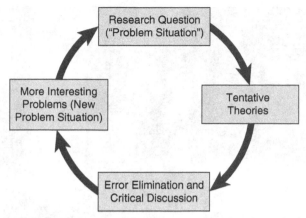

FIGURE 1.1   Karl Popper's representation of human knowledge.

CONNECTING ACADEMIC
CONVERSATIONS ACROSS DISCIPLINES

Conversations in two or more disciplines could be connected either in practice or theory. For instance, industrial sculpture requires artists to have a significant knowledge of engineering practices in addition to their creative abilities. Developing a deep understanding of the materials and mechanical concepts that influence this approach to art can help us analyze a work like Anthony Caro's *Midday* (Figure 1.2). *Interdisciplinary* questions might include:

- How is Caro's creativity inspired—or limited—by the materials and size of his project?
- If Caro describes his sculpture as "drawing in space," can this approach tell us anything about structural engineering as well as art?

Another example of interdisciplinarity is the field of biomedical ethics, which combines approaches from medicine and philosophy. This field is growing quickly in response to demands from healthcare providers, geneticists, and stem cell researchers to understand interdisciplinary issues, like the impact of new medical technologies on traditional aspects of medical care. Their questions include:

- How can ethical investigation help scientists see the potential impact of the Human Genome Project, which seeks to map out humans' DNA structure?

FIGURE 1.2   Anthony Caro's *Midday.*

- How do new medical technologies, such as life support systems, impact patients' rights to determine the course of their own medical care, including when to die?
- How do technological innovations in medicine, which may be developed by computer scientists or physiologists, impact the daily practices of nurses and doctors?

How might an artist and an engineer see eye to eye when discussing this structure? Is it art? Is it a building? How can two or more discourse communities meet around a shared idea or issue?

These examples show how researchers can combine the work of two or more fields as they explore an issue. As you develop your own ideas and gather sources, be sure to consider possible interdisciplinary connections that will help you best understand and contribute to the conversation.

Activity 2: Imagine a Subject in Relation to Potential Areas

Follow up on your list from the beginning of this chapter and think about issues drawn from your personal interests, the questions being asked in your academic major, and the problems faced in the profession that you are thinking of entering. How might those issues connect to academic conversations? Below is a list of major academic fields and selected subdivisions where you might see such connections.

- **Physical Sciences:** biology, chemistry, genetics
- **Education:** elementary education, secondary education, special education
- **Applied Sciences:** engineering, computer sciences, physics
- **Medicine:** forensics, optometry, dentistry, obstetrics, dietetics
- **Humanities:** philosophy, literature, history, cultural studies, foreign languages
- **Fine Arts:** theater, film, visual arts, music, sculpture, dance
- **Social Sciences:** psychology, sociology, geography
- **Business:** marketing, human resources, administration, international commerce

For each issue you chose, identify at least three academic conversations the issue belongs to. Draw from the above list or add other areas that better fit your issues.

For example, if you are interested in issues related to online social networking (such as *Twitter*, *Facebook*, newsgroups, and online dating services) consider how:

- In the field of **Business**, marketing researchers test ways of connecting advertising to users through their profiles and preferences.
- In the field of **Applied Sciences**, computer scientists design and improve on the programs that support online social networking.
- In the field of **Social Sciences**, psychologists study the effects on the mind of using (and perhaps overusing) online social networks.
- In the field of **Medicine**, optometrists investigate challenges to eye and vision health related to computer overuse.

Strategies for Seeing the Academic Conversation

1. Collaborate with other members of your academic communities, informally through conversation and formally through the exchange of texts.

2. See research as the pursuit of solutions and clarity and of problems and complexity.

3. Consider both subject matter and rhetorical aspects of your ideas.

4. Use research to help make new knowledge by participating in the conversation.

5. Investigate issues within one or more academic conversations.

2

Building a Knowledge Base and Reading for Informative Purposes

---

CHAPTER OBJECTIVES

In this chapter you'll learn to:

- Recognize that texts provide useful information, such as facts, statistics, dates, and examples
- Review and practice familiar reading skills
- Use informational sources to build a knowledge base on a particular subject or issue
- Connect informational texts in order to identify and explore points of debate on an issue

An academic conversation usually begins with developing a foundation of relevant, useful, and credible information. This chapter focuses on texts that are probably familiar to you from your previous research and writing experiences. You'll see ways of using texts to locate and collect information, and to build your own knowledge base about a particular subject or issue. You'll also learn how to use your knowledge base to develop questions that lead to and result in successful academic research projects.

People read for many reasons—for pleasure (blogs, novels, comics, fan fiction), to study for a class (textbooks, articles), to get information (choosing the best laptop or presidential candidate, learning how to use the latest e-reader device), or debate an issue (convincing someone of your position on a social or political controversy). People also read for different *purposes*. There is a difference between skimming a novel while on vacation and re-reading the same novel multiple times to study for an exam or write a paper for a literature course.

Reading is guided by purpose.

Academic writers must have a purpose that goes beyond simply reporting facts if they are to fully and effectively enter a conversation. However, it's difficult to make much progress in the research process without a firm foundation in the facts surrounding a particular issue or question. Because familiarity with facts and data is such an important starting place, we'll look first at sources with which you are likely familiar that provide foundational facts and data. In later chapters, we'll look more closely at sources generally used in academic research and writing.

STARTING WITH THE FACTS

It's hard to imagine how to get started in any endeavor without essential building blocks of information, which can motivate us first to investigate and then to participate in a larger conversation. All researchers have to find the facts they need, and even expert researchers depend on other experts to provide the building blocks that can spark new contributions to their communities. This is true in many professions and situations. Consider how the producer of a news program who is responsible for a segment on a current event, such as a political campaign, a piece of legislation, or an international crisis, depends on information drawn from the Internet, newspapers, corporate press releases, executive and government profiles, and reference books. With a foundation built from these sources, the producer can help a host report on an issue credibly and responsibly, or ask informed questions while interviewing guest experts.

Many people depend on the opinions and claims of experts to inform their choices and actions.

Academic researchers also use informational sources to *situate* themselves in a conversation with a body of basic knowledge and ideas.

Experts can provide us with a foundation of accepted knowledge about an issue.

A sociologist, for example, might make a series of observations about a particular place, a particular group of people, or a particular social behavior, and then design a research project that seeks to discover how those observations fit together and why they are important. A physicist may observe an unusual phenomenon in the laboratory, or in his or her reading come across an unusual observation made by another researcher, and then seek to understand the cause and importance of the conflict between expectations and observations. These professional researchers have built their expertise on foundations of basic knowledge provided by experts who came before them and whose work is collected in many of their field's general resources, such as textbooks, encyclopedias, dictionaries, and other reference works. Those sources have helped them to learn how a sociologist or physicist looks at the world, and how to distinguish between situations and problems that have already been covered by researchers and those that demand further attention and new contributions.

READING INFORMATIONAL TEXTS TO BUILD KNOWLEDGE

Think about the kinds of reading you've done in the past to complete a research project either for school or to satisfy your own curiosity about an issue. Whenever you turn to books, magazines, and electronic sources, like Wikipedia.org, you should consider the credibility of those sources. For example, Wikipedia is popular and convenient, but it may also be unreliable since it is "open source" and most entries can be changed by anyone, without regard to their expertise or authority on an issue. In later chapters, we will explore ways of harnessing the power of the Internet for research projects. For now, we turn our attention to *print sources* that researchers use to collect information. It's important, even in the early stages of a research project, to seek out information—and later arguments—by authors who are considered credible. Try to ensure that the people you choose and depend on to help you build a knowledge base for research projects can give you information that is as correct, as relevant, and as current as possible. These authors are likely to have the credentials comparable to other experts, that is, degrees and peer recognition based on their publications and other contributions to their fields.

Seek out credible informants as you build a knowledge base for your research projects.

As you recall your own reading experiences, consider the following questions:

- How did you decide what to read first?
- Did you encounter any controversies in your reading, and, if so, how did you resolve them?
- Why did you accept or reject information and claims you found in your reading?

- How did you decide which parts of the readings were most important or least important to answering your question?
- When did you know you had enough material to come to a conclusion?

Think about the amount of information that you've acquired in the courses you are taking now or took recently, particularly the "surveys" on which the first year or two of college tend to focus. Those introductory courses you take early in college are designed to give you a body of essential knowledge—facts, procedures, theories, and so on—about a subject or field that will allow you to participate fully in later courses as a major or future specialist. Some of the following fields and issues might—or soon will—be familiar to you:

- **Psychology:** Essential concepts (such as the oedipal conflict), key movements (Freudian and Adlerian psychoanalysis), and significant events (the 1971 Stanford Prison Experiment)
- **Mathematics:** Basic operations (balancing equations), essential formulas (the quadratic equation), and useful processes (such as mathematical proofs)
- **Biology:** Key concepts (cell parts and their functions, the components of DNA), essential theories (evolution), and basic classification systems (Linnaean and Evolutionary taxonomy)
- **Literature:** Geographic divisions (such as British, American, and African literature), key authors (Virginia Woolf, Ernest Hemingway, and Toni Morrison)
- **Sociology:** Major figures (Emile Durkheim and Max Weber), and key concepts (historical materialism, functionalism, and action theory)
- **U.S. History:** Important people (Thomas Jefferson, William Randolph Hearst, and Malcolm X) and major events (King Philip's War, the Montgomery Bus Boycott, and the Cuban Missile Crisis)

For the remainder of this chapter, we'll use one of the topics from the previous list as a hypothetical issue to demonstrate some of the preliminary steps that researchers follow when they begin a project. Because it is significant to American history, and because it finds its way into many academic conversations, imagine that we need to learn about relationships between Native Americans and people of European origin during colonial times. We'll want to start the project with a background in some basic facts about the time period.

As we work through a hypothetical case in this chapter, apply examples to the issues and questions that interest you, or use them to spark new ideas and issues you might be interested in exploring later. How might the path we take on one issue help you begin your own project?

Encyclopedias: Collections of Information

If you're like many students, you've already used online and print encyclopedias to find information for research projects. Take a moment to read the following excerpts from the encyclopedia *Colonial America.* As you read, consider not only *what* kinds of facts and data are being presented in the entries, but also *how* those facts and data are being presented. Keep in mind, then, the two aspects—subject matter (the "what"), and rhetorical (the "how")—of constructing meaning in academic research.

Look for hierarchical and sequential organization of your informational sources.

Like most sources of its kind, *Colonial America* is designed to help readers find information efficiently, so it's organized hierarchically, by dividing, then subdividing aspects of U.S. history. Specifically, *Colonial America* divides many of its sections first according to significant themes in early American history and then presents information sequentially by year. For example, in the section "Military and Diplomatic Affairs," we find the following entry for the years 1675–1676:

> King Philip's War is a brutal war fought in New England between English colonists and Native Americans. While native warriors achieve some success and destroy several colonial towns, the war ends when Metacom, known to the colonists as King Philip, is killed.[1]

The section on "The Colony of Massachusetts" is similarly divided, so that we read the following entry for the years 1615–1620:

> The total native population of southern New England, which had been as high as 75,000, is cut in half by a series of epidemics. In some localities, the devastation is even greater—from 75 to 90 percent in the most extreme cases. This stunning decline dramatically alters native community life and paves the way for English colonization in the area.[2]

You may have noticed that each entry offers readers a set of facts that relate to a date in the case of the first passage and a place in the case of the second. You may have noticed that

Do your sources collect or connect information?

while these entries *collect* pieces of information and facts, they do not *connect* them with explanations that develop relationships between events over time or due to particular causes and effects. A researcher who is inspired to explore connections and relationships can begin with a collection of information and develop a problem that leads to inquiry-driven research.

AS YOU READ:

✓ Keep a notebook with facts, names, dates, and other information.

✓ Decide whether your sources collect or connect information.

✓ Record questions you have about the information you find.

Textbooks: Connecting Information

Another type of source that should be familiar from your earlier and current school experiences is the textbook. In the following excerpt from *America: A Concise History*, the authors describe King Philip's War, which we saw briefly covered in the first encyclopedia entry above. As you read this longer textbook excerpt, compare the two types of sources. Think about how the information is organized and developed. You should also consider the way the textbook uses details and connects the issues it raises.

> By the 1670s there were three times as many whites as Indians in New England. The English population now totaled some 55,000, while the number of Indians had plummeted: from an estimated 120,000 in 1570, to 70,000 in 1620, to barely 16,000. To Metacom, leader of the Wampanoags, the future looked grim. When his people copied English ways by raising hogs and selling pork in Boston, Puritan officials accused them of selling at "an under rate" and placed restrictions on their trade. When they killed wandering livestock that damaged their cornfields, authorities denounced them for violating English property rights. Like Opechancanough and the Susquehannocks in Virginia and Popé in New Mexico, Metacom finally concluded that only military resistance could save Indian lands and culture. So in 1675 Metacom (whom the English called King Philip) forged a military alliance with the Narragansetts and Nipmucks and attacked white settlements throughout New England. Bitter fighting continued into 1676, ending only when Indian warriors ran short of guns and powder, and Mohegans and Mohawks in alliance with the Massachusetts Bay government ambushed and killed Metacom.[3]

The textbook excerpt goes beyond simply listing bits of information as the encyclopedia
does, and connects informational elements
with *narrative*. The textbook explains connec-
tions by incorporating storytelling strategies, so that the authors can:

> *Narrative is used to
> connect pieces of
> information.*

- Show a *sequence of events* over time, such as the rate of the indige-
  nous population's decline in three fifty year increments
- Speculate on the *mindset* of important figures, such as Metacom,
  who sees a "grim" future for his people
- Develop *connections* between two or more events, such as the
  declining population inspiring a number of strategies by the
  Wampanoags
- Provide *causes* for events, such as the diminishing supplies of
  Metacom's army leading to the end of fighting

This passage also provides readers with additional details that add
depth and life to data that may otherwise seem lifeless and uninterest-
ing. For instance, our encyclopedia entry simply claims that the war
ends when Metacom is killed, while our textbook entry shows that
Metacom was killed because of an alliance between the English and
rival Native American groups. Another difference is that, while the encyclopedia describes events in the present tense, the textbook uses past
tense in its narrative to show the sequence of events over time, and
their cause and effect relationships.

USING INFORMATIONAL TEXTS TO DEVELOP QUESTIONS

We can also see that even as the textbook entry answers questions
that we might have about connections and relationships between particular events and people, it also can prompt new questions:

- Would this war have been avoided if laws were applied equally
  to both English and Native American traders, like the hog farm-
  ers described in the passage?
- Would the English have been victorious without the assistance of
  Native American groups—the Mohegans and Mohawks?
- Why did some groups of Native American people join with
  Metacom and other groups with the English?
- How did other groups of European colonists choose sides in the
  conflict?

Use existing (old) information and knowledge to develop new issues and questions to pursue.

In fact, we can probably come up with any number of interesting questions (new problem situations), since we are limited only by our own imaginations in developing new issues from old knowledge. In order to answer those new questions, we could, perhaps, first search the rest of *America: A Concise History* to see if they are answered in a different section. We would probably also want to look at other sources to see if they offered different perspectives on the same or a similar event, group of people, and particular moments of contact and crisis between two or more societies.

REFLECTING ON AN EVOLVING KNOWLEDGE BASE

Let's pause for a moment to consider some uses for information that we've uncovered thus far in our exploration of encounters between European colonizers and Native Americans in the 1600s. In reading only a handful of passages from two texts, we've acquired a lot of data concerning these encounters. To start, we have sets of facts, such as:

- Important people and groups: English, Puritans, Wampanoags, Mohawks, Opechancanough, Metacom, and so on
- Significant dates and periods: 1615–1620 and 1675–1676,
- Locations: Boston and Virginia
- Noteworthy themes: business practices, cultural conflict, warfare, disease, and the like.

More importantly, our encyclopedia and textbook provide us with descriptions of events that show the significance of the facts that we've acquired. They tell us, for example, about:

- Economic relationships and tensions between English colonizers and Native Americans
- The effect of alliances between indigenous groups and colonizers
- How disease and population decline first motivated indigenous attempts to assimilate into colonizers' culture, and then their military resistance against it;
- The rise and fall of Metacom's campaign

Arrange building blocks of information in meaningful ways.

The facts that you have accumulated from the encyclopedia and textbook can work like a vocabulary list for a new language. These facts, as do words, supply the essential building blocks that may then be put into some kind of order—as words can be connected into a sentence—and used to make meaning. It's important then to begin thinking about the strategies that you can use to arrange those building blocks of information in ways to make and strengthen an argument.

AS YOU READ:

✓ Collect new vocabulary and new meanings.

✓ Keep track of new ideas, facts, and their relationships.

✓ Make connections to come up with your own questions.

Activity 1: Report on Your Knowledge Base

Following this chapter's information gathering process, use at least two sources to draft a brief report (of a paragraph or so) on one of the topics or issues that you described in Activity 1 in Chapter 1. You can turn to encyclopedias and textbooks, and to other sources, such as newspapers and credible websites, like those hosted by educational institutions (.edu) and the government (.gov). Use these sources to build a knowledge base that includes the most significant people, places, dates, statistics, conflicts, cause-and-effect relationships, and other data that you find worth describing.

As you write your report, ask yourself the following questions:

- Which pieces of information are included in both (or all) of your sources?
- Which pieces of information appear in only one source?
- What conclusions can you draw from these comparisons?
- Can your comparisons help you to develop critical questions that would lead to an academic research project?

BUILDING ON INFORMATION

We can look at these collections of points and information in more than one way. Considering the amount of information presented about King Philip's War in our two sources thus far, a writer might already be equipped to write a satisfactory (although brief) report on an important conflict between Native Americans and European colonizers, the relationship between the declining indigenous population and their attempts to survive, or some other issue. Depending on the writer's style and ability to

Write to share information you've acquired with others.

Seek out additional sources to confirm or challenge the information and explanations found in a single source.

write vividly, this report may present information in an interesting way, but it's unlikely to add any critical insights or make any contributions to the conversation about these cultures and their relationships over time.

But, what if the information that we've found and the interpretations suggested by our two sources conflict with our own ideas and interpretations of historical events? Is there anything new or surprising in the information presented in our sources? Are there perspectives, issues, or features of seventeenth-century European–Indian encounters that challenge what you expected to find? In cases of conflict, a researcher who is skeptical about one or two sources could consider testing and comparing the information found in competing sources. New sources could provide additional details to support the claims of older sources, or those new sources could provide alternative explanations to support a contrasting position. Whether you find yourself agreeing or disagreeing with a first source, or set of sources, a search for additional sources can help deepen the knowledge that you have about an issue.

Metacommentary

We might find, too, that in our search for new data, connections, and alternative explanations, we can start making generalizations about the sources themselves. For example, as University of Vermont historian James Loewen argues in his book, *Lies My Teacher Told Me*, even though the textbooks students in the United States use to learn about American history try to be different from each other, from his perspective they begin to look much the same. He shows how certain shared perspectives shape the ways that textbook writers tell a story (like the story of the United States) and, more importantly, impact their audiences by presenting history through a certain set of values. Our history textbooks, he writes, "actually make students stupid"![4] How do they have this effect?

Returning to the issues covered by our informational sources above, Loewen shows how textbooks cover the population decline of indigenous people in the 1600s:

"The American Republic," the authors of *The American Pageant* tell us on page one, "was from the outset uniquely favored. It started from scratch on a vast and virgin continent, which was so sparsely peopled by Indians that they were able to be eliminated or shouldered aside." Henry Dobyns and Francis Jennings have pointed out that this archetype of the "virgin continent" and its corollary, the "primitive tribe," have subtly influenced estimates of precontact populations to match the stereotype. The tiny Mooney estimate thus "made sense"—resonated with the archetype. Never mind that the land was, in reality, not a virgin wilderness but recently widowed.

How do the twelve textbooks, most of which were published in the 1980s, treat this topic? Their authors might let readers in on the furious debate of the 1960s and 1970s, telling how and why estimates changed. Instead, the textbooks simply state numbers—very different numbers! "As many as ten million," *American Adventures* proposes. "There were only about 1,000,000 North American Indians," opines *The American Tradition*. "Scattered across the North American continent were about 500 different groups, many of them nomadic." Like other Americans who have not studied the literature, the authors of history textbooks are still under the thrall of the "virgin land" and "primitive tribe" archetypes; their most common Indian population estimate is the discredited figure of one million, which five textbooks supply. Only two of the textbooks provide estimates of ten to twelve million, in the range supported by contemporary scholarship. Two of the textbooks hedge their bets by suggesting one to twelve million, which might reasonably prompt classroom discussion of why estimates are so vague. Three of the textbooks omit the subject altogether.

The problem is not so much the estimates as the attitude. Only one book, *The American Adventure*, acknowledges that there is a controversy, and this is only in a footnote. The other textbooks seem bent on presenting "facts" for children to "learn." Such an approach keeps students ignorant of the reasoning, arguments, and weighing of evidence that go into social science.[5]

Lies My Teacher Told Me is an example of *metacommentary* because it analyzes not only a particular fact or set of facts, but goes further to analyze an entire group of sources that present information. The more data Loewen accumulates from each of his U.S. history textbooks, the more he begins to realize that he can develop an analysis of all the books as they work together to form a genre of U.S. history textbooks—at least as the subject is taught to high school and early college students. We can even take this idea of metacommentary further, since the concern isn't confined to the subject area of history alone, but may be part of an approach to knowledge that shapes the ways we are encouraged to use the information we acquire in reading.

Thus, even if they first appear to be, informational sources are not simply collections of facts waiting to be found and repeated. Instead, they present *particular* facts, explanations, and perspectives at the

How we understand and use facts can either inspire or prevent further exploration into critical questions and perspectives.

expense of others, which, together, could lead either to very different meanings and interpretations or to more complex and challenging experiences for readers.

We can begin to see beyond facts as an end in themselves and develop an *approach to facts* that opens up new possibilities for exploration. If we limit our own research purpose to collecting facts, we can miss opportunities to pursue the issues that may be of greater significance—as well as being far more interesting and exciting. If we read just to learn facts, then we risk losing sight of the controversial give-and-take process in which professional researchers—historians, anthropologists, sociologists, and others—are engaged as they make unique contributions to academic conversations.

THINKING CRITICALLY ABOUT INFORMATION

A critical mindset can lead to metacognitive questions and open up new opportunities for researchers.

This critical approach to information is important to readers and researchers in every academic field—and to issues in our everyday lives. As science writers John Hatton and Paul Plouffe explain it, "students in the sciences are seldom asked to think about the nature of scientific knowledge and the ways in which science 'knows.' ...Such thinking, of course, cannot help but lead to a closed and essentially rigid view of science and its practitioners."[6] Adopting that closed view can make us less skeptical about information that we take from the world around us. Think about the messages that we get that sound valid or scientifically based, such as "four out of five dentists recommend Brand X toothpaste," or "veterinarians found that most cats prefer the taste of Brand Y cat food." A critical approach helps us see these informational claims as selective uses of information designed to convince us of something that may seem less certain once we scratch the surface.

We can think about using this mindset to expand the discussion even further across the range of academic conversations that stretches from the humanities to the physical sciences and from business to fine arts. Because each academic conversation involves a unique discourse community, each has a language of its own and a specialized way of seeing the world that is distinct from other conversations and their discourses. Although each of our examples of informational texts come from the field of U.S. history, you might consider how the same people, time period, and issues would be seen and represented in other academic conversations, such as archeology, economics, agricultural sciences, geography, medicine, anthropology, and the fine arts. Are there ways of seeing issues that would be unique to these fields, and aspects of those issues that stand out—or drop into the background—because of the interests specific to them?

AS YOU READ:

✓ Consider how facts are used differently between texts.

✓ Think skeptically about the information you find.

✓ Imagine how other fields would use the same data.

FINDING MOTIVATION

Academic researchers are motivated beyond the need to just find information, even if they begin with a modest goal. However, they aren't expected to come up with these motivations on their own. Informational sources help researchers find issues and ask questions that are consequential—those they and their readers find are worth the time and energy required for critical exploration. Like professional researchers, you should consider using informative texts to jumpstart a project by providing you with a firm foundation of credible information that helps you to develop questions—opportunities—to participate in the ongoing academic conversation that encompasses your project.

Your academic research projects may start with information, but they will be further motivated by your desire to explore and explain the significance of that information with your own arguments. You will take information that appears objective or self-evident from *Create informed questions from your evolving knowledge base.* one perspective and activate it by investing it with meaning and making valuable connections from one source to another. In the next chapter, we follow a professional researcher as she moves from an early goal of collecting information in order to share it with her students, to ultimately developing a critical, investigative project out of her engagement with the sources that she has gathered. This extended example of scholarly writing—and the process that makes it possible—helps us see how any question, or search for explanations and new connections, can lead us into compelling research journeys of our own.

Strategies for Reading Sources for Information and Knowledge Building

1. Use sources to build a body of information about an issue that interests you. Encyclopedias, textbooks, and other sources designed for a general audience help researchers collect facts and data and understand how ideas, events, and people are connected.

2. Find informative sources that are credible: written by people who are respected by their peers and who have sufficient knowledge about the issue.

3. Build a list of issues identified and explored in your sources. What features, people, places, relationships, causes and effects, and so on are considered important in your sources?

4. What kinds of questions emerge from the information in general audience sources? Where are the gaps? What do you think they leave unsaid as they describe their topics? Are certain perspectives or values given less attention?

5. Find new informational sources with varied perspectives and explanations. Begin generalizing about their approaches to your area of interest.

6. Evaluate what you read. Identify information and explanations that are more convincing or clear and those that are less so.

7. Imagine the academic conversations you can join. Investigate particular fields and areas of scholarship in order to make a contribution to the knowledge that you've found so far.

3

Integrate Academic
Reading and Writing

CHAPTER OBJECTIVES

In this chapter, you'll learn to:

- See academic activity as a process rather than a product
- Use a recursive approach for reading and writing
- Develop active reading strategies
- Practice reading and responding to a piece of academic writing

---

Academic conversations come to life when we read and respond to the ideas of others and invite them to respond to our ideas in turn. In every field, the conversation depends on a give-and-take process between members of a community who share personal, professional, and academic interests they explore together, typically through the exchange of texts. Focusing on the active reading process, this chapter provides strategies for reading academic texts and ways to connect reading with writing. As you integrate your reading and writing practices, you start a dialogue with one or more academic texts. This dialogue prepares you to continue this conversation through your own critical engagement.

A process approach to academic writing and reading can conflict with the habits that many of us bring to college from our earlier school experiences—habits that many of us spend significant time unlearning.

For instance, think about the writing that emphasizes a finished *product* rather than an engaged *process*. A product focus may emphasize grammatical correctness rather than content or a required number of sources rather than their quality or relevance. Focusing on research products can also lead to reporting on topics without developing any personal investment, or to following a set structure, such as the five-paragraph model with no opportunity to experiment with other approaches. The process approach is significantly different because it encourages writers to focus less on getting the product right the first time, and more on exploring ideas that are valuable to them.

READING AND WRITING AS A PROCESS

Although much of your reading and writing takes place in isolation—with books, articles, and other texts—a successful process approach to writing also depends on the people around you (see Figure 3.1).Writers benefit when they share work and get and give feedback to guide each new draft and revision. They also need time to reflect on their writing, to review and build on earlier projects as they work on later ones. As linguist Erik Eriksson explains, reflection and conversation allow writers to tap into deep mental structures that lead "to new associations, and ultimately new ideas."[2] Experience shows that this *recursive* process of reading, writing, and collaborating leads to stronger end products.

FIGURE 3.1 Although the technology—from books to laptops, for instance—has changed, the coffee shop remains a hub for conversations, just as it was for intellectuals and students during the eighteenth century (left). Students today have access to e-mail, cell phones, Facebook, and the like. Some even take entire courses online. Nevertheless, they still benefit from face-to-face conversations with other students and their instructors about texts, ideas, and their writing projects (right).

Student Voice

June, who researched gender imbalances in retail sales jobs, describes how she came to value reading in the conversation:

I liked realizing that I wasn't in it alone, and I learned that no one, scholars and students alike, writes a strong paper alone. This really made me feel comfortable and made the reading and writing process more enjoyable.

A process orientation to writing can be daunting because it's riskier than focusing on the finished product alone. With a process approach, you often have to begin writing without knowing exactly what you're going to say or how to say it. You have to read not simply to fill your paper with information but to *discover* new ideas and *choose* how you want to engage with the texts you read. These qualities lead you to more freedom as a writer and to new ways of thinking as you work through the process.

ESSENTIAL FEATURES OF THE WRITING PROCESS

There is no one approach to successful drafting and composition. For example, some writers compose on a computer, while others may need a pencil or pen to write early drafts.

Writers may draft their early work in strict isolation or draft with a writing group. They may talk out their ideas before writing or mentally wrestle with them while on a walk, working out in the gym, and the like. Some writers plan and outline early on, while others free write ideas to find their voice, leaving structure, grammar, spelling, and style for later.

As you compare these approaches with your own, you'll realize that the writing process isn't a formula that can be easily reproduced. However, all successful writers share some basic strategies that can help you begin:

- **Time:** Writers give themselves plenty of time to allow their ideas to percolate. They also create opportunities to work on their projects in stages rather than all at once.
- **Focus:** Writers design the focus of a project for a given situation, audience, and purpose. They refine and clarify their focus throughout the writing process.

- **Drafting:** Writers expect to produce multiple drafts of a project.
- **Revising:** Writers often make large-scale changes to a project with each new draft. In doing so, they make many improvements (moving paragraphs around, choosing different words, correcting grammar and spelling, and even taking on a new voice).
- **Collaborating:** Writers solicit feedback from their colleagues. They test their ideas. They brainstorm. They may even get up and discuss their ideas before a live audience.
- **Daring:** Writers are willing to take risks, going out on a limb to find their place in a conversation.

Writers share these basic strategies, but each writer may not follow the same pattern. When faced with different situations, expectations, and responsibilities—a formal research paper, a newspaper editorial, or an autobiographical reflection—a writer adjusts the process for the situation.

Academic writers also have many ways of meeting the particular challenges of research projects. They may read many sources to have a clear sense of the conversation before they begin to write, or develop arguments alongside each source they encounter. They may begin with the history of an idea or debate, or with the most current sources. With each approach, writers use research to enter and contribute to conversations with other experts in their field. As you combine critical reading with engaged writing, you will be motivated to participate in the conversation, adding your voice, moving the conversation forward, and inviting readers to participate with you.

Student Voice

Craig describes how process strategies changed the way he approaches research writing.

I have written several research papers in past classes, but none like this. Usually, when I write a research paper, I gather all my information, then sit down and write the majority of the paper in one day. In this class, we did it differently: we planned, researched, and developed, and then we planned, researched, and developed some more. Although sometimes I wanted to pull my hair out from frustration with this new writing method, I eventually grew to understand the reasons behind the steps.

READING IN THE CONVERSATION

A process approach is necessary for strong writing. Process is just as important in reading, especially when you face the unique challenges posed by academic arguments.

> *Process strategies are used in writing and reading.*

Process reading frees you from having to "get it" all at once. As you work your way through a text for the first time, you may skim to identify the big ideas, just as you might brainstorm to sketch ideas for a writing project. Once you have the big ideas in mind, a more substantive read-through (later "reading drafts") can draw your attention to specific paragraphs, passages, or rhetorical moves in the text, just as you keep sight of your own thesis and goals when you develop a particular example in your writing.

The following text illustrates the interrelationship of reading and writing in the research process. In this article, "'Indians': Textualism, Morality, and the Problem of History,"[3] literary theorist Jane Tompkins uses a research narrative to show how she gathers sources and incorporates strategies of personal reflection and revision as she develops an argument. As you read, think about process features—time, focus, drafting, revising, collaborating, and daring—that Tompkins demonstrates as she works out her thoughts about encounters between European colonists and Native Americans in the 1600s.

In your first reading draft, work through the article slowly on your own or in a group. Look first for compelling points and clear examples in the article. Take time to reread difficult sentences and passages. We discuss specific strategies for reading academic writing later in this chapter. For now, use the strategies you already have at hand and keep track of those you find helpful.

As you read, use these questions as a guide:

- How much *prior knowledge* is expected of readers? How do those without prior knowledge get into the conversation?
- Does it surprise you that this scholarly article opens with a *personal anecdote*? Why are so many personal experiences, perceptions, and reactions incorporated into the analysis?
- Who are the essay's *readers*? Are they already inclined to agree with these arguments? Are they skeptics?
- What *cues* help guide readers through the argument?
- Which parts of the article do you find convincing? Think about how *evidence* is used and organized. Follow the movement from one point to the next or from one part of the essay to the next. Which approaches would you use if you were exploring the same research problem?

"Indians": Textualism, Morality, and the Problem of History

Jane Tompkins

The essay opens with a personal reflection. What do you think motivated this strategy?

1 When I was growing up in New York City, my parents used to take me to an event in Inwood Park at which Indians—real American Indians dressed in feathers and blankets—could be seen and touched by children like me. This event was always a disappointment. It was more fun to imagine that you *were* an Indian in one of the caves in Inwood Park than to shake the hand of an old man in a headdress who was not overwhelmed at the opportunity of meeting you. After staring at the Indians for a while, we would take a walk in the woods where the caves were, and once I asked my mother if the remains of a fire I had seen in one of them might have been left by the original inhabitants. After that, wandering up some stone steps cut into the side of the hill, I imagined I was a princess in a rude castle. My Indians, like my princesses, were creatures totally of the imagination, and I did not care to have any real exemplars interfering with what I already knew.

Why might people relate to Indians as though they were children, or essentially childlike?

2   I already knew about Indians from having read about them in school. Over and over we were told the story of how Peter Minuit had bought Manhattan Island from the Indians for twenty-four dollars' worth of glass beads. And it was a story we didn't mind hearing because it gave us the rare pleasure of having someone to feel superior to, since the poor Indians had not known (as we eight-year-olds did) how valuable a piece of property Manhattan Island would become. Generally, much was made of the Indian presence in Manhattan; a poem in one of our readers began: "Where we walk to school today / Indian children used to play," and we were encouraged to write poetry on this topic ourselves. So I had a fairly rich relationship with Indians before I ever met the unprepossessing people in Inwood Park. I felt that I had a lot in common with them. They, too, liked animals (they were often named after animals); they, too, made mistakes—they liked the brightly colored trinkets of little value that the white men were always offering them; they were handsome, warlike, and brave and had led an exciting, romantic life in the forest long ago, a life such as I dreamed of leading myself. I felt lucky to be living in one of the places where they had definitely been. Never mind where they were or what they were doing now.

3   My story stands for the relationship most non-Indians have to the people who first populated this continent, a

The personal story is connected to a piece of scholarship.

relationship characterized by narcissistic fantasies of freedom and adventure, of a life lived closer to nature and to spirit than the life we lead now. As Vine Deloria, Jr. has pointed out, the American Indian Movement in the early seventies couldn't get people to pay attention to what was happening to Indians who were alive in the present, so powerful was this country's infatuation with people who wore loincloths, lived in tepees, and roamed the plains and forests long ago.[1] The present essay, like these fantasies, doesn't have much to do with actual Indians, though its subject matter is the histories of European-Indian relations in seventeenth-century New England. In a sense, my encounter with Indians as an adult doing "research" replicates the childhood one, for while I started out to learn about Indians, I ended up preoccupied with a problem of my own.

4   This essay enacts a particular instance of the challenge post-structuralism poses to the study of history. In simpler language, it concerns the difference that point of view makes when people are giving accounts of events, whether at first or second hand. The problem is that if all accounts of events are determined through and through by the observer's frame of reference, then one will never know, in any given case, what really happened.

The personal story helps to frame the research project.

5   I encountered this problem in concrete terms while preparing to teach a course in colonial American literature. I'd set out to learn what I could about the Puritans' relations with American Indians. All I wanted was a general idea of what had happened between the English settlers and the natives in seventeenth-century New England; post-structuralism and its dilemmas were the furthest thing from my mind. I began, more or less automatically, with Perry Miller, who hardly mentions the Indians at all, then proceeded to the work of historians who had dealt exclusively with the European-Indian encounter. At first, it was a question of deciding which of these authors to believe, for it quickly became apparent that there was no unanimity on the subject. As I read on, however, I discovered that the problem was more complicated than deciding whose version of events was correct. Some of the conflicting accounts were not simply contradictory, they were completely incommensurable, in that their assumptions about what counted as a valid approach to the subject, and what the subject

---

[1]See Vine Deloria, Jr., *God Is Red* (New York, 1973), pp. 39–56.

The essay's central question is introduced and connected to an event that motivated the project. Research materials include both secondary and primary sources.

itself was, diverged in fundamental ways. Faced with an array of mutually irreconcilable points of view, points of view which determined what was being discussed as well as the terms of the discussion, I decided to turn to primary sources for clarification, only to discover that the primary sources reproduced the problem all over again. I found myself, in other words, in an epistemological quandary, not only unable to decide among conflicting versions of events but also unable to believe that any such decision could, in principle, be made. It was a moral quandary as well. Knowledge of what really happened when the Europeans and the Indians first met seemed particularly important, since the result of that encounter was virtual genocide. This was the kind of past "mistake" which, presumably, we studied history in order to avoid repeating. If studying history couldn't put us in touch with actual events and their causes, then what was to prevent such atrocities from happening again?

6   For a while, I remained at this impasse. But through analyzing the process by which I had reached it, I eventually arrived at an understanding which seemed to offer a way out. This essay records the concrete experience of meeting and solving the difficulty I have just described (as an abstract problem, I thought I had solved it long ago). My purpose is not to throw new light on antifoundationalist epistemology—the solution I reached is not a new one—but to dramatize and expose the troubles antifoundationalism gets you into when you meet it, so to speak, in the road.

The essay's structure and purpose are introduced.

Activity 1: Reflect on the Introduction

After reading the first six paragraphs of this essay, discuss the following questions as a class or in small groups:

- Which points did you understand or identify within the section?
- What was hard to understand at first? Work together to make sense of unfamiliar words and challenging passages.
- Which words or passages in the section remain confusing?
- What do you think the essay is going to be about? As a group, find a thesis statement.
- Where can you see a plan for the article's structure and argument?

As you read, start identifying and organizing ideas in the essay:

- Which are the big ideas and themes?
- How do smaller ideas and themes work alongside the bigger ones?

7   My research began with Perry Miller. Early in the preface to *Errand into the Wilderness*, while explaining how he came to write his history of the New England mind, Miller writes a sentence that stopped me dead. He says that what fascinated him as a young man about his country's history was "the massive narrative of the movement of European culture into the vacant wilderness of America."2 "Vacant?" Miller, writing in 1956, doesn't pause over the word "vacant," but to people who read his preface thirty years later, the word is shocking. In what circumstances could someone proposing to write a history of colonial New England *not* take account of the Indian presence there?

Paragraphs 7–11 focus on the article's first source. The time and place in which Miller writes shapes what he sees (and what he doesn't see) in important ways.

8   The rest of Miller's preface supplies an answer to this question, if one takes the trouble to piece together its details. Miller explains that as a young man, jealous of older compatriots who had had the luck to fight in World War I, he had gone to Africa in search of adventure. "The adventures that Africa afforded," he writes, "were tawdry enough, but it became the setting for a sudden epiphany" (p. vii). "It was given to me," he writes, "disconsolate on the edge of a jungle of central Africa, to have thrust upon me the mission of expounding what I took to be the innermost propulsion of the United States, while supervising, in that barbaric tropic, the unloading of drums of case oil flowing out of the inexhaustible wilderness of America" (p. viii). Miller's picture of himself on the banks of the Congo furnishes a key to the kind of history he will write and to his mental image of a vacant wilderness; it explains why it was just here, under precisely these conditions, that he should have had his epiphany.

9   The fuel drums stand, in Miller's mind, for the popular misconception of what this country is about. They are "tangible symbols of [America's] appalling power," a power that everyone but Miller takes for the ultimate reality (p. ix). To Miller, "the mind of man is the basic factor in human history," and he will plead, all unaccommodated as he is among the fuel drums, for the intellect—the intellect for which his fellow historians, with their chapters on "stoves or bathtubs, or tax laws," "the Wilmot Proviso" and "the chain store," "have so little respect" (p. viii, ix). His preface seethes with a hatred of the merely physical and mechanical, and this hatred, which is really a form of moral outrage, explains not

2Perry Miller, *Errand into the Wilderness* (Cambridge, Mass., 1964), p. vii; all further references will be included in the text.

only the contempt with which he mentions the stoves and bathtubs but also the nature of his experience in Africa and its relationship to the "massive narrative" he will write.

10   Miller's experiences in Africa are "tawdry," his tropic is barbaric because the jungle he stands on the edge of means nothing to him, no more, indeed something less, than the case oil. It is the nothingness of Africa that precipitates his vision. It is the barbarity of the "dark continent," the obvious (but superficial) parallelism between the jungle at Matadi and America's "vacant wilderness" that releases in Miller the desire to define and vindicate his country's cultural identity. To the young Miller, colonial Africa and colonial America are—but for the history he will bring to light—mirror images of one another. And what he fails to see in the one landscape is the same thing he overlooks in the other: the human beings who people it. As Miller stood with his back to the jungle, thinking about the role of mind in human history, his failure to see that the land into which European culture had moved was not vacant but already occupied by a varied and numerous population, is of a piece with his failure, in his portrait of himself at Matadi, to notice *who* was carrying the fuel drums he was supervising the unloading of.

11   The point is crucial because it suggests that what is invisible to the historian in his own historical moment remains invisible when he turns his gaze to the past. It isn't that Miller didn't "see" the black men, in a literal sense, any more than it's the case that when he looked back he didn't "see" the Indians, in the sense of not realizing they were there. Rather, it's that neither the Indians nor the blacks *counted* for him, in a fundamental way. The way in which Indians can be seen but not counted is illustrated by an entry in Governor John Winthrop's journal, three hundred years before, when he recorded that there had been a great storm with high winds "yet through God's great mercy it did no hurt, but only killed one Indian with the fall of a tree."[3] The juxtaposition suggests that Miller shared with Winthrop a certain colonial point of view, a point of view from which Indians, though present, do not finally matter.

[3]This passage from John Winthrop's *Journal* is excerpted by Perry Miller in his anthology *The American Puritans: Their Prose and Poetry* (Garden City, N.Y., 1956), p. 43. In his headnote to the selections from the *Journal*, Miller speaks of Winthrop's "characteristic objectivity" (p. 37).

Activity 2: Collect Ideas

At this point, the essay's first source has been analyzed. What ideas and information have been found thus far, and what questions motivate further research? As you read, be aware of:

- **Words and ideas you find important:** Why do you choose particular words and ideas over others? What clues signal importance?

- **Words and ideas you find intriguing:** Which ideas are controversial or problematic? Which require further evidence or support from sources?

- **Words and ideas you find confusing:** Can you make sense of these by reading further, examining the context, or discussing them in groups?

As you read, begin marking the text. Try to identify places where the author:

- Describes arguments in the sources she finds

- Develops her own responses to the sources

A decade separates the publication of Vaughan's and Miller's books; Vaughan's work seems "definitive" in a new era of historical research.

12   A book entitled *New England Frontier: Puritans and Indians, 1620–1675*, written by Alden Vaughan and published in 1965, promised to rectify Miller's omission. In the outpouring of work on the European-Indian encounter that began in the early sixties, this book is the first major landmark, and to a neophyte it seems definitive. Vaughan acknowledges the absence of Indian sources and emphasizes his use of materials which catch the Puritans "off guard."[4] His announced conclusion that "the New England Puritans followed a remarkably humane, considerate, and just policy in their dealings with the Indians" seems supported by the scope, documentation, and methodicalness of his project (*NEF*, p. vii). The author's fair-mindedness and equanimity seem everywhere apparent, so that when he asserts "the history of interracial relations from the arrival of the Pilgrims to the outbreak of King Philip's War is a credit to the integrity of both peoples," one is positively reassured (*NEF*, p. viii).

13   But these impressions do not survive an admission that comes late in the book, when, in the course of explaining why works like Helen Hunt Jackson's *Century of Dishonor* had spread misconceptions about Puritan treatment of the Indians, Vaughan finally lays his own cards on the table.

---

[4]Alden T. Vaughan, *New England Frontier: Puritans and Indians, 1620–1675* (Boston, 1965), pp. vi–vii; all further references to this work, abbreviated *NEF*, will be included in the text.

A conversation develops among sources: Vaughan (source #2) responds to Miller (source #1); Higham (source #3) responds to Vaughan. What are some of the reasons for their disagreements? On which issues do they agree?

The root of the misunderstanding [about Puritans and Indians] . . . lie[s] in a failure to recognize the nature of the two societies that met in seventeenth century New England. One was unified, visionary, disciplined, and dynamic. The other was divided, self-satisfied, undisciplined, and static. It would be unreasonable to expect that such societies could live side by side indefinitely with no penetration of the more fragmented and passive by the more consolidated and active. What resulted, then, was not—as many have held—a clash of dissimilar ways of life, but rather the expansion of one into the areas in which the other was lacking. [*NEF*, p. 323]

14   From our present vantage point, these remarks seem culturally biased to an incredible degree, not to mention inaccurate: Was Puritan society unified? If so, how does one account for its internal dissensions and obsessive need to cast out deviants? Is "unity" necessarily a positive culture trait? From what standpoint can one say that American Indians were neither disciplined nor visionary, when both these characteristics loom so large in the enthnographies? Is it an accident that ways of describing cultural strength and weakness coincide with gender stereotypes—active/passive, and so on? Why is one culture said to "penetrate" the other? Why is the "other" described in terms of "lack"?

15   Vaughan's fundamental categories of apprehension and judgment will not withstand even the most cursory inspection. For what looked like evenhandedness when he was writing *New England Frontier* does not look that way anymore. In his introduction to *New Directions in American Intellectual History*, John Higham writes that by the end of the sixties

> the entire conceptual foundation on which [this sort of work] rested [had] crumbled away . . . Simultaneously, in sociology, anthropology, and history, two working assumptions . . . came under withering attack: first, the assumption that societies tend to be integrated, and second, that a shared culture maintains that integration. . . . By the late 1960s all claims issued in the name of an "American mind" . . . were subject to drastic skepticism.[5]

---

[5]John Higham, intro. to *New Directions in American Intellectual History*, ed. Higham and Paul K. Conkin (Baltimore, 1979), p. xii.

16   "Clearly," Higham continues, "the sociocultural up-heaval of the sixties created the occasion" for this reaction.[6] Vaughan's book, it seemed, could only have been written be-fore the events of the sixties had sensitized scholars to ques-tions of race and ethnicity. It came as no surprise, therefore, that ten years later there appeared a study of European-Indian relations which reflected the new awareness of social issues the sixties had engendered. And it offered an entirely different picture of the European-Indian encounter.

17   Francis Jennings' *The Invasion of America* (1975) rips wide open the idea that the Puritans were humane and con-siderate in their dealings with the Indians. In Jennings' ac-count, even more massively documented than Vaughan's, the early settlers lied to the Indians, stole from them, mur-dered them, scalped them, captured them, tortured them, raped them, sold them into slavery, confiscated their land, destroyed their crops, burned their homes, scattered their possessions, gave them alcohol, underminded their systems of belief, and infected them with diseases that wiped out ninety percent of their numbers within the first hundred years after contact.[7]

Source #4: 18   Jennings mounts an all-out attack on the essential de-
Jennings. How   cency of the Puritan leadership and their apologists in the
does Jennings   twentieth century. The Pequot War, which previous historians
contribute   had described as an attempt on the part of Massachussetts Bay
to the   to protect itself from the fiercest of the New England tribes, be-
conversation?   comes, in Jennings' painstakingly researched account, a delib-
Who does he   erate war of extermination, waged by whites against Indians.
agree with,   It starts with trumped-up charges, is carried on through a se-
and who does   ries of increasingly bloody reprisals, and ends in the massacre
he disagree   of scores of Indian men, women, and children, all so that
with?   Massachussets Bay could gain political and economic control
    of the southern Connecticut Valley. When one reads this and
    then turns over the page and sees a reproduction of the Bay
    Colony seal, which depicts an Indian from whose mouth issue
    the words "Come over and help us," the effect is shattering.[8]

---

[6]Ibid.

[7]See Francis Jennings, *The Invasion of America: Indians, Colonialism, and the Cant of Conquest* (New York, 1975), pp. 3–31. Jennings writes: "The so-called settlement of America was a resettlement, a reoccupa-tion of a land made waste by the diseases and demoralization introduced by the newcomers. Al-though the source data pertaining to populations have never been compiled, one careful scholar, Henry F. Dobyns, has provided a relatively conservative and meticulously reasoned estimate con-forming to the known effects of conquest catastrophe. Dobyns has calculated a total aboriginal popu-lation for the western hemisphere within the range of 90 to 112 million, of which 10 to 12 million lived north of the Rio Grande" (p. 30).

[8]Jennings, fig. 7, p. 229; and see pp. 186–229.

Source #5:   19   But even so powerful an argument as Jennings' did
Axtell.   not remain unshaken by subsequent work. Reading on,
Contemporary   I discovered that if the events of the sixties had revolution-
events (here   ized the study of European-Indian relations, the events of
the 1970s)   the seventies produced yet another transformation. The
have the   American Indian Movement, and in particular the founding
power to   of the Native American Rights Fund in 1971 to finance In-
shape   dian litigation, and a court decision in 1975 which gave the
historical   tribes the right to seek redress for past injustices in federal
knowledge.   court, created a climate within which historians began to
                       focus on the Indians themselves. "Almost simultaneously,"
                       writes James Axtell, "frontier and colonial historians began
                       to discover the necessity of considering the American na-
                       tives as real determinants of history and the utility of ethno-
                       history as a way of ensuring parity of focus and impartiality
                       of judgment."[9] In Miller, Indians had been simply beneath
                       notice; in Vaughan, they belonged to an inferior culture; and
                       in Jennings, they were the more or less innocent prey of
                       power-hungry whites.

Source #6:   20   But in the most original and provocative of the ethno-
Martin   histories, Calvin Martin's *Keepers of the Game*, Indians became
                       complicated, purposeful human beings, whose lives were
                       spiritually motivated to a high degree.[10] Their relationship to
                       the animals they hunted, to the natural environment, and to
                       the whites with whom they traded became intelligible within
                       a system of beliefs that formed the basis for an entirely new
                       perspective on the European-Indian encounter.

                              [. . .]

                21   At this point, dismayed and confused by the wildly di-
                       vergent views of colonial history the twentieth-century
                       historians had provided, I decided to look at some primary
                       materials. I thought, perhaps, if I looked at some firsthand
                       accounts and at some scholars looking at those accounts, it
                       would be possible to decide which experts were right and
                       which were wrong by comparing their views with the evi-
                       dence. Captivity narratives seemed a good place to begin,
                       since it was logical to suppose that the records left by whites
                       who had been captured by Indians would furnish the sort of
                       firsthand information I wanted.

---

[9]James Axtell, *The European and the Indian: Essays in the Ethnohistory of Colonial North America* (Oxford, 1981), p. viii.
[10]See Calvin Martin, *Keepers of the Game: Indian-Animal Relationships and the Fur Trade* (Berkeley and Los Angeles, 1978).

Activity 3: Connect Sources

At this point, six sources dealing with European–Indian relationships have been analyzed. In groups, discuss how these sources work individually and in conversation. Consider how the author:

- Describes each new source
- Separates information and data from her commentary
- Moves from one source to the next
- Builds connections between sources
- Develops her own arguments by analyzing sources

As you read further, continue developing your marks on the text. Look for opportunities to:

- Identify important points in sources and how an author responds
- Respond in your own ways to claims made in sources or by an author
- Imagine counterarguments to one or more of these claims

Firsthand accounts ("primary sources") are introduced to better understand the research problem.

22   I began with two fascinating essays based on these materials written by the ethnohistorian James Axtell, "The White Indians of Colonial America" and "The Scholastic Philosophy of the Wilderness."[11] These essays suggest that it would have been a privilege to be captured by North American Indians and taken off to Canada to dwell in a wigwam for the rest of one's life. Axtell's reconstruction of the process by which Indians taught European captives to feel comfortable in the wilderness, first taking their shoes away and giving them moccasins, carrying the children on their backs, sharing the scanty food supply equally, ceremonially cleansing them of their old identities, giving them Indian clothes and jewelry, assiduously teaching them the Indian language, finally adopting them into their families, and even visiting them after many years if, as sometimes happened, they were restored to white society—all of this creates a compelling portrait of Indian culture and helps to explain the extraordinary attraction that Indian culture apparently exercised over Europeans.

The debate among historians is repeated in primary sources.

23   But, as I had by now come to expect, this beguiling portrait of the Indians' superior humanity is called into question by other writings on Indian captivity-for example, Norman

---

[11]See Axtell, "The White Indians of Colonial America" and "The Scholastic Philosophy of the Wilderness," *The European and the Indian*, pp. 168–206 and 131–167.

Heard's *White into Red*, whose summation of the comparative treatment of captive children east and west of the Mississippi seems to contradict some of Axtell's conclusions:

> The treatment of captive children seems to have been similar in initial stages. . . . Most children were treated brutally at the time of capture. Babies and toddlers usually were killed immediately and other small children would be dispatched during the rapid retreat to the Indian villages if they cried, failed to keep the pace, or otherwise indicated a lack of fortitude needed to become a worthy member of the tribe. Upon reaching the village, the child might face such ordeals as running the gauntlet or dancing in the center of a throng of threatening Indians. The prisoner might be so seriously injured at this time that he would no longer be acceptable for adoption.[12]

24   One account which Heard reprints is particularly arresting. A young girl captured by the Comanches who had not been adopted into a family but used as a slave had been peculiarly mistreated. When they wanted to wake her up the family she belonged to would take a burning brand from the fire and touch it to her nose. When she was returned to her parents, the flesh of her nose was completely burned away, exposing the bone.[13]

25   Since the pictures drawn by Heard and Axtell were in certain respects irreconcilable, it made sense to turn to a first-hand account to see how the Indians treated their captives in a particular instance. Mary Rowlandson's "The Soveraignty and Goodness of God," published in Boston around 1680, suggested itself because it was so widely read and had set the pattern for later narratives. Rowlandson interprets her captivity as God's punishment on her for failing to keep the Sabbath properly on several occasions. She sees everything that happens to her as a sign from God. When the Indians are kind to her, she attributes her good fortune to divine Providence; when they are cruel, she blames her captors. But beyond the question of how Rowlandson interprets events is the question of what she saw in the first place and what she considered worth reporting. The following passage, with its

---

[12]J. Norman Heard, *White into Red: A Study of the Assimilation of White Persons Captured by Indians* (Metuchen, N.J., 1973), p. 97.
[13]See ibid., p. 98.

abrupt shifts of focus and peculiar emphases, makes it hard to see her testimony as evidence of anything other than the Puritan point of view:

> Then my heart began to fail: and I fell weeping, which was the first time to my remembrance, that I wept before them. Although I had met with so much Affliction, and my heart was many times ready to break, yet could I not shed one tear in their sight: but rather had been all this while in a maze, and like one astonished: but now I may say as, Psal. 137.1. *By the Rivers of Babylon, there we sate down; yea, we wept when we remembered Zion.* There one of them asked me, why I wept, I could hardly tell what to say: yet I answered, they would kill me: No, said he, none will hurt you. Then came one of them and gave me two spoon-fulls of Meal to comfort me, and another gave me half a pint of Pease; which was more worth than many Bushels at another time. Then I went to see King Philip, he bade me come in and sit down, and asked me whether I woold smoke it (a usual Complement nowadayes among Saints and Sinners) but this no way suited me. For though I had formerly used Tobacco, yet I had left it ever since I was first taken. It seems to be a Bait, the Devil layes to make men loose their precious time: I remember with shame, how formerly, when I had taken two or three pipes, I was presently ready for another, such a bewitching thing it is: But I thank God, he has now given me power over it; surely there are many who may be better imployed than to ly sucking a stinking Tobacco-pipe.[14]

What Rowlandson sees or can't see during her captivity is significant. How does analysis in this section recall an earlier section of the essay?

26   Anyone who has ever tried to give up smoking has to sympathize with Rowlandson, but it is nonetheless remarkable, first, that a passage which begins with her weeping openly in front of her captors, and comparing herself to Israel in Babylon, should end with her railing against the vice of tobacco; and, second, that it has not a word to say about King Philip, the leader of the Indians who captured her and mastermind of the campaign that devastated the white population of the English colonies. The fact that Rowlandson has

[14]Mary Rowlandson, "The Soveraignty and Goodness of God, Together with the Faithfulness of His Promises Displayed; Being a Narrative of the Captivity and Restauration of Mrs. Mary Rowlandson (1676)," in *Held Captive by Indians: Selected Narratives, 1642–1836*, ed. Richard VanDerBeets (Knoxville, Tenn., 1973), pp. 57–58.

just been introduced to the chief of chiefs makes hardly any impression on her at all. What excites her is a moral issue which was being hotly debated in the seventeenth century: to smoke or not to smoke (Puritans frowned on it, apparently, because it wasted time and presented a fire hazard). What seem to us the peculiar emphases in Rowlandson's relation are not the result of her having *screened out* evidence she couldn't handle, but of her way of constructing the world. She saw what her seventeenth-century English Separatist background made visible. It is when one realizes that the biases of twentieth-century historians like Vaughan or Axtell cannot be corrected for simply by consulting the primary materials, since the primary materials are constructed according to *their* authors' biases, that one begins to envy Miller his vision at Matadi. Not for what he didn't see—the Indian and the black—but for his epistemological confidence.

27   Though it is probably true that in certain cases Europeans did consciously tamper with the evidence, in most cases there is no reason to suppose that they did not record faithfully what they saw. And what they saw was not an illusion, was not determined by selfish motives in any narrow sense, but was there by virtue of a *way* of seeing which they could no more consciously manipulate than they could choose not to have been born. At this point, it seemed to me, the ethnocentric bias of the firsthand observers invited an investigation of the cultural situation they spoke from. Karen Kupperman's *Settling with the Indians* (1980) supplied just such an analysis.

28   Kupperman argues that Englishmen inevitably looked at Indians in exactly the same way that they looked at other Englishmen. For instance, if they looked down on Indians and saw them as people to be exploited, it was not because of racial prejudice or antique notions about savagery, it was because they looked down on ordinary English men and women and saw them as subjects for exploitation as well.[15] According to Kupperman, what concerned these writers most when they described the Indians were the insignia of social class, of rank, and of prestige. Indian faces are virtually never described in the earliest accounts, but clothes and hairstyles, tattoos and jewelry, posture and skin color are. "Early modern Englishmen believed that people

---

[15]See Karen Ordahl Kupperman, *Settling with the Indians: The Meeting of English and Indian Cultures in America*, 1580–1640 (Totowa, N.J., 1980), pp. 3, 4.

can create their own identity, and that therefore one communicates to the world through signals such as dress and other forms of decoration who one is, what group or category one belongs to."[16]

29   Kupperman's book marks a watershed in writings on European-Indian relations, for it reverses the strategy employed by Martin two years before. Whereas Martin had performed an ethnographic analysis of Indian cosmology in order to explain, from within, the Indians' motives for engaging in the fur trade, Kupperman performs an ethnographic study of seventeenth-century England in order to explain, from within, what motivated Englishmen's behavior. The sympathy and understanding that Martin, Axtell, and others extend to the Indians are extended in Kupperman's work to the English themselves. Rather than giving an account of "what happened" between Indians and Europeans, like Martin, she reconstructs the worldview that gave the experience of one group its content. With her study, scholarship on European-Indian relations comes full circle.

An entire paragraph is used to transition from gathering research materials to developing a conclusion. Readers are invited to consider their own judgment and interpretation of these ideas.

30   It may well seem to you at this point that, given the tremendous variation among the historical accounts, I had no choice but to end in relativism. If the experience of encountering conflicting versions of the "same" events suggests anything certain it is that the attitude a historian takes up in relation to a given event, the way in which he or she judges and even describes "it"—and the "it" has to go in quotation marks because, depending on the perspective, that event either did or did not occur—this stance, these judgments and descriptions are a function of the historian's position in relation to the subject. Miller, standing on the banks of the Congo, couldn't see the black men he was supervising because of his background, his assumptions, values, experiences, goals. Jennings, intent on exposing the distortions introduced into the historical record by Vaughan and his predecessors stretching all the way back to Winthrop, couldn't see that Winthrop and his peers were not racists but only Englishmen who looked at other cultures in the way their own culture had taught them to see one another. The historian can never escape the limitations of his or her own position in history and so inevitably gives an account that is an extension of the circumstances from which it springs. But it seems to me that when one is

[16]Ibid., p. 35.

confronted with this particular succession of stories, cultural and historical relativism is not a position that one can comfortably assume. The phenomena to which these histories testify—conquest, massacre, and genocide, on the one hand; torture, slavery, and murder on the other—cry out for judgment. When faced with claims and counterclaims of this magnitude one feels obligated to reach an understanding of what actually did occur. The dilemma posed by the study of European-Indian relations in early America is that the highly charged nature of the materials demands a moral decisiveness which the succession of conflicting accounts effectively precludes. That is the dilemma I found myself in at the end of this course of reading, and which I eventually came to resolve as follows.

The research process increases self-awareness about earlier approaches to the research question and sources.

31   My problem presupposed that I couldn't judge because I didn't know what the facts were. All I had, or could have, was a series of different perspectives, and so nothing that would count as an authoritative source on which moral judgments could be based. But, as I have just shown, I did judge, and that is because, as I now think, I did have some facts. I seemed to accept as facts that ninety percent of the native American population of New England died after the first hundred years of contact, that tribes in eastern Canada and the northeastern United States had a compact with the game they killed, that Comanches had subjected a captive girl to casual cruelty, that King Philip smoked a pipe, and so on. It was only where different versions of the same event came into conflict that I doubted the text was a record of something real. And even then, there was no question about certain major catastrophes. I believed that four hundred Pequots were killed near Saybrook, that Winthrop was the Governor of the Massachusetts Bay Colony when it

---

Activity 4: Anticipate

A resolution to the research problem is forecasted for the next section. Recalling the introduction and other important moments in the article, how do you think it will conclude? Consider the article's thesis, purpose, and the sources gathered and developed to this point.

As you wrestle with these questions individually or in groups, take a moment to imagine a conclusion you might develop, had you explored a similar problem with these sources. Consider, for example, concluding with an answer to the research problem or a new question. You may also give your reasons for choosing one approach over another.

happened, and so on. My sense that certain events, such as the Pequot War, did occur in no way reflected the indecisiveness that overtook me when I tried to choose among the various historical versions. In fact, the need I felt to make up my mind was impelled by the conviction that certain things had happened that shouldn't have happened. Hence it was never the case that "what happened" was completely unknowable or unavailable. It's rather that in the process of reading so many different approaches to the same phenomenon I became aware of the difference in the attitudes that informed these approaches. This awareness of the interests motivating each version cast suspicion over everything, in retrospect, and I ended by claiming that there was nothing I could know. This, I now see, was never really the case. But how did it happen? . . .

32   At this point something is beginning to show itself that has up to now been hidden. The notion that all facts are only facts within a perspective has the effect of emptying statements of their content. Once I had Miller and Vaughan and Jennings, Martin and Hudson, Axtell and Heard, Rowlandson and Wood and Whitaker, and Kupperman; I had Europeans and Indians, ships and canoes, wigwams and log cabins, bows and arrows and muskets, wigs and tattoos, whisky and corn, rivers and forts, treaties and battles, fire and blood— and then suddenly all I had was a meta-statement about perspectives. The effect of bringing perspectivism to bear on history was to wipe out completely the subject matter of history. And it follows that bringing perspectivism to bear in this way on any subject matter would have a similar effect; everything is wiped out and you are left with nothing but a single idea—perspectivism itself.

33   But—and it is a crucial but—all this is true only if you believe that there is an alternative. As long as you think that there are or should be facts that exist outside of any perspective, then the notion that facts are perspectival will have this disappearing effect on whatever it touches. But if you are convinced that the alternative does not exist, that there really are no facts except as they are embedded in some particular way of seeing the world, then the argument that a set of facts derives from some particular worldview is no longer an argument against that set of facts. If all facts share this characteristic, to say that any one fact is perspectival doesn't change its factual nature in the slightest. It merely reiterates it.

34   This doesn't mean that you have to accept just any-body's facts. You can show that what someone else asserts to be a fact is false. But it does mean that you can't argue that someone else's facts are not facts *because they are only the prod-uct of a perspective*, since this will be true of the facts that you perceive as well. What this means then is that arguments about "what happened" have to proceed much as they did before post-structuralism broke in with all its talk about lan-guage-based reality and culturally produced knowledge. Reasons must be given, evidence adduced, authorities citied, analogies drawn. Being aware that all facts are motivated, believing that people are always operating inside some par-ticular interpretive framework or other is a pertinent argu-ment when what is under discussion is the way beliefs are grounded. But it doesn't give one any leverage on the facts of a particular case.[17]

Although the   35   What this means for the problem I've been addressing
research   is that I must piece together the story of European-Indian re-
process   lations as best I can, believing this version up to a point, that
began with   version not at all, another almost entirely, according to what
information-   seems reasonable and plausible, given everything else that I
seeking, it   know. And this, as I've shown, is what I was already doing in
shifts focus by   the back of my mind without realizing it, because there was
showing that   nothing else I *could* do. If the accounts don't fit together
"the subject of   neatly, that is not a reason for rejecting them all in favor of a
[the] debate   metadiscourse about epistemology; on the contrary, one en-
has changed."   counters contradictory facts and divergent points of view in
The article   practically every phase of life, from deciding whom to marry
ends not by   to choosing the right brand of cat food, and one decides as
filling the gaps   best one can given the evidence available. It is only the na-
in historical   ture of the academic situation which makes it appear that
knowledge,   one can linger on the threshold of decision in the name of an
but with an   epistemological principle. What has really happened in such
entirely new   a case is that the subject of debate has changed from the ques-
challenge.   tion of what happened in a particular instance to the ques-
tion of how knowledge is arrived at. The absence of pressure to decide what happened creates the possibility for this change of venue.

---

[17]The position I've been outlining is a version of neopragmatism. For an exposition, see *Against Theory: Literary Studies and the New Pragmatism*, ed. W. J. T. Mitchell (Chicago, 1985).

The change of venue, however, is itself an action taken. In diverting attention from the original problem and placing it where Miller did, on "the mind of man," it once again ignores what happened and still is happening to American Indians. The moral problem that confronts me now is not that I can never have any facts to go on, but that the work I do is not directed toward solving the kinds of problems that studying the history of European-Indian relations has awakened me to.

The preceding text illustrates how, especially for academic researchers, the process of reading and writing is *recursive*. A narrative focus on the research process shows the importance of gathering and analyzing sources without committing to one position or another. Finding many different explanations and testing them against each other allow researchers to critically evaluate sources and make strategic decisions about how to develop their own arguments. The process of struggling with ideas in sources can lead to engaged participation in the conversation.

> *Reading and writing are interrelated activities that work together recursively.*

The research narrative also shows that reading and writing are interrelated. Each new source sends researchers back to sources read previously and invites constant revision of earlier ideas and interpretations.

ACTIVE READING

Academic prose presents unique challenges to readers, especially those who aren't already initiated in the academic conversation. Because their purpose is critical rather than simply informative, academic texts demand active readers who are prepared to look up unfamiliar words, decode complicated arguments, and work hard to arrive at conclusions.

Since these texts demand constant critical engagement, we have to build new strategies for active reading. You may already underline or highlight passages when you read, so that you can summarize an argument, thesis, and main points. If you've highlighted an academic text, go back and scan a couple of those

> *Academic prose demands careful, active, and critical readers who participate in the process of making meaning.*

passages. Do you recall why you thought those passages were significant? Do you recall what you were thinking as you highlighted? You
may find that it's hard to remember details, even when you return to the
text immediately after reading.

Used alone, underlining and highlighting can be limiting because they do not require a reader's critical engagement. Highlighting can help you identify important parts of a text, but doesn't help
you to recall later *why* you highlighted those parts or *how* the parts fit
into a larger argument. In other words, highlighting identifies an
author's significant points, but it doesn't help us return to the text for
new purposes.

According to writing scholar John Gage, active readers engage
self-consciously with texts and are willing to be "swayed" by strong arguments.[4] We can develop new strategies and add to older ones in
order to enhance our reading experiences and become more conscious,
active readers who are open to considering ideas rather than accepting
or rejecting them at face value. In the rest of this chapter, we'll look at
some of the following active reading strategies:

- Marking the text with notes and comments
- Maintaining a reading log
- Reading consciously
- Summarizing the argument
- Asking questions about the argument
- Finding answers in the text
- Identifying and defining unfamiliar terms
- Copying significant and memorable passages
- Using the author's notes to find additional ideas and sources

Use Margins to Annotate Texts

In the example below, a student used active reading strategies to
engage with Tompkins's introduction. The student underlined unfamiliar words and made notes, or "annotations," in the margin that help
track the argument and anticipate questions about claims and issues
raised while reading:

Fantasies of
Indians are
narcissistic
for white
people? Why?

My story stands for the relationship most non-Indians have to the people who first populated this continent, a relationship characterized by narcissistic fantasies of freedom and adventure, of a life lived closer to nature and to spirit than the life we lead now. As Vine Deloria, Jr. has pointed out, the American Indian Movement in the early seventies couldn't get people to pay attention to what was happening to Indians who were alive in the present, so powerful was this country's infatuation with people who wore loincloths, lived in tepees, and roamed the plains and forests long ago. The present essay, like these fantasies, doesn't have much to do with actual Indians, though its subject matter is the histories of European-Indian relations in seventeenth-century New England. In a sense, my encounter with Indians as an adult doing "research" replicates the childhood one, for while I started out to learn about Indians, I ended up preoccupied with a problem of my own.

Transition to
purpose of
essay:
understanding
the
importance of
point of view

This essay enacts a particular instance of the challenge post-structuralism poses to the study of history. In simpler language, it concerns the difference that point of view makes when people are giving accounts of events, whether at first or second hand. The problem is that if all accounts of events are determined through and through by the observer's frame of reference, then one will never know, in any given case, what really happened.

Why
"automatically"?
Why Miller?

I encountered this problem in concrete terms while preparing to teach a course in colonial American literature. I'd set out to learn what I could about the Puritans' relations with American Indians. All I wanted was a general idea of what had happened between the English settlers and the natives in seventeenth-century New England; post-structuralism and its dilemmas were the furthest thing from my mind. I began, more or less automatically, with Perry Miller, who hardly mentions the Indians at all, then proceeded to the work of historians who had dealt exclusively with the European-Indian encounter. At first, it was a question of deciding which of these authors to believe, for it quickly became apparent that there was no unanimity on the subject. As I read

Who to
believe?

on, however, I discovered that the problem was more complicated than deciding whose version of events was correct. Some of the conflicting accounts were not simply contradictory, they were completely incommensurable, in that their assumptions about what counted as a valid approach to the subject, and what the subject itself was, diverged in fundamental ways. Faced with an array of mutually irreconcilable points of view, points of view which determined what was being discussed as well as the terms of the discussion, I decided to turn to primary sources for clarification, only to discover that the primary sources reproduced the problem all over again. I found myself, in other words, in an epistemological quandary, not only unable to decide among conflicting versions of events but also unable to believe that any such decision could, in principle, be made. It was a moral quandary as well. Knowledge of what really happened when the Europeans and the Indians first met seemed particularly important, since the result of that encounter was virtual genocide. This was the kind of past "mistake" which, presumably, we studied history in order to avoid repeating. If studying history couldn't put us in touch with actual events and their causes, then what was to prevent such atrocities from happening again?

For a while, I remained at this impasse. But through analyzing the process by which I had reached it, I eventually arrived at an understanding which seemed to offer a way out. This essay records the concrete experience of meeting and solving the difficulty I have just described (as an abstract problem, I thought I had solved it long ago). My purpose is not to throw new light on antifoundationalist epistemology—the solution I reached is not a new one—but to dramatize and expose the troubles antifoundationalism gets you into when you meet it, so to speak, in the road.

"secondary" and "primary" sources

The moral cost if we don't understand history

Dramatizing the problem of point of view

Record comments and questions as you read.

Annotations help prepare for later visits to the text by outlining key points in the argument. *Comment* notes can remind the reader of places where the stakes, or the significance, of key issues are described. *Question* notes can remind the reader to find out if answers are given later in the argument or left for readers to deduce. Your annotations on the text may be developed into more extensive notes in a *reading log*, where you can keep a permanent record of responses, questions, and reactions sparked by your reading.

Student Voice

Cindy, who read a number of law articles dealing with medical malpractice, explains how paragraph-by-paragraph summary helped her to read more actively.

I found that summarizing paragraphs I read and noting my thoughts next to them improved my comprehension and memory of difficult passages, my ability to develop my thoughts on the reading, and my vocabulary.

Summarizing Texts

Whenever you encounter a long or especially complex text, track your reading by summarizing each paragraph or main idea in your reading log. You can summarize either by paragraph or by section.

Summary by Paragraph: The "Map" Think of a paragraph-by-paragraph summary as a map that describes a text's "layout." This kind of summary helps you quickly return to a particular point or example without having to reread the entire text. For example:

- **Paragraph 1:** Many Americans share childhood fantasies about Indians of the past that make them incapable of seeing Indians in the present. Historical research reflects rather than solves this problem—like it's impossible to learn about actual Indians.
- **Paragraph 2:** Maybe it's impossible to completely know about the past, because everything we have is the point of view of one person (or group) or another. What about the facts?
- **Paragraph 3:** Research begins with historians (Miller and others) who focus on Puritan–Indian relationships and come up with very different accounts. The solution could be in primary (first-person) texts, but they are just as conflicted as the historical sources. Is it impossible to know what happened? There's a moral problem if we can't know for sure, but we think we know—maybe this is where the narcissism in par. 1 comes from?
- **Paragraph 4:** The rest of the essay is forecasted: describing and analyzing the research process, then coming up with a solution.

Summary by Section: The "Path"   You can also track major moves in a text, identifying "chunks" of meaning you can revisit and analyze in more detail in later readings. Rather than going paragraph by paragraph through a text, you might want to look more closely at types of sources, focus on the motivation for research, or trace the movement from analysis to conclusion. For example:

- **Section 1** (paragraphs 1–6): The essay's motivation: help students challenge fantasies of Indians and of European–Indian encounters. Research problem: understand the role of point of view—the "troubles" of "antifoundationalism."
- **Section 2** (paragraphs 7–11): Surveying history texts written in the 1950s and 1960s.
- **Section 3** (paragraphs 12–24): Seeing how historians become "sensitized to questions of race and ethnicity" in the 1960s and 1970s.
- **Section 4** (paragraphs 25–33): Shifting from historians to first-person accounts.

If your paragraph-by-paragraph summary works like a *map* of the text, this section-by-section summary includes fewer details but helps you follow the unique *path* an author takes through sources and examples.

Tracking Subject, Organization, and Purpose in Texts

You can also use detailed notes in your reading log to track the *subject* and *purpose* of each paragraph or section. Make sure that you can recall both the claims (the "what") and the purpose (the "why") of important paragraphs and passages.

Recall that Tompkins became perplexed by her first set of sources, and shows readers how she used these tracking strategies to organize and make sense of ideas. Her approach for wrestling with the texts she found includes:

1. Reading each source for ideas and information
2. Connecting sources to understand the critical issues in history, encountering an "impasse"
3. Revising the research question and seeking more sources

We can visualize the argument as an evolutionary process that moves from a simple *informative* purpose to a more complex *critical* purpose, and concludes with a challenge for readers to reflect on their own perspectives and judgment strategies:

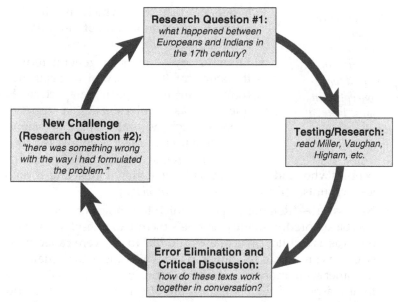

FIGURE 3.2   Jane Tompkins's research process.

Define Unfamiliar Terms

Record unfamiliar words or concepts in your reading log, and develop definitions using a college dictionary or another reference text, such as a specialized dictionary or encyclopedia devoted to an academic discipline. You can also search for definitions on the Internet using online dictionaries (e.g., *Merriam-Webster Online* at www.m-w.com) and encyclopedias (e.g., *Wikipedia* at wikipedia.org). University course websites (URLs that end in .edu) may also include reference pages devoted to a particular discipline or subject area. The following are some unfamiliar words found in Tompkins's article that can easily be defined using the Internet, a college library reference section, or books on your own shelves:

> *This process illustrates a strong critical thinking model (see Chapter 1): Begin with a researchable question, develop theories through reading, test their validity and credibility, and then develop a more interesting question that starts the process again.*

- Epistemological—"relating to the study of knowledge" (*New Webster's Dictionary*)[5]
- Incommensurable—"having no common measure, utterly disproportionate" (*New Webster's Dictionary*)[6]
- Antifoundationalism—"a term applied to any philosophy which rejects a foundationalist approach; i.e., an anti-foundationalist is one who does not believe that there is some fundamental

Online reference sources are good places to begin understanding specialized terms and concepts, but they must be used critically.

belief or principle which is the basic ground or foundation of inquiry and knowledge" (*Wikipedia*)[7]

- Ethnohistory—"refers in general terms to the study of the history of a social group from an anthropological perspective. Frequently, this involves using a variety of sources, such as oral history, missionary documents, and travel accounts, to reconstruct the social history of marginalized peoples who tend to form the subject matter of most anthropological accounts." (*Encyclopedia of Anthropology*)[8]

- Narcissism—"Relationships in which the choice of one's partner was based predominantly on one's picture of oneself as one is, as one was as a child, or as one would like to be, were called narcissistic, in contrast to relationships in which the actual qualities of the other were more important. In terms of self, narcissism refers to any aspect of the complex state of self-esteem, and includes such things as overweening pride, arrogance, and sensitivity to insult."(*Oxford Encyclopedia of Psychology*)[9]

Every field has its own reference texts to help you understand the terms and concepts that you will encounter in reading, writing, and discussion. Sometimes, as the definition of "narcissism" shows, the explanations can seem as challenging as the terms themselves. As you connect unfamiliar terms with their uses in an academic conversation, you will develop working definitions that aid your reading and that you can confidently use in your own work.

Activity 5: Define Unfamiliar Terms

Identify an unfamiliar word or concept in an academic text. Then, define it in one or two sentences using resources, such as *Merriam-Webster Online*, the *Oxford English Dictionary*, *Wikipedia*, or an academic reference work.

Recording Significant Passages

Your reading log is a good place to record passages from sources that you plan to incorporate as quotations or paraphrases in your own writing projects. Passages you find convincing, controversial, challenging, or unique provide opportunities to develop your own insight and engagement.

Activity 6: Revisit a Difficult Passage in a Source

Identify a passage (of at least one paragraph) in an academic text that you found particularly challenging or thought-provoking. Revisit the passage and read it slowly, noting specific parts that are more easily understood than others. Use those familiar elements as anchors to build your comprehension of the more difficult elements and, finally, the entire passage.

In about one page, engage with the passage in two ways:

- Describe the *subject* of the passage, its point, examples, and other important details.

- Describe the *purpose* of the passage in the context of the entire essay. Is its purpose to introduce a source, provide an example, transition between major parts, or summarize a section?

After fully engaging with the passage, explain how your new understanding helps you to better understand the entire text.

Sample Student Responses

The following student writers chose to examine the same passage from Tompkins's essay.

Connecting Perspectives

I chose paragraph 30 in the Tompkins essay to reread and try to understand better. What first caught my attention (and caught me off guard) was Tompkins's beginning statement, which seemed to focus on and sympathize with Rowlandson's ordeal of tobacco addiction. Because of that first connection, I had a hard time following the connection Tompkins makes at the end of the paragraph about how this related to Miller's vision at Matadi. After reading through the paragraph and picking up a few details in the surrounding paragraphs, it began to make more sense.

Tompkins looks at the parts of the captivity experience Rowlandson focuses on in her narrative, especially the role of Indians. Tompkins points out here that Rowlandson's views were really limited and did not describe the whole picture. The best example is when the Indians offered her food and a smoke from one of their pipes in an attempt to ease her fright; however, Rowlandson rejects their offers and begins to discuss the immoral habit of smoking. Rowlandson's "way of constructing the world" made her focus on the moral temptation of smoking so extreme that, as Tompkins points out, her story "has not a word to say about King Philip," one of the most important Native American leaders of the time. Tompkins shows how these missing details compare to the "biases of twentieth-century historians like Vaughan and Axtell," who try to correct Miller's vision of Matadi but end up reflecting a lot of their own biases. Just like Rowlandson or Miller, the historians see the past through their present values and experiences. Tompkins comes to the conclusion that, just like the historians she had been reading, the first-person accounts also "made a poor source of evidence for the nature of European-Indian relations."

This paragraph works in a couple different ways with the whole essay. First, Tompkins's evaluation of Rowlandson's experience challenges her expectation that the first-person narrative would be a more "truthful" account. The captivity narratives and other examples from colonial times challenge the validity and reliability of the captivity narrative genre. Then, the same principle also reminds readers of the debates between the previous "experts" on the subject, such as Miller, Vaughan, and Axtell. By using these specific examples, Tompkins is able to transition into the rest of her paper and make her way to a conclusion. Even though her conclusion did not present new historical information, it was still insightful and interesting because of the way she showed the limits of perspective.

What Does Smoking Have to Do with Tompkins?

While reading Tompkins essay, I found a couple of paragraphs to be confusing, but the section I really wanted to understand was paragraphs 29 and 30, which were about Rowlandson's captivity experiences. It's actually a quote by Rowlandson that most confused me, and the first time I read it I wasn't quite sure why Tompkins included it. To me, it seemed like a paragraph about smoking, but what did smoking have to do with Tompkins's questions about history? In the long quote, Rowlandson describes her hardships dealing with the Indians. She tells us how she breaks down for the first time since her capture, and cries in front of the Indians. She then quotes the Bible, comparing herself to exiled Jews in Psalms: "By the rivers of Babylon, there we sate down; yea, we wept when we remembered Zion." I knew the Bible verse, but at first I had no idea what this woman was talking about. Then I realized that she was saying she missed her home, she missed her people, and she was afraid of what the future would bring. After the woman's breakdown, the Indians tried to comfort her with food. When that didn't work, they sent her to their leader, King Philip, who asked her to smoke with him. Rowlandson then describes her past use of tobacco and how since she had joined the Puritans she no longer needed it. Now, from her perspective, the devil was trying to tempt her in her moment of weakness. By the end of the paragraph, Rowlandson shows how grateful she is that God has now given her the power to overcome her addiction with the "stinking tobacco pipe."

I had no idea what this had to do with anything Tompkins had previously talked about. How did this Puritan woman's story fit in with the other scholars Tompkins used? I read into the next paragraph, and it was there that the story fit in. I guess I was so baffled the first time I read it that I completely missed her point.

Tompkins explains how incredible it was that this
Puritan woman had been through this whole ordeal
of being captured by the Indians, and was able to
meet with the chief Indian, but all she could
comment on was the moral issue of tobacco smoking. Even though the Indians tried to comfort her
by feeding her, and complimented her by letting
her smoke with the "chief of chiefs," she saw the
whole experience as a test of personal morals.

Tompkins included Rowlandson's story because
it fits perfectly into her theory that it's hard
to know what really happened in the past because
everyone sees things differently. Their time periods, whether during colonial times or in the
present, and their beliefs, like Rowlandson's
dislike of smoking and Miller's experiences in
Africa, affect their viewpoints. After slowing
down and taking a section of a confusing passage
and paying closer attention to it, I found how
well it actually helps Tompkins to move forward
and get the point across in a new way.

Retrace the Author's Steps: Notes and Bibliography

An author's bibliography and explanatory notes provide further
support for readers. For instance, in paragraphs 34–36, Tompkins summarizes Karen Kupperman's argument that English colonizers' understanding of social class explains why they exploited Indians and other
Europeans. She provides references to Kupperman's book *Settling with
the Indians* and notes the specific pages where she found this information. To find out more about this particular aspect of the argument, you
could read those passages yourself. As you read *Settling with the Indians*, Kupperman's references would lead to more sources and help you
follow this thread of discussion into the larger academic conversation.

Many authors also write extensive ex-
planatory notes, where they describe issues or   *Chapter 7 features*
ideas that relate to the argument but are outside   *discusson on using*
its immediate scope. In her final note, Tompkins   *notes in your own*
names her critical position as "neopragmatism,"   *research projects.*
but tells us that a discussion of that concept isn't
her purpose. The note allows her to cite a key text, Mitchell's book
Against Theory, to help interested readers explore the neopragmatist

position in more detail. When read alongside the main text, these explanatory notes help to develop a more complete sense of the conversation surrounding every issue or research question. Since authors often use notes to show readers aspects of an issue that remain blind spots, or aspects that haven't yet been fully worked out, they can be especially helpful in sparking new research projects.

INTEGRATE ACADEMIC READING AND WRITING

At this point, you can see how reading academic texts requires a recursive approach. You'll find that the reading process is much like the writing process because it takes a number of attempts—that is, "drafts"—to grasp an author's points, arguments and important details. These reading drafts often include:

1. A first draft to identify the thesis and important points
2. A second draft to develop a more complex understanding of the argument, and map out the relationship between sources
3. Another draft to identify key rhetorical moves (organization, appeals, and transitions) an author makes to persuade readers
4. Subsequent drafts to identify opportunities for engagement, response, and participation in the conversation.

Strategies for Becoming an Active Reader

1. Keep a dictionary or similar reference work near you as you read.

2. Read in multiple "drafts."

3. Identify confusing points to reread later for understanding.

4. Identify transitional words and passages to track the development of an argument.

5. Mark points in the text where you agree or disagree with the author.

6. Take complete notes in a reading log. Write out especially compelling passages you can quote in your own writing projects.

7. Plan to reread important sections.

8. Find points of connection and dissent between texts.

9. Use bibliographies and explanatory notes to read further in the conversation.

4

Develop a Research Question

CHAPTER OBJECTIVES

In this chapter, you'll learn how to:

- Begin the process of choosing a subject area for research
- Practice one or more brainstorming strategies
- See a subject area and research question on a scale of abstraction
- Connect a subject area to one or more academic conversations
- Identify a manageable aspect of the conversation to explore in research projects

---

Academic writers are rarely satisfied with just accumulating and reporting information. Their passion for issues leads to conversations with other writers whose work they read closely and evaluate carefully in order to develop their own arguments and contribute to an ongoing discussion. The process you take is very similar. You will explore an issue that intersts you through critical thinking, reading, and response. This chapter shows you the first stages of choosing an issue, developing one or more possible research questions, and beginning your research process with easily accessible sources.

The activities in this chapter will help you identify personal, academic, and professional areas of interest and develop them into compelling and researchable questions for your writing projects. Although your instructor will place constraints on these assignments, you can often emphasize certain elements and strategies to shape your research and writing according to your interests. Even if your instructor assigns a subject area for your research writing, you may be able to find an angle that can connect it to the particular issues and conversations that motivate you.

FIND A SUBJECT AREA AND CREATE A RESEARCH QUESTION

Research questions can often reflect your personal interests and everyday experiences. What issues concern, motivate, and challenge you? What campus and community issues spark your curiosity? Are you interested in certain types of music, or a particular film genre or director? Do any political or social issues get your attention? Are you attracted to new technologies? Are teachers in your courses discussing any issues you would like to know more about?

Research projects evolve from combining your personal interests and assignment goals.

As you get started, simply build a list of topics and issues. Get as many ideas on paper as you can. Don't worry about quality at this point, or about how an issue might fit into more than one subject area or conversation. Steroid use in college sports, to use one example, concerns the fields of sports medicine, higher education policy, and sociology—there are many possible ways to write about it inside these discplines or across them. Similarly, automobile fuel technology relates to engineering, environmental sciences, public policy, and economics. Part of the process of refining your research question is directing your interests into one or more academic conversations.

One topic or issue can lead researchers in many directions.

Once you generate a list of possible issues, identify those that most interest you. Develop more focus by asking yourself the following questions:

Develop subject areas and issues into questions.

- What issues lead to interesting questions?
- Which of these questions spark intense debates?
- What contributions can you make to a conversation by exploring one of these questions?
- Who would be interested in reading about one of these issues and learning about your answer?

Activity 1: Discuss Possible Research Issues in Groups

Individually, compile a list of at least five subject areas and at least three issues within each area. Then, identify three issues that are the most interesting to you. For each issue, write down three to five questions that seem the most promising for research. In groups, discuss how each question could apply to a specific area or academic conversation.

Student Voice

Julie, whose research focused on the relationship between psychology and religion, describes a common apprehension about beginning the research process and how she overcame it.

In past research writing courses, starting a project was always the most difficult part for me. I just couldn't get into my topic. Now that I know I can research and write about issues meaningful to me, I find it easier to start researching and writing about my ideas right away, since I'm interested in my project from the start.

CONNECT PERSONAL AND ACADEMIC GOALS

Let's say your instructor has described the writing projects for your course. If so, think about the topics and questions that will best meet course goals. Beginning the process with issues that truly interest you will motivate you to learn something new, explore a problem you're been wrestling with in a new way, or argue for a position you hold on an issue. Of course, you will have other personal and academic goals tied to writing assignments. You want to get good scores on your writing projects and in the course, learn more about your anticipated major or profession, and learn how to write and communicate more effectively. You will also want to develop research questions that are likely to interest your readers.

You may be surprised to learn that almost any everyday question can be explored through academic conversations. Table 4.1 lists and describes some recent research projects undertaken by students like yourself. These examples are listed under certain academic fields, but the questions asked can apply or be adapted to other fields as well. The students developed open-ended research questions first—that is, questions that had no simple yes or no answers and no easy solutions.

TABLE 4.1   Student Research Projects

Agricultural Sciences, Public Policy

- What are the effects of transplanting wolves into the Intermountain West? Do the environmental benefits outweigh the risks of negative impact on farming and ranching?
- How is suburban sprawl affecting farming and farming communities in the United States?

Biology

- Are there scientifically proven benefits to eating organic foods, such as milk produced without Bovine Growth Hormones?
- How much connection is there between vaccination and increased incidents of autism among infants and children?

Cultural Studies, Art and Popular Culture

- How do explicit (sexual or violent) language and content in popular music affect listeners' behavior? Are children affected differently than adults?
- How did the growing popularity of rap music in the late 1980s affect its artistic integrity?
- Is graffiti better seen as an art form or a crime?
- Can playing video games (especially first-person shooting games) really have any negative consequences on players?
- Why is there a debate over photography as a legitimate art form?

To see examples of such student papers, read "Violent Video Games" in Chapter 11 and "Thinking Outside the X-Box" in Chapter 12.

Earth Sciences

- Have technological developments helped seismologists to track and predict earthquakes (such as the one in Haiti in 2010) more effectively today than in the past?
- What is the debate about "peak oil," and what are some alternatives to fossil fuels?

See the student paper "Hope for a Hydrogen Economy" in Chapter 12.

Economics, International Relations

- Is water going to replace oil as the most valuable natural resource? How is entrepreneurial control over water affecting people across the globe?
- How will the Sarbanes-Oxley Act affect corporate bookkeeping practices? How will the act affect investors?

TABLE 4.1   *(continued . . .)*

Education

- How are high stakes testing requirements changing public education in the United States?
- Who is shaping the debate over teaching "intelligent design" in public schools? How are scientists participating in the debate? ◄———————
- How are charter schools and vouchers changing people's access to education? How beneficial are vouchers to poor people compared to public schools?

> *These issues are addressed In Chapter 08, which features excerpts by* New Yorker *writer Margaret Talbot and biologists Michael Antolin and Joan Herbers.*

Film

- How did the science fiction genre develop over time, and how does it compare to other film genres?
- How are gender issues—specifically the relationships between male and female teens or young adults—portrayed in horror films?
- How have movies, like Westerns, affected perceptions of Native Americans? How do Native Americans look at movies that are supposed to be about them? Have Native Americans made historical films in response?

History

- How can authoritarianism—as in Germany in the 1930s—become the dominant political system in a democratic society?
- What social and political conflicts lead to forming the United States's Electoral College system?

Journalism

- How has political journalism changed with media consolidation over the last decade, and how biased is political reporting?

Law

- What are the legal risks of doctors and hospital staff apologizing for medical mistakes? Can apologies reduce the rate of malpractice suits? ◄———

> *Follow one student, Cindy, as she writes about this topic using assignments in this book.*

TABLE 4.1   (*continued . . .*)

Public Health

- How does preimplantation genetic diagnosis work, and what are its benefits and risks?
- What is the history behind fluoridation of drinking water? Why does fluoridation remain a contested issue? What's the science behind fluoridation, and do scientists debate its value?
- What are the ethical and economic stakes of performance-enhancing drugs among professional athletes?

Technology, Computer Science

- Do traffic cameras prevent people from running red lights? How well do they work and what are the technical challenges to perfecting them?
- How do political concerns affect people's access to the Internet in some countries, as with the conditions placed on Google's ability to provide service in China?
- Is increased dependence on technology (self-checkout at grocery stores, iPods, cell phones, MySpace and Facebook, etc.) making young people antisocial?

Brainstorming Your Research Question

Brainstorming activities help you think about broad subject areas and imagine ways they relate to particular issues and concerns. Brainstorming helps you imagine ideas in broader or narrower contexts, which can open up surprising new directions and perspectives to explore through research. It helps you break subjects out of isolation and bring them into contact with like and unlike ideas. It helps you identify aspects of an issue to focus your research and keep it manageable.

As you brainstorm possible research topics, think about the following questions and strategies.

- What kinds of questions are important to your major? Talk with a professor or graduate student in your anticipated major about their research interests. What discussions or debates are they following in the field? Discuss with them the interests that drew you to the major. How might one of your own questions be explored through research?

- What issues and questions are important in the profession you plan to pursue? Can you talk with a working professional who has insight on current issues facing a particular business or industry? Can one or more of those issues be investigated through academic research?

- Think about the magazines you read, or news sites and blogs you follow online. Scan the table of contents in a recent copy of your favorite magazine and identify an issue that interests you and that could be developed through academic research.

- Are there current events you are curious about? One way you might generate lots of possible research questions in a relatively short time is to pick up an issue of a large daily newspaper and scan the contents. Note how editors divide issues into interest areas for particular discourse communities—international relations, economics, culture, sports, and so on—that could bring you into conversations taking place in your discipline, major, or profession.

VISUALIZE YOUR RESEARCH QUESTION

Clustering, or *idea mapping,* helps writers diagram research topics from a number of perspectives. These diagrams can be developed in various levels of detail and tied to particular academic disciplines. Figure 4.1 shows a cluster diagram based on a newspaper article discussing the increasing rates of premature babies born in the United States. The student writer used this cluster to imagine the possible causes of the increase and identify the conditions that allow more premature babies to survive.

Cluster diagrams help writers consider many different perspectives and subtopics related to a larger issue or question. Clusters also help writers see possible connections between the different aspects of an issue, such as in the relationship between premature births and access to insurance in Figure 4.1. They can spark connections and tie issues to particular academic fields, including:

- Researching medical or public policy journals to understand how doctors and and public health officials connect access to health care with health concerns

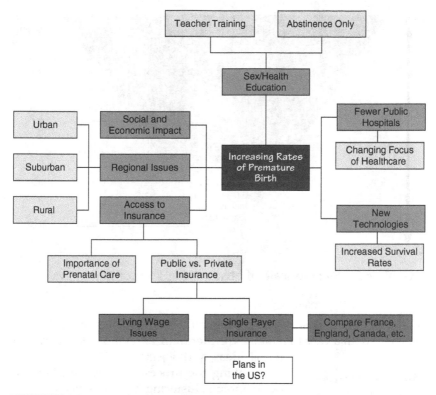

FIGURE 4.1   Sample cluster diagram: "Premature births"

- Comparing premature birth rates between the United States and countries with public medical systems and speculating on possible connections between medical funding and outcomes
- Learning how new medical technologies increase survival rates for premature births and might pose new challenges for pediatric health care professionals

NARROW AND BROADEN YOUR RESEARCH QUESTION

Biologists use an especially valuable technique for organizing their subjects on a *scale of abstraction*. The Scientific Classification System allows them to place any single object of study into a discipline-specific scale that takes the object out of isolation and places it into broader and narrower relationships with like and unlike objects as shown in Figure 4.2.

While the cluster diagram allows researchers to think about a wide *range of connections* between a subject and related issues, the scale

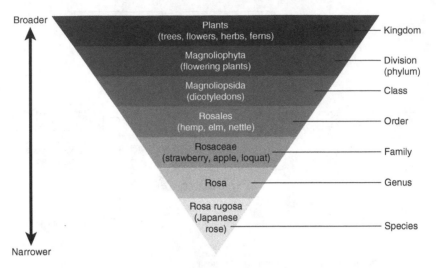

Broader

Narrower

Plants
(trees, flowers, herbs, ferns) — Kingdom

Magnoliophyta
(flowering plants) — Division
(phylum)

Magnoliopsida
(dicotyledons) — Class

Rosales
(hemp, elm, nettle) — Order

Rosaceae
(strawberry, apple, loquat) — Family

Rosa — Genus

Rosa rugosa
(Japanese
rose) — Species

FIGURE 4.2 Sample scale of abstraction: The common rose

of abstraction makes *particular connections*, because it provides researchers with a way to imagine the hierarchical relationships between terms, ideas, and objects.

Anticipate the scope of your project.

Taking the process one step further, we can combine clustering and classification into a *concept map* that visualizes the movement from a broad subject area to subtopics by describing the connections between them. The more you reflect on and identify the specific relationships between ideas, the easier it is to choose a manageable *scope* for your project, and, at the same time, anticipate connections that can be developed as needed.

For example, imagine a writing project examining the new technologies that increase survival rates for premature babies. To develop the project beyond that initial idea, issues from a cluster diagram can be incorporated, and logical connections between one subtopic and another can then be developed. If, for instance, new technologies allow for higher survival rates, are those technologies available to people in every region, or do differences in access between urban, suburban, and rural areas play important roles in whose premature babies are most likely to survive? Consider the map of possible connections in Figure 4.3.

To develop ideas in more detail and make more connections, we could continue adding aspects and relationships as necessary, positioning them hierarchically and purposefully to each other.

A scale of abstraction helps *contextualize* a project in relation to other possible subjects and aspects, and helps anticipate the kind and amount of *detail* that will be incorporated into the projects. Although

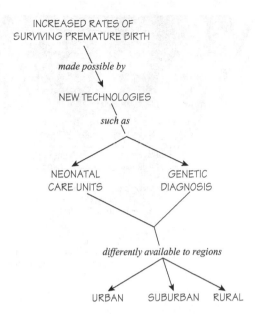

FIGURE 4.3 Sample concept map: Premature birth survival rates

your most important task right now is to come up with some interesting topics and questions for research projects, it is likely that you will find yourself either having to narrow your question to make it more manageable, or to broaden its scope to ensure that you can meet the requirements of your writing assignments.

Scales of abstraction can be adapted to any subject. For example, a film studies student who became interested in the work of the American director Stanley Kubrick was immediately challenged by the need to narrow his interests in order to keep his research project manageable. First, he found that the director's films spanned from the 1950s to 1990s, making it impossible to deal with all of his films in depth. Additionally, following some preliminary research, the student discovered that Kubrick is highly regarded by film scholars, so he had to make some decisions about how to approach the large body of scholarship on the director's films and begin his project with a manageable scope. The student developed a scale of abstraction that helped him conceptualize a number of possible organizing strategies and research questions as shown in Figure 4.4.

The student knew that he wanted to write about Kubrick's 1987 film, *Full Metal Jacket,* but he was unable to find enough academic work just on that film. Working upward on the scale of abstraction, he could consider his first choice in a number of broader contexts so that he could fulfill class requirements while still focusing on issues that interested him the most. The student ultimately chose to look at *Full*

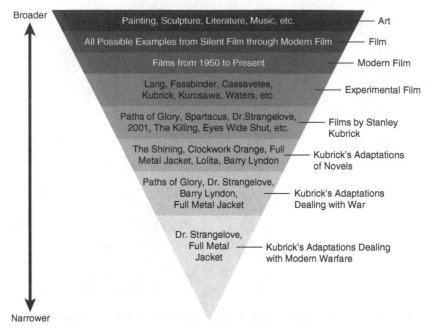

Broader

Painting, Sculpture, Literature, Music, etc. ——— Art

All Possible Examples from Silent Film through Modern Film ——— Film

Films from 1950 to Present ——— Modern Film

Lang, Fassbinder, Cassavetes,
Kubrick, Kurosawa, Waters, etc. ——— Experimental Film

Paths of Glory, Spartacus, Dr.Strangelove,
2001, The Killing, Eyes Wide Shut, etc. ——— Films by Stanley
Kubrick

The Shining, Clockwork Orange, Full
Metal Jacket, Lolita, Barry Lyndon ——— Kubrick's Adaptations
of Novels

Paths of Glory, Dr. Strangelove,
Barry Lyndon,   ——— Kubrick's Adaptations
Full Metal Jacket   Dealing with War

Dr. Strangelove,
Full Metal ——— Kubrick's Adaptations Dealing
Jacket   with Modern Warfare

Narrower

FIGURE 4.4   Sample scale of abstraction: Kubrick films

Metal Jacket in relation to Kubrick's other films about warfare, but the scale opened up a number of additional ways to think about the film:

- because it is a film about boot camp and combat during the Vietnam War, he could have looked at *Full Metal Jacket* in relation to other American films about the war (*Apocalypse Now*, *The Deer Hunter*, *Platoon*, *Forrest Gump*, and even the *Rambo* movies)
- he could have worked only with films that were supportive of the Vietnam War or of war generally
- he could have compared only films that challenged war generally, or US involvement in Vietnam specifically
- he might have investigated the cultural significance of the Vietnam War in the United States during the 1980s and considered the importance of Kubrick's film (again perhaps turning to *Platoon* for comparison)
- he might have viewed films about, and read academic treatments of, the Vietnam War in world cinema (in Europe and Asia, for example)
- he might have considered the film in relation to Asian and Asian-American perceptions of the Vietnam War

Because the possibilities for interesting and viable research projects in any field are practically endless, prewriting and brainstorming strategies such as clustering, classifying, and concept mapping are all valuable tools for helping researchers to visualize and manage projects in early stages. Additionally, these prewriting techniques help prevent much of the frustration students can experience early in the research process, when they begin searching for sources only to become either quickly overwhelmed by the amount of research material available or, just as quickly, dejected by an apparent lack of material. In the next chapter, we'll look more closely at strategies for further limiting and expanding the scope of your project once you begin searching for sources. For now though, the challenge is in finding the area and question that both interests you and meets the requirements of the assignment set out by your instructor.

Activity 2: Envision an Issue on a Scale of Abstraction

At this point, you have thought of one or more possible topics you can choose for your research project. Take an area of interest—or a question, if you've gotten that far—and build a scale of abstraction around it. As you build your scale, try to position an issue or question in such a way that you can think of at least three levels of abstraction above (broader) and below (narrower).

Note: In the process of building your scale, you may realize that overly broad subjects, such as abortion, euthanasia, and gun control, are not usually practical for the kinds of inquiry-oriented research projects that you'll do in this course. Sometimes instructors place these three, along with certain others, off-limits for their students' research projects because many of us have trouble getting out of the most general conceptions of the issues (abortion is always wrong, private gun ownership should be illegal, and so on) and into inquiry-focused questions that will be more productive for working in academic conversations.

Student Voice

Cindy, a pre-law student, explains how building a scale of abstraction helped her to narrow her topic and develop a compelling research question.

My greatest challenge in writing this paper was refocusing and refocusing again on a narrow enough area to stay within the parameters of what was practical for my time and abilities. I was interested in a lot of the legal issues related to medical malpractice, but that was too broad for a semester project. The scale of abstraction helped me to focus my research project on the legal risks of doctors and hospital staff apologizing for medical mistakes.

FIND BROADER CONTEXTS FOR LOCAL ISSUES

A student in a recent writing course became interested in a local highway project that was the subject of a lot of controversy. Because its planned route was through protected wetlands, many people in the community were concerned with the impact of the highway on the local ecosystem and with the project's legality. Other community members favored the project because of the positive impact on traffic it was anticipated to have. The student wanted to fully understand the issue so that she could develop her own informed opinion, but she couldn't find much information about the particular highway project outside of local newspapers. Rather than abandoning her interests, the student worked upwards on the scale of abstraction to see the project in a *broader context*, and position the local issue in a variety of possible ways, such as:

- in the field of **public policy**, looking at the impact of highway building on traffic flow
- in the field of **environmental sciences**, looking at the impact of highway building on wetlands
- in the field of **political science**, looking at the impact of a voter referendum process on public debate
- in the field of **law**, looking at how the enforcement of protected lands is achieved and maintained.

KNOW YOUR PURPOSE

In further shaping your research question, think about what you plan to accomplish. You may want to achieve an in-depth knowledge of an academic debate or controversy. You may want to integrate—or compare and contrast—the work of researchers in more than one academic field. You may want to test a theory or solution, or understand a particular case in order to generalize about a larger problem. You may use your research to conduct your own field or laboratory investigation.

You will begin locating and reading sources for your research projects shortly. If you already have a preliminary purpose in mind, you can do much of your organizational work as you read. Anticipating your purpose early in the process will make it easier to agree and disagree with your sources.

AS YOU READ:

✓ List aspects or subtopics of larger issues

✓ Pose questions about issues and ideas

✓ Anticipate a purpose

✓ Connect new sources to old ones

✓ Share ideas and plans with your classmates and instructor

DEVELOP A RESEARCH QUESTION:
A CASE STUDY

After reading local and national newspapers and watching the news on TV, a student became interested in issues of surveillance in U.S. society. She noticed on a daily basis that there were a number of news stories on surveillance in the national and world sections of the paper and that editorial writers were regularly presenting their opinions on those stories. Two of those pieces are reproduced in this section. The first is an editorial from the *New York Times* that criticized the New York Police Department for allegedly infiltrating and surveilling protests. The second, from the *Associated Press State & Local Wire*, reports on a February 2007 ruling by the U.S. District Court against indiscriminate police surveillance in New York City.

See Chapter 13 for more readings on surveillance.

Editorial: Surveillance, New York Style[1]

It's a sad day when a police force generally known for its professionalism is caught using underhanded tactics to spy on and even distort political protests and mass rallies. Yet that is precisely what an archive of videotapes shows New York City police officers or people working with them doing at seven public gatherings since August 2004. The sorry tale was laid out by Jim Dwyer in yesterday's Times in an article based on civilian and police videotapes gathered by a forensic analyst critical of the tactics.

The most disturbing instance of improper behavior occurred last year during the Republican National Convention when a sham arrest of a man secretly working with the police set off a bruising confrontation with demonstrators.

The man, who had vivid blond hair, was holding a sign at a march of poor people when the police suddenly moved to arrest him. Onlookers shouted at the police to let him go, and officers in riot gear responded by pushing against the crowd. Protesters were put on the ground, and at least two were arrested. Meanwhile, the blond-haired man spoke quietly with the police and was quickly led away. The same man was videotaped at an arrest scene a day earlier calling out words that seemed intended to rile the bystanders.

This was a deliberate effort to incite violence that would in turn justify a tough police response.

Another disturbing incident occurred last year when a police helicopter, attempting to track bicycle riders at night through the Lower East Side, recorded nearly four minutes of a couple's intimate moments on the secluded terrace of a Second Avenue penthouse. The night-vision camera did not catch the couple's most personal moments, but the invasion of privacy proved deeply upsetting and brought a formal complaint from one of the victims. It was a sobering reminder for those who generally favor surveillance, as the penthouse owner does, that covert spying often sweeps up innocent victims.

The questionable police tactics may have been fostered by a national mood that favored tough antiterrorism measures after Sept. 11, 2001, even if that meant an erosion of civil liberties. The same impulse to overreach that led the Bush administration to intercept Americans' international communications without warrants, and that emboldened the F.B.I. to spy on groups like Greenpeace and Catholic Worker members, was surely at work in New York when the police spied on people protesting the Iraq war, bicyclists riding in a mass rally and even mourners at a street vigil.

Mayor Michael Bloomberg's record on free speech is already pretty poor. Unless he wants to make a disregard for New Yorkers' rights part of his legacy, he should make sure that the police understand what civil liberties mean in a democracy.

Source: New York Times, December 23, 2005. Judge Bans Routine NYPD Videotaping of Political Protests

Judge Bans Routine NYPD Videotaping of Political Protests

What happened
in the 1980s?
Where?

More than 20 years after a court settlement framed guidelines for police investigations of political activities, a federal judge rapped police for videotaping demonstrations.

U.S. District Judge Charles S. Haight said New York Police Department videotaping of two recent protests was as egregious as police conduct at

Historical
connection—
Vietnam War

anti-Vietnam War demonstrations 35 years ago that led to permanent court oversight of police surveillance and intelligence collecting methods at large gatherings.

The judge said Thursday that police cannot routinely videotape demonstrations when

Demonstrators
OK if it's politi-
cal activity—
instead of
what?

they involve purely political activity. He said the city had violated the Handschu guidelines, named for the lead plaintiff in a case that included 1960s radical activist Abbie Hoffman and others as plaintiffs. The guidelines date

1985—
Handschu"
ruling, NYC

to 1985.

"Solely politically based investigations are flatly prohibited by the guidelines," the judge wrote. "In other words, there must always be a legitimate law enforcement pur-

Law enforce-
ment or
politics—who
decides?

pose[;] having a purpose of investigating political activity exclusively for its own sake is never allowed."

The city was not punished for the videotaping of the two recent protests, but the judge said it would be held in con-

tempt of court for future violations and could be fined.

New York Civil Liberties Union executive director Donna Lieberman said the ruling "should restore the expectation that New Yorkers can participate in lawful demonstrations without fear of being placed in political dossiers."

The judge said the city cannot be stopped from videotaping demonstrators on First Amendment grounds, despite the plaintiffs' contention that being videotaped by police at peaceful protests is unpleasant and unsettling and inhibits their activities.

"These sentiments, while understandable in human terms, fall well short" of what is needed to assert a constitutional claim, the judge said.

City law department special counsel Gail Donoghue said it was significant that the judge rejected the plaintiffs' long-standing argument that the videotaping violates the First Amendment.

The judge rejected the city's argument that it could not be found to violate the Handschu guidelines unless it had also violated the Constitution.

The judge
supports and
rejects parts
of both
arguments

"If all the Handschu guidelines do is forbid NYPD conduct that the Constitution forbids, those involved in the case have been wasting their time," the judge said. "I reject that interpretation. It is entirely appropriate for a consent decree or guidelines such as these to prohibit police activity which the Constitution would allow."

He sided with lawyers for the class who complained that police procedures regarding videotaping that were implemented in September 2004 amounted to police deciding they can videotape political demonstrations whenever they want.

He said the police department acted improperly when it videotaped demonstrators in December 2005 in a march organized by advocates for the homeless outside Mayor Michael Bloomberg's residence. He said the department also erred when in March 2005 it videotaped participants in a Harlem rally.

Lawyers for the class had also protested the videotaping of monthly Critical Mass bicycle demonstrations throughout the city, but the judge said those demonstrations could be videotaped if police obtained authorization for videotaping from the department's deputy commissioner of intelligence.

"It is clear that some Critical Mass bikers thought the best

way to get their message across was to engage in the unlawful and dangerous practices of running red lights and impeding automobile traffic," the judge said.

The consent decree that created the Handschu guidelines settled a 1971 lawsuit brought by the Black Panther Party, alleging that police engaged in widespread surveillance of legitimate political activity and distributed the information to other law enforcement groups.

The Handschu guidelines were modified after the Sept. 11, 2001, terrorist attacks to help the police department investigate terrorism or terrorism-related crimes.

The judge said a police statement of the importance of videotaping large well-advertised public gatherings, airports, bridges, tunnels and subway lines had the "unintended consequence of showing that more modest and unheralded political gatherings, such as the Coalition for the Homeless demonstration, are less likely to attract terrorists bent upon destruction or to deter terrorism by the open and public display of video recorders and cameras."

Key events: homeless protest Dec. 2005, and Harlem rally Mar. 2005 (about what?)

Key events: Critical Mass demonstration (back to NYT editiorial)

Police collecting/ distributing info on Black Panthers— why?

Patriot Act passed about then?

Find out more about this group

Or are they saying demonstrations can attract terrorists?

Are homeless people and bike riders terrorists? Might they be? How do police decide? Maybe they're right?

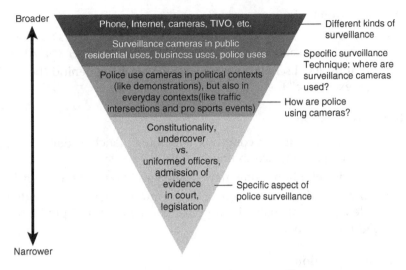

FIGURE 4.5   Scale of abstraction: Police surveillance

These readings lead her to choose "surveillance" as her research subject, but she also knew that "surveillance" is too broad—too high on the scale of abstraction as shown in Figure 4.5—to be manageable for her class projects.

In order to limit the scope of the issue and turn it into a research question, she first *listed the aspects* of surveillance in the newspaper articles and editorials, and then *developed some possible questions* stemming from those aspects.

Key aspects and concepts

- Cameras in public spaces
- Electronic eavesdropping
- Political demonstrations
- Handschu Case—NYC
- Data mining
- COINTELPRO—Black Panther Party
- Constitutional protection/interpretation
- Unitary executive theory
- Definitions of terrorism
- Church Committee
- New technologies
- Patriot Act—after September 11, 2001

Legal questions

- How do new surveillance practices affect laws (such as the Fourth Amendment) and legal conventions (like lawyer-client privilege)?
- What do legal scholars say about the reasoning behind the "unitary executive" theory?

Technical questions

- How do advances in computer technology (such as data storage) enhance surveillance abilities?
- Why do cell phones pose new challenges to personal privacy?
- How do advances in consumer electronics (such as handheld video cameras) enable both police surveillance and public oversight of the police?

Historical questions

- Why was COINTELPRO developed?
- What were the effects of surveillance on civil rights movements?
- Have groups on the political left been equally affected by surveillance as groups on the right?
- What are the similarities between surveillance practices of the 1950s, '60s,'70s, and now?

Cultural questions

- How do cameras in public places (such as the Super Bowl in 2003 or city streets) impact the people in those places?
- How do social networking sites (*Facebook*, *Twitter*, etc.) enable surveillance, and even stalking?
- How do public surveillance programs affect family relationships and social organizations?

Speculative questions

- Will new access to documents (library and medical records, for instance) by government agencies affect people's behavior? How?
- Would more government oversight on the Internet have positive effects, such as limiting hate speech or reducing pornography?

Once she decided on police use of cameras in public places as her subject and understanding the effects of those cameras as her research purpose, she was ready to find a set of sources, learn more about the subject, and, when necessary, further narrow aspects and questions to keep her projects manageable.

**Activity 3: Develop Possible Research Topics
from Everyday Sources**

In small groups or as a class, read these two articles as though you were a researcher seeking an issue to explore further. Discuss your questions about the articles as well as the key words and concepts that sound interesting to you.

MAKE A TENTATIVE RESEARCH PLAN

Once you have narrowed your topic, developed a compelling question, and decided on an academic field to explore, you should develop a tentative plan for research. Your instructor has probably given you an overview of the kinds of writing assignments that you will do at this point in the term, so now is a good time to begin planning how to rally the resources you already have around you.

- Are you currently taking any courses related to your research question? If so, plan to visit with your instructor after class or during office hours. Use your meeting to test possible angles on the question that you're already considering, and describe ways you might both widen and narrow your focus. Ask your instructor for advice about your project, your research question, and additional or alternative directions you might take. Because your instructor is an expert in the field, he or she will also tell you about the books, journals, and other resources that will help you succeed.

- Are any of your classmates considering similar subjects or questions tied to the same academic field? You may find that a classmate in your chemistry or psychology course is taking a writing course like yours as well, and is thinking about ways to integrate the two. Keep in touch with these students and find ways of working together to share research, read drafts of each other's writing projects, revise past assignments, or simply talk at the planning stages of future projects.

- Do you know anyone personally or know of a family friend who works in a professional field related to your research question? How might you incorporate his or her professional expertise into your academic work? Are there opportunities for first hand observation of a professional setting that will give you practical experience and add "real world" examples to your research writing?

RESEARCH PITFALL

Students who are required to write multiple research projects in one term may wish to turn in a single paper for credit in more than one course. This practice may constitute plagiarism unless you ensure that your project is approved by each instructor involved and that each instructor is aware of your intention to submit the same paper for credit. To learn more about this and other kinds of plagiarism, see pages 139–142 in Chapter 6.

Activity 4: Test Your Research Plan

Share your research plan with other students. Survey your classmates to find those who are interested in pursuing similar projects and consider building a writing group with them. What additional questions are classmates interested in? Do they have ideas for angles on the topic or approaches to research you might add to your plan?

   If possible, share your research plan with your instructor. Over years of teaching, your instructor has seen many topics and writing projects and has a good idea of effective approaches.

We'll discuss interviewing and other field research strategies in Chapter 11. For now, think about the people around you who can help you get your research journey started. Finally, because your projects in this course will probably require a significant amount of academic research, consider how much you know about the campus library (or libraries), and the resources available to you there. The next chapter focuses on the specialized skills required to locate and read the academic texts related to your research question.

Strategies for Developing a Research Question

1. Start with issues that truly interest you. Consider issues related to your personal, academic, and professional interests and plans.
2. Connect issues to one or more academic fields or conversations.
3. Broaden and narrow your topic: use a scale of abstraction and other prewriting techniques.
4. Anticipate your research purpose: consider the goals of your writing projects.
5. Use everyday sources (newspapers, blogs, magazines, etc.) to generate details, ideas, and potential questions related to your issue.
6. Share ideas with classmates, your instructor, and others to find issues of common interest, get starting points for your research, and generate additional aspects of and directions for your research writing projects.

5

Locate and Evaluate Sources

CHAPTER OBJECTIVES

In this chapter, you'll learn how to

- Use library facilities
- Find research materials on and off campus
- Manage search strategies
- Check research materials for relevance, credibility, and readability
- Build a research archive for writing projects

As a quick Internet search shows, it's easy to find information about any topic. The difficulty posed by Internet searches is in evaluating this information and selecting trustworthy and credible sources. It takes additional skill to sift through the vast amount of available material and find those sources valued by the academic community. This chapter shows you how to choose and manage the best research material so that you can effectively enter into academic conversations.

By now, you've learned some of the preliminary steps to help start your project, such as choosing an issue and reflecting on what you already know and what interests you. You may have talked to other students in your writing class to share with them what you know and to identify the interests of potential readers. You may have drafted a research plan and anticipated the goals of your project. You may have received feedback from your instructor to ensure that you have chosen a viable issue with a manageable scope. Your research plan may include *field research,* which can include observing people and locations related to your research question and conducting interviews. While field research is discussed later in the book, this chapter focuses on *textual research,* with special emphasis on scholarly sources used in academic research writing.

Opportunities for field research are described in more detail in Chapter 11.

The process of finding sources can take many forms, and your work will be shaped by the resources available at your campus. This chapter begins with an overview of research strategies suitable for campuses with large library holdings. Special attention is then given to electronic search systems developed for the academic community, research databases that harness the power of the Internet for particularly academic purposes.

Let's begin with a broad overview of the types of sources available to you, from the most general, popular audience materials to those especially for specialized audiences of scholars and student researchers (see Table 5.1).

TABLE 5.1   Types of Research Sources

Type of Source	*Description*
The Open Internet	The broadest possible range of general and specialized materials: • Loosely sorted by domain (.com for commercial websites, .edu for educational, and .gov for government institutions) • Difficult to determine authors' credentials and biases • Authors may appear credible through good website design as much as through credible information and arguments
General Audience Texts	Periodicals and books appealing to a wide readership and general interests: • Published for profit by commercial presses • Aimed to inform and entertain • Appeal primarily to consumers and advertisers • Magazines such as *The New Yorker* and *Time* appeal to a broad audience with sections covering movie and theater reviews, news and current events, food reviews and recipes, essays and profiles of various public figures

TABLE 5.1 (*continued . . .*)

Trade and Special-Interest Periodicals	Articles and advertising addressing interests of a particular profession, trade, or community: • Examples include *Forbes* magazine (investment and entrepreneurship), *Low Rider* (cars, style, and music), and the *Advocate* (lesbian, gay, bisexual, and transgender—LGBT—issues) • Published by for-profit and nonprofit companies • Niche marketed to specific audiences • Driven by advertising
Discipline-Specific Reference Texts	Encyclopedias, dictionaries, and other guides: • Used to inform readers of specialized terms, concepts, and issues of interest to a particular academic area • For example, for philosophers the *Cambridge Dictionary of Philosophy* and the *Routledge Encyclopedia of Philosophy*; for biologists, the *Encyclopedia of Evolution* and the *Encyclopedia of Molecular Biology*
Scholarly Journals and Books	Peer-reviewed writing in specialized academic language: • For scholars and other members of the academic community • Usually published by a university, academic, or professional publisher • Not for profit • Advertising limited to journals and books, conferences, and other events related to the field

PEER REVIEW—THE STANDARD OF ACADEMIC CREDIBILITY

As you may have noticed in Table 5.1, scholarly texts are distinguished from others by *peer review*. Typically, when an academic researcher is ready to present work to colleagues, he or she sends a manuscript to the editorial board of a journal or book publisher, who in turn sends it to fellow specialists in the area of the author's research. To determine whether it should be published, peers read and evaluate the manuscript; they judge its contribution to the field and assess the strengths and weaknesses of its argument. As they review submissions they often provide constructive suggestions to the author to help guide revisions and increase the chance of publication. This review process ensures that the manuscript advances the academic conversation in its particular field, unlike commercial publications, whose primary goals are to sell copies and attract advertisers.

In academic writing, the peer review process is designed to ensure that published scholarship meets a field's criteria of accuracy, quality of argument, and relevance. This does not mean that peer-reviewed scholarship simply argues a single point that everyone agrees on. Reviewers ensure that a writer makes a *significant* and *credible* contribution to the conversation on a particular subject or question.

What Peer Reviewers Look For

- Accuracy of data
- Credibility of research
- Quality of argument
- Relevance of findings
- Value of contribution to the field
- Use of the field's conventions

Peers also ensure that the writer practices *conventions* agreed on by scholars in the discipline. For example, even though both philosophers and medical doctors participate in studies of biomedical ethics, the criteria for publication in philosophical and medical circles are quite different. The kinds of data, methods of argumentation, and even acceptable styles, are so different that the philosopher and doctor would likely have a hard time publishing in the other's field without first learning new conventions.

As you become involved with the academic conversation surrounding your own research question, you will see how each field uses conventional practices of argument, form, style, and documentation. Reading in your research field will help you identify sources that reflect those conventions, and help you to read and understand arguments efficiently. Those conventions will also help guide you to make convincing contributions to the conversation, just as the expert researchers in your field did when they were beginning their careers.

The peer review process also plays an important role in business and government. When agencies decide to provide start-up funding for a project, or consider whether to continue funding an existing project, they often turn to outside reviewers who add expertise and objectivity to decisions. Peer review helps organizations to ensure neutrality and to avoid conflicts of interest and favoritism. In the U.S.

Academics and other professionals use peer review as a system of checks and balances.

Office of Science and Technology Policy, for instance, each agency in the office may draft its own process, but all are guided by the "fundamental concept of a review of technical or scientific merit by individuals with sufficient technical competence and no unresolved conflict of interest." For another example, consider the way an appeal in the legal system works like a peer review process, where the decisions of one judge are subject to review by peers at the local, regional, and national levels, all the way to the U.S. Supreme Court.

HOW PEER REVIEW WORKS

The United Kingdom's Parliamentary Office of Science and Technology provides a flow chart that shows authors how their manuscripts will be reviewed.[1]

WHAT IS PEER REVIEW?

Peer review is a system whereby research—or a research proposal—is scrutinised by (largely unpaid) independent experts (peers). In general, the process serves a technical (ensuring that the science is sound) and a subjective function (is the science interesting, important and/or groundbreaking?). The flowchart below gives a brief overview of how the process works to select science for funding and publication, although in practice, there is considerable variation in peer review processes between funding bodies and journals.

Manuscript or grant proposal (application) arrives at appropriate funding body or journal ← May be considered by in-house peer review team and either rejected or passed on to next stage

↓

Application is sent to appropriate (largely unpaid) external peer reviewers (referees)

↓

Referees comment on application and make a recommendation (grade) regarding ← its suitability for publication or funding   Author may be permitted to respond to the referees' comments at this stage

↓

All comments are returned to journal editor or funding body committee for consideration ← Peer review panels consider referees' comments

↓

Application is accepted or rejected.

LIBRARY RESEARCH

If you attend a large research university, you have access to countless sources—reference materials, government documents, journals, books, databases, and more—for virtually any academic field you choose. But access is one thing. You need to navigate the unique characteristics of your campus library system. Many universities have library facilities spread across campus—even in different parts of a city or state—and each can have a specific purpose or serve an academic discipline such as medicine, engineering, and law. Different facilities can be devoted to the particular needs of undergraduates, graduate students, faculty, and academic researchers. Some facilities may house collections on special topics or the papers of particular authors. Each of these facilities may have unique cataloguing and lending policies that users must learn and follow in order to maintain privileges.

Campuses with large research holdings employ librarians who are specialists in particular fields. When you choose to work in an unfamiliar library, they are the authorities who can help with cataloguing, holding, and lending *Get help at your library's reference desk.* practices of their facilities. Reference librarians are most likely to be on top of new technologies for finding the best materials and can assist you in using the library efficiently. They typically know where you can find the most useful reference works, introductory texts, and academic journals related to your research question. The research librarian and his or her colleagues, who represent the other specialized branches and functions of the library, truly complement the expertise of your instructors.

Professional Voice

Nicole Spar, a specialist librarian, explains her work with researchers.

My job is to help researchers get their work done in the most productive and efficient ways possible. That means, among other things, making sure that they have access to the print and online resources they need and that they know how to get to those resources. Even though I'm really there to help students and faculty with their work, one of the best parts of my job is that I feel like I'm constantly learning, both about new aspects of old questions and about entirely new issues. And, since we always have new students and faculty coming through our doors, there's a constant sense of newness and discovery in the library. I imagine it's the same kind of feeling a wilderness guide has in helping people successfully get through strange (and often scary) places for the first time!

Use Subject Headings

Beginning researchers may get frustrated when they use terms that do not match those used by library catalogs and online databases. In order to see how information is organized, your research librarian might show you how to

Use LCSH to identify a topic and related areas.

use the *Library of Congress Subject Headings* (LCSH). These volumes show you how your research topic and question fit into the Library of Congress classification system, the standard of library organization in the United States. LCSH can also help you find ways to think about your topic, showing you connections that exist between your subject and related areas. These connections, in turn, help you to anticipate ways of narrowing and broadening the scope of your research project.

Figure 5.1 shows how the LCSH organizes subject areas alphabetically using a *scale of abstraction* that places subjects in relation to broader and narrower areas. In this case, we follow the path that one student took to research surveillance, particularly the use of cameras in public spaces by police. LCSH divides the broad subject area of surveillance into *subfields*

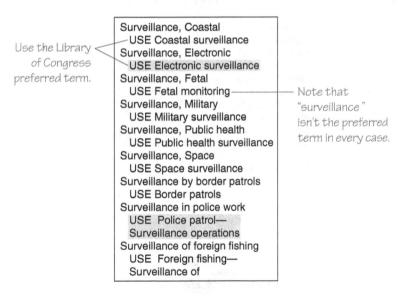

FIGURE 5.1   Sample LCSH entry: Surveillance

From this point, our student could continue to the entry for either of *LCSH*'s preferred terms for her subject: "electronic surveillance" or "police patrol—surveillance operations." She turned first to the listing

See Chapter 4 for more on using scales of abstraction to shape your projects.

that connects surveillance to police work because uses of surveillance cameras by police interested her most.

The entry for "surveillance operations" appears as a subdivision of the broader subject area of "police patrol" (see Figure 5.2). Each LCSH entry follows a standard format; so once users know what to look for and what the abbreviations mean, they are very easy to scan for relevance.

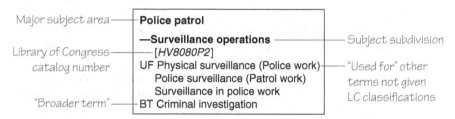

FIGURE 5.2   Sample LCSH entry: Surveillance operations

These aspects of surveillance didn't quite hit the mark, so the student went to *LCSH*'s other preferred term and found a subject description and terms that more closely matched her interests as shown in Figure 5.3.

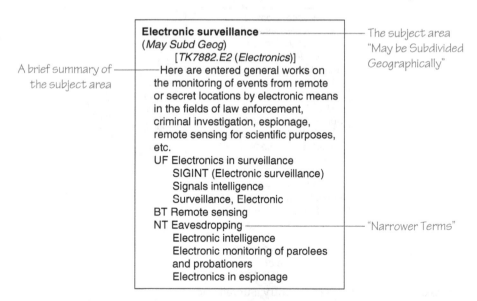

FIGURE 5.3   Sample LCSH entry: "electronic surveillance."

You can use the catalog number to find the library's book and journal holdings in your subject area. Since your library's holdings are organized by subject according to the Library of Congress system, once

---

Glossary of LCSH Terminology

- USE: *Use* the preferred term to organize material
- UF: This term is *used for* others
- NT: *Narrower terms* are available
- BT: *Broader terms* are available
- May Subd Geog: The subject area is *subdivided geographically*

---

you find a book or journal that matches your interests, it can be well worth your time to compare those nearby. Quickly scanning the tables of contents and indexes in those texts will give you a sense of their potential value to your project. This work may also help you make connections that were not apparent on first glance from LCSH and help you to develop new directions for your projects.

We'll see shortly how online research databases use LCSH and similar approaches to organize their materials and to help users perform the most effective searches.

ONLINE RESEARCH

When you hear about "online research," the first thing that comes to mind is *Google* or a similar search engine that matches a word or phrase with billions of webpages. The Internet has become for many of us the first—and sometimes the only—way we find information and answer questions. The Internet provides immediate access to almost unlimited amounts of information on just about any issue. But while the open Internet can be a great place to get general information about topics and areas of interest, it's not the best place to pursue specialized academic research. For example, while *Google* can find the latest in entertainment news or today's stock market results, it will not be the best way to locate critical academic work in media studies or economics to help us understand these issues in more depth.

Using the Internet effectively can take discipline, and it's easy to get sidetracked by topics that won't contribute to your writing goals. As you might have discovered in your own experience, the Internet can cause you to lose sight of what you started looking for, especially when you're diverted by reading irrelevant information or following links that never go anywhere productive. There's no reason to make the research project more complicated by shifting your attention to unnecessary or unhelpful activities.

Stay focused: avoid getting sidetracked when you use the Internet for research.

Fortunately, scholars, university consortiums, and academic presses have created online databases to serve academic researchers— and they can supplement the research materials available in any campus library. General and discipline-specific databases connect researchers to materials in their areas of interest, from bibliographic information to abstracts of scholarly books and articles, and, in many cases, even full texts of academic articles and books. For the rest of this chapter, we discuss the nature and use of databases that are common to many U.S. colleges and universities. We will also learn how to manage the materials that they provide.

Online databases offer some advantages over research libraries, such as allowing access to material from home and campus computer labs. However, students who use databases, either by choice or necessity, will face challenges and possible pitfalls that their counterparts using research libraries will avoid. As we explore these databases, we'll look at techniques for ensuring that the materials you choose are best for the writing projects in your course.

Research with Online Databases—the Basics

Libraries usually subscribe to many online research databases (see Figure 5.4). *Academic Search Premier* is one of the best to start with

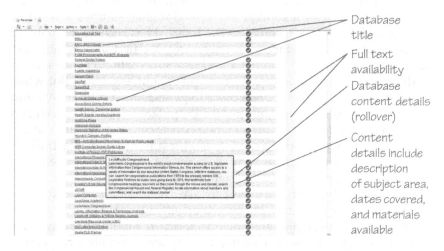

FIGURE 5.4   A library's list of available online databases

if you are uncertain about the ideal subject area for your research question or the range of possible areas your question falls into. The *Academic Search Premier* database can search across disciplines, from the sciences to humanities, from technology to the fine arts. It can search the broadest range of sources, from newspapers and magazines to scholarly journals.

The search page of the database (see Figure 5.5) includes features that will already be familiar to Internet users. Simple keyword searches (a subject, a title, an author, and so on) work much like Google or Yahoo! search engines to locate all the matching sources in the database. This basic search on *Academic Search Premier* locates results from the widest range of sources in the database, regardless of availability.

If you can access *Academic Search Premier* or a similar database at the library or from another location, try doing some keyword searches for the issues and questions that you're considering for your research projects, concepts being discussed in your courses, current events, or whatever subject interests you. If you've already had a chance to look at the LCSH entries related to your research question, try running searches with those terms.

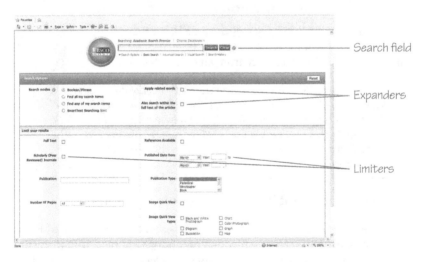

FIGURE 5.5 Academic Search Premier Basic Search page

TABLE 5.2   Database Features: Limiters

1. **Publication Date.** Your instructor might ask that your research use only, or at least include, recently published sources. Online databases allow you to include publication dates in searches, either to find the most recent material or to search within a specific period.

2. **Full-Text Resources.** Many databases allow you to limit your search so that all results are linked to full-texts of sources. When choosing to limit your search to full texts, consider the amount of time that you have to locate and read materials against the time it takes to get articles or books through interlibrary loan services on your campus.

3. **Scholarly/Peer-Reviewed Sources.** As you narrow your research project from a subject area to a particular question, you will increasingly focus on scholarly sources. Databases that cast a very broad research net like *Academic Search Premier* allow researchers to limit their results to types of sources. They might begin a research project with newspaper articles and general audience periodicals to become familiar with current issues and debates, and then recast a search to find only academic articles and books.

Student Voice

Trent, whose research projects focused on deforestation in tropical regions of the world, explains how he determines the credibility of a source from an online database.

Since Academic Search Premier can search for a lot of different kinds of sources, I learned that even though an article is in the database, it isn't necessarily scholarly. I still have to look at the bibliography to see if the author has used credible sources, like from scholarly journals and university publishers. Another way to be sure that an article is scholarly enough is checking whether it has been peer reviewed.

Expand and Limit Terms with Boolean Operators

As we explore online research databases, we need to look at techniques for ensuring that the materials you choose are best suited for the writing projects of your course. Because *Academic Search Premier*, like many other online databases, provides access to a wide variety of materials, you'll often find an overwhelming number of sources when you use a single decontextualized search term ("Internet," "health care," "climate change," "surveillance," and so on). Fortunately, these databases allow you to use Boolean operators (see Figure 5.6) to *combine* two

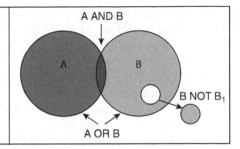

AND, OR, and NOT are examples of "Boolean operators." Boolean logic is a conventional way to build sets of information, and is especially useful in combining and excluding terms and concepts in the process of gathering research materials.

FIGURE 5.6 Boolean operators

or more terms with "AND" in order to narrow results. Thus, if our "surveillance" researcher is overwhelmed by the results of a single term search, she can combine terms until the number of sources she has to scan and select from is more manageable. Perhaps "surveillance AND public" will limit the search sufficiently; but more terms could be added for increased specificity—"surveillance AND public AND camera."

Alternately, you can link two or more terms with "OR" to search for sources that use the terms either together or separately. If a first

---

Activity 1: Expand and Limit Terms

Using your research topic or question—or a temporary one provided by your instructor—make a list of terms you associate with it. For example, if you wanted to research the impact of increased standardized testing in U.S. schools, your terms would probably include "standardized test," "United States," and perhaps "No Child Left Behind" (the legislation that mandates standardized testing in the United States)—all suitable for online library catalog and database searches.

Once you have your list of terms in place, first add three or more "AND" words that will help you narrow your search, such as "AND Texas" if we wanted to look at the impact of standardized testing in one state, or "AND teachers" if we wanted to look at their unique role.

Then add three or more "OR" words that will help you expand your search, such as "OR California" if we wanted to broaden our regional focus from above, or "OR parents" if we wanted to look at two important stakeholders in testing mandates.

Finally, add three or more "NOT" words to your original term, such as "NOT national" if we wanted to limit our search above to testing at the state and school district levels only.

Consider visualizing the relationship between your terms in a diagram like the one in Figure 5.6, or in another kind of chart. Some databases offer researchers the option of visual searching, which presents results using Venn diagrams and other charts, tables, and images.

search using a single term fails to return enough useful sources, you can add one or more *related* terms with OR to broaden your search.

Finally, you can also use "NOT" to *exclude* certain aspects of a broader search. "Surveillance NOT police" or "bird NOT seagull" would be two examples.

We can study two Boolean linked searches, one using AND and one using NOT, to compare the results pages produced by each search. In Figure 5.7, the first 10 sources are

> *In contrast to the "NOT" search results below, the "AND" search results are tightly focused on issues of criminal justice.*

1. The French Riots: Questioning Spaces of Surveillance and Sovereignty. By: Ossman, Susan; Terrio, Susan. International Migration, 2006, Vol. 44 Issue 2, p5-21, 17p; DOI: 10.1111/j.1468-2435.2006.00361.x; (AN 20791269)
Check LinkSource for more information
Add

2. SPIES AMONG US. (cover story) By: Kaplan, David E.; Ekman, Monica M.; Marek, Angie C.; D. E. K. U.S. News & World Report, 5/8/2006, Vol. 140 Issue 17, p40-49, 8p, 6c, 1bw; (AN 20638998)
Notes: This title is held locally, Call Number JK1.U65, 1977 to present
HTML Full Text   Check LinkSource for more information
Add

3. Book Reviews. By: WAKEFIELD, ALISON; PLESHKOVA, OLGA; CODD, HELEN; PALMER, EMMA J.; BRIDGEMAN, JO; BARROWS, RANDEL; SHARPE, GILLY. Howard Journal of Criminal Justice, May2006, Vol. 45 Issue 2, p223-238, 16p; DOI: 10.1111/j.1468-2311.2006.00417.x; (AN 20515714)
Check LinkSource for more information
Add

4. The Real Color of Money: Controlling Black Bodies in the NBA. By: Leonard, David J.. Journal of Sport & Social Issues, May2006, Vol. 30 Issue 2, p158-179, 22p; DOI: 10.1177/0193723506286725; (AN 20649583)
Check LinkSource for more information
Add

5. Terror Case May Offer Clues Into Police Use Of Informants. By: Rashbaum, William K. New York Times, 4/24/2006, Vol. 155 Issue 53559, pB1-B4, 2p; (AN 20741100)
Notes: Print Journal Held Locally, Newspaper, 2 months, also ProQuest, 1995 to present
Check LinkSource for more information
Add

6. How Patriot Act Helped Convict Man In Baby-Food Ring. (cover story) By: McKinnon, John D.. Wall Street Journal - Eastern Edition, 4/4/2006, Vol. 247 Issue 78, pA1-A6, 2p, 1 chart, 1bw; (AN 20352450)
Notes: This title is held locally, ProQuest 1985+
Check LinkSource for more information
Add

7. Lockheed Martin Applies Surveillance Technology for US Marines in Iraq. Microwave Journal, Apr2006, Vol. 49 Issue 4, p47-47, 2/3p; (AN 20597150)
PDF Full Text (125K)   Check LinkSource for more information
Add

8. The Spectre of Crime: Photography, Law and Ethics. By: Biber, Katherine. Social Semiotics, Apr2006, Vol. 16 Issue 1, p133-149, 17p; DOI: 10.1080/10350330500487802; (AN 20070137)
Cited References (29)
Check LinkSource for more information
Add

9. Military Intelligence. By: Welch, Matt. Reason, Apr2006, Vol. 37 Issue 11, p11-11, 1/3p; (AN 20062174)
HTML Full Text   Check LinkSource for more information
Add

10. City Defends Surveillance Of Protesters. By: Preston, Julia. New York Times, 3/29/2006, Vol. 155 Issue 53533, pB3-B3, 1/8p; (AN 20609476)
Notes: Print Journal Held Locally, Newspaper, 2 months, also ProQuest, 1995 to present
Check LinkSource for more information
Add

FIGURE 5.7   Results from a database search using the AND operator

those returned by an "AND" search, "surveillance AND police." In Figure 5.8, the first 10 sources are those returned by a "NOT" search, "surveillance NOT police."

1. Response of a tethered aerostat to simulated turbulence. By: Stanney, Keith A.; Rahn, Christopher D.. Communications in Nonlinear Science & Numerical Simulation, Sep2006, Vol. 11 Issue 6, p759-776, 18p; DOI: 10.1016/j.cnsns.2005.01.001; (AN 19843436)

   Check LinkSource for more information
   Add

2. Expression of the membrane complement regulatory protein CD59 (protectin) is associated with reduced survival in colorectal cancer patients. By: Watson, Nicholas F.; Durrant, Lindy G.; Madjd, Zahra; Ellis, Ian O.; Scholefield, John H.; Spendlove, Ian. Cancer Immunology, Immunotherapy, Aug2006, Vol. 55 Issue 8, p973-980, 8p, 3 charts, 1 graph, 1c; DOI: 10.1007/s00262-005-0055-0; (AN 20620504)

   Check LinkSource for more information
   Add

3. An immune edited tumour versus a tumour edited immune system: prospects for immune therapy of acute myeloid leukaemia. By: Chan, Lucas; Hardwick, Nicola R.; Guinn, Barbara-ann; Darling, Dave; Gäken, Joop; Galea-Lauri, Joanna; Ho, Aloysius Y.; Mufti, Ghulam J.; Farzaneh, Farzin. Cancer Immunology, Immunotherapy, Aug2006, Vol. 55 Issue 8, p1017-1024, 8p, 2 diagrams; DOI: 10.1007/s00262-006-0129-7; (AN 20620491)

   Check LinkSource for more information
   Add

4. Sweet's syndrome on the area of postmastectomy lymphoedema. By: García-Río, I.; Pérez-Gala, S.; Aragüés, M.; Fernández-Herrera, J.; Fraga, J.; García-Díez, A. Journal of the European Academy of Dermatology & Venereology, Jul2006, Vol. 20 Issue 4, p401-405, 5p, 1 chart, 3c; DOI: 10.1111/j.1468-3083.2006.01460.x; (AN 20287190)
   Cited References (19)

   Check LinkSource for more information
   Add

5. Estimation of life expectancy of wood poles in electrical distribution networks. By: Datla, S.V.; Pandey, M.D.. Structural Safety, Jul2006, Vol. 28 Issue 3, p304-319, 16p; DOI: 10.1016/j.strusafe.2005.08.006; (AN 19912753)

   Check LinkSource for more information
   Add

6. Acoustic imaging using a volumetric array. By: Rigelsford, J.M.; Tennant, A.. Applied Acoustics, Jul2006, Vol. 67 Issue 7, p680-688, 9p; DOI: 10.1016/j.apacoust.2005.11.005; (AN 20013019)

   Check LinkSource for more information
   Add

7. Tumor immune escape mechanisms: impact of the neuroendocrine system. By: Lang, Kerstin; Entschladen, Frank; Weidt, Corinna; Zaenker, Kurt S.. Cancer Immunology, Immunotherapy, Jul2006, Vol. 55 Issue 7, p749-760, 12p, 2 diagrams; DOI: 10.1007/s00262-006-0126-x; (AN 20279783)

   Check LinkSource for more information
   Add

8. Surgical influence of pancreatectomy on the function and count of circulating dendritic cells in patients with pancreatic cancer. By: Takahashi, Kanji; Toyokawa, Hideyoshi; Takai, Soichiro; Satoi, Sohei; Yanagimoto, Hiroaki; Terakawa, Naoyoshi; Araki, Hiroshi; A-Hon Kwon; Kamiyama, Yasuo. Cancer Immunology, Immunotherapy, Jul2006, Vol. 55 Issue 7, p775-784, 10p, 3 charts, 1 diagram, 3 graphs; DOI: 10.1007/s00262-005-0079-5; (AN 20279792)

   Check LinkSource for more information
   Add

9. Effects of Salmonella enterica serovars Typhimurium (ST) and Choleraesuis (SC) on chemokine and cytokine expression in swine ileum and jejunal epithelial cells. By: Skjolaas, K.A.; Burkey, T.E.; Dritz, S.S.; Minton, J.E.. Veterinary Immunology & Immunopathology, Jun2006, Vol. 111 Issue 3/4, p199-209, 11p; DOI: 10.1016/j.vetimm.2006.01.002; (AN 20621641)

   Check LinkSource for more information
   Add

10. Immunohistochemical markers augment evaluation of vaccine efficacy and disease severity in bacillus Calmette–Guerin (BCG) vaccinated cattle challenged with Mycobacterium bovis. By: Johnson, Linda; Gough, Julie; Spencer, Yvonne; Hewinson, Glyn; Vordermeier, Martin; Wangoo, Arun. Veterinary Immunology & Immunopathology, Jun2006, Vol. 111 Issue 3/4, p219-229, 11p; DOI: 10.1016/j.vetimm.2006.01.016; (AN 20621643)

    Check LinkSource for more information
    Add

FIGURE 5.8 Results from a database search using the NOT operator

Specify with Quotation Marks

As you may already know from using *Google* and other Internet search engines, searches with multiple terms will find all of the terms appearing on the same page, regardless of their relationship to each other. To manage your search, try combining terms within *quotation marks* in order to find occurances of the exact phrase. In the Activity 1 search, rather than searching for every occurrence of both "standardized" and "test" terms, a researcher could combine "standardized test" in quotation marks to find better matched sources.

Read the Academic Search Premier Title Screen

Continuing with our surveillance research example with *Academic Search Premier*, "surveillance AND public AND camera" returned about a hundred results, not all about police surveillance. In fact, of the first ten titles listed in the search, only a few were about police surveillance, while others were about issues in science and medicine (issues like following disease spread, showing population growth, and tracking effects of climate change). After scanning titles for those most relevant to the issue or question, a researcher can click on the title to get more detailed information and choose the best sources for a project.

For example, the detail page shown in Figure 5.9 describes an article by Catherine Yang, Kerry Capell, and Otis Port from the magazine *BusinessWeek*.

The detail page includes a number of links that lead to other works by an author, other articles in a journal, and subject terms, which can help researchers develop their ideas through new searches.

1. **Subject Terms.** Discovering the best subject terms for your search can be a challenge. Online databases often suggest alternative subject headings related to each search term. Glance over these subject headings to find a better term than the one you used—or combine them to better refine your search. Note that one of the terms we saw in LCSH, "police patrol—surveillance operations," appears in Figure 5.9. By clicking that link, you can instantly run a new search using that LCSH term.
2. **Author Links.** Many online databases also support hyperlinked author searches. It may be that an author has written other pieces that will interest you. Click the name to find more work by the same author.
3. **Source Title.** In some databases, the journal title may be linked so that you can search for results within that title alone. When

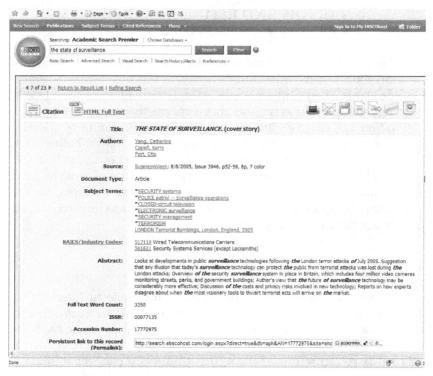

FIGURE 5.9   Academic Search Premier: Detail page for a surveillance article

you search within a title, you may find a special issue in which a number of scholars converse about a topic of shared interest. You may also see historical aspects or trends of a conversation by understanding how it has developed over time in a single journal.

4. **Links to Notes and Bibliography.** Links to notes may be embedded in the article text so that readers do not have to continually scroll up and down through the entire article to read a footnote or to see a source in the bibliography.

5. **Links to Key Passages and Pages.** Some databases provide readers with links to article pages where search terms appear. This feature can be especially handy in databases that offer files of very long articles, in which only a section or two of the whole might deal specifically with the research question. As you can imagine, this is also a feature that can be abused or tempt researchers to read passages out of context.

NARROW AND REFINE SEARCHES— A CASE STUDY

Let's look at some of the ways to scan and select sources as you develop your research question.

Students often find that one of the first challenges they face in their research projects is not—as they expect—that materials are difficult to find, but that they are overwhelmed by the amount of material. Whether your research takes you to campus libraries or online databases, it is especially important to practice refining your search so that your workload remains manageable, given the scope of your research project and the time you have to complete it. As an example, we can look at the strategies used by a student who wanted to research the impact of steroid use in college sports.

Combining

When this student began her search with the term "steroids" in *Academic Search Premier*, she got back over 13,000 sources—this, of course, was far more than she was prepared to scan, let alone read! But since few of the articles were about sports, adding "sports AND" to the original keyword reframed the search to directly connect steroids to sports, and reduced the number of results from the initial thirteen thousand to about 1,400—a reduction of almost 90 percent.

Limiting

Our student researcher was still left with too many sources after she had combined the terms "steroids" and "sports." Her initial searches led her to a wide range of materials, from articles in local and national newspapers, to special-interest magazines and articles written by scholars for academic audiences. Since her research project would include some scholarly sources, she used database tools to increase the chances that she would find the kinds of materials required by her instructor. The "scholarly (peer reviewed) sources" option on the search page returned 232 results, while the full-text availability option further reduced the number to 68.

At this point, our student had additional options to limit her search so that she would not have to read over 60 scholarly articles about sports and steroids. Often, instructors will ask students to use only, or primarily, recent sources in their research projects. Since every database allows users to enter date limiters, using *currency* as a search criterion can be another effective way to frame a search.

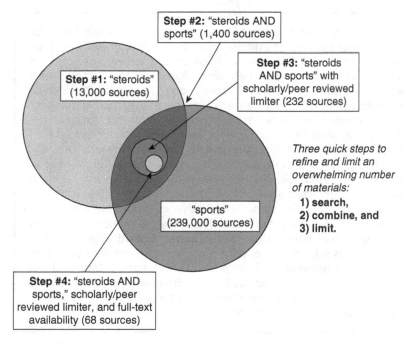

Step #2: "steroids AND sports" (1,400 sources)

Step #1: "steroids" (13,000 sources)

Step #3: "steroids AND sports" with scholarly/peer reviewed limiter (232 sources)

"sports" (239,000 sources)

Three quick steps to refine and limit an overwhelming number of materials:
1) **search,**
2) **combine, and**
3) **limit.**

Step #4: "steroids AND sports," scholarly/peer reviewed limiter, and full-text availability (68 sources)

FIGURE 5.10   Visual relationship of search terms and results

Evaluate Material for Relevance and Difficulty

In preparing for your own projects, consider reading article abstracts as a way of *scanning* and *screening* sources. An *abstract* provides a summary of an article, usually in about 100 to 250 words. Abstracts allow researchers to get an overview of an article's point and purpose, to quickly judge its relevance to a particular question, and to rapidly build connections with other sources.

One of the articles our student researcher found was "Adolescent Anabolic Steroid Use, Gender, Physical Activity, and Other Problem Behaviors," published in 2005 in the journal *Substance Use and Misuse*. The article abstract (see Figure 5.11) was especially useful in helping the student gauge her ability to read and decode the argument, and to understand the author's purpose and major points.

Besides the concept of "strain theory," there is little in this abstract that cannot be understood by the average college reader. However, compare that abstract to another source in the search, "Multi Residue Screening of Intact Testosterone Esters and Boldenone Undecylenate in Bovine Hair Using Liquid Chromatography Electrospray Tandem Mass Spectrometry" shown in Figure 5.12.

To test the comparative value of strain theory and problem behavior theory as explanations of adolescent anabolic steroid use, this study examined gender-specific relationships among steroid use, physical activity, and other problem behaviors. Based on the United States Centers for Disease Control and Prevention's 1997 Youth Risk Behavior Survey, a nationally representative sample of over 16,000 U.S. public and private high school students, binge drinking, cocaine use, fighting, and sexual risk-taking were associated with higher odds of lifetime steroid use. In gender-specific analyses, steroid use was strongly associated with female lighting and smokeless tobacco use as well as male sexual risk. Neither athletic participation nor strength conditioning predicted odds of steroid use after controlling for problem behaviors, nor did steroid-using athletes report more frequent use than steroid-using nonathletes. The study's limitations and policy implications were noted. These data suggest that other problem behaviors such as substance use, fighting, and sexual risk are better predictors of adolescent steroid use than physical activity. Interventions to prevent steroid use should not be limited to male participants in organized sports programs, but should also target adolescents identified as at risk for other problem behaviors.

FIGURE 5.11   Article abstract: "Adolescent Anabolic Steroid Use: Gender, Physical Activity, and Other Problem Behaviors"

The abuse of esters of natural androgenic steroids in cattle fattening and sports is hard to control via routine urine testing. The esters are rapidly hydrolysed in vivo into substances which are also endogenously present in urine. In veterinary control strange findings of 17β-testosterone and 17α-testosterone in urine are often ignored because of the lack of statistically sound reference data of naturally occurring levels. An interesting alternative for inconclusive urine analyses in veterinary control can be provided by the analysis of the administered steroids themselves, i.e. the analysis of intact steroid esters in hair. Unfortunately, the analysis of intact steroid esters is complicated not only by the vulnerability of the esters which precludes alkaline hydrolysis of the hair, but also by the wide polarity range of short and long-chain esters yielding very poor recoveries for either the one or the other. In this study, a multi-steroid esters LC/MS/MS screening method is presented for trace analysis of the synthetic intact esters of 17β-testosterone and the undecylenate ester of 17β-boldenone in bovine hair. The method, requiring only 200mg of pulverised hair, features a mild digestion procedure using tris (2-carboxyethyl)phosphine hydrochloride (TCEP) and the use of four deuterium-labelled steroid esters as internal standards covering the wide polarity range of the analytes. In spiked hair samples for most of the analytes the limit of detection and the accuracy using isotope dilution were 2–5ng/g and 97–105%, respectively. The applicability was demonstrated using hair samples from a controlled experiment in which six bovines were injected intramuscularly with two different doses of two commercial mixtures of testosterone esters, and with two different doses of boldenone undecylenate. Depending on the dose all administered testosterone- and boldenone esters were found to be incorporated in bovine hair ...

FIGURE 5.12   Article abstract: "Multi Residue Screening of Intact Testosterone Esters and Boldenone Undecylenate in Bovine Hair Using Liquid Chromatography Electrospray Tandem Mass Spectrometry"

Both articles are aimed toward academic audiences, but the abstracts show the different amounts of specialized language and prior knowledge needed for reading and comprehension. Comparing journal titles—*Substance Use and Misuse* versus *Journal of Chromatography B*—further suggests different assumed audiences for each article.

Connect Preliminary Research and Purpose

At this point, our student could narrow her search again, not only because she wanted to avoid becoming overwhelmed by the language used in her sources, but also because the first article was relevant to her age group and to experiences that were close to her own. That abstract also raised critical questions by challenging assumptions about the people who use, or are prone to using, steroids. Is it true, for instance, that participation in sports is not the best indication of risk among adolescents who may be using steroids? This claim would go against the widely held belief that student athletes are their main users. If true, then parents, teachers, and peers would have to adjust their preconceptions accordingly.

At this point, equipped with a key article and its abstract, our student could begin to refine her purpose by planning a persuasive research essay in which she would argue against common—but apparently mistaken—beliefs about which adolescents are likely to be using steroids.

FIND THE DATABASE THAT'S RIGHT FOR YOUR RESEARCH

In the process of finding the *Academic Search Premier* database through your library website, you may have already uncovered a complete list of research technologies at the library. If you haven't yet, search the library's website until you find the complete list. Your institution may have as few as 10 databases that are the most useful and relevant or over a hundred databases that connect you to the widest possible range of materials. As we have seen, databases such as Academic Search Premier can provide access to a variety of sources and many disciplines. Other databases are focused specifically to lead researchers to *particular kinds of documents*—such as LexisNexis Congressional, which searches government records—or to *particular fields*—such as MEDLINE, which covers medical publications and data.

If your library offers access to a wide range of databases, you probably can find one or more that allow you to research the question you have in mind and direct your research into a specific academic field. Using discipline-specific databases will help your time management, because you will be likely to find relevant materials with far less sifting than you would in a general database. Additionally, your discipline-specific search will help you to maintain the focus of your research project within a single academic conversation.

Whenever possible you should search more than one database. Each is licensed to access a specified, limited pool of information, and no one database can provide you with access to every book, journal, report, and other texts related to your research. Although you are certain to find some overlap between databases, each has blind spots. Even when you hit the "jackpot" (*Academic Search Premier*'s 13,000 sources on steroids), you should still search additional databases and use as many related search terms as possible. That way, you increase the chances of finding the most relevant texts for your research writing projects from the broadest range of contenders. Even though you'll end up using only a fraction of those sources in your projects, you can approach writing assignments with the confidence of having selected the best available materials.

FULL-TEXT ARTICLES

Let's turn now to finding full-text articles from online databases. The full text limiter can prevent frustration early in the research process by leading you to sources you can begin reading immediately.

PDF and HTML Formats in Online Delivery

Most online databases provide access to full-text articles, which appear in two formats: PDF and HTML. Depending on the database or the original source of the article, both formats may be available, but usually we're offered only one. Let's compare the two by examining PDF and HTML versions of an article from the *Harvard Journal of Law and Public Policy* about the relationship between the Patriot Act and surveillance abilities of law enforcement. The PDF version of the article (Figure 5.13) is a *facsimile* of its original print version; thus, as we read a page online, it's just as though we were reading the article in a campus law library.

In contrast, in the HTML version of the same passage (Figure 5.14), we are given only the article's *text*. Although the HTML version includes the complete text of the article, its format adds challenges for writers who cannot accurately cite page numbers of quoted, paraphrased, or summarized passages. Fortunately, if the writer is unable to obtain a copy of the original print source through other electronic delivery methods or a hard copy from the interlibrary loan service, there are ways to cite and document online sources, which are discussed in detail in Chapter 7.

Some HTML-formatted articles provide indications of page breaks, so that even if we cannot read a facsimile of the original article, we have a way of "seeing" the pages and properly citing passages used for quotations, paraphrases, and summaries. Figure 5.15 shows a portion of an article from the *The Future of Children* which uses bold type in square brackets to show page breaks in the original print version. Additionally, this article, unlike the HTML version of our law review article, includes hyperlinks to the author's notes. In longer articles especially, this is a handy feature that allows readers to move quickly from text to notes and back again.

Save Your Sources and Record Your Research Process

Always be sure to print, save, or e-mail to yourself articles that are relevant to your projects. During the early stages of your research process, it might be best—both economically and environmentally—to save materials on your computer or portable drive, and only print when it is useful to do so. Be sure to take careful notes on paper as well because printed articles from online databases may occasionally lack all the citation information that you will need for a bibliography. Additionally, in case there are any problems with an electronic file, you should make careful notes of the databases and the search terms used so that you can to relocate your sources. Especially if your campus library provides access to many search engines, it can be easy to forget how you found a particular source, or a particular version. Your reading log will be the best place to keep track of your research process as you gather and read sources.

FISA generally requires the government to have advance judicial approval for such surveillance. To get judicial approval for electronic surveillance under the original FISA, a high-ranking government official with intelligence responsibilities had to certify to a court that "the purpose of the surveillance was to obtain foreign intelligence information."[10] Some lower federal courts interpreted this provision to mean that the "primary purpose" of the proposed surveillance had to be gathering foreign intelligence, rather than gathering evidence for a criminal prosecution.[11] This "primary purpose" test assumed incompatibility between the purpose of gathering foreign intelligence and the purpose of gathering evidence for a prosecution. To satisfy the primary purpose test, the Department of Justice accordingly adopted procedures limiting contact between foreign intelligence agents in the FBI and federal prosecutors. Those procedures came to be interpreted restrictively by the Justice Department and the court responsible for issuing FISA surveillance orders, the Foreign Intelligence Surveillance Court ("FISA Trial Court"). The restrictive interpretation produced what the public came to call "the wall."[12] The wall thus was mainly the result of (1) lower courts' interpretation of the original FISA's "purpose" provision; (2) the Justice Department's procedures for implementing the lower courts' interpretation; and (3) the restrictive interpretation of those procedures by Department officials and the FISA Trial Court.[13]

The wall caused trouble before 9/11 but did not attract public or congressional attention until afterwards.[14] For example, the wall hurt

---

[10] 50 U.S.C. § 1804(a)(7)(B) (1980).

[11] *See infra* notes 210–23 and accompanying text.

[12] *See infra* notes 227–86 and accompanying text.

[13] "The wall" originally referred to restrictions on intelligence sharing internal to the U.S. Department of Justice. *See, e.g., 9/11 Comm'n Staff Statement No. 9*, at 4–5 (*available at* http://www.9-11commission.gov/staff_statements/ staff_statement_9.pdf) (stating that internal Justice Department procedures to separate foreign intelligence functions from law enforcement functions "became known as the 'wall'"); *see also infra* notes 227–86 and accompanying text. The phrase came to be used in a broader sense to mean "a series of restrictions" between foreign intelligence and law enforcement that existed "between and within" various federal agencies and that was "constructed over sixty years as a result of legal, policy, institutional, and personal factors." HOUSE PERMANENT SELECT COMMITTEE ON INTELLIGENCE AND THE SENATE SELECT COMMITTEE ON INTELLIGENCE, REPORT OF THE JOINT INQUIRY INTO THE TERRORIST ATTACKS OF SEPTEMBER 11, 2001, S. REP. NO. 107-351 & H.R. REP. NO. 107-792, at 363 (Dec. 2002) (pagination from unclassified version of report) [hereinafter REPORT OF THE JOINT INQUIRY]; *see also* Hill, *Joint Inquiry Staff Statement, supra* note 3, at 21–26 (referring to "the many 'walls' that have been built between the agencies over the past sixty years").

[14] *See, e.g.,* Hill, *Joint Inquiry Staff Statement, supra* note 3, at 14 ("The walls that had developed to separate intelligence and law enforcement often hindered efforts to

---

FIGURE 5.13   A PDF-formatted article from an online database: *Harvard Journal of Law and Public Policy*

intelligence information. (n9) The FISA generally requires the government to have advance judicial approval for such **surveillance**. To get judicial approval for **electronic surveillance** under the original FISA a high-ranking government official with intelligence responsibilities had to certify to a court that "the purpose of the **surveillance** was to obtain foreign intelligence information." (n10) Some lower federal courts interpreted this provision to mean that the "primary purpose" of the proposed **surveillance** had to be gathering foreign intelligence, rather than gathering evidence for a criminal prosecution. (n11) This primary purpose test assumed incompatibility between the purpose of gathering foreign intelligence and the purpose of gathering evidence for a prosecution. To satisfy the primary purpose test, the Department of Justice accordingly adopted procedures limiting contact between foreign intelligence agents in the FBI and federal prosecutors. Those procedures came to be interpreted restrictively by the Justice Department and the court responsible for issuing FISA **surveillance** orders, the Foreign Intelligence **Surveillance** Court ("FISA Trial Court"). The restrictive interpretation produced what the public came to call "the wall." (n12) The wall thus was mainly the result of (1) lower courts' interpretation of the original FISA's "purpose" provision; (2) the Justice Department's procedures for implementing the lower courts' interpretation; and (3) the restrictive interpretation of those procedures by Department officials and the FISA Trial Court. (n13)

Search terms
are boldfaced.

The wall caused trouble before 9/11 but did not attract public or congressional attention until afterwards. (n14) For example, the wall hurt the investigation of whether Wen Ho Lee stole classified information from the Los Alamos National Laboratory. (n15) It was the 9/11 attacks, however, that made the general public aware of the wall, because of its apparent role the government's failure to prevent the 9/11 attacks. (n16) Right after 9/11, the Justice Department asked Congress to amend the "purpose" provision of the original FISA to eliminate the primary purpose test. Under the Department's proposal, instead of certifying that "the purpose" of proposed FISA **surveillance** was to obtain foreign intelligence information, the government would have to certify that obtaining (n17) foreign intelligence was "a purpose" of the proposed **surveillance**. Rather than adopt that proposal, Congress amended the original FISA in the Patriot Act to require the government to show that obtaining foreign intelligence information is "a significant purpose" of the proposed **surveillance**. (n18) Congress thus struck a compromise between the Department of Justice and supporters of the primary purpose test.

The case on which this article focuses arose when the Justice Department changed its procedures to implement the Patriot Act's "significant purpose" amendment. The new procedures reflected the Department's view that the Patriot Act eliminated the primary purpose test. Thus, the Department's procedures

FIGURE 5.14   An HTML-formatted article from an online database: *Harvard Journal of Law and Public Policy*

Many studies have found what social scientists call curvilinear relations between hours of TV viewed and achievement. In other words, up to a certain threshold number of hours viewed, TV viewing is linked positively with achievement; above that threshold the link becomes negative. A meta-analysis of more **[End Page 64]** than 1 million students by Micha Razel suggests that the optimal number of hours of TV viewed daily decreases as children get older; for a nine-year-old two hours a day is optimal, whereas for a seventeen-year-old it is half an hour.[8]

Research that takes into account relevant characteristics of the children under study, such as their IQ and socioeconomic status, typically finds no significant link between hours of TV viewing and achievement.[9] IQ, in particular, plays a large role in the association between TV watching and achievement; students with lower IQ scores, for example, watch more television, on average.[10]

Bold text indicates page breaks in the original print version.

Footnotes are hyperlinked in the text.

FIGURE 5.15   An HTML-formatted article excerpt showing page breaks: *The Future of Children*

Activity 2: Store and Manage Files Electronically

Create and manage an archive of files on your computer or portable hard drive (some campuses also provide storage space for students accessible online from any computer). Organize your research materials in a logical way, such as:

- Author
- Sources on particular subtopics
- Sources for and against your anticipated position

Note that many databases provide enough information on search and title screens (including article abstracts, subject headings, and publication date) to assist in early organization.

MOVE BEYOND ONLINE ACCESS

By comparing a general search against one that's restricted to full-text availability, limiters strongly impact the number of sources available to you. Although a limitation can be useful in some cases, it can also restrict finding the very best sources for research projects. In this section we'll look at additional strategies for finding and acquiring sources that take advantage of every available way to access materials.

Locating Materials in the Library

Many databases don't provide access to the full text of every source. Some databases offer very limited full-text access—and some offer none at all. These databases should not be discounted; instead, you should learn how to navigate the holdings in your campus library and use *article delivery* and *interlibrary loan* services, which your reference librarian can explain to you.

Your first step beyond online databases is checking your library's holdings. Some databases, including *Academic Search Premier,* can be linked to your library system, allowing you to jump directly from the database to the library catalog and find materials on campus. If you cannot link directly to call numbers of books and journals, you might also see the notice "print journal held locally" in the search results page. In this case, you simply run a separate search in the library catalog for the title of the book or journal (not for a specific book chapter or journal article) to find the call number and check its availability (see Figure 5.16).

Interlibrary Loan and Article Delivery

Whether you work in a campus library or use online databases, you are likely to find citations of materials that are not immediately available. For example, if you are researching a literary subject and use a comprehensive, discipline-specific database such as the *Modern Language Associ-*

RESEARCH PITFALL

If you want to find a book chapter or journal article in the library, in order to match up with the catalog system you must *search for the title of the entire book or journal* rather than the title of an individual piece.

Activity 3: Navigate Campus Library

Go to your main campus library and familiarize yourself with the Library of Congress system and with the organization of library holdings. Ask a librarian for help in finding the disciplines related to your research topic or question.

The journal is held in the library; call number is included

Users have the option of finding the newspaper in the library or reading an HTML-formatted version of the article

FIGURE 5.16   Results from an *Academic Search Premier* search showing documents available locally (i.e., in the library's holdings)

ation International Bibliography, you may find few of its cited materials online or in the library stacks. Even if you have access to relatively large holdings on campus, you may find that crucial materials are either missing or checked out and not due back in the library until after your research project is over. Instead of feeling discouraged from reading those materials, you should use other means to access them.

> *Search: Article Delivery; Interlibrary Loan; Nearby academic and public libraries; and Ask your librarian for help.*

Fortunately, colleges and universities are members of interlibrary loan networks that provide access to the combined holdings of all affiliated libraries. The research librarian can explain the procedure and provide you with the necessary form to make article delivery and interlibrary loan requests. Be sure to request materials early in your research to ensure that you get them in time.

Sometimes you can avoid the interlibrary loan waiting period with a minor amount of travel. If you live in an area with a number of colleges, check to see if students at your school also have library privileges at nearby campuses. In some cases, you will even find that catalog systems in a region are linked together, so you can get a call number and check availability from home or your campus library. Rather than waiting for material to be shipped to your school, a bike or subway ride—or even a walk—on your own can get you to the material much faster.

Strategies for Searching in Libraries and Online Databases

1. Cast a wide net and discover the range of material available in catalogs and databases—and the variety of ways in which your topic can be pursued.

2. Combine related "framing" terms to narrow results and use multiple terms and Boolean operators (AND, NOT, OR) to shape your search.

3. Limit results to scholarly materials.

4. Limit results by date of publication and get the most recent materials possible.

5. Use database-supplied search terms to expand or refine your search.

6. Read article titles and abstracts to identify the most likely sources and skim for difficulty.

7. When appropriate, limit by full-text availability.

8. Repeat these strategies in more than one campus library and in more than one database.

6

Incorporate Source Material into Your Writing

> **CHAPTER OBJECTIVES**
>
> In this chapter, you'll learn how to:
> - Purposefully use source material, such as quotations, paraphrases, and summaries
> - Incorporate quotations to support your writing
> - Distinguish a paraphrase from a summary and when to use each
> - Embed and develop source material clearly
> - Add citations to source material
> - Avoid plagiarism through careful note-taking and attribution

Academic writers depend on the work of others as they develop their own positions and arguments. The incorporation of this prior work is at the heart of academic research writing—and the effective use of quotation, paraphrase, and summary brings the academic conversation to life. In this chapter, we learn how to use and attribute sources in your writing.

Many beginning writers are wary of using quotations and other source materials in their work. They may believe that it stifles creativity and originality, or they may have been chided by past teachers for

overusing sources. They may be rightly cau-
tious about allowing research material to overshadow their own voices. However, there are
more empowering ways to use material from
sources. Effectively incorporating sources
shows your active participation in the academic conversation surrounding your research. Whether you agree or disagree with sources,
using their ideas, language, and points of view supports your analysis
and makes your responses credible. Your challenge is to use sources
purposefully so that they enhance rather than overshadow what you
want to say in your writing.

> *Use sources to enhance, not replace, your ideas.*

THE PURPOSE OF SOURCE MATERIAL

Beginning research writers often find themselves incorporating
material from sources without clearly explaining its role in their own
work. They may assume that a quotation by an expert speaks for itself,
and that its purpose is as apparent to the reader as it is to them. Sea-
soned research writers ensure that each source is relevant, that it adds
to their credibility, and that they have something to say about it. They
clearly integrate sources into their work and help readers see the role
that each source plays in a point or an argument.

Source materials should always be used *purposefully*. The sources
you use should contribute to your argument, and be clearly integrated
into your writing. Without context, readers are unprepared to connect
material with what they have previously read, and it becomes jarring,
even confusing. *Freestanding source material* that lacks adequate context
and purpose can sidetrack readers from the argument, leaving them to
guess the point you are trying to make with it. It is important not only
to use your sources but also to develop strategies for incorporating
them purposefully into your writing.

Deciding how to use your sources depends on the roles you want
them to play and the amount of detail you plan to incorporate into your
project.

Summaries

If you are using the source to introduce
your readers to the conversation, provide
background information, or describe essential issues in a debate, a summary can quickly
establish a foundation of shared knowledge.
Summaries describe the central argument

> *Use summaries to quickly establish background information, describe positions in a debate, and build common knowledge with readers.*

and major points of a source and often lead to more detailed examinations. All summaries require a writer to accurately *compress* a long piece of writing, such as an article or even a book, into brief passage. A writer must be able to distill the most important claims and illustrations that will allow readers to understand the source and prepare them for the writer's own purpose. Often, a writer also includes one or more direct quotations from the source so that readers have a sense of the language of the original text and credibility of the writer's summary. By summarizing one or more sources, a writer can introduce readers to the conversation and prepare them for his or her contribution to it.

Review of Literature

Longer papers using many sources often include a *review of literature* that summarizes a broader academic conversation. This review introduces the important people involved in the conversation, summarizes what are they saying, and describes key points of agreement and disagreement. The review of literature can demonstrate a writer's understanding of the current state of the conversation and help invite readers to explore the conversation together.

Summaries and literature reviews help strong writers work methodically to establish shared knowledge with readers and prepare for more detailed engagement with research. Having established credibility as an accurate reader, a writer can then use additional details to explain reasons for supporting or challenging each source.

Manage the Voices in an Academic Conversation: The Talk Show Host Paradigm

"Host" your sources, as a talk show host would his or her guests.

Imagine being a talk show host who must get a number of guests on stage, let them have their share of air time, satisfy the audience, and wrap up the show on schedule. Use this image to help you incorporate material from outside sources—your "guests"—without losing sight of your own voice and the larger purpose of your essay—the "show." You want to give your sources their time on stage, but you don't want them to take over the show in the process. As a good "host," it is your responsibility to keep the audience's interest, to stay on topic, and balance your use of source "guests" with your central role in the conversation.

This managing role also allows you to choose *how* you bring your sources into the conversation with you—and with each other. Consider these questions as you make your choices:

- Will you work in a "he said/she said" style, alternating between sources that support and oppose a position in a debate?
- Will you group together all of the authors on one side of a debate and then build a group of authors holding an alternative view?
- As you develop your own position in a debate or solution to a problem, should you give authors who support your position more "air time" or less?
- Should you introduce sources you oppose first so that you gradually build support for the position you plan to take—or establish the strength of your position first and then introduce counterarguments?

Evaluate Strengths and Weaknesses of Sources

Effective writers often incorporate sources because they make strong claims that can either be supported or challenged. Writers may even support *and* challenge passages from the same source. Your evaluations of the strengths and weaknesses of each source help you take a credible position in your writing. Your criteria for evaluating a source include:

- **Currency:** When the source appeared and how current the information is
- **Credentials:** The validity of the author's professional or academic background and authority in the field
- **Logic:** The strength of an argument and credibility of sources used
- **Relevance:** How a source helps you make your own contribution to the conversation

Support your Position with Relevant Sources

Once you evaluate your sources, consider incorporating parts that provide evidence, prove, support, and, where necessary, contradict the positions you take on an issue. Select parts of sources based on which elements you wish to emphasize, which are especially interesting, and which offer the most convincing evidence to support your position.

As you read, use sources to add weight to your personal experiences, reinforce points made in another source, add emphasis to your position, and provide credible evidence for your argument.

Counter Arguments

Sources can also be used to develop strong counter arguments. Specific evidence helps you avoid making sweeping generalizations that are difficult to support and are typically unconvincing. Relevant, well-chosen passages from your sources can enhance your reasoned disagreements. Your counter arguments can show how sources make incorrect assumptions, use insufficient, old, or irrelevant evidence, contradict themselves, and use flawed logic.

USE QUOTATIONS

Quotations—an author's exact words—are used to add emphasis, especially when the source material is so vivid and well written that no rewording can improve it. Shorter quotations are distinguished from your words by quotation marks, while longer (*block*) quotations are off-set from the main text.

Effective writers contextualize quotations, so that each quote plays a clear role in the argument. Writers use a set of rhetorical *moves*, key techniques and strategies, to incorporate quotations. Typically, these moves are made through *signal phrases*—ways of introducing, explaining, and developing source materials—that show purpose to readers.

Signal Phrases

Common signal phrases have been highlighted in the following examples. (Page numbers in parentheses are a convention of the Modern Language Association [MLA] citation style, discussed later in this chapter.) These phrases help readers anticipate how a research writer plans to use the quoted passage in his or her own argument.

Introduce an Author

After introducing an author's full name and his, her, or their work, use the author's last name to set up quotations, as in the following example by education scholars Thomas Mackey and Trudi Jacobson:

According to Breivik, "the best place to start information literacy planning is with general education or core curriculum, where

concerns for competencies that all students should acquire provide a natural home for the discussion of information literacy
abilities" (44).[1]

Additional phrases that indicate *attribution* of authorship include:
"As Breivik claims," "Breivik argues," "Breivik asserts," and the like.

Describe an Author's Credentials

Here, journalism scholar Trudy Lieberman describes Tara
O'Toole's academic credentials and professional affiliation, which add
authority to her observations:

> "This isn't just any story," points out Dr. Tara O'Toole, who heads
> the Center for Biosecurity at the University of Pittsburgh Medical
> Center. "We are in a whole new era, the end of American hege-
> mony, in which we are vulnerable to attack. And that makes people
> very uncomfortable."[2]

Identify the Type of Source

Describe the type of source—a book, article, report, interview,
personal conversation, or e-mail—as in this example from James
Gomez's study of Internet surveillance in Asian nations:

> The Electronic Privacy Information Center (EPIC) and the Pri-
> vacy International report entitled *Privacy and Human Rights 2003*
> identified global trends in governmental and legislative surveil-
> lance following 9-11. Those were: increased communications sur-
> veillance; weakened data protection regimes; increased data
> sharing; and increased profiling and identification. RSF, EPIC,
> and Privacy International are in agreement that: "None of the
> above trends are necessarily new; the novelty is the speed with
> which these policies gained acceptance, and in many cases, be-
> came law" (EPIC 27).[3]

Identify Aspects of a Source

Here, the writer describes historical characteristics of a source as a
way of introducing the quotation:

> The publisher and editor of *Campaigns and Elections*, which has
> evolved from a public information to a trade journal, celebrates
> this process as one in which "technology—and not candidates,
> consultants, or the press—is driving change" (5).[4]

Provide Context

Summarize the larger point being made by the writer, identify specific research methods, or describe the subject area of the source:

> Patricia Bellia studies the connections between existing surveillance law and new technologies to conclude that "if electronic surveillance cases were to plainly expose the limits of surveillance law, they would generate a more fruitful legislative debate about the propriety of true data privacy legislation, whether broadly or narrowly conceived" (1286).[5]

Connect to Other Sources for Affirmation

In this passage, Mikko Tuhkanen develops a theme with quotations from multiple sources:

> According to Dale Cockrell, the blackface tradition emerged among the lower classes whose ranks were not racially segregated in the early days of minstrelsy (84–86). Similarly, such forms of cultural expression as music and dance were "creolized at the level of common urban people" (86). We can indeed understand minstrelsy as a *creolized* cultural form, in the sense in which Edouard Glissant uses the term. Put simply, creolization refers to ongoing cultural mixing, the "unceasing process of transformation" (142).[6]

Words and phrases that signal *affirmation* or *emphasis*: additionally, furthermore, moreover, similarly, likewise, indeed.

Connect to Other Sources for Refutation

In this passage, English professor Sherry Linkon uses key words and signal phrases to move from one author's analysis to another's:

> Graff suggests that part of the problem is that many students see "standard academic practices" as "bizarre, counterintuitive, or downright nonsensical" (44). Students don't value the process or the outcome, the academic argument about ideas, nor do they know how to use the "conventional formulations that characterize written argument" (168). Yet before they can formulate an argument, students need to develop critical interpretations of texts. However, as educational psychologist and historian Samuel L. Wineburg suggests, we also don't teach this adequately: "Profes-

sors may assume that their students are stupid or suffer from a learning disability. Often the truth is much simpler. No one has ever bothered to teach them some basic but powerful skills of interpretation" (B20).[7]

Words and phrases that signal *contrast* or *counterpoint*: however, but, nevertheless, on the contrary, on the other hand.

Ellipsis and Insertions

To make quoted passages flow easily with your work, or to connect separate parts of a longer passage, use ellipses (...) to cut words and square brackets ([/]) to add or alter them.

For example, here a writer wants to quote from the following passage by Lemi Baruh, but cut the explanation in the middle of the sentence:

> Unlike conventional mass media which, to a large extent, rely on a combination of aggregate audience viewing data—such as ratings, shares, GRPs, reach, and frequency (Webster et al., 2000)—and demographic data, interactive media provide the means through which technology and content providers can get real-time information about audience behavior.[8]

The quotation with ellipses would look like this:

> According to Baruh, television, newspapers, and similar media "rely on a combination of aggregate audience viewing data ... and demographic data" to develop audience profiles (60).

If the writer expects that readers are unlikely to know what the abbreviation "GRP" stands for, the same passage from Baruh could be altered to aid comprehension. The writer uses square brackets to add words which integrate the passage and the introduction, ellipses to indicate missing words in the quoted passage, and finally another set of square brackets to define GRPs.

> According to Baruh, mass media "rely on a combination of aggregate audience viewing data ... [including] ratings, shares, GRPs [Gross Rating Points], reach, and frequency" (60).

RESEARCH PITFALL

Research writers must fairly represent a source's original meaning and convey its original context. The following examples are from an excerpted newspaper article that compares statements by two politicians and how these statements were misused for political purposes.

Context Fabrication: Two Examples

Example 1

- Who: Andy Luger, DFL-endorsed candidate for Hennepin County attorney.

- What he said: "We have complaints from neighbors that I have been hearing throughout this campaign about the fact that we're not getting people off the streets."

- How the National Republican Senatorial Committee (NRSC) introduced Luger's quote: "Andy Luger, the endorsed DFL candidate to succeed Amy Klobuchar as Hennepin County attorney, details widespread complaints he has received that Klobuchar is 'not getting people off the streets.'"

- What Luger said about the NRSC press release: "An untrue and unfair characterization ... Pure and simple, neighborhood groups, people active in crime watch programs, are upset that repeat offenders were not getting more time in prison. They were not complaining about Amy Klobuchar or her office."

Example 2

- Who: Former Hennepin County Attorney Mike Freeman, Luger's opponent.

- What he said: "We need to target better some of the more violent offenders and some more of the repeat offenders."

- How the NRSC introduced Freeman's quote: "Freeman, also says Klobuchar hasn't held 'repeat offenders'and 'violent offenders' accountable."

- What Freeman said about the NRSC press release: "It's falsely misleading ... Typical fodder from a partisan national campaign committee that knows nothing about Minnesota. It's a systemwide problem and it needs a systemwide response. I was talking about police officers, investigators, judges, prosecutors. This wasn't a specific criticism of Amy, it was calling for a systemwide approach."

CITE QUOTATIONS AND OTHER
SOURCE MATERIAL

Because quotations use unique ideas and exact words drawn from your research material, they must include citations which allow readers to find passages in the original sources. The Modern Language Association (MLA) style requires parenthetical citations that include the page number(s) where source material is located, and, in some cases additional information.

If your introduction of the source material does not clearly identify the author, then his or her last name should be included in the parenthetical citation:

> Because of new approaches to data collection and methodology, "confidence bands, model checking, and errors-in-variables problems can all now be handled" in the study of issues such as global climate change (Samworth 290).

If you are incorporating material from multiple texts by the same author, and if you don't identify the title of the source, include it in the parenthetical citation:

> For much of his career, the French philosopher Jean Baudrillard has explored problems relating to "the total misunderstanding on the part of Western philosophy ... of the relation between Good and Evil" (*Spirit* 13).

The title of Baudrillard's book, *The Spirit of Terrorism*, has been shortened to a signal word that will distinguish it from other Baudrillard sources used in the essay, such as the book *Simulacra and Simulation* and the article "Divine Europe." The signal word has been italicized to indicate a book title; it would be in quotations for an article title.

If a quotation is introduced without naming the author or the title of the work, and if more than one source by the author is being used, the parenthetical citation must include the author's last name, an indication of the title, and the page number:

> The practice of psychoanalysis is centered on the analyst's ability to overcome the patient's resistances, "in uncovering these as quickly as possible, in pointing them out to the patient and inducing him by human influence ... to abandon his resistance" (Freud, *Beyond* 18).

Here, the source author, Sigmund Freud, is named in the parenthetical citation because he has not been otherwise introduced. Because this paper uses more than one source by Freud, a key word from the

title, *Beyond the Pleasure Principle* is required. Finally, as in every parenthetical citation, the page on which the quoted material appears is also
included.

*Your citations guide
readers to the original
sources.*

When deciding which elements are
needed as you use sources, check your citation
against the amount of contextual information
readers have in leading up to the quotation.
Ensure that your reader has all the information
needed to locate the source in your bibliography and to find the page or
pages on which the source material appears.

RESEARCH PITFALL

Be sure to include page numbers, author names, and source titles whenever you take notes in your reading log. See Chapter 3 for more information on starting a reading log, and Chapter 9 for advice on using reading
logs in the research process.

Electronic sources present a number of additional citation challenges. We will look in more detail at ways of referencing websites,
chat room discussions, online articles, and other electronic sources in
Chapter 7.

Cite Authors Quoted in Source Material

As you research, you're likely to come across quoted passages in
your sources that you would like to incorporate in your writing projects. Style guides have rules for these special cases to indicate when a
writer uses quotes removed from their original source. In MLA style,
the source of the quotation is indicated by the abbreviation"qtd. in," as
in the following example. Here, a researcher has read Sherry Linkon's
article, "The Reader's Apprentice," and wants to use a passage from
Gerald Graff's book *Clueless in Academe* that is cited by Linkon. The researcher may incorporate the second hand quotation as:

> Gerald Graff claims that college students find "standard academic
> practices" to be "bizarre, counterintuitive, or downright nonsensical"
> (qtd. in Linkon 248).

The citation points to where the passage appears in Linkon's article
rather than Graff's book, because the writer may only cite those sources
he has read. Also, by using "qtd. in," the writer shows that he relies on

Linkon for this particular representation of Graff's book. The writer's bibliography will also list Linkon's article rather than Graff's book as the source of this quotation.

If you find that a secondary quotation plays an important role in your research projects, consider reading the original source to ensure that you fully understand its meaning.

SUMMARIZE AND PARAPHRASE

It can be tempting to use quotations every time you incorporate source material. Because experts often make their claims more elegantly and are likely to have more credibility than beginning researchers, quotations may be overused because they easily add instant credibility and volume to student writing.

But that ease is deceptive. Using quotations excessively can distract readers from your contribution to the conversation, or even hinder your ability to develop your own contribution. Returning to the talk show host example, the host who lets the "guests" do all the talking is barely present for his or her own show. Excessive quotation can distract readers from the way *you* write. When you do not need a source's exact words, and to avoid monotonous or excessive use of quotations, incorporate source material with *summary* and *paraphrase*.

Summaries

Summaries are concise restatements that allow you to quickly sketch out the thesis or main points of a source. A short summary of one or two sentences will provide a broad overview of a source, while a longer summary, which may be a paragraph or even a few pages, will explain main points and include key supporting arguments and examples from the source. A summary demands careful selection of what to include, and what to leave out. As you make these choices, work to keep your summary objective and give readers an accurate representation of the source.

A summary is used to *situate* readers in a discussion, give context, historical background, or an overview of essential points. In the following example, Hal Neidzviecki situates his readers by summarizing a classic text by Gustave Le Bon on people's behavior in crowds:

> In his 1895 text *The Crowd*, Le Bon began a new field of study: how to psychologically control large groups of people. Le Bon characterized the masses as intrinsically dangerous, unpredictable, and irrational rabble. But, he also suggested that because of and

Summary elements:
1. *Introduce the source*
2. *Identify key points*
3. *Include a representative quotation*
4. *Describe the conclusions*

despite their volatility, crowds could be manipulated. "Whatever be the ideas suggested to crowds," noted Le Bon, "they can only exercise effective influence on condition that they assume a very absolute, uncompromising shape." Le Bon, father of mass psychology and patron saint of propaganda, had a clarion call that would come to affect future billions: *Dumb it down!*[9]

Notice how Niedzviecki summarizes an entire book in a few sentences. The first sentence restates Le Bon's thesis and places his book in a specific year. The second and third sentences summarize Le Bon's major subpoints and themes. The fourth sentence includes a quotation to show Le Bon's ideas in his own words. The final sentence describes the conclusion and implications of Le Bon's study. The summary is brief but informative enough so that Niedzviecki can pursue his own goal of showing the influence of Le Bon on other thinkers of the late nineteenth century, as his next sentence demonstrates:

Summary purpose: Showing the influence of a major text in the field

Le Bon's theories found plenty of attention, not to mention sympathetic followers. Foremost among them was Gabriel Tarde, who compared the crowd's actions to an epileptic fit.[10]

Summaries prepare readers for a writer's contribution, which can include examining an aspect or subpoint in detail, linking to one or more additional sources, and agreeing or disagreeing with an author's conclusions. Chapter 9 will introduce you to other strategies for summarizing.

Paraphrase

Paraphrases are restatements of source material in your own words. They are best used when the point of a source is important, but its exact language is not. Because a paraphrase is a restatement, it will run about the same length as the original text.

Paraphrases are used to help readers understand your discussion of a source, especially when its language may be overly technical, difficult, archaic (old), or possibly confusing to nonspecialists. An effective paraphrase replaces or reuses keywords from the original to make them more accessible to readers. You can also reorganize the original, rearranging phrases and sentences to clarify the flow of ideas.

Here is an example of an original source followed by its paraphrase:

ORIGINAL SOURCE:

The lawyer saith what men have determined; the historian what men have done. The grammarian speaketh only of the rules of speech; and the rhetorician and the logician, considering what in nature will soonest prove and persuade, thereon give artificial rules, which are still compassed within the circle of a question according to the proposed matter. The physician weigheth the nature of a man's body, and the nature of things helpful or hurtful unto it. And the metaphysic, though it be in the second and abstract notions, and therefore be counted supernatural, yet doth he indeed build upon the depth of nature. Only the poet, disdaining to be tied to any such subjection, lifted up with the vigor of his own invention, doth grow in effect another nature, in making things either better than nature bringeth forth, or, quite anew, forms such as never were in nature.

—"Apologie for Poetry, "
Sir Philip Sidney, 1595

PARAPHRASE:

In his 1595 essay, "Apologie for Poetry," Sir Philip Sidney compares lawyers, who study the will of the people, with historians, who are interested in the people's past. Grammarians, he continues, study the rules of language, while rhetoricians and logicians develop theories based on speculations tied to nature. Physicians are interested in the human body and understanding it in health and sickness, and philosophers, even though they examine the supernatural, develop theories from their knowledge of nature. Sidney concludes by claiming that poets are alone in rejecting natural limitations to produce new natures, either by improving what is or by inventing altogether new ideas through their creative efforts.

The passage from Sidney presents some challenges, particularly diction (vocabulary), and syntax (word order), for readers not familiar with late sixteenth-century English. The paraphrase works by replacing archaic words with contemporary ones, such as "study" for "saith" and "speaketh," and "develop theories" for "give artificial rules." In the last sentence, the paraphrase reworks the original syntax to simplify the passage for today's audience. The paraphrase also provides regular attributions of authorship ("he continues" and "Sidney concludes") to remind readers that they are not reading the writer's ideas, but rather the reworking of an original source. To avoid the appearance of plagiarism (see page 139), this periodic attribution is necessary.

As with Sidney's archaic language, the specialized language of academic fields can also present challenges for readers outside the discipline. When it is not necessary to use an exact quotation, paraphrases ease readers' comprehension of sources so that their efforts can be spent on following arguments rather than on deciphering unfamiliar language. Consider this passage from Mary Louise Pratt's article "Arts of the Contact Zone," followed by a paraphrase that recasts her words and ideas in a more familiar form:

ORIGINAL SOURCE:

Autoethnographic texts are not, then, what are usually thought of as autochthonous forms of expression or self-representation (as the Andean *quipus* were). Rather, they involve a selective collaboration with and appropriation of idioms of the metropolis or the conqueror. These are merged or infiltrated to varying degrees with indigenous idioms to create self-representations intended to intervene in metropolitan modes of understanding. Autoethnographic works are often addressed to both metropolitan audiences and the speaker's own community. Their reception is thus highly indeterminate.[11]

PARAPHRASE:

To illustrate the "contact zone," Pratt shows how colonized people create new writing techniques to represent themselves. People, like the indigenous Andeans under Spanish rule, strategically draw on their cultural traditions, such as "quipus" texts and oral histories, and on those of conquerors. As Pratt goes on to explain, new strategies for self-representation challenge colonizers' ways of seeing the world. Because these "merged" texts speak to different audiences at once, Pratt concludes that their message is less certain than texts that speak to one audience alone (77).

Although paraphrasing can be an effective way to use sources in your writing, it's just as important to keep your purpose and audience in mind. Perhaps for one audience, the writer anticipates more interest in Sidney's point than his precise language; thus, the passage from "Apologie for Poetry" need not be quoted word for word. However, another audience, scholars of sixteenth-century English literature, might be very interested in Sidney's original language and organization and do not need help to clarify the passage's meaning.

Writers can also mix paraphrase and quotation as in this example, where Jane Tompkins discusses the work of historian Perry Miller:

> The fuel drums stand, in Miller's mind, for the popular misconception of what this country is about. They are "tangible symbols of [America's] appalling power," a power that everyone but Miller takes for the ultimate reality (ix). To Miller, "the mind of man is the basic factor in human history," and he will plead, all unaccommodated as he is among the fuel drums, for the intellect—the intellect for which his fellow historians, with their chapters on "stoves or bathtubs, or tax laws,""the Wilmot Proviso" and "the chain store,""have so little respect" (viii, ix).

Summaries, paraphrases, and quotations play a significant role in research writing. Use the following guidelines to consider methods of bringing sources into your own work:

- **What to quote, summarize, or paraphrase.** Quote when no rewording is necessary. Summarize to relay information quickly. Paraphrase to clarify language.
- **Where to introduce your sources.** Will your argument be a comparison, problem/solution, or development of a new idea?
- **Why the source material appears in your writing.** Tie the source to your argument by explaining its purpose.
- **How your sources connect to each other.** Use signal phrases to connect the source to your argument. (See the seven examples demonstrated earlier in this section.)
- **When to be a good host.** Using the talk show host paradigm, keep the audience in mind by staying on topic and balancing sources with your own voice.

Activity 1: Write a Paraphrase

Paraphrase a passage (of three to four sentences) selected from one of your research texts or one chosen by your instructor. Make the passage accessible to an audience of nonspecialists, which may include your instructor and classmates. As you draft your paraphrase, be sure to:

- *Replace* specialized terms and concepts
- *Simplify* syntax without losing the overall meaning of the original
- Provide *attribution* of authorship to indicate that you're paraphrasing someone else's words

EMBED SOURCE MATERIAL:
THE HOURGLASS APPROACH

A paragraph that uses a quote, paraphrase, or summary typically begins with a broad statement that introduces the topic of the paragraph. The writer clearly transitions from the preceding paragraph by describing the relationship between old and new points. Gradually, the writer narrows the focus of the paragraph, moving toward a specific example or illustration drawn from the source. The writer develops the significance of the source material to give it a purpose in the paragraph, then connects the paragraph point to a larger thesis before moving on to the next paragraph.

Embedding source material in this way can be visualized as an hourglass (see Figure 6.1)—the author moves from a broad, general statement toward the neck of the hourglass, where source material is used, and then develops its broader significance.

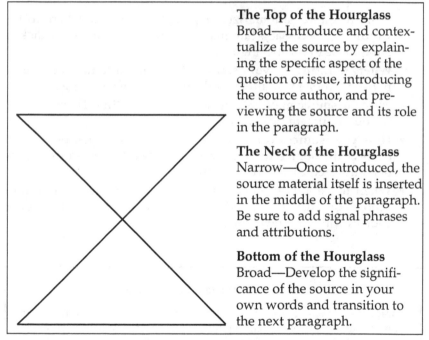

The Top of the Hourglass
Broad—Introduce and contextualize the source by explaining the specific aspect of the question or issue, introducing the source author, and previewing the source and its role in the paragraph.

The Neck of the Hourglass
Narrow—Once introduced, the source material itself is inserted in the middle of the paragraph. Be sure to add signal phrases and attributions.

Bottom of the Hourglass
Broad—Develop the significance of the source in your own words and transition to the next paragraph.

FIGURE 6.1   The Hourglass approach.

In the following excerpt from "The Influence of Anxiety: September 11, Bioterrorism, and American Public Health,"[12] writer Nicholas B. King uses the hourglass approach to introduce his sources and develop their significance. (You can read King's entire essay in Chapter 13.)

"Similar" refers back to the point of the preceding paragraph, reminding readers of prior knowledge and signaling that a comparison will be developed here.	Proposed responses to bioterrorism have similar historical analogs. In the past, outbreaks of epidemic disease have sometimes led to the curtailment of civil liberties, from compulsory vaccination and treatment to detention and isolation of those deemed threatening to the public's health. As Alan Kraut, Barron Lerner, and Judith Walzer Leavitt have ably demonstrated, the brunt of such restrictions have frequently been borne by the poor and socially marginalized, and protection of public health has often been conflated with attempts to maintain social order and control "difficult" populations.[7] Recent	"Historical" indicates the kind of comparison to be made. **Broad** King transitions from the preceding paragraph and introduces the topic of this paragraph. **Narrow** King's sources illustrate the particular point of this paragraph, answering the question of whose civil liberties are curtailed.
King again uses the transition word "similarly" to signal his development of the point made by the authors he cites.	recommendations have similarly sought to balance civil liberties with public health. One controversial piece of model legislation, prepared for the Centers for Disease Control and Prevention (CDC), expands the state's power to seize hospitals and private property; compel vaccination and treatment of individuals; and quarantine those who refuse medical examination, testing, vaccination, or treatment.[8]	**Broad** King applies these historical studies to current issues.

AS YOU WRITE:

✔ Use the hourglass approach to practice integrating sources smoothly with your own ideas.

Activity 2: Draft a Paragraph with Embedded Source Material

Choose a quotation from one of your research texts, or one assigned by your instructor, and draft a paragraph using the hourglass approach.

Start with a broad claim, perhaps about the topic, or the context of the quotation you've chosen.

Then, work toward the quotation itself, which will be the narrowest point of the hourglass.

(Continued)

Next, explain the broader significance of the quotation with additional development or by adding your own examples.

Finally, link the paragraph topic to your thesis.

As you develop your paragraph, signal the narrowing and broadening moves you're making.

Sample Paragraph Using the Hourglass Approach

In the beginning of her essay, Jane Tompkins describes the ways people's perspectives shape their understanding of history. In fact, Tompkins's first example is drawn from her own childhood experiences with Native Americans in New York City during the 1950s. Even though Tompkins had regular opportunities to see "real" Indians, she recalls how her fantasies were more powerful than reality: "My Indians … were creatures totally of the imagination, and I did not care to have any real exemplars interfering with what I already knew" (5). Even when the real person was standing right in front of her, Tompkins chose to hold on to the more comforting fantasy, and she goes on to show how professional historians are similarly swayed by their beliefs and perspectives when they study the past. Tompkins's examples of historical research are especially important, because she is able to show readers that what historians see is shaped by values like patriotism and ethnocentrism, just like the Indians she saw in her childhood were shaped by fairy tales and simplistic stories about the past.

Broad
The writer introduces a topic from the source: the significance of perspective

Narrower
Describes the context in the source

Narrowest
Illustrates point with key quote

Broader
Develops example into larger significance

Broadest
Revisits main point to transition into next paragraph—perhaps developing a more contemporary example (regarding immigration, poverty, gay people, etc.) to illustrate how perspective can affect reality

AVOID PLAGIARISM

Plagiarism occurs when a writer uses another person's words or ideas without giving
credit to the source. Writers face significant
risks when they plagiarize, whether intention-
ally or unintentionally. Students may lose the

> *The exact words and unique ideas of others must be cited to avoid plagiarism.*

opportunity for credit on the plagiarized as-
signment; they can also face long-term damage to their academic careers, including failing the course and receiving institutional sanctions
such as probation, suspension, and expulsion. On a larger scale, the academic community is harmed when its conventions, which depend on
the integrity of each member, are violated.

Plagiarism can be avoided when you acknowledge the sources
that you incorporate into your writing by using the citation conventions described thus far and in greater detail in the next chapter. Not
only will good citation habits prevent plagiarism, they will also testify
to your credibility as a researcher. Therefore,
plagiarism is to be avoided not only because it
is a significant violation of academic integrity,
but, more importantly, because the failure to
adequately document sources undermines
your credibility as a researcher.

> *Good citation habits enhance your contributions to the conversation.*

Attribute Authorship in Quotation, Paraphrase, and Summary

Be sure to attribute authorship not only to direct quotations, but
also to paraphrases and summaries. Attribution is required any time
you use ideas unique to your sources and ideas that fall outside of
your audience's general knowledge. Of course, this last issue is a judgment call for writers because they must reasonably assess the knowledge of their readers. For example, a physicist working in quantum
mechanics can write for a physics journal and assume that a highly
specialized body of knowledge is shared by her audience. Conversely,
a physicist working on similar problems who writes for philosophers
of science, may have to provide more context to situate readers in a
conversation outside of their specialty. If you are simply stating facts
that are in the realm of general knowledge—the altitude of Mount
Rainier, the distance between London and Rome, and so on—you do
not need to cite a source, but any sources used to *interpret* and *explain*
facts must be cited.

Essential Strategies for Avoiding Plagiarism

Entering into conversation with your sources requires constant integration of your ideas with those of others. The process also requires you to carefully distinguish between the two by attributing and citing every use of your source material. In order to avoid plagiarism, ensure that:

- The *idea* **is your own.** Clearly and fairly attribute any new ideas you get from your sources, whether in print, online, or in the field.
- The *language* **is your own**. Whenever you include the exact words of your source, use quotation marks to show the difference between your words and those of others.
- The *sentence structure* **is your own.** Paraphrases must alter the arrangement of ideas from the original source and not the words alone.

The Role of Ethical Note Taking

Your reading log will be a lifesaver as you compile and manage sources for research projects.

Prevent the misuse of others' work by taking careful notes as you read, clearly identifying exact quotations, paraphrases, and summaries, and distinguishing source material from your own observations and responses. If you copy quotations or draft summaries and paraphrases in your reading log, take a few extra minutes to briefly contextualize source material as you use it. Careful note taking now helps you to distinguish the words and ideas of the source from your own when you draft an essay. At the same time, you will also anticipate using your sources purposefully in your writing projects.

Activity 3: Identifying and Revising Unacceptable Uses of Source Material

Read the following passage about the ways children can be treated by teachers and school administrators:

> Instead of labeling kids, let's talk about them as potential leaders, affirm their strengths, and believe they can do good, brave, remarkable things. The path to safer, less violent

schools lies less in our control over children than in appreci-
ating their need to have more control in their lives, to
feel important, to be visible, to have an effect on people and
situations.

—"10 Ways to Move Beyond Bully-Prevention"
by Lyn Mikel Brown

Each of following cases contains unacceptable attempts to use
Brown's words in quotations or paraphrases. Either individually or in
groups, suggest one or more ways of revising each sentence, for example:

According to Brown, we have to stop just labeling kids as
bullies and start talking about them as potential leaders (48).

This sentence incorporates specific phrases by Brown, but doesn't
use quotation marks to distinguish Brown's words from the writer's.
Suggested revision:

According to Brown, we have to stop just "labeling kids"
as bullies and start "talk[ing] about them as potential
leaders" (48).

CASE 1

We must start believing that young people can do brave, remarkable things and gain more control over their own lives.

By not attributing the source, the writer unfairly takes credit for
Brown's idea.

CASE 2

We should stop treating kids as bullies, writes Lyn Brown,
and begin creating less violent schools and treating kids as
potential leaders (48).

The writer alters Brown's sentence structure and accurately summarizes Brown's point, but uses some of Brown's words without quotation
marks.

CASE 3

Brown argues that we should start valuing students' desire
to shape their lives (48).

This sentence is unacceptable because it replaces Brown's words
with synonyms, but copies the original sentence structure.

(*Continued*)

CASE 4

> Start treating kids, argues Brown, "as potential leaders, appreciating their need to have more control over their lives" (48).

The writer doesn't indicate the fusing of two disconnected parts of Brown's longer passage.

CASE 5

> I disagree with Brown, who claims that "labeling kids" helps them "to feel more important" (48).

The writer correctly puts Brown's words in quotation marks, but misrepresents Brown's meaning by inaccurately connecting two parts of the original.

Strategies for Incorporating Source Material

1. Use source material: quotations, paraphrases, and summaries bring the conversation to life.

2. Take precise notes as you read to ensure accurate citations.

3. Introduce and contextualize material in your own words. Avoid freestanding quotations.

4. Relate quotations, paraphrases, and summaries to the point of the paragraph or section.

5. Evaluate sources. Show readers your ability to understand sources' strengths and weaknesses.

6. Relate sources to your research question. Connect voices in the conversation to each other.

7. Cite every source.

7

Prepare Bibliographies

CHAPTER OBJECTIVES

In this chapter, you'll learn how to:

- Understand the purpose of a bibliography
- Locate information for a bibliography entry
- Style a parenthetical citation or footnote reference
- Prepare a bibliography in an accepted style
- Write entries for websites, listservs, and other electronic sources
- Write content notes

In this chapter, we examine how to create a bibliography from the sources used in research and writing. If you keep an up to date reading log with a record of your research and the materials you integrated into your writing, you will already have much of the information you need for a formal bibliography.

First, let's consider why a bibliography is a valuable resource for your audience and not simply a required attachment tacked to the end of a research paper. It serves a purpose beyond giving your instructor a way to check your sources and test your mastery of mysterious conventions.

THE PURPOSE OF REFERENCES

If "surveillance" was the only reason to write bibliographies, they probably wouldn't be of much use beyond the classroom. Yet, scholars, research writers, and other members of the academic community also use bibliographies in their own work. A record of sources shows readers how a research project is situated in the academic conversation. It documents the research process and prompts further research on the part of readers. A comprehensive and accurate reference list provides conventionally organized evidence of the research behind the writing. To see how this works, review the bibliographies of your sources and consider how they aid further research by helping you locate additional sources, adopt a particular approach in your research, and reveal new directions for it to take.

Reference lists and bibliographies summarize a writer's research journey.

The references in your sources can provide new leads, especially if you become stuck in the research process or have trouble finding useful sources. Furthermore, it is the paper trail that helps readers join you and build on your contribution to the academic conversation. Your bibliography can even provide future students with new ways of thinking about their own research and writing.

THE WORKING BIBLIOGRAPHY

Throughout your research, keep a working bibliography of the sources that you intend to use in your writing projects. Your working bibliography should include a complete and accurate record for each type of source as described in Table 7.1.

BIBLIOGRAPHIC STYLES

Academic writers typically choose bibliographic styles that match the conventions of their fields. The most common styles, denoted by their initials, include:

- **MLA**—*The MLA Style Manual and Guide to Scholarly Publishing*, 7th ed. (2009), by the Modern Language Association. This style is primarily used in the humanities, such as English literature.
- **CMS**—*Chicago Manual of Style*, 15th ed. (2003), by the University of Chicago Press. This style, which includes two systems of preparing references and the option of using footnotes or endnotes, is

TABLE 7.1   Basic source information for articles, books, and
electronic source material

Articles	*Books*	*Book Chapter*	*Electronic Sources*
• Library call number	• Library call number	• Library call number	• URL (Internet "address")
• Article author	• Author(s)	• Chapter author	• Page title
• Article title	• Title	• Chapter title	• Site title
• Periodical title	• Publisher	• Book editor	• Site author(s) and/or sponsor(s)
• Volume number	• Place of publication	• Publisher	• Publication date and/or last update
• Issue number	• Publication year	• Place of publication	• Date you access the source
• Issue date	• Other information as available (edition number, translator, editor, etc.)	• Publication year	• Complete print information (for electronic versions of print sources)
• Inclusive page numbers		• Inclusive page numbers	

used across the disciplines in the humanities and sciences, including history and mathematics.

- **APA**—*Publication Manual of the American Psychological Association,* 6th ed. (2009), by the American Psychological Association. This is often the preferred style of the social sciences.
- **CSE**—*Scientific Style and Format: The CSE Manual for Authors, Editors, and Publishers,* 7th ed. (2006), by the Council of Science Editors. This is the preferred style for the physical and applied sciences.

Realize, too, that a style is not restricted to a particular discipline. APA style can been used, for example, in ecology, mathematics, and the humanities. CMS, the most universal in this list, can be used for virtually every discipline and is often adapted for unique uses. Professional writers may use additional guidelines, or entirely different approaches, at the request of a particular editor, journal, or academic press. If you have the opportunity to practice the bibliographic style related to your research field, expect that some of the sources you read might not conform precisely to their conventions. Resist the temptation to simply copy approaches of your sources, and be prepared to convert entries as required for the style of your bibliography. Finally, if your instructor has a particular style or variation of a style that he or she wants you to follow, do so regardless of your research field.

LOCATING SOURCE INFORMATION FOR BIBLIOGRAPHY ENTRIES

You need to know where to find the information used for citing and documenting sources. In this section, we discuss print (books, journals, newspapers, and magazines) and electronic sources.

Print Sources

Books

Information for books appears in the initial pages—often called the front matter— and includes the title page and the page immediately following, the copyright page. More often than not the copyright page will have all the information you need if the title page does not: title, subtitle, the author's or editor's name, the place of publication, the publisher, and the date (see Figure 7.1).

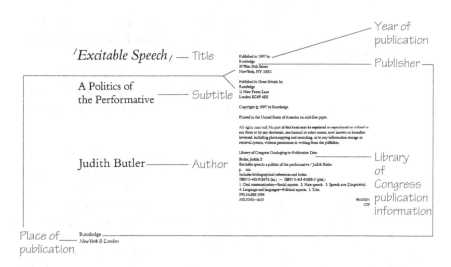

FIGURE 7.1 Sample title page (left) and copyright page (right) from a book.

Academic Journals

The cover and the table of contents of an academic journal will typically feature the full name of the journal, the volume and issue numbers, and the month, season and year of publication (see Figure 7.2). The other important information you need is the name of the author, the article title, and the page range of the article, which may be found in the table of contents or in each article. It is also important to determine if page numbers continue from one issue to the next through a volume, or if each issue is individually numbered.

Pagination varies between journals that begin each issue with page 1 and those that continue page numbers from one issue to the next through a year (see Figure 7.2).

Many academic journals reprint publication information on the first page of each article in an issue to help researchers who obtain sources online, through interlibrary loan, or in reprint form.

General Audience Periodicals

General audience periodicals, such as *Time*, the *New Yorker*, and the *Nation*, provide bibliographic information on the front or back cover and the table of contents, including the name of the author, the title of the article, the name of the periodical, volume and issue numbers, and the date of issue (see Figure 7.3). Figure 7.3 shows

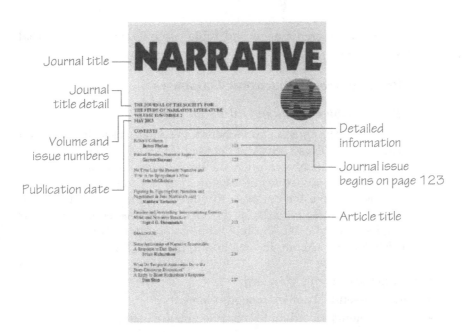

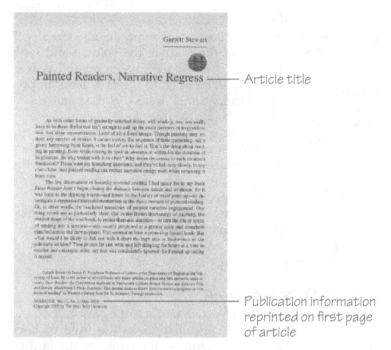

Article title

Publication information
reprinted on first page
of article

FIGURE 7.2   Sample contents page (top) and first page of an article
(bottom) from a scholarly journal.

the combined copyright page and table of contents for the journal
Rethinking Schools.

Print Sources in Electronic Databases

Publication Details in Online Databases

Academic Search Premier and other online databases include citation
information in results screens and detailed title screens (see Figures 7.4
and 7.5). Because databases often include source information not required by bibliographic style guides, you must be careful to avoid copying and pasting from the database to your bibliography. Additionally,
online databases may not order or format elements as required by your
style guide—even the MLA online bibliography does not provide entries in MLA form. To compile a bibliography entry, prepare to:

- *Identify* the elements you need
- *Separate* essential from extraneous elements
- *Order* elements according to the style you are using

RETHINKING SCHOOLS is a nonprofit, independent magazine advocating the reform of elementary and secondary public schools, with an emphasis on urban schools and issues of equity and social justice. We stress a grassroots perspective combining theory and practice and linking classroom issues to broader policy concerns. We are an activist publication and encourage teachers, parents, and students to become involved in building quality public schools for all children. Published by Milwaukee-area teachers and educators with contributing writers and editors from around the country, Rethinking Schools focuses on local and national reform.

■

EDITORS
Wayne Au, Bill Bigelow, Terry Burant
Linda Christensen, David Levine,
Stan Karp, Larry Miller, Hyung Nam,
Bob Peterson, Kelley Dawson Salas,
Stephanie Walters

EDITORIAL ASSOCIATES
Rita Tenorio, Kathy Williams

MANAGING EDITOR
Fred McKissack

CURRICULUM EDITOR
Bill Bigelow

BUSINESS MANAGER
Michael Trokan

OFFICE MANAGER
Michaele A. Datsko

ART DIRECTOR
Patrick JB Flynn

PROOFREADER
Jennifer Morales

PEOPLE WHO HELPED WITH THIS ISSUE
Carole Dede, Beth Kaplan, Larry Hoffman,
Jamie Spagnolo, Aaria Troiano

■

RETHINKING SCHOOLS Vol 23, No. 3 (ISSN 0895-6855) is published four times a year between (September and June) for $17.95 a year by Rethinking Schools, Limited. 1001 East Keefe Avenue, Milwaukee, WI 53212-1710. Periodicals postage pending at Milwaukee, WI. POSTMASTER: Send address changes to RETHINKING SCHOOLS. P.O. Box 2222, Williston, VT 05495-9940. Rethinking Schools is published by Rethinking Schools, Limited, a nonprofit, tax-exempt organization. It is listed in the Alternative Press Index. Rethinking Schools is a member of Community Shares of Greater Milwaukee, an alternative workplace giving federation in Milwaukee, Wis. One-year subscriptions are $17.95. Bulk order subscriptions are available at substantially reduced prices. Occasionally Rethinking Schools makes its mailing list available for educational promotions. If you do not want your name given out, contact us. Rethinking Schools would like to acknowledge the support of the Communitas Charitable Trust, Frederick Douglass Edhlund Fund, the Ford Foundation, Sheilah's Fund, the Tides Foundation, and New Visions Foundation. Rethinking Schools is printed at Royle Printing, Sun Prairie, Wis. Newsstand circulation is through Disticor Magazine Distribution Services, call 905-619-6565 or fax 905-619-2903.

Rethinking Schools
1001 East Keefe Avenue, Milwaukee, WI 53212
Phone: 414-964-9646 | Fax: 414-964-7220
Editorial email: Fred.McKissack@gmail.com
Subscriptions/business: RSBusiness@aol.com
www.rethinkingschools.org
©2009 RETHINKING SCHOOLS, LTD.

Rethinking

SPRING 2009

COVER ILLUSTRATION BY DAVID McLIMANS

COVER STORY

Arne Duncan
and the Chicago Success Story: Myth or Reality?

BY JITU BROWN,
ERIC (RICO) GUTSTEIN,
AND PAULINE LIPMAN

Yes, he played basketball with the president, but there's more to know—and be worried about— when it comes to the new Secretary of Education **10**

FIGURE 7.3   Sample inside cover page from a magazine.

Annotation callouts: "Volume and issue numbers", "Table of Contents", "Date of publication"

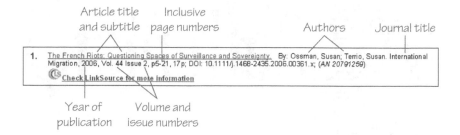

FIGURE 7.4   Academic Search Premier results screen showing the elements for an MLA-style entry: Ossman and Terrio.

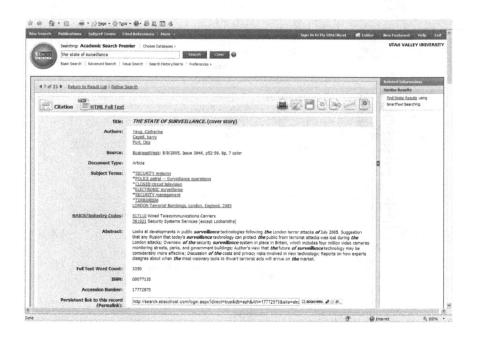

FIGURE 7.5   Academic Search Premier title screen: Yang, Capell, and Port.

Using the results screen listing in Figure 7.4 you can create the following MLA-style bibliography entry:

Ossman, Susan, and Susan Terrio. "The French Riots: Questioning Spaces of Surveillance and Sovereignty." *International Migration* 44.2 (2006): 5–21. Print.

Entries in an MLA-style Works Cited page must include a description of a source's medium (print, web, film, etc.).

To write an MLA bibliography entry from the Academic Search Premier title screen shown in Figure 7.5, select and transpose the following elements:

Yang, Catherine, Kerry Capell, and Otis Port. "The State of Surveillance." *BusinessWeek* 8 Aug. 2005: 52–59. Print.

The following sections are a selection of examples for how to cite different kinds of print and electronic sources. The same sources are used for MLA, APA, CMS, and CSE to show comparative differences in the order of names, punctuation, capitalization, and the like.

PARENTHETICAL CITATION SYSTEMS—MLA AND APA

Attributions and parenthetical citations in the text include the page number and, depending on the kind of citation, may also include the names of the author(s), the title of the source (MLA), or the date of the publication (APA). Attributive tags and parenthetical citations must contain enough information to help readers find the correct bibliographic entry and the page(s) where the cited passage appears in the source. These citations direct readers to the bibliography, where sources are arranged in alphabetical order according to the primary author's last name.

Attributive tags (see Chapter 6) help writers introduce quotations, paraphrases, and summaries, by connecting them to authors and sources.

Because an author's last name is the essential piece of information readers need to move from text to bibliography, be sure to either attribute each source clearly or include the name in your parenthetical citation.

Identifying Multiple Works by One Author

If you use more than one source by the same author, your reader will need additional information to distinguish between them in the text and in the bibliography. For example, a historian of science may use two books by Karl Popper—*Quantum Theory and the Schism in Physics* and *The Open Universe*—both of which were published in 1982. The writer plans to use material from page 114 in *Quantum Theory and the Schism in Physics,* and from page 68 in *The Open Universe.*

In the MLA system, if the author's last name and the source title are not mentioned through attribution, parenthetical citations distinguish between the two books by including a keyword from each title: (Popper, *Quantum* 114) and (Popper, *Open* 68).

In the APA system, citations include the author's last name, the page number, and the source's publication date, which are usually enough to distinguish between multiple sources by the same author. If two texts are cited that have been published in a single year by the same author, they are distinguished with a lower-case letter after the year: (Popper, 1982a, p. 114) and (Popper, 1982b, p. 68). The author-date system used in the References will have the years labeled with the same letters.

WORKS CITED AND REFERENCES LISTS

Bibliographies appear in separate, final sections of a text called "Works Cited" in MLA and "References" in APA. In both MLA and APA styles, these sections include only those sources used in the text. Entries are double-spaced throughout and begin on the page's left margin. Entries that exceed one line are indented five spaces (or a tab) after the first line. The final element in each MLA style entry is the medium of publication (print, web, television, film, etc.).

Documenting Print Sources in MLA Style

Books

Begin with the author's name or authors' names (primary author's last name first), followed by the title of the book (italicized), the place of publication, the publisher, and the year of publication.

BY ONE AUTHOR

Butler, Judith. *Excitable Speech*. New York: Routledge, 1997. Print.

BY TWO OR THREE AUTHORS

Bartholomae, David, and Anthony Petrosky. *Ways of Reading: Words and Images*. New York: Bedford, 2003. Print.

BY MORE THAN THREE AUTHORS

Name the primary author, followed by "et al." to indicate additional authors.

Durrant, Sam, et al. *Postcolonial Narratives and the Work of Mourning*. Albany: SUNY P, 2004. Print.

EDITED COLLECTION

Roof, Judith, and Robyn Wiegman, eds. *Who Can Speak? Authority and Critical Identity*. Urbana: U of Illinois P, 1995. Print.

AUTHOR AND EDITOR

Nietzsche, Friedrich. *Hammer of the Gods*. Ed. Stephen Metcalf. London: Creation, 1995. Print.

AUTHOR AND TRANSLATOR

Diderot, Denis. *The Indiscreet Jewels*. Trans. Sophie Hawkes. New York: Marsilio, 1993. Print.

MORE THAN ONE WORK BY THE SAME AUTHOR

Works are alphabetized by first word (excluding "the," "a," "an," etc.) of the title. Subsequent entries are denoted by three em dashes. Do not repeat the author's name.

Popper, Karl. *The Open Universe: An Argument for Indeterminism*. Totowa, NJ: Rowman, 1982. Print.

———. *Quantum Theory and the Schism in Physics*. Totowa, NJ: Rowman, 1982. Print.

Periodicals

As in entries for books, begin with the author's name or authors' names (primary author's last name first), followed by the article title in quotation marks, the title of the periodical (italicized), the volume and issue numbers, the year, and the pages on which the article appears. In this section, entries document journal articles accessed in print, rather than online.

Works cited entries for online sources are described in the next section.

SCHOLARLY JOURNAL WITH CONSECUTIVE PAGINATION

Walby, Kevin. "Open-Street Camera Surveillance and Governance in Canada." *Canadian Journal of Criminology and Criminal Justice* 47.4 (2005): 655–83. Print.

JOURNAL WITH ISSUES INDIVIDUALLY PAGINATED

Schumacher, Yorck Olaf, and Michael Ashenden. "Doping with Artificial Carriers: An Update." *Sports Medicine* 34.3 (2004): 141–50. Print.

MONTHLY MAGAZINE ARTICLE

The issue date (month and year) replaces the volume number.

Cornehls, Jim. "The War on Civil Liberties Continues." *Z Magazine* July-Aug. 2006: 37-41. Print.

WEEKLY/BI-WEEKLY MAGAZINE ARTICLE

The issue date (day, month, year) replaces the volume number.

Talbot, Margaret. "Darwin in the Dock." *New Yorker* 5 Dec. 2005: 66–77. Print.

NEWSPAPER ARTICLE

Include the complete issue date (and, if applicable, the edition); if the article runs over nonconsecutive pages, include the first page followed by a plus sign.

Lichtblau, Eric, and James Risen. "US Officials Cite Legal Rationale on Spying Effort." *New York Times* 20 Jan. 2006: A1+. Print.

EDITORIAL

Add the word "Editorial" after the title.

"Surveillance, New York Style." Editorial. *New York Times* 23 Dec. 2005: A26. Print.

Anonymous sources like this editorial are alphabetized by title.

Personal Interviews

PERSONAL INTERVIEW

"TS" refers to a typescript, such as a letter or memo.

Begin with the name of the person interviewed (last name first), describe the type of interview (telephone, e-mail, personal interview, etc.), and include the date.

Chin, Frank. Personal Interview. 30 Mar. 2002.
Curran, Paul. Letter to the Author. 27 Sep. 2006. TS.

PUBLISHED INTERVIEW

Begin with the name of the person interviewed, followed by either the title of the interview or "Interview," then complete the entry according to the source type.

Gavrielatos, Angelo. "Australia Battles Privatization: An Interview with Angelo Gavrielatos." *Rethinking Schools* 21.2 (2006): 11–15. Print.
Weiss, Russ. Letter. *New York Times* 19 April 2007: A26. Print.

Documenting Print Sources in APA Style

Books

Begin with the (primary) author's last name and initial(s), followed by the year of publication, the title of the book (italicized), the place of publication, and the publisher. Only proper nouns and the first word in a title, and in a subtitle if applicable, are capitalized. Note that the initials of the author's first and middle names are used. Also note that multiple-author entries are alphabetized and are connected by ampersands (&).

BY ONE AUTHOR

Butler, J. (1997). *Excitable speech*. New York: Routledge.

BY TWO OR THREE AUTHORS

Bartholomae, D., & Petrosky, A. (2003). *Ways of reading: Words and images*. New York: Bedford/St. Martin's.

BY MORE THAN THREE AUTHORS

Include all names up to six authors, after which you may use "et al." as in MLA style above.

Durrant, S., Coetzee, J.M., Harris, W., & Morrison, T. (2004). *Postcolonial narratives and the work of mourning*. Albany: State University of New York Press.

EDITED COLLECTION

Roof, J., & Wiegman, R. (Eds.). (1995). *Who can speak? Authority and critical identity*. Urbana: University of Illinois Press.

AUTHOR AND EDITOR

Nietzsche, F. (1995). *Hammer of the gods*. (S. Metcalf, Ed.). London: Creation Books.

AUTHOR AND TRANSLATOR

Diderot, D. (1993). *The indiscreet jewels*. (S. Hawkes, Trans.). New York: Marsilio.

MORE THAN ONE WORK BY THE SAME AUTHOR

Multiple works by one author are ordered by date of publication (most recent first); works published in the same year are alphabetized according to the first major word in the title and distinguished by lowercase letters (a, b, c, etc.).

Popper, K. (1982a). *The open universe: An argument for indeterminism*. Totowa, N.J.: Rowman and Littlefield.
Popper, K. (1982b). *Quantum theory and the schism in physics*. Totowa, N.J.: Rowman and Littlefield.

Periodicals

Begin with the author's name (last name first and initials of first and middle names), followed by the date of publication, the article title, the title of the periodical and volume number in italics, and the pages on which the article appears.

SCHOLARLY JOURNAL WITH CONSECUTIVE PAGINATION

Walby, K. (2005). Open-street camera surveillance and governance in Canada. *Canadian Journal of Criminology and Criminal Justice 47*, 655–683.

JOURNAL WITH ISSUES INDIVIDUALLY PAGINATED

The issue number, in plain text, follows the volume number.

Schumacher, Y. O., & Ashenden, M. (2004). Doping with artificial carriers: An update. *Sports Medicine 34*(3), 141–150.

MONTHLY MAGAZINE ARTICLE

Include the publication month(s) (and the day of weekly magazines), the volume number in italics, and the inclusive page numbers.

Cornehls, J. (2006, July-August). The war on civil liberties continues. *Z Magazine 19*, 37–41.

WEEKLY/BI-WEEKLY MAGAZINE ARTICLE

Talbot, M. (2005, December 5). Darwin in the dock. *The New Yorker 81*, 66–77.

NEWSPAPER ARTICLE

Include the complete issue date (and, if applicable, the edition); list the section and the inclusive pages, using the abbreviation "p." or "pp." as appropriate.

Lichtblau, E., & Risen, J. (2006, January 20). U.S. officials cite legal rationale on spying effort. *New York Times*, pp. A1, A14.

EDITORIAL

Unsigned articles are alphabetized according to the first major word in the title and completed using the form appropriate to the type of source.

Surveillance, New York style. (2005, December 23). *New York Times*, A26.

LETTER TO THE EDITOR

Include the complete issue date and "Letter to the editor" in square brackets after the title, if available, or after the date.

Weiss, R. (2007, April 19) [Letter to the editor]. *New York Times*, A26.

Published Interviews

Begin with the name of the person interviewed, followed by either the title of the interview or "[Interview]," then complete the entry according to the source type.

Gavrielatos, A. (2006, Winter). "Australia Battles Privatization: An Interview with Angelo Gavrielatos." *Rethinking Schools 21*, 11–15.

Personal Interviews/Correspondence

Personal interviews and correspondence are cited only in the text. Follow appropriate attributive tags with parenthetical citations which include a descriptive phrase, such as "personal communication," and the date.

> Like other civil rights activists of the time, novelist Frank Chin recalls that he had become "fed up with the Bay Area" by the late 1970s (personal interview, March 30, 2002).

FOOTNOTE/ENDNOTE SYSTEMS—CMS AND CSE

The Chicago Manual of Style features Documentation I ("Humanities" style) and Documentation II (author-date) styles of reference lists. CMS also allows writers to use documentary footnotes or endnotes for source citations and various kinds of additional notes that may add further information for the reader. CMS Documentation II features parenthetical citation similar to APA style as well as a bibliography of only the sources cited like APA and MLA styles. CMS Documentation I— which is a Notes-Bibliography System—is a foot- or endnote system used to cite references with specific notes and an alphabetized bibliography. Readers are directed to these notes by superscript arabic numbers, inserted following the closest punctuation after a piece of source material. The first time a source is cited, the note includes a complete bibliographic entry; later citations are shortened, with the author's last name, a truncated version of the title, and always the referenced page or pages.

The style recommended by the Council of Science Editors, CSE uses a separate reference section organized numerically in the order of each source's appearance in the text. CSE reference numbers appear immediately following the citation. The number assigned to an individual source repeats each time it is used throughout the text. It is also common to see multiple superscript numbers appearing at once in CSE papers, since a writer's point often references more than one source.

CMS and CSE references are formatted with reference numbers on the left margin, and the entry beginning one space from the number. Entries are double-spaced in both styles.

Documenting Print Sources in Chicago Style

Books

Begin with the author's name or authors' names, followed by the title of the book (italicized), the place of publication, the publisher, and the year of publication.

In a typical CMS entry page numbers of cited material are included as the last element.

BY ONE AUTHOR

Judith Butler, *Excitable Speech* (New York: Routledge, 1997), 164.

BY TWO OR THREE AUTHORS

David Bartholomae and Anthony Petrosky, *Ways of Reading: Words and Images* (New York: Bedford/St. Martin's, 2003), 87.

BY MORE THAN THREE AUTHORS

Include all names up to four authors, after which you may use "et al." following the first author's name.

Sam Durrant, J.M. Coetzee, Wilson Harris, and Toni Morrison, *Postcolonial Narratives and the Work of Mourning* (Albany: State University of New York Press, 2004), 203–205.

EDITED COLLECTION

Judith Roof and Robyn Wiegman, eds., *Who Can Speak? Authority and Critical Identity* (Urbana: University of Illinois Press, 1995), 14.

AUTHOR AND EDITOR

Friedrich Nietzsche, *Hammer of the Gods*, ed. Stephen Metcalf (London: Creation Books, 1995), 92.

AUTHOR AND TRANSLATOR

Denis Diderot, *The Indiscreet Jewels*, trans. Sophie Hawkes (New York: Marsilio, 1993), 36.

MORE THAN ONE WORK BY THE SAME AUTHOR

Since notes are arranged in order of a source's appearance, each work is given a complete listing when it is referenced in the text. After the first appearance of an author's full name and work, the last name and a truncated version of the title may be used.

Karl Popper, *The Open Universe: An Argument for Indeterminism* (Totowa, N.J.: Rowman and Littlefield, 1982), 182.

Popper, *Quantum Theory and the Schism in Physics* (Totowa, N.J.: Rowman and Littlefield, 1982), 65.

Periodicals

As in entries for books, begin with the author's name or authors' names, followed by the article title in quotation marks, the title of the periodical in italics, the volume number, the year, and the pages on which the article appears.

SCHOLARLY JOURNAL WITH CONSECUTIVE PAGINATION

Kevin Walby, "Open-Street Camera Surveillance and Governance in Canada," *Canadian Journal of Criminology and Criminal Justice* 47 (2005): 655-83.

JOURNAL WITH ISSUES INDIVIDUALLY PAGINATED

The issue number (abbreviated "no.") follows the volume number.

Yorck Olaf Schumacher and Michael Ashenden, "Doping with Artificial Carriers: An Update." *Sports Medicine* 34, no. 3 (2004): 141–50.

MONTHLY MAGAZINE ARTICLE

Entries may include the volume number. If so (as in Cornehls's article), the date of publication is placed in parentheses and separated from the pages with a colon; if not (as in Talbot's article), the date of publication follows immediately after the magazine title and then by the pages on which the article appears. If your instructor does not prefer one approach over the other, choose one and stay with it throughout your paper.

Jim Cornehls, "The War on Civil Liberties Continues," *Z Magazine* 19, no. 7-8 (July–August 2006): 37–41.

WEEKLY/BI-WEEKLY MAGAZINE ARTICLE

Margaret Talbot, "Darwin in the Dock," *The New Yorker*, December 5, 2005, 66-77.

NEWSPAPER ARTICLE

Include the complete issue date (and, if applicable, the edition); include either the section in, or all pages on, which the article appears.

Eric Lichtblau and James Risen, "U.S. Officials Cite Legal Rationale on Spying Effort," *New York Times*, January 20, 2006, A1, A14.

EDITORIAL

"Surveillance, New York Style," Editorial, *New York Times*, December 23, 2005, A26.

Personal Interviews/Correspondence

Begin with the name of the person interviewed, describe the type of interview (telephone, email, personal interview, etc.), and include the date.

Frank Chin, personal interview with the author, March 30, 2002.
Paul Curran, letter to the author, September 27, 2006.

Published Interviews/Correspondence

Begin with the name of the person interviewed, followed by either the title of the interview or "interview by" (without quotation marks) and the interviewer's name, then complete the entry according to the source type.

Angelo Gavrielatos, "Australia Battles Privatization: An Interview with Angelo Gavrielatos," *Rethinking Schools* 21, no. 2 (2006): 11-15.
Russ Weiss, letter to the editor, *New York Times*, April 19, 2007, A26.

Documenting Print Sources in CSE Style

Books

Begin with the author's or authors' last name(s) and first initial(s), followed by the title of the book, the place of publication, the publisher, the year of publication, and the number of pages in the source.

BY ONE AUTHOR

As in APA style, only proper nouns and the first word of the title are capitalized; the title is in plain text. A colon separates the location and publisher; a semicolon separates the publisher and year of publication.

Butler J. Excitable speech. New York: Routledge; 1997. 185 p.

BY TWO OR THREE AUTHORS

Bartholomae D, Petrosky A. Ways of reading: Words and images. New York: Bedford/St. Martin's; 2003. 457 p.

BY MORE THAN THREE AUTHORS

Entries for books with up to ten authors include each author by name; after the first ten are named, other authors are indicated by "and others."

Durrant S, Coetzee JM, Harris W, Morrison T. Postcolonial narratives and the work of mourning. Albany (NY): State University of New York Press; 2004. 146 p.

EDITED COLLECTION

Roof J, Wiegman R, editors. Who can speak? Authority and critical identity. Urbana (IL): University of Illinois Press; 1995. 251 p.

AUTHOR AND EDITOR

Nietzsche F. Hammer of the gods. Metcalf S, editor. London: Creation Books; 1995. 235 p.

AUTHOR AND TRANSLATOR

Diderot D. The indiscreet jewels. Hawkes S, translator. New York: Marsilio; 1993. 285 p. Translation of: Les bijoux indiscrets.

MORE THAN ONE WORK BY THE SAME AUTHOR

Since notes are arranged in order of a source's appearance, each work is given a complete listing when it is referenced in the text.

Popper K. The open universe: An argument for indeterminism. Totowa, N.J.: Rowman and Littlefield; 1982. 185 p.

Popper. Quantum theory and the schism in physics. Totowa, N.J.: Rowman and Littlefield; 1982. 229 p.

Periodicals

As in entries for books, begin with the author's name or authors' names (up to ten), followed by the article title, the title of the periodical, the year, the volume number, and the pages on which the article appears.

SCHOLARLY JOURNAL WITH CONSECUTIVE PAGINATION

Only proper nouns and the first word in the article title are capitalized. After the first word, the journal title is abbreviated when possible, and articles (the, a, an, etc.) are omitted. The year, volume number, and page range have only punctuation marks—no spaces—separating them.

Walby K. Open-street camera surveillance and governance in Canada. Canadian J Criminol Crim Just 2005;47:655–683.

JOURNAL WITH ISSUES INDIVIDUALLY PAGINATED

The issue number, in parentheses, follows the volume number.

Schumacher YO, Ashenden M. Doping with artificial carriers: an update. Sports Med 2004;34(3):141–150.

MONTHLY MAGAZINE ARTICLE

If volume and issue numbers are available (as in Cornehls's article), the entry is just like a journal paginated by issue; if not (as in Talbot's article), the date of publication follows immediately after the magazine title and is followed in turn by the pages on which the article appears.

Cornehls J. The war on civil liberties continues. Z Mag 2006;19(7–8):37–41.

WEEKLY/BI-WEEKLY MAGAZINE ARTICLE

Talbot M. Darwin in the dock. New Yorker 2005 December 5:66–77.

NEWSPAPER ARTICLE

If not part of its title, include the newspaper's location in parentheses after the title, as in Journal and Courier (Lafayette, IN). Also include the complete issue date (and, if applicable, the edition); indicate the section by "Sect," and list all pages on which the article appears.

Lichtblau E, Risen J. U.S. officials cite legal rationale on spying effort. New York Times 2006 Jan 20; Sect A:1, A:14.

EDITORIAL

Unsigned articles begin with [Anonymous], and the type of source is described in square brackets after the article title.

[Anonymous] Surveillance, New York style. [editorial] New York Times 2005 Dec 23; Sect A:26.

LETTER TO THE EDITOR

Begin with the author's name. Include "letter to the editor" in square brackets after the title, if available. Complete the citation as with similar periodicals.

Weiss R. [Letter to the editor]. New York Times 2007 Apr 19; Sect A26.

Published Interviews

Begin with the name of the person interviewed, followed by either the title of the interview or "Interview" (without quotation marks). Include the interviewer's name, followed by "interviewer" (without - quotation marks), then complete the entry according to the source type.

Gavrielatos A. Australia battles privatization: an interview with Angelo Gavrielatos. Miner B, interviewer. Rethinking Schools 2006;21(2): 11–15.

Personal Interviews/Correspondence

Personal interviews and correspondence are not cited as references, although they can be mentioned in a separate appendix section after the references section.

DOCUMENT ELECTRONIC SOURCES AND ONLINE DATABASES

Materials in Online Databases

Each style recommends a special format for material accessed through online databases. Typically, databases supply all the information needed to write bibliography entries.

For example, this *Academic Search Premier* results screen leads readers to an HTML version of the article:

Title:	THE PATRIOT ACT AND THE WALL BETWEEN FOREIGN INTELLIGENCE AND LAW ENFORCEMENT.
Source:	Gardner, William. *Harvard Journal Of Law And Public Policy* Volume: 28 Issue: 2 (2005-03-01) p. 319–463. ISSN: 0193-4872

The bibliography entry will include all information from the print version. To show that you read an online version, the print citation is followed by other information, which may include:

- The name of the database
- The database URL
- The date the material was published online
- The date you accessed it

MLA

MLA style includes information about both the original print source and the online source; also include the date you accessed the online version. The URL is optional; however, if it is used, place in angle brakets (</>).

Seamon, Richard Henry, and William Dylan Gardner. "The Patriot Act and the Wall between Foreign Intelligence and Law Enforcement." *Harvard Journal of Law and Public Policy* 28 (2005): 319–463. *Academic Search Premier.* Web. 28 Jul. 2008.

APA

APA style includes information about the print source, adding "[Electronic version]" after the article title.

Seamon, R., & Gardner, W.D. (2005). The Patriot Act and the wall between foreign intelligence and law enforcement [Electronic version]. *Harvard Journal of Law and Public Policy 28* (2005): 319–463.

CMS

The Chicago Manul of Style's Documentation I includes information about the print source, the URL, and the date you accessed the online version.

Richard Henry Seamon and William Dylan Gardner, "The Patriot Act and the Wall Between Foreign Intelligence and Law Enforcement," *Harvard Journal of Law and Public Policy* 28 (2005): 319–463, http://web.ebscohost.com/ehost/detail?vid=4&hid=4&sid=240d0a9d-3dd1-4324-9e1d35ee075d410f%40 sessionmgr13&bdata= JnNpdGU9ZWhvc3QtbGl2ZQ%3d%3d#db=aph&AN=16901261 (accessed 28 July 2008).

CSE

CSE includes information about the print source, the URL, and the date you accessed the online version.

Seamon RH, Gardner WD. 2005. The Patriot Act and the wall between foreign intelligence and law enforcement. Harvard J Law Pub Pol 2005;28: 319–463. In: EBSCO [database on the Internet]. Ipswich (MA): EBSCO Industries; c2010 [cited 2008 July 28]. Available from: http://search .ebscohost.com/.

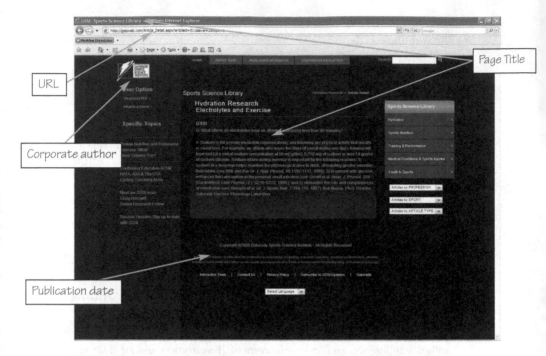

FIGURE 7.6   Page from Gatorade Sports Science Institute website.

Websites

You can use materials from the open Internet—government and commercial websites, chat rooms, and so on—in your writing projects. Bibliography entries for websites should include as much information as possible to help readers retrace your steps.

For example, a writer uses the website in Figure 7.6 to research the effects of performance-enhancing substances on athletes. Like many commercial websites, this one contains information that the author needs for a detailed reference.

MLA

MLA style includes the author's name, article or page title in quotation marks, website name, publication date, Web medium, and access date. The URL is optional; however, if it is used, place in angle brakets (</>).

Gatorade Sports Science Institute. "Hydration Research: Electrolytes and Exercise." *Sports Science Library*. 2008. Web. 27 July 2008. <http://gssiweb.com/Article_Detail.aspx?articleid=511&level=2&topic=1>.

APA

Include the author's name, publication date, article or page title, website name, access date, and URL.

Gatorade Sports Science Institute (2008). Hydration research: Electrolytes and exercise. *Sports Science Library*. Retrieved July 27 2008, from http://gssiweb.com/Article_Detail.aspx?articleid=511&level=2&topic=1

CMS

Include the author's name, article or page title, website name, URL, and access date.

Gatorade Sports Science Institute, "Hydration Research: Electrolytes and Exercise," *Sports Science Library*, 2008, http://gssiweb.com/Article_Detail.aspx?articleid=511&level=2&topic=1 (accessed July 27, 2008).

CSE

Include the author's name, publication (or last revision) date, page title, site title, URL, and access date.

Gatorade Sports Science Institute. Hydration research: Electrolytes and exercise. [Internet]. Sports Science Library web site. 2008. [cited 2008 Jul 27]. Available from: http://gssiweb.com/Article_Detail.aspx?articleid=511&level=2&topic=1.

Chat Rooms and Listservs

Internet discussions—on social networking sites (such as *Twitter* and *Facebook*), blogs, chat rooms, bulletin boards, discussion threads, and e-mail lists—can be valuable sources for your research projects. These are listed in the bibliography with as much relevant information as you can find about an author, the discussion subject, and the hosting website.

For example, a writer follows the online discussion below (see Figure 7.7) for information from diesel enthusiasts about using waste vegetable oil to fuel their cars and trucks:

MLA

MLA style includes the author's name if available, title of posting in quotation marks, type of source, posting date, host/forum name, Web medium, and access date. The URL is optional; however, if it is used, place in angle brakets (</>).

Axel. "Re: Filtering WVO." Online posting. 27 January 2006. *Bio Fuels Forum*. Web. 2 December 2009. <http://www.biofuelsforum.com/svo_users/146-filtering_wvo.html>.

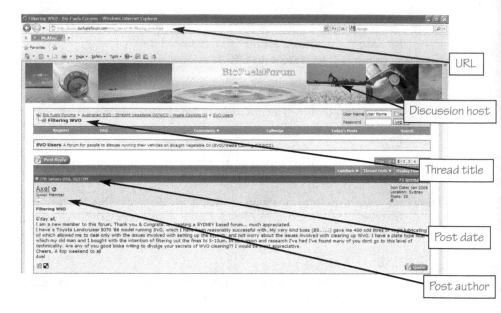

FIGURE 7.7   Page from an online discussion board.

APA

APA style includes the author's name if available, posting date, title of posting, host/forum name, and URL.

Axel (2006, January 27). Re: Filtering WVO. Message posted to Bio Fuels Forum, archived at http://www.biofuelsforum.com/svo_users/146-filtering_wvo.html.

CMS

CMS includes the author's name if available, title of posting in quotation marks, posting date, URL, and access date.

Axel, "Re: Filtering WVO." January 27, 2006, http://www.biofuelsforum.com/svo_users/146-filtering_wvo.html (accessed December 2, 2009).

CSE

CSE includes the author's name if available, posting date, title of posting, type of source, date of access, and URL.

Axel. 2006 27 Jan. Re: Filtering WVO. [Internet: Online posting]. 2 December 2009. Available from: http://www.biofuelsforum.com/svo_users/146-filtering_wvo.html.

CONTENT NOTES

In addition to bibliographic notes that provide citations for your sources, there are other kinds of footnotes and endnotes that can be very useful to your readers, giving them additional information that may not fit in the text proper. *Content* notes, for example, allow writers to insert comments and explanations that need to be made outside of the main discussion. There are many reasons to include these notes— additional information about a particular idea, concept, scholarship, source, and the like—a few of which are discussed next.

Illustrate a Concept

In his article "What's New About the 'New Surveillance'?: Classifying for Change and Continuity," sociologist Gary Marx uses the note in Figure 7.8 to expand common descriptions of surveillance, explaining how observational techniques are not limited to vision alone. Note 5 allows Marx to introduce an additional sense and to illustrate it with an example that will be familiar to all readers, making it optional for the reader to interrupt the flow of the main discussion.

To be sure the visual is usually an element of surveillance, even when it is not the primary means of data collection (e.g., written accounts of observations, events and conversations, or the conversion to text or images of measurements from heat, sound or movement). Yet to "observe" a text or a printout is in many ways different from a detective or supervisor directly observing behavior. The eye as the major means of direct surveillance is increasingly joined or replaced by hearing, touching and smelling.[5] The

---

[3] The self-restraint and voluntary compliance favored in liberal democratic theory receives a new dimension here. The lme between the public and the private order maintenance becomes hazier. The border may be blurred in the sense that there can be a continuous transmission link between sender and receiver as with brain waves or scents. Other broken and reconstructed borders are discussed in Marx, 1997. Consider also a federally funded "Watch Your Car" program found in 11 states in 2001. In this program vehicle owners attach a decal to their car inviting police to pull them over late at night to be sure the car is not scolen. To the exteot that this "co-production" of social order becomes established it is easy to imagine individuals wearing miniature video, audio location and biological monitors sending data outward to protective sources. New borders? and forms of neutralization will of course appear, but it will be a new senses-transcending ball game and we will become more aware of the extent to which the limits of the physical world shape cognition and norms.
[4] William Holden nicely captures this in his self-analysis in die film *Picnic*, "What's the use, baby? I'm a bum. She saw through me like an x-ray machine."
[5] Taste is the most under-utilized of the senses for surveillance. Drug agents sometimes taste a suspect substance. I don't know about the validity of biting a stone to determine if it is a diamond (technically this may be closer to feel than to taste but doesn't fit either that well. It involves cognition). Historically the tasters who sampled the food and drink of elites to see if they were poisoned are one example I will learn more about. Evaluating the performance of a chef by tasting the product, a chef's self-monitoring by sampling a dish before serving and a baking contest in which there is a taste test arc ofher examples.

FIGURE 7.8   Sample content footnote from an article.

Demonstrate Knowledge of Context

In his article "The Influence of Anxiety: September 11, Bioterrorism, and American Public Health," Nicholas B. King uses the note in Figure 7.9 to demonstrate awareness of directions his argument might have taken and familiarity with texts that may have been used in his project. The note allows King to keep his argument on track but point to other possible claims and readings.

For historians, the tone of these recommendations is immediately recognizable. Flush with the promise of the bacteriological revolution, early twentieth-century American public health began to turn its attention and funding from broad preventive measures toward clinical medicine, laboratory science, and the early detection of disease. As a number of historians have argued, the subsequent redirection of funding from public health toward biomedical research contributed to the abandonment of social and structural remedies, and the eventual dismantling of the public health infrastructure in the 1980s under the pressure of Reagan-era budgetary constraints.[10]

The rhetorical and institutional equation of national security with public health is also hardly novel.[11] The U.S. Public Health Service's flagship institution, the CDC in Atlanta, Georgia, was established (as the "Malaria Control in War Areas") in 1942 as a "Sentinel for Health" to investigate and control infections among soldiers, and "to keep malaria from spreading to the armed forces from its reservoir in the civilian population."[12] Its Epidemic Intelligence Service (EIS), established in 1951 to "investigate outbreaks of disease in strategic areas," has long served as an invaluable arena for training scientists and epidemiologists.[13] In 1999, one CDC official argued in the journal

---

[10] There is some controversy over the "narrowing hypothesis" in public health. A number of historians have argued that the bacteriological revolution led public health to narrow its focus to laboratory science and the efficient location, identification, and eradication of germs, while others contend that public health has maintained a broad social focus throughout the century. See, among others, Barbara Rosenkrantz, "'Cart before Horse': Theory, Practice, and Professional Image in American Public Health, 1870–1920," *J. Hist. Med. Allied Sci.,* 1974, 29, 55–73; Elizabeth Fee, "Public Health and the State: The United States," in *The History of Public Health and the Modern State,* ed. Dorothy Porter (Amsterdam: Editions Rodopi B.V., 1994), 224–75; Georgina D. Feldberg, *Disease and Class Tuberculosis and the Shaping of Modern North American Society* (New Brunswick, N.J.: Rutgers University Press, 1995); and Nancy Tomes, *The Gospel of Germs: Men, Women, and the Microbe in American Life* (Cambridge: Harvard University Press, 1998).

FIGURE 7.9   Sample content footnote from an article.

A Glimpse "Backstage"

Imagine your research project as a performance, like a stage play or television program. The main text and core argument are the portions of your research and thinking you want your audience to "see," or the show itself. As you put your show on stage, consider using explanatory notes as a way to give your readers a glimpse "backstage" at the ideas and sources that make your main argument work. Those behind-the-scenes looks give readers a sense of your process of selection in choosing the sources you incorporate into your final essay, show that you understand there are multiple possible ways of looking at your research topic and question, and see that your selection process was well informed.

> *Explanatory notes give readers a glimpse "backstage."*

If your instructor asks you to incorporate content notes into your writing projects, consider some of these uses:

- Provide background on an issue related, but not central, to your argument
- Describe a source or idea that might distract readers if included in your argument
- Direct readers to additional sources
- Suggest possible directions readers could take in their own research

Anticipating Notes in the Reading Log

As you track your sources in a reading log, consider keeping a list of ideas, arguments, and points that are interesting, but unlikely to appear in your research projects. You might see patterns emerging, inspiring questions you can hint at in your notes, or discover background in a debate that would be useful or even necessary for readers who are not yet full participants in your research conversation.

Strategies for using and Writing References Effectively

1. Locate bibliographic material in print and online sources.
2. Select and reorder material according to the needs of the citation system.
3. Include URLs and other additional information for online sources.
4. Use content notes when appropriate.

8

Explain Academic Terms and Concepts

CHAPTER OBJECTIVES

In this chapter, you'll learn how to:

- Understand terms and concepts
- Identify specialized terms and concepts used in an academic conversation
- Define terms using discipline-specific reference works such as dictionaries and encyclopedias
- Explain terms used in the academic conversation

Writers and readers depend on shared language to communicate effectively as they exchange ideas. Definition plays an especially important role in effective academic research writing. Writers expect readers to participate in wrestling with compex ideas, but they may not want readers reaching for the dictionary or puzzling through unfamiliar terms so often that their point is lost. Academic writers, from students writing for professors to professors writing for each other, often expect that their audience is already familiar with specialized language. However, other readers may not be so well equipped. These readers depend on clear definition of essential terms and concepts, on a writer's ability to *define, explain,* and *show* the meaning of ideas used in a discussion.

Each area of research has unique ways of understanding and expressing ideas, and as you gain expertise in the conversation you should consider the needs of your classmates and instructor, who may not share your familiarity. This chapter helps you invite readers *Defining specialized terms and concepts anticipates and meets readers' expectations.* into the academic conversation by building a common foundation of key terms and concepts used in your research field.

ACQUIRE SPECIALIZED KNOWLEDGE THROUGH EXPLORING POSSIBLE DEFINITIONS

Definitions help readers understand terms and concepts—even ones that may seem familiar from their use in everyday contexts—that have special meaning and application when used within a particular academic community. In the passage below, English professor Virginia Blum studies contestants on MTV's reality program, *I Want a Famous Face*,[1] and explains their emotional responses to cosmetic surgery:

> The economy of love enacted on *I Want a Famous Face* suggests that the enhanced self-esteem (read self-love) and self-confidence desired by all of the participants are structurally always out of reach after being wholly turned over to a consumer culture that depends on just this bottomless pit of wounded narcissism.

To follow Blum's argument, we have to understand the key word "narcissism." You may not be steeped in the language of psychology, but you may know that "narcissism" essentially means "self-centered." Or, you may recall the ancient Greek story of Narcissus, the youth who falls in love with his own reflection. These connections can help you make preliminary sense of the passage, but developing the term's particular psychological meanings will clarify Blum's *discipline-specific* use. A dictionary or encyclopedia of psychological terms would explore "narcissism" by *describing* the term's history in the field, *explaining* the term through related words and phrases, and *showing* the term's application by experts in the field. This discipline-specific knowledge would enhance your ability to fully appreciate Blum's analysis of the tension between desire and loss ("wounded narcissism") experienced by *I Want a Famous Face* contestants.

In order to explain a court battle over teaching science in Pennsylvania high schools, *New Yorker* reporter Margaret Talbot shows readers

Activity 1: Identify Elements in Definitions

Take a preliminary trip to the library and locate dictionaries, encyclopedias, and other reference works related to fields that you're interested in
(art, elementary education, physics, anthropology, etc.). If you haven't yet
chosen a field of interest, continue with the example above by finding reference works in psychology and reading two or more entries for "narcissism." Describe a typical entry by answering the following questions:

- How does the reference work *define* terms?
- How does the reference work incorporate *examples* with definitions?
- How does the reference work *compare* terms to others used in the
  field?

the importance of understanding an apparently simple term in its academic context:

What does "theory" mean inside and outside of scientific conversations?
Considering how often it is said that evolution
is "just" a theory, for instance, it is clear that
many people either do not know or do not accept the scientific definition of a theory. The
lawyers for the pro-evolution side went to
great lengths to make the point that, although
all science is provisional, a scientific theory is a powerful explanation
that unites a large body of facts and relies on testable hypotheses.[2]

Talbot identifies "theory" as a key term in the debate and describes
different meanings for general and academic audiences. Assuming that
her readers, like "many people," may also not understand its special
academic use, Talbot pauses in her story about the court case to explain
what scientists mean when they talk about a "theory." Having built
shared knowledge with her readers, Talbot may
now return to her story about the conflict over
Definition builds shared knowledge between author and readers.
teaching evolution, which in large part turns out
to be a debate over definition. Without this
pause, Talbot's audience might miss the larger
significance of her story.

UNDERSTANDING SPECIALIZED DEFINITIONS

Definitions also play an important role in writing for academic
audiences, as in the following passage by Colorado State University
biology professors Michael Antolin and Joan Herbers[3]. Challenges to

science teaching in local school districts motivated them to write an extended definition of "science" and invite readers to share the language of their academic conversation with others outside the scientific community:

We start with definitions. In order to discuss science education, we must define what makes up scientific inquiry. We find William Overton's (1982) language in the court decision in the case of McLean versus Arkansas Board of Education (529 F. Supp. 1255 [ED Ark. 1982]) to be clear, concise, and practical:

Core definition of "Science"

Essential characteristics of science: (1) It is guided by natural law; (2) It has to be explanatory by reference to natural law; (3) It is testable against the empirical world; (4) Its conclusions are tentative, that is, are not necessarily the final word; and (5) It is falsifiable.

Appeal to authority

The same definition was used in the Supreme Court decision in 1987 to put a permanent injunction against so-called equal time laws, which required creation science to be taught if evolution is included in science classrooms (Edwards vs. Aguillard, 482 U.S. 578 [1987]). Overton's five criteria have tremendous heuristic value, although some philosophers of science exclude falsifiability as a necessary criterion (Depew and Weber 1995; Gould 1999; Pennock 1999). Falsifiability cannot be applied to explanations of single historical events like those from paleontology, geology, or astronomy in the same way it is applied to present-day experiments that can be replicated. Even so, individual predictions and hypotheses based on historical explanations can be falsified if they fail to be supported by observations of the natural world. Thus, Overton's definition of scientific inquiry is extremely useful for teaching about the scientific method, the interdependence of experiments and observations, and the limits of the scientific enterprise.

Historical context and example

Qualify with possible exception

Apply definition to evolution as example of scientific inquiry

Within that context, we define the theory of evolution as a series of explanations of natural forces that result in descent with modification of living organisms (see also Linhart 1997). A nonexhaustive list of study topics subsumed by the theory of evolution includes: adaptation by natural selection; genetic drift and changes that result from chance events in small populations; mutation and neutral variation within and between populations; rates of change within lineages; rates of divergence between lineages; phylogenetic relationships among populations and species; and analysis of the history of life as recorded by geology, the fossil record,

Evolution explained with examples

and analysis of DNA. A list of topics addressed by creationists would be much longer because the diversity of opinion on how supernatural forces might shape our world far outstrip the differences among scientists (Numbers 1993; Scott 1997). We define special creationism as the idea that supernatural forces play a direct and leading role in shaping the history of life (Johnson 1993). Within that rubric, creation science refers to the idea of an Earth that is no more than 10,000 years old and was created ex-nihilo in six days by a monotheistic God; on this Earth no new kinds have arisen since the period of creation and that a single flood of staggering force shaped layers of rocks and trapped the organisms that are fossilized within them. Clearly, creation science posits evidence consistent with a literal reading of the Judeo-Christian Bible (Overton 1982); it thereby deviates not only from scientific evolution theory but also from every other creation scenario.

Counter definition: "Special creationism"

Examples of "Creation science"

Comparison: "Creation science" doesn't meet scientific criteria

Writing in the academic journal *Evolution*, Antolin and Herbers define science in multiple ways so they can appeal to readers from various backgrounds and with varying amounts of prior knowledge. We can identify several steps Antolin and Herbers take to build their definition:

- They begin with a *core definition* they find to be "clear, concise, and practical."
- They present *examples* and situations that illustrate the core definition.
- They provide *context*, showing readers the history of the term's current definition.
- They *appeal to authority*, showing how the definition was used in the *Edwards v Aguillard* Supreme Court decision.
- They *qualify* their definition, showing how some branches of science and some methods of scientific inquiry may not use all five aspects of the broad definition.
- They *apply* their definition to a particular case, the study of evolution.
- They *compare* arguments of science to arguments of belief.

Antolin and Herbers also develop a *counter-definition* that allows them to demonstrate the value of creation arguments. Through counter-definition, Antolin and Herbers show how arguments of science and belief are differently validated, and they explain why the two modes of study are not compatible within science's unique domain.

Careful and clear definitions—with examples—play important roles in other fields as well. Because academic writing uses specialized

Marx's entire essay is reprinted in Chapter 13.

language in ways that often differ from every-day uses, definitions of terms and concepts help bring readers into the conversation. In the next passage, sociologist Gary Marx explains how the standard dictionary definition of "surveillance" should be revised for academic examinations of the "new surveillance."[4] As you read, try to identify the techniques that Marx uses to build his definition:

General dictionaries provide inadequate definitions

One indicator of rapid change is the failure of dictionary definitions to capture current understandings of surveillance. For example in the *Concise Oxford Dictionary* surveillance is defined as *"close observation, especially of a suspected person."* Yet today many of the new surveillance technologies are not *"especially"* applied to *"a suspected person."* They are commonly applied *categorically.* In broadening the range of suspects the term "a suspected person" takes on a different meaning. In a striking innovation, surveillance is also applied to contexts (geographical places and spaces, particular time periods, networks, systems, and categories of person), not just to a particular person whose identity is known beforehand.

Which aspects have to be reexamined?

Aspects and examples of the old surveillance

Aspects and examples of the new surveillance

The dictionary definition also implies a clear distinction between the object of surveillance and the person carrying it out. In an age of servants listening behind closed doors, binoculars, and telegraphic interceptions, that separation made sense. It was easy to separate the watcher from the person watched. Yet self-monitoring has emerged as an important theme, independent of the surveilling of another. In the hope of creating self-restraint, threats of social control (i.e., the possibility of getting caught) are well-publicized with mass media techniques. A general ethos of self-surveillance is also encouraged by the availability of home products such as those that test for alcohol level, pregnancy, menopause and AIDS. Self-surveillance merges the line between the surveilled and the surveillant. In some cases we see parallel or co-monitoring, involving the subject and an external agent. The differentiation of surveillance into ever more specialized roles is sometimes matched by a rarely studied de-differentiation or generalization of surveillance to non-specialized roles. For example regardless of their job, retail store employees are trained to identify shoplifters and outdoor utility workers are trained to look for signs of drug manufacturing.

A new definition to account for new aspects	A better definition of the new surveillance is *the use of technical means to extract or create personal data.* This may be taken from individuals or contexts. In this definition the use of "technical means" to extract and create the information implies the ability to go beyond what is offered to the un-
The importance of technology	aided senses or voluntarily reported. Many of the examples extend the senses by using material artifacts or software of some kind, but the technical means for rooting out can also be deception, as with informers and undercover police. The
The importance of patterns	use of "contexts" along with "individuals" recognizes that much modern surveillance also looks at settings and patterns of relationships. Meaning may reside in cross-classifying dis- crete sources of data (as with computer matching and profil-
Expanding the definition to include systems	ing) that in and of themselves are not of revealing. Systems as well as persons are of interest. This definition of the new surveillance excludes the routine, non-technological surveillance that is a part of everyday life such as looking before crossing the street or
Counter examples: what's excluded in the new definition?	seeking the source of a sudden noise or of smoke, as well as the routine attentiveness to others that is fundamental to being a social being and to interaction central to the symbolic interaction tradition. An observer on a nude beach or police interrogating a cooperative suspect would also be excluded, because in these cases the information is volunteered and the unaided senses are sufficient.

In the rest of the article, Marx develops his definition into a socio- logical argument about the new surveillance's impact on information and privacy. Marx first shows his understanding of a key term to bring readers into the conversation, so that he can go on to develop more complex ideas and build a persuasive case for his claims. Whenever possible, he chooses familiar examples, like home pregnancy tests and crossing the street, so that his new definition is accessible to a wide au- dience.

The kind of definition practiced by scholars in their writing is also practiced all the time in college classrooms. You can probably think of a recent class meeting (perhaps even today) when you or a classmate stopped an instructor to ask for clarification. Your instructor probably used techniques of *defining, explaining,* and *showing* to shed light on a new term or concept. Because you are writing for readers who may not

How do your instruc- tors use definition strategies in class?

share your expertise in a field, you will have to make specialized terms and concepts accessi- ble for a varied audience, while conveying their discipline-specific meanings and uses.

AS YOU READ:

✓ When do you need to define new terms and concepts so that you can understand a passage or text?

✓ How do authors share knowledge with readers by defining, explaining, and showing meaning when they use discipline-specific language?

✓ How can you use the strategies of experienced writers as you introduce and define new terms and concepts for your audience?

Activity 2: Find Terms and Concepts in Your Classes

Keep a record of discipline-specific terms and concepts used in your courses. How do you know which ones are especially important to understand? How do your instructors work to explain new or specialized ideas in class? Do you encounter these terms and concepts during lectures, in textbooks, or in outside readings related to the field?

DEVELOPING A MULTIDIMENSIONAL DEFINITION: A WRITING ASSIGNMENT AND PEER REVIEW

This section features a project in which you take a position of authority in your writing by playing the role of teacher. You will assist your readers in building the foundations and examples necessary to share your understanding of the specialized language used in an academic conversation. As a way of inviting the reader into your academic conversation, focus on your own process of becoming familiar with the concept. Explain how experts—including youself—use the term and why a special definition is crucial to understanding the text in which you first encountered the term.

WRITING ASSIGNMENT

I. First, identify a term or concept that has specific academic meaning and would be unfamiliar to a general audience. Choose your term from either:

1. An academic text in your area of interest or one selected by your instructor
2. A classroom experience in which you encountered a new term or concept

II. Second, using specialized reference works, such as discipline-specific dictionaries and encyclopedias, clearly define the concept and explain its significance. Use examples to show the use or function of the concept in context.

III. Finally, explain the importance of your new discipline-specific knowledge for understanding the text or experience that first motivated you.

Student Voice

Marcus chose to explore his interest in art and started with a set of possible terms to define: "ready-made," "found art," "assemblage," "avant-garde," and "pop art." Here he describes the process of narrowing his topic and working toward a definition.

I decided to define the term "ready-made." I knew I wanted to write about something in the art field, and I've been interested for a while in the question of what makes something art. When someone picks up trash off the street, frames it, and calls it art, by definition it is, but why? Are we justified in calling art anything that is discovered in this way? Are we being too liberal with what we consider art? These questions led to more specific questions, which eventually led me to study the art and philosophy of Marcel Duchamp, whose ready-made installations helped to redefine the nature of art.

Drafting

Explain Your Concept's Context and Function

Once you have identified the term or concept that you want to work with, describe the context in which it appears in your source, or the event in which you first encountered the term.

Activity 3: Introduce Your Term and Its Significance

Answer the following questions as you introduce your term and consider its context and function:

- Why is defining this concept useful for understanding a source or larger issue in the field?
- Did you get clues for defining the term when it was introduced in the source?

- What was your first impression of the term's meaning?
- Did you understand the term on your first encounter, or did you have to read the text multiple times in order to understand it? Through multiple readings, could you infer the meaning?

Develop Introductory and Supporting Definitions

By explaining your first encounter with the term, you help readers share your initial experience of unfamiliarity. Once you relate that experience, recount your process of working from unfamiliarity to expertise. The first step in that process is linking the term to definitions in general dictionaries and encyclopedias, and on reliable Internet pages. If, for instance, you wanted to test Talbot's definition of "theory" in her *New Yorker* article, you might turn first to a general dictionary, which includes a number of possible meanings. In Figure 8.1, the definitions found at *Merriam-Webster Online* include, but are not limited to, the scientific uses described by Talbot. Some, like "abstract thought: speculation," include both theoretical frameworks of science and belief, as expert biologists Antolin and Herbers explain them. We must go beyond the general dictionary to arrive at the specialized definition Talbot uses to show why science excludes some of these theoretical frameworks.

Related terms are highlighted and hyperlinked

Synonyms (similar words) and antonyms (opposing words) are highlighted and hyperlinked

Main Entry: **the·o·ry** ◀))
Pronunciation: 'thE-&-rE, 'thir-E
Function: *noun*
Inflected Form(s): *plural* **–ries**
Etymology: Late Latin *theoria*, from Greek *theOria*, from *theOrein*
1 : the analysis of a set of facts in their relation to one another
2 : abstract thought: **SPECULATION**
3 : the general or abstract principles of a body of fact, a science, or an art <music *theory*>
4 a : a belief, policy, or procedure proposed or followed as the basis of action <her method is based on the *theory* that all children want to learn> b : an ideal or hypothetical set of facts, principles, or circumstances -- often used in the phrase *in theory* <in *theory*, we have always advocated freedom for all>
5 : a plausible or scientifically acceptable general principle or body of principles offered to explain phenomena <the wave *theory* of light>
6 a : a hypothesis assumed for the sake of argument or investigation b : an unproved assumption : **CONJECTURE** c : a body of theorems presenting a concise systematic view of a subject <*theory* of equations>
synonym see HYPOTHESIS

FIGURE 8.1   Entry from Merriam-Webster Online Dictionary (www.m-w.com).

As you continue the process, consider supplementing your introductory definition with a print encyclopedia or a commonly used Internet encyclopedia, such as *Wikipedia* (wikipedia.org). These reference works offer more detailed definitions and more extensive examples than found in a dictionary. The *Wikipedia* entry in Figure 8.2 begins by distinguishing the scientific meaning of theory from common usage.

Theory has a number of distinct meanings in different fields of knowledge, depending on the context and their methodologies. In common usage, people use the word "theory" to signify "conjecture", "speculation", or "opinion." In this sense,"theories" are opposed to "facts" — parts of the world, or claims about the world, that are real or true regardless of what people think.

Related terms are highlighted and hyperlinked

In science, a theory is a proposed description, explanation, or model of the manner of interaction of a set of natural phenomena, capable of predicting future occurrences or observations of the same kind, and capable of being tested through experiment or otherwise verified through empirical observation. It follows from this that for scientists "theory" and "fact" do not necessarily stand in opposition. For example, it is a fact that an apple dropped on earth has been observed to fall towards the center of the planet, and the theory which explains why the apple behaves so is the current theory of gravitation.

Etymology
The word 'theory' derives from the Greek 'theorein', which means 'to look at'. According to some sources, it was used frequently in terms of 'looking at' a theatre stage, which may explain why sometimes the word 'theory' is used as something provisional or not completely resembling real. The term 'theoria' (a noun) was already used by the scholars of ancient Greece. Theorein is built upon 'to theion' (the divine) or 'to theia' (divine things) 'orao' (I see), ie 'contemplate the divine'. 'Divine' was understood as harmony and order (or logos) permeating the real world surrounding us.

Science
In scientific usage, a *theory* does not mean an unsubstantiated *guess* or *hunch,* as it often does in other contexts. A theory is a logically self-consistent model or framework for describing the behavior of a related set of natural or social phenomena. It originates from and/or is supported by experimental evidence (see scientific method). In this sense, a theory is a systematic and formalized expression of all previous observations that is predictive, logical and testable. In principle, scientific theories are always tentative, and subject to corrections or inclusion in a yet wider theory. Commonly, a large number of more specific hypotheses may be logically bound together by just one or two theories. As a general rule for use of the term, theories tend to deal with much broader sets of universals than do hypotheses, which ordinarily deal with much more specific sets of phenomena or specific applications of a theory.

FIGURE 8.2   Entry from Wikipedia, the online encyclopedia (wikipedia.org).

> **RESEARCH PITFALL: CRITICALLY EVALUATE ONLINE SOURCES**
>
> Wikis, such as the Internet encyclopedia Wikipedia, are websites where users collaborate to write and edit entries. Wikipedia entries are often reliable, but when they get into controversial issues or political topics, personal opinion and agenda can affect explanations. If you use an Internet encyclopedia like Wikipedia, be sure to evaluate the site with a critical eye.

Put the Term in the Conversation

Once you have established context and provided a general definition of your term or concept, you can develop a discipline-specific, academic definition.

As you develop your term or concept from one context to another, show its unique uses in the academic conversation. In the case of "inclusion" (see the Student Voice about Whitney), the special education encyclopedia *adds* a new definition to others. Alternately, in the case of "theory" (see Figure 8.3), the scientific encyclopedia *eliminates* many definitions found in the general dictionary. In both cases, academic reference works explore in detail only the aspects that are relevant to the particular conversations of special education and science.

Show how the discipline-specific source is necessary to explain a special term in uniquely academic ways.

Student Voice

Whitney chose to focus her definition project on the term "inclusion," a common word that, as she found, has specialized meanings within the field of education. Here Whitney describes how she moved from a general to a conversation-specific definition of her term.

Most people understand the term "inclusion" from its use in day-to-day contexts. But I wanted to explore the meanings of this term within my field, elementary education. When I started my research, I found that none of the desktop dictionaries I consulted address the term's education-specific meaning. Strangely, only a couple of the specialized reference works I found have entries for "inclusion." Through more research, I found that the term is specific to the special-education field. Once I located a special-education encyclopedia, I was able to find a clear and complete definition of "inclusion," which gives an overview of the term's history and its significance in the field.

Activity 4: Find a Discipline-Specific Definition

- First, locate your field in the reference section of your campus library. Reference sections are broadly divided (science, humanities, education), and then subdivided into specialties (science, for instance, into chemistry, biology, botany, geology, and so on).
- Second, use reference works in your field to find one or more definitions of your term. You may include in your paper quoted portions of the definition you found; however, you must also explain the definition in your own words, in language your readers are likely to understand.

Definitions may be similar in general and academic reference works, but their focus and specificity can change.

Return again to the scientific use of "theory," described in Talbot's *New Yorker* article and Antolin and Herbers's *Evolution* article. One definition is found in the *Academic Press Dictionary of Science and Technology*,[5] which is one of many discipline-specific reference works

Theory
Science. An explanation for some phenomenon that is based on observation, experimentation, and reasoning.
Mathematics. The collection of definitions, principles, theorems, and rules of calculation associated with a class of mathematical objects. (From the Greek term meaning "a viewing;" "a way of considering.") *Theory*, in popular use, is often assumed to imply conjecture or speculation, as in "Evolution is just a theory." In scientific use, however, to describe an explanation as a *theory* does not indicate it is uncertain. Progressing in degrees of uncertainty, a *law* is based on many observations of a natural phenomenon that demonstrate it to be true without exception; e.g., the second *law* of thermodynamics states that heat cannot flow spontaneously from a cooler body to a warmer one. A *theory* is developed from extensive observation and reasoning to explain a phenomenon; e.g., Einstein's *theory* of relativity postulated that the speed of light represents an upper limit or velocity for any particle having mass; this has since been experimentally confirmed. A hypothesis is a preliminary explanation for an observed phenomenon that may or may not be supported by more extensive observation; e.g., the current hypothesis that the earth's climate is gradually becoming warmer because of the effects of burning fossil fuels.

Separating scientific and mathematical uses of the term

Showing the origin of the term with etymology

Distinguishing between common and specialized uses of the term

Classifying similar and dissimilar terms

Connecting each term in the class to an example

FIGURE 8.3   Discipline-specific reference work entry: "Theory" in *Academic Press Dictionary of Science and Technology*.

Activity 5: Explain Your Term

In your own words, explain your term's:

- **Function:** How does it work? What does it do?
- **Purpose:** What's it for? How was it developed? Are its historical and current purposes the same?
- **Classification:** In what category of things or ideas does your term belong?
- **Composition:** How is it organized?
- **Comparison:** What's it like? How is it distinguished from related terms?
- **Negation:** How is your specialized definition different from the general? How is the academic definition limited? What terms and concepts are opposed to yours?

As you consider these questions, anticipate what your readers already know or assume about the term. For comparison, consider that science writers in this chapter use evolution to explain scientific work and define "theory" in comparison—and in contrast—to popular conceptions of the term. Because it is a common reference for readers within and outside science's conversations, evolution is an effective example for an audience interested in both general and specialized understandings of the term.

---

devoted to the sciences (see Figure 8.3). Each reference work structures its definitions in the same way, but the examples become increasingly specialized and more closely connected to academic uses in the discipline-specific works. As you can see, these reference works are the keys to understanding a term's specific academic meanings and uses.

Develop Your Own Examples

In the academic writing samples shown thus far, effective examples help to illustrate an unfamiliar term or concept by placing it in a familiar context. Once you have a strong working definition in place, begin illustrating the term or concept with examples. Try to connect your academic definition to situations, experiences, and activities that will help readers better visualize your term at work.

Activity 6: Find an Example for Your Term

Now that you have a working academic definition, develop at least one example that illustrates the use or function of the concept. To get started, answer the following questions:

- Are there everyday situations to which you can apply the concept?

- Can you, as Marx does with surveillance, describe a situation that shows the concept in a familiar way for nonspecialist readers?
- Would a particular image or comparison help bring the concept to life for readers?

Reconnect Your Definition in Context

Finally, reconnect the definition to the term's role in the source or event that motivated you.

Activity 7: Integrate Your Term into the Conversation

Connect your specialized definition back to the text or event that motivated your writing project. Show how your understanding of the term has changed or expanded. Answer the following questions as a guide:

- Did a complete academic definition change your initial understanding of the situation in which you first encountered the term?
- Were you compelled to reread some, or even all, of the source once you had a new definition in place?
- How does your newly acquired expertise in the conversation help you work your way through the rest of the passage or the entire text?

For an example of this move in practice, let's return to Talbot's definition, now placing it in the context of the passages that precede and follow it:

Why is a definition important to understanding the debate?

If we accept one definition, what consequences must we also accept?

You sometimes hear it said that a courtroom is not a proper venue for debating science. In this case, it proved to be an ideal forum. For one thing, it allowed for the close questioning of Michael Behe, the Lehigh University biochemist who is the leading intellectual of intelligent design (and one of the movement's few working scientists). Under cross-examination by Eric Rothschild, a dogged lawyer for the plaintiffs, Behe conceded, for example, that a definition of science that could be expanded to embrace intelligent design could, by the same token, embrace astrology. And he was unable to name any peer-reviewed research generated by intelligent design, though the movement has been around for more than a decade.

How do
scientists use
the term?

What is it?

What is it
not?

Counter-
example:
argument of
inference

The trial also allowed the lawyers to act as proxies for the rest of us, and ask of scientists questions that we'd probably be too embarrassed to ask ourselves. In a courtroom, you must lay an intellectual foundation in order to earn a line of questioning—and so the lawyers stripped matters neatly back to the first principles of science. Considering how often it is said that evolution is "just" a theory, for instance, it is clear that many people either do not know or do not accept the scientific definition of a theory. The lawyers for the pro-evolution side went to great lengths to make the point that, although all science is provisional, a scientific theory is a powerful explanation that unites a large body of facts and relies on testable hypotheses. As Padian testified, it's not "something that we think of in the middle of the night after too much coffee and not enough sleep."

Intelligent design is an argument by inference. If we walk down the beach and see the words "John loves Mary" in the sand—an example offered by the intelligent-design textbook "Of Pandas and People"—we can infer that someone wrote them. We can make a similar inference, the textbook claims, when we look at the inner workings of some of nature's niftier products.

Revise and Edit

Now that you have all the parts for your definition project, it's time to put them together and prepare the essay for peer review and submission. The following sections are suggestions to consider as you organize, edit, and format your essay.

Organize

- Consider opening your essay with a "common sense" definition of your term that reflects your first, or "naïve," understanding. How might this approach help you engage with your reader and establish common ground for the essay?
- Consider opening with an anecdote—a story of your first encounter with the term. Did it confuse you? Did you have a relatively accurate sense of its meaning from the beginning? Did you try to work out the term's meaning on your own? If so, how?
- Test a couple of organizational strategies for linking definitions. Would it be more effective to begin with the discipline-specific definition, and then contrast it with more general ones, or to move from the general to the specific?

Edit

- Look for *wordy* sentences and passages that can be compressed for clarity.

  Chapter 14 discusses editing strategies.

- Examine your *transitions*, making sure that you move from point to point (or paragraph to paragraph) clearly and effectively.
- Check for paragraph *unity*, ensuring each paragraph has a clear focus.
- Check for essay *coherence*, ensuring that each paragraph makes a point that contributes to your definition.

Format

- Ensure that you are using the appropriate heading or title page for the style that your instructor has assigned, or as used in your discipline.
- Check the margins of your paper for conformity to your style guide.
- If you need a header with page numbers, your name, and other information, include it now.

Activity 8: Test Your Project in Group Conversation

Find one student in class who shares interest in your field and one who is unfamiliar with it. In conversation with them, test the structure and elements of your definition project.

1. Describe to the group your tentative:

Introduction

- Explain the context, event, or reading in which you first encountered the term.

Definitions

- Explain your general dictionary/encyclopedia definition (outside the conversation).
- Explain your specialized dictionary/encyclopedia definition (in the conversation).
- Discuss how each definition works, focusing on the elements of the specialized definition that you will use in your paper (function, purpose, comparison, application, etc.).

Example(s)

- Restate examples from your selected reference works.
- Develop your own examples.

2. Ask the group to identify parts of your tentative project that work well and parts that could use further development. Do group members have suggestions for improvement? How could you incorporate their suggestions? Use the peer review form in Figure 8.4.

MULTIDIMENSIONAL DEFINITION
FORMAL PEER REVIEW

Writing Project goals: 1) identify a term or concept that has a unique academic meaning; 2) explain your own understanding of the term, taking your audience from general to specialized meanings; 3) develop your own examples to illustrate the meaning and application of the term for nonspecialist readers.

Peer Reviewers: Avoid replying to the following questions with yes/no answers alone; instead, make constructive notes on a separate sheet of paper (or type and print them out) as you read your partner's draft. As you read, imagine the kinds of comments and suggestions you would like to have on your paper in order to do the best job possible on the assignment. If you have time, discuss comments with your partner to clear up any questions.

INTRODUCTION

1. Has the writer clearly introduced the term or concept being defined?
2. Do you have a sense of the writer's first encounter with the term? Did s/he first encounter it in an article, a book, a website? Who is the source author? In which discipline is the source author working?
3. How might the writer clarify the story of his or her initial encounter?

GENERAL DEFINITION

4. Was the writer able to find general definitions for the term in a dictionary or encyclopedia?
5. Does the writer show how the general definition helps or hinders understanding the term's specialized meaning?
6. Does the writer effectively transition from the general definition to the discipline-specific one?
7. Does the writer give you an indication of why s/he had to move from one definition to the other?

SPECIALIZED DEFINITION

8. Has the author included a definition of the term from one or more academic reference works? Has the writer clearly named the field and included the title of the reference work(s)?
9. Has the writer incorporated quotations from the reference work(s)? Is there a balance between quotation and the writer's own explanation?

EXAMPLE(S) AND CONCLUSION

10. Does the writer use effective examples to illustrate the term? Do you think these examples will be easily understood by a non-specialist audience, including the writer's classmates and instructor?

FIGURE 8.4 Multidimensional definition formal peer review. (*continued*)

11. Has the writer returned to the original source to explain how definition has helped him/her to more effectively understand a specific passage or the entire argument?
12. Has the process of definition added to the writer's understanding of the discipline?

ORGANIZATION AND MECHANICS

13. Help the writer revise by identifying parts of the paper that you found confusing and that s/he could develop in more detail, or more clearly.
14. Point out passages that are wordy or distracting. How could the writer revise passages to make them work more effectively?
15. Identify misspelled words, punctuation errors, and run-on and fragment sentences. When you can, help the writer correct mistakes.

FIGURE 8.4   Multidimensional definition formal peer review (*continued*)

Activity 9: Incorporate Experts' Definition Strategies

Find a professor on campus who works in the field you've chosen and visit him or her during office hours. Ask the professor to explain your concept and related terms. Make a list of the examples that he or she uses that would help clarify the concept for your audience.

WRITING SAMPLES

In this section, you can read definition papers written by students. As you research and write this project, think about incorporating effective strategies used by one or both of these student writers. Also, as you read classmates' drafts, note which strategies are especially effective and consider which you could incorporate into your own draft.

The first student writer, Cindy, is planning to study law and had read about the legal concerns facing victims of Hurricane Katrina, which struck the Gulf Coast in 2005. As she read Adam Scales's article, "How Will Homeowners Insurance Litigation after Hurricane Katrina Play Out?," Cindy began noting the terms and concepts lawyers use to find responsibility in cases of injury or damage. She chose to define "proximate cause" because it is the key to understanding whether or not insurance companies have to pay damages in the Gulf Coast region. Her paper describes the process of moving from the first appearance of the term in Scales's article through her development of definitions and examples, and then finally returning to the original context equipped with a deeper, discipline-specific understanding.

Cindy H.
Dr. Richmond
College Writing
16 September 2008

Understanding Proximate Cause

On September 15th, 2005, the Mississippi Attorney General filed a lawsuit

against several insurance companies who insured residents in the state of

Mississippi. According to an article written by Adam Scales entitled "How Will

Homeowners Insurance Litigation after Hurricane Katrina Play Out?" the

floodwaters from Hurricane Katrina destroyed residents' homes and, since their

insurance policies do not cover floods, "vulnerable homeowners are being

pressured into accepting partial payments and signing away their rights." What

is the basis for the Attorney General bringing a suit? While several factors are

involved, Scales, Chair of the Association of American Law Schools Section on

Insurance Law, states "At the core of this dispute is the legal doctrine of

'proximate cause.'"

What is "proximate cause"? *Webster's II New Riverside University*

Dictionary defines "proximate" as "closely related in space, time, or order."

Therefore, "proximate cause" refers to a cause that is closely related in space,

time, or order. Within the discipline of law, the definition gets more specific and

restricted. *The Law Dictionary* defines the term "proximate cause" as "that

which in natural and continuous sequence unbroken by any new independent

cause produces an event, and without which the injury would not have

occurred" (Gifis 69). After reading the definition in *The Law Dictionary*, I had

some idea of what the term meant, but it wasn't until I read the further

explanations in a couple of dictionaries and a textbook specific to the field of

law that I was able to more deeply grasp the definition. Following are the

insights that I gained.

"Proximate cause" is a key term in any legal case involving liability.

Liability is the context within law where this term is used; "proximate cause" might be used, for instance, when trying to establish who or what should bear the liability for some injury or damage. "Proximate cause" is synonymous with "legal cause," which refers to a cause from a legal standpoint. For example, to the doctor who treated a patient who sustained fatal injuries in an automobile accident, the patient died from shock and loss of blood. To a lawyer retained by the family of that deceased patient, the person's death was caused by the reckless driving of the individual in the other car, or, in other words, that driver's reckless driving was the proximate cause of the patient's death (Garner 139).

The definition of "proximate cause" refers to a "natural and continuous sequence unbroken" (Gifis 69). An example of a broken sequence would be as follows: X shoots Y who is then hospitalized and is recovering nicely. But then Y receives poor medical treatment and soon dies. That poor medical treatment would break the continuous sequence and it would become the proximate cause of Y's death, not the fact that X shot Y (Garner 139). One might pose the question, "The very fact that Y received medical care in the first place broke the 'continuous sequence,' so why was the 'natural and continuous sequence' not considered broken at that point?" The answer is that, in law, only *damaging* acts break the "natural and continuous sequence," thereby overriding the original cause. The following example also illustrates this condition: If you cause a potted plant to drop off of a second-floor windowsill and it hits someone on the head and injures that person, you are liable for that injury. But, if the potted plant, which you caused to fall, simply lands on the sidewalk and a stranger picks up the broken pieces and tosses them into the parking lot without looking, consequently striking and damaging a car, the stranger (not you) is liable for the damage to the car.

In addition to passing the "natural and continuous sequence unbroken" requirement, a proximate cause must pass the "but for" requirement to show that the injury would not have occurred "but for" that action or event, thus fulfilling the second part of the definition of "proximate cause," which states, "without which the injury would not have occurred" (Gifis 69). For example, "but for" X shooting Y, Y would not have sustained gunshot injuries. While one might argue that "but for" the production of the gun, Y would not have sustained gunshot injuries in the first place, X's act of shooting Y was *injurious* and therefore broke the continuous sequence, making the gun manufacturer no longer liable from a proximate cause standpoint.

Courts are often the setting in which determinations are made as to whether an individual or business has legal liability for the injury or damage someone else sustained. Legal liability can be very difficult to determine. Adam Scales states, "Proximate cause has long been the bane of law students required to learn it, and lawyers and judges required to apply it." Consider the following scenario:

> Suppose Arnie carelessly leaves a campfire burning. The fire not only burns down the forest but also sets off an explosion in a nearby chemical plant that spills chemicals into a river, killing all the fish for a hundred miles downstream and ruining the economy of a tourist resort. Should Arnie be liable to the resort owners? To the tourists whose vacations were ruined? These are questions of proximate cause that a court must decide. (Miller and Urisko 226)

The courts will ultimately rule in the case that the Mississippi Attorney General has brought against insurance companies for not covering damage from floodwaters resulting from Hurricane Katrina. This case is much like the hypothetical example of the patient who died from shock and loss of blood resulting from an automobile accident proximately caused by a reckless driver. The reckless driver is liable for the victim's death. By the same reasoning, the hurricane is responsible for the damage to many of the homes in Mississippi, even though the floodwaters, not the storm itself, caused the damage. If the courts agree, then homeowners whose insurance policies cover hurricanes will be compensated for their loss even though the floodwaters were the direct cause of the damage because the hurricane will be deemed the proximate cause.

WORKS CITED

Garner, Bryan A. "Proximate cause." *A Dictionary of Modern Legal Usage.* 2nd ed. New York: Oxford UP, 1995. Print.

Gifis, Steven H. "Proximate cause." *Law Dictionary.* 4th ed. Hauppauge, NY: Barron's, 1996. Print.

Miller, Roger LeRoy, and Mary Meinzinger Urisko. *West's Paralegal Today.* 3rd ed. Clifton Park, NY: Delmar, 2004. Print.

"Proximate." *Webster's II New Riverside University Dictionary.* Boston: Houghton, 1988. Print.

Scales, Adam. "How Will Homeowners Insurance Litigation after Hurricane Katrina Play Out?" *FindLaw.* Web. 11 Sept. 2006

Carmell, our second writer, chose the term "post-structuralism," which she encountered in Jane Tompkins's article, "'Indians': Textualism, Morality, and the Problem of History," which is included in Chapter 3. Since this term plays an important role in Tompkins's argument, Carmell wanted to understand as much of its academic use and significance as possible.

Carmell H.C.
Mr. Osman
College Writing
17 March 2007

Post-Structuralism: The Paradox of Not Knowing the "Known"

In her essay, "'Indians': Textualism, Morality, and the Problem of History," Jane Tompkins addresses a specific difficulty of "post-structuralism," stating: "This essay enacts a particular instance of the challenge post-structuralism poses to the study of history" (102). She goes on to explain that it is difficult, perhaps even impossible, to arrive at a solid understanding of an event in history, or even of history itself. This difficulty is due to the fact that some scholars recognize the possibility of multiple perceptions and contexts, that there may be no "absolute truth." Initially, this is what I thought Tompkins's problem was in trying to understand who and what the Indians were. However, upon closer reading, I found that she meant something different. What was this difference?

Understanding "post-structuralism" is essential to understanding Tompkins's entire thesis and conclusion. In questioning the "truth" of history and yet still wanting to understand it, her thesis itself is an example of the challenge post-structuralist thought poses to a critical investigation of the past. The term "post-structuralism" was familiar to me but the definition and concept were not. Because it was key to her entire essay and to fill in a context for the term, I had to reread this paragraph in the essay many times and pause to think about what she was saying. I first found a general definition for "post-structuralism" in the *Merriam-Webster Online Dictionary*: "a movement or theory (as in literary theory or psychoanalysis) that sees inquiry not as the objective exploration of stable structures (as the self) but rather as a relative undertaking shaped by discursive and interpretive practices."

This definition explains Tompkins's conundrum in a simple way. Not only was she unable to find a consensus on which to base her initial project of discovering the truth about European-Indian encounters, but she had to ask what exactly the difference in their viewpoints were, whether they were important, and how these answers bore on her present understanding and purpose. For example, as she researched white experiences with Native Americans, she found different pictures of who and what the Native Americans were. Unable to arrive at any final agreement, she was forced to look for a new question altogether. Her revised thesis acknowledged this lack of consensus and the larger fundamental question it exposed; she changed the entire goal of her research.

Understanding structuralism first helped me to understand post-structuralism. Both the *Dictionary of Philosophy and Religion* and the *Cambridge Dictionary of Philosophy* provide insights into these two philosophies. Structuralists assume that common foundations underlie all reality, that stable ideas underlie all of the conceptual systems we create, such as philosophy, art, science, religion, politics, economics, and even the family. Meaning is best understood by getting at a thing's or idea's essential structure or through comparisons to similar structures.

Post-structuralism is characterized by systems that are always unstable, by meanings that are always in flux—the opposite of structuralism. For example, the philosopher "Foucault . . . focused on the generation of the 'subject' by the various epistemic discourses of imitation and representation, as well as on the institutional roles of knowledge and power in producing and conserving particular 'disciplines' in the natural and social sciences" (Audi 883). It is difficult to define post-structuralism because its very nature is subject to and relative to whatever is being discussed at the time; there is nothing solid or certain against which to define it. Without some stable subject or solid ground, as structuralism was based on, one is never certain "where" one actually is. This is the difficulty Tompkins faced: "post-structuralist thinkers were perhaps less concerned with the organization of social phenomena than with their initial constitution and subsequent dynamics. Hence the problematics of the subject and history . . . [and] temporality itself . . . [are] engaged" (Audi 884). Post-structuralists investigate the unresolved dilemmas of "subject" and "history," rather than trying to find the one concrete foundation on which we stand.

Tompkins's question is specifically to "the difference that point of view makes when people are giving accounts of events, whether first or second hand. The problem is that if all accounts of events are determined through and through by the observer's frame of reference, then one will never know, in any given case, what really happened" (102). Therefore, Tompkins would be unable to argue any conclusion using history as a concrete foundation for her argument.

From Tompkins's point of view then, a post-structuralist understanding of history is essential for critical inquiry of any kind. But the realization that all facts are relative and all we have left is the discussion about relativity is the problem she faces. But how can one argue against reality? Where would one even begin? I think Tompkins's point is well made: "If the accounts don't fit together neatly, that is not a reason for rejecting them in favor of a metadiscourse about epistemology. . . . What has really happened in such a case is that the subject of debate has changed from the question of what happened in a particular instance to the question of how knowledge is arrived at" (118). Tompkins finishes the essay not by presenting a conclusion but by asking a larger question: "The moral problem that confronts me now is not that I can never have any facts to go on, but that the work I do is not directed toward solving the kinds of problems that studying the history of European-Indian relations has awakened me to" (119). The differences between accounts and perspectives showed Tompkins how her work was no longer targeted toward the structuralist goal of discovering one historical truth. Post-structuralism helped her critically re-examine her direction and her methods to find a new approach for accomplishing her work.

WORKS CITED

Audi, Robert. "Post-structuralism." *The Cambridge Dictionary of Philosophy.* Cambridge: Cambridge UP, 1995. Print.
"Post-structuralism." *Merriam-Webster Online Dictionary.* Web. 12 March 2006.
Tompkins, Jane. "'Indians': Textualism, Morality, and the Problem of History." *Critical Inquiry* 13 (1986): 101–19. Print.

Note the ways in which Carmell's approach to the writing assignment differs from Cindy's. Cindy opens with Hurricane Katrina, an event many of her readers will find familiar, and then introduces an unfamiliar, discipline-specific term related to Katrina's effects. In contrast, Carmell opens by describing Tompkins's use of "post-structuralism" and keeps her focus on Tompkins's essay. Cindy and Carmell also take different approaches to developing examples; while Cindy uses everyday scenarios to illustrate "proximate cause," Carmell chooses examples that stay close to Tompkins's area of interest.

9

Summary and Critical Engagement

"For me, nothing happens, or could happen, until I imagine myself within a discourse—a kind of textual conversation/confrontation with people whose work matters to me and whose work, then, makes my own possible."

—*David Bartholomae*[1]

CHAPTER OBJECTIVES

In this chapter, you'll learn how to:
- Summarize academic writing
- Identify and use appropriate rhetorical appeals
- Read "with" and "against" the grain
- Use a reading log in summary and critical engagement

According to writing scholar David Bartholomae, academic writing "happens" when a reader works first to comprehend and then to accurately and critically engage with the texts he or she reads. Although reading and responding to academic texts can be challenging, those skills are important in getting the most out of the college experience. This chapter shows you how to work with an academic text to build critical reading and response skills that you can apply to multiple texts in later writing projects. The skills and strategies you will learn and practice here provide you with the foundation for developing research projects in any academic field, which, in turn, ensure that you fully enter into academic conversations with your research materials.

Using a source from your own research, or one assigned by your instructor, you begin this chapter's writing project by *summarizing* the text, explaining the author's thesis, argument, vocabulary, key points and subpoints, and other features, to explain the conversation for readers who do not yet share your familiarity with it. In the second part of the project, you bring your own voice into the conversation by developing an informed and sustained critical response to the text. Being critical doesn't mean that you have to disagree or take exception with the author's arguments; instead, your strong response will incorporate multiple *engagement* skills that demonstrate your ability to use the text as a means to participating in a larger academic conversation.

> *Together, summary and critical engagement help you converse with your sources.*

STRATEGIES FOR BUILDING CRITICAL LITERACY

Summary and engagement skills are essential to your academic research writing in this course and throughout your college career. According to Linda Flower, the noted rhetoric professor and author, engaging with academic texts opens a "door to critical literacy" by connecting key strategies of *summary, interpretation, evaluation,* and *critical response.*[2] These strategies help connect critical reading to writing, because, Flower explains: "students are reading to create a text of their own, trying to integrate information from sources with ideas of their own, and attempting to do so under the guidance of a purpose they must themselves create."

Since readers are at the center of critical engagement, an important part of your task is choosing your own ways to engage with a comparatively lengthy, specialized text, and then develop and pursue your own purpose. As we see, both summary and response portions of the writing project depend on the

> *Summary and engagement are guided by your own decisions, emphasis, and purpose.*

choices that you make in selecting and emphasizing elements of the academic text that are important to you. The summary portion of the project will demonstrate your ability to identify and accurately represent ideas that you encounter in a text; while your engaged response will

> ## WRITING ASSIGNMENT
>
> Working with an academic text in your area of interest (or one selected by your instructor), describe, evaluate, and engage with its argument:
>
> 1. Introduce the text: name the author and his, her, or their credentials; name the title of the text and the source in which it appears, including the date of publication.
> 2. Summarize the thesis and main points of the text, being sure to give balanced attention to all aspects of the argument.
> 3. Through critical reflection, engage with the text by responding to its argument, purpose, and claims.

show you how to "speak back" to the text in your own voice. This purposeful summary–response process motivates you to break free of simplistic commentary ("I liked it," "I don't agree," and so on) and express yourself with meaningful, active participation in an academic conversation.

SUMMARIZING—THE CORE OF ACADEMIC WRITING

In order to effectively enter into conversation with their sources, successful academic writers must be able to clearly explain information and arguments, and build the foundation for their full engagement. Through summary, you accurately and convincingly represent

Summaries build shared knowledge between writers and readers.

what you read to give your audience a body of *shared knowledge* on which you can build your own credible arguments. The length of an effective summary can vary depending on the purpose and length of the writing project, and the role the source plays; it may be as short as a sentence or as long as a book chapter, and may include every length in between. Regardless of length, every effective summary describes a source as objectively as possible, and presents relevant information in a clear, condensed form.

As you read, think about the context of your source, and the author's motivation for writing. For example:

- Is the author responding to specific ideas or pressures from peers in the field?

- How would you describe the historical or cultural moment in which the author is writing?
- Does the author explain why or how they chose to write about a particular problem or challenge?
- Does the author include personal experiences or anecdotes to illustrate their motivations?

Showing readers how an author begins, or *situates*, a text can be an effective way to start your summary. Often you will see similar contextual introductions in critical readers and anthologies, where editors explain the role of a key text by a major author, or place a reading in context with other authors and texts from the same time. Your own contextual introduction will help readers understand the point and purpose of your source and the event or question that motivated the author to write. Accurately describing the historical context of the source may help you imagine the author's audience as well, and guide you to identifying blind spots and shortcomings in the argument.

> *Context helps readers understand your source author's motivations.*

Summarize with Purpose

Summary writing is essential practice for your own comprehension skills, helping you to understand what you read and to clearly and accurately represent the content of academic texts in your own words. The critical engagement project begins with a summary of your source. This is your opportunity to demonstrate your understanding of the text you've chosen and prepare for your response in the second part of the writing project. A strong summary ensures that your responses to the argument later in the essay are based on a credible reading and description of your source.

> *Through summary, you present yourself as a credible reader of your sources.*

Like taking the time to accurately understand new terms and concepts through definition, summary techniques habituate writers to working slowly and carefully through a text. By ensuring their understanding of small chunks of meaning (terms and concepts, the point of a key sentence or paragraph, or the purpose of an example), writers can follow their development into an argument and ensure an accurate understanding of the larger points and purpose of a source. Thus, when it is time for you to move beyond descriptive strategies like definition and summary and into critical responses of your own, you will have a sound and credible basis for your entry into the conversation.

The first sentence in your summary will introduce the author, give an indication of his, her, or their credentials, and mention the source in which the piece appears. You might begin the summary process by simply:

1. **Describing** the author's purpose or thesis
2. **Mapping** out the source's argument
3. **Explaining** key examples used and points made in the text
4. **Restating** the author's conclusion

In a longer summary, you might also consider incorporating some representative quotations from the text, so that you provide your readers with examples of the author's own voice. In any summary, you want to make good decisions about selecting the specific information you want to include to help your audience understand the text and to prepare them for your own engagement.

Anticipate Critical Responses

While demonstrating your understanding of the text as a whole and bringing the author's voice into the summary whenever possible, you should also anticipate your own responses. Prepare your readers for the second part of the essay by including examples, subpoints, and other details from the source that you find particularly interesting and that you plan to support or challenge later. Because your space for summary is limited and the source that you use is likely to be complex, you will not be able to include every detail. You may, however, want to start with a paragraph-by-paragraph summary and then choose a small number of points to emphasize, by combining or reordering points drawn from groups of paragraphs.

> *See Chapter 3 for summaries by paragraph and by section.*

Track the Author's "Moves"

When the structure and organization of a text is as important or interesting as its claims, use active reading strategies to select and emphasize an author's transitions from one point to another in the argument. Even if your source is not divided into parts with section headings or subtitles, you should try to break it into manageable chunks on your own. After reading the text you've chosen for this project, identify a small number (probably two to four) of subpoints that help you to describe the major transitions in the argument and prepare readers for your later responses.

> *Active reading strategies are discussed in Chapter 3.*

As you choose, recall how important transitions are to following the "turns" in a long or complex argument. Note how the author works from one chunk of the argument to the next and whether he or she does so in a logical and convincing way. You might consider describing the ways your author connects parts of the text—sources and examples, for instance—to build a compelling argument. Or, even if each chunk of the argument is convincing on its own, might you show the author's less convincing turns so that you can return to that feature of the argument in your response?

Moves and signal phrases are introduced in Chapter 5.

Track the Author's Sources

An author's choice of sources can tell us a lot about the context and foundations of an argument. For instance, if an author gives special weight to a single source (or author, or school of thought) in the introduction, and turns repeatedly to the same source throughout the text, you might show why that source is so important in the argument. A brief description of key sources in your summary can set the stage for your own interpretation and analysis of the author's use of research in your response.

ESSENTIAL SUMMARY STRATEGIES

1. Introduce the author, title, and source.
2. Accurately describe the author's thesis.
3. Clearly and concisely describe the argument.
4. Incorporate brief quotations to show the source author's voice at work.
5. Give balanced attention to the entire text.
6. Remain objective in your descriptions.

Activity 1: Adapt Your Focus to Summary Length

At this point, you should have chosen the text you plan to summarize. After reading the text at least once, write three summaries of varying lengths: one sentence, two to three sentences, and a full paragraph. Figure 9.1 shows three examples of length. Why and how do you adjust your focus and make choices about which information to include and which to exclude?

In his essay "'Here's Lookin' at You': Video Surveillance and the Interpellated Body," John Gunders looks at the frequent exposure of the public to video surveillance and the ethics involved with surveillance. **(32 words)**

In "'Here's Lookin' at You': Video Surveil-   *Gunders's entire*
lance and the Interpellated Body," John Gun-   *essay is reprinted in*
ders shows how governments and private   *Chapter 13.*
businesses have begun a campaign to "protect citizens" from crime and abuse. They
argue that the use of hidden cameras will make the world a safer place. Gunders shows the other, often overlooked, side of the argument by asking questions about the effectiveness of cameras and the risks of voyeurism. **(68 words)**

With video surveillance and closed circuit security systems becoming more and more prevalent, John Gunders shows how surveillance tapes have been used as evidence, as in the case of convicting the two ten-year-old killers of toddler James Bulger in 1996. However, in "'Here's Lookin' at You': Video Surveillance and the Interpellated Body," Gunders also addresses the risks of voyeurism that come with the advantages of abundant security cameras. Even though security cameras can provide valuable evidence in modern court cases, they also intrude into the privacy that people expect in their everyday lives. Gunders argues that even innocent people are seen as law breakers or potential law breakers when they don't conform to "social standards" (24). Do the risks of hidden cameras outweigh the problems of voyeurism and increased pressure to conform? **(132 words)**

FIGURE 9.1   Three Sample Summaries.

RHETORICAL ANALYSIS—ETHOS, LOGOS, AND PATHOS

Consider supplementing a point-by-point summary of the text with an explanation of the *appeals* the author uses to reach readers. By identifying *classical rhetorical appeals,* we can see a variety of techniques used to bring readers into an academic conversation and persuade them to accept arguments supporting an author's claims. Ancient rhetoricians, such as Aristotle in Greece and Cicero in Rome, divided appeals into three types: the ethical (*ethos*), the logical (*logos*), and the emotional (*pathos*); as Cicero argued, audiences respond best to "language agreeable to the ear and arguments suited to convince." While each type of appeal may be effective in its place, we will focus first on ethos and logos, the two most often used in conventional academic writing, and then turn to pathos.

Ethos

> *Ethos: establishing trust between writer and audience.*

Ethos describes strategies authors use to establish credibility, so that they can create and maintain *trust* between themselves and their audience.

In making ethical appeals, academic writers cite established authorities and demonstrate their familiarity with their field's conventions of organization, vocabulary, and argument. These appeals may take the form of a literature review or an introductory section (a paragraph or chapter, depending on the length and scope of the project) that refers to generally accepted knowledge, or cites respected authors.

You begin the critical engagement project by establishing your credibility through objective and accurate representations of your source in the summary. Later, especially in writing projects that require you to use multiple sources, you establish credibility within the conversation by acknowledging and explaining multiple views and positions taken by experts on your research question.

Ethos and Conventions of the Conversation

Beginning research writers often overlook one of the most important aspects of establishing credibility: using the *conventions* of argument valued in their research field. This is a significant challenge, because they have to use academic language and strategies as experts do, but before they feel at home in foreign and forbidding conversations. As David Bartholomae explains this challenge:

> The student has to appropriate (or be appropriated by) a specialized discourse, and he has to do this as though he were easily and comfortably one with his audience, as though he were a member of the academy or an historian or an anthropologist or an economist.

In your research writing, you'll have to play the part of an expert even if you don't feel fully prepared to participate in the conversation as an equal. Although challenging, this is a process of acculturation—or *appropriation*—that all academic writers experience, and ethical appeals are means of using the conventions of a new discourse community.

Ethos and Personal Reflection

In establishing connections, a writer can also use anecdotes and other images or references that appeal to readers' shared experiences. By drawing on familiar events, cultural practices, and people, writers can establish strong connections with an audience that they can build into shared academic experiences. While anecdotes and other references to common experience can be effective opening appeals, writers must ensure that connections with the audience are not entirely built on personal experience. In fact, researchers use their sources to prevent simple *universalizing* of personal experiences or observations—the logical fallacy of "hasty generalization" described below—and connect them to the academic conversation.

Logos

Logos describes strategies authors use when they appeal to the audience's powers of reason. Once authors have established a rapport with their readers, they reinforce their credibility with logical and sound arguments. Authors ensure that their arguments use evidence that is *useful, relevant,* and *current* enough to meet their purposes and audience expectations. Different academic fields may not value each kind of evidence in the same way, so as you read your sources, be aware

Logos: using reason to persuade.

of the particular kinds of evidence authors use so that you will be able to effectively enter the conversation. Credible evidence you can use to develop a sound, logical argument includes:

- Historical records
- Statistics
- Lab reports
- Interviews
- Expert opinions
- Case studies
- Personal observations
- Citations of scholarship

Your voice and responses play important roles in the conversation, so being logical does not necessarily mean being unbiased. Instead, your argument, which includes evaluation and critical engagement, simply has to be systematic and well reasoned. Professional academic writing is no different; writers do not undermine their claims when they include personal observations, but they do have to develop compelling arguments and maintain their credibility as logical thinkers.

Logical Fallacies

Although it is not possible to explain all the kinds of evidence you can use as you explore your question, we can see here the kinds of logical fallacies you might encounter in your research materials, and should avoid including in your own writing.

Either/Or Reasoning   This is a claim that reduces complex issues or questions to two simple positions. As you have probably realized by now, almost all academic writing—whether scientific, philosophical, or technical—is concerned with problematizing issues, concepts, and theories and then wrestling with complexity. Thus, a writer who represents an issue as a simple debate between two exclusive positions can be intellectually dishonest.

> Healthcare costs in the United States are rising rapidly while the quality of care is decreasing for many patients; however, we are faced with either maintaining the system as it is or abandoning it for a system entirely funded by the federal government.

While federally funded healthcare might be one possible alternative to the current system, surely there are many other possibilities. The writer avoids the underlying complexity of the issue in order to set up an argument that she is guaranteed to win with little intellectual investment.

Hasty Generalization   This is a claim based on insufficient evidence. Typical hasty generalizations include stereotyping, drawing a conclusion with too little evidence, and mistaking a personal or unique experience for a universal truth:

> Since my astronomy professor was late to office hours today, she doesn't care about keeping to a schedule.

Here, the author uses an exception to the norm to argue that the norm itself doesn't exist. It is a claim that uses the evidence of a single case to generalize outward into a claim in which it is an example, but probably not a representative or sufficient one.

Slippery Slope   This is a claim asserting that taking one step in an unfavorable direction inevitably leads to a catastrophic conclusion.

> We must not encourage research on embryonic stem cells. Although the research may start with looking for cures for diseases, soon researchers will be creating spare human parts, and then ultimately human clones, until human life becomes absolutely meaningless.

Like the either/or argument and the hasty generalization, the slippery slope argument makes a claim that overlooks other possible developments and outcomes. While this catastrophic conclusion about stem cell research might ultimately come to pass, it is not inevitable.

Non Sequitur **("it does not follow")**   A non sequitur makes a conclusion that does not follow logically from the premise.

> I always got A grades on my papers in high school, so I deserve A grades on my college papers.

The writer mistakenly argues that because a case was true in the past it must be true in the present even though the situation has changed.

Straw Man   This is an argument that uses easily discredited caricatures, distortions, or exaggerations of opponents' positions.

> Senator Wilson opposes our plans to build a fenceon the US-Mexico border. Since he intends to do nothing to protect Americans we cannot support him.

The author misrepresents Wilson's position by exaggerating it, then by arguing against the misrepresented position claims to have refuted Wilson's actual position.

   An author may also make a straw man argument by inventing a fictitious person who holds the position to be discredited. By discrediting the fictitious person, the author claims to have discredited the position itself.

Mistaking Statistical Correlation for Causal Relation   This is a claim that uses a statistic to argue a conclusion that suits the writer's position but does not necessarily follow.

> SAT scores are significantly higher among students who own five or more pairs of shoes than students who own fewer pairs of shoes. If you buy your children five or more pairs of shoes they will have higher test results.

Some relationship probably does exist between the two facts, but is the correlation, as the writer claims, a *necessary* one? If there are also statistical links between family income and test scores, the number of shoes owned might be incidental to another, more meaningful relation. This writer has overlooked other possible correlations and variables in order to make her argument.

   Fad diets and other popular health trends often take advantage of mistaken correlations.

> Our study showed that 53% of cancer patients who ate three spears of asparagus every day saw their disease go into remission.

This claim suggests to readers that if they too ate asparagus every day their disease would go into remission. Unfortunately, the isolated statistical correlation obscures other factors, including those with more medical credibility—perhaps the same fifty three percent are the cancer patients who had chemotherapy or other medical treatments!

Mistaking Sequence for Causality (*"post hoc ergo propter hoc"*)   In mistaking sequence for causality, a claim asserts that, because one event happened after a second, the second was caused by the first.

> In 1999, a group of teenagers who participated in Internet chat groups and online gaming shot fellow students at Columbine High School in Colorado; therefore, some parents argued, using the Internet caused the attack.

While this assertion *may* be true, or *might* be a partial explanation for the event, certainly we can think of other possible causes. Writers can enhance their credibility by carefully considering the complexities of cause-and-effect relationships; even if one conclusion is emphasized, a credible writer acknowledges that the conclusion is one of multiple possibilities.

Pathos

Pathos describes strategies authors use in appealing to the audience's emotions. Although pathos is used effectively by many writers, it is rarely the primary mode of argu-

Pathos: appealing to emotions, values and beliefs.

ment in standard academic writing. Because it does not appeal to logic and reason, you should use pathos sparingly, if at all, in your research projects.

To anticipate the move you're about to make from summary to response, we can see how literary theorist Jane Tompkins uses rhetorical analysis to prepare for critical engagement. Searching for information about relations between American Indians and European colonists in the 1600s, she evaluates the following source based on its appeals to pathos:

Tompkins provides essential source information: author, title, and date of publication.

> My research began with Perry Miller. Early in the preface to *Errand into the Wilderness*, while explaining how he came to write the history of the New England mind, Miller writes a sentence that stopped me dead. He says that what fascinated him as a young man about his country's history was "the massive narrative of movement of European culture into the vacant wilderness of America." "Vacant?" Miller, writing in 1956, doesn't pause over the word "vacant," but to people who read his preface thirty years later, the word is shocking.

In what circumstances could someone proposing to write a history of colonial New England *not* take account of the Indian presence there?

> Tompkins focuses on a key challenge in the book and explains how Miller answers the question he posed.

The rest of Miller's preface provides an answer to this question, if one takes the trouble to piece together its details. Miller explains that as a young man, jealous of older compatriots who had had the luck to fight in World War I, he had gone to Africa in search of adventure. "The adventures that Africa afforded," he writes, "were tawdry enough, but it became the setting for a sudden epiphany" (vii). "It was given to me," he writes, "disconsolate on the edge of a jungle of central Africa, to have thrust upon me the mission of expounding what I took to be the innermost propulsion of the United States, while supervising, in that barbaric tropic, the unloading of drums of case oil flowing out of the inexhaustible America" (viii). Miller's picture of himself on the banks of the Congo furnishes a key to the kind of history he will write and to his mental image of a vacant wilderness: it explains why it was just there, under precisely these conditions, that he should have had his epiphany.

> Tompkins shows how Miller mistakenly takes his personal experience to be generally valid.

The fuel drums stand, in Miller's mind, for the popular misconception of what this country is about. They are the "tangible symbols of [America's] appalling power," a power that everyone but Miller takes for the ultimate reality (ix). To Miller, "the mind of man is the basic factor in human history," and he will plead, all unaccommodated as he is among the fuel drums, for the intellect—the intellect for which his fellow historians, with their chapters on "stoves and bathtubs, or tax laws," "the Wilmot Proviso" and "the chain store," "have so little respect" (viii, ix). His preface seethes with a hatred of the merely physical and mechanical, and this hatred, which is really a form of moral outrage, explains not only the contempt with which he mentions the stoves and bathtubs but also the nature of his experience in Africa and its relationship to the "massive narrative" he will write.

> Tompkins identifies the emotional argument at work in Miller's understanding of American history.

Although Tompkins's response to Miller's book continues for two more paragraphs, you can get an idea of her use of rhetorical analysis in this excerpt. In fact, she uses a number of the techniques you will be asked to practice in this chapter's writing assignment. First, she introduces the work with its author, title, and publication date. She summarizes a key passage—about Miller's motivation to write

U.S. history—and proceeds to analyze the passage's point and purpose, its strengths and weaknesses, and the kinds of appeals it makes. She then shows how features of the passage she has chosen to focus on are repeated throughout Miller's book.

In moving from an objective description to critical engagement, which gives her an opportunity to respond to the source, Tompkins pays a lot of attention to analyzing the appeals it uses. If emotional appeals to the audience (shared values of patriotism, morality, and nostalgia) are used instead of reason and logic, perhaps we should think twice about the value of Miller's claims and conclusions. We would at least want to find more sources that use different appeals to help us confirm or further challenge this initial evaluation.

CRITICAL ENGAGEMENT: OCCUPYING A POSITION OF AUTHORITY

Once you have written your summary and established your credibility as an accurate reader of the text, it's time to draft your response.

Overcome Apprehensions about Entering the Conversation

Critical engagement requires that you to go beyond reporting on a text and assume a position of authority from which you can ask questions, examine details, agree and disagree knowledgably, and provide your own response. Careful, active, critical reading and accurate summary give you the foundation from which you can respond credibly and fully engage with the text. The engaged response is your opportunity to participate with your source in the academic conversation.

> *Reading carefully and asking questions helps you participate in the conversation.*

You may still have some apprehensions about responding to your text as an equal in the conversation—or, to use Bartholomae's word, "appropriating" the position of an equal. Keep in mind that the scholars you encounter throughout your college career probably haven't read every text and studied every possible aspect of their field. The scope of their knowledge about the conversation may be comparatively larger than yours, but they too have made risky decisions to enter it without complete knowledge or certainty. Since every aspiring participant must decide at some point to jump into the conversation, if you begin developing your authority now, it will become more natural as you continue in the research process.

Narrate the "Pressure" of the Reading Experience: From Detachment to Investment

Critical engagement happens when you are compelled to respond to your reading, when you become invested in the conversation and motivated to share your thoughts with readers. Consider some of the following questions as you plan your response:

- Where do you agree with the author, and why?
- Where do you disagree with the author, and why?
- Where is the author most convincing?
- Which examples, illustrations, and evidence best support the author's claims?
- Where has the author avoided or overlooked credible challenges to claims?
- How does the author encourage you to think differently about an issue?
- How does the author help you better support a position you already hold on the issue?
- Did the author prompt you to change your mind about an idea or question?

You need not have the last word on these questions as you wrestle with them in your responses. Instead, engaged responses show how your voice and ideas participate in a conversation that will continue long after you've left it.

Student Voice

As she began her project on youth mentoring programs, Andi recalls that reading with a critical eye gave her confidence to add her voice to the conversation:

> *I've always taken what I read at face value, accepted what I was told, and left it at that. But since the academic conversation is about asking questions and exploring new possibilities, I can find holes or places where the argument is incomplete, and it's OK to recognize and respond to them.*

CREATE A READING LOG

The often long, complex arguments of academic texts pose unique challenges to readers. Like many students, you may have found yourself losing track of an author's points each time you reach the end of a paragraph; or, you may have had trouble following an argument that builds over many pages and may, at first, appear to grow in many directions. These kinds of challenges are faced by beginning and expert researchers alike, and there are strategies that help them manage material in their sources and organize their thinking about a question as it evolves over time. As you plan and draft your critical engagement essay, you should keep a reading log that organizes material from your source and helps track your responses.

See Chapter 3 for an introduction to reading logs.

Activity 2: Anticipate Points for Later Engagement

You can get a head start on your responses by identifying places in the text where you feel compelled to participate in the conversation. In your reading log, write brief reactions to the following questions:

- Does the author's argument challenge any of your beliefs? If so, what beliefs are being challenged—political, religious, ethical, cultural, economic?
- Has the author caused you to think more deeply or in new ways about an issue you thought you fully understood?

Use your log to record your reading process and focus on the content of a text by noting important points in the source, keeping track of unfamiliar terms and concepts, and showing how the author supports a thesis or solves a problem. As you work on the critical engagement project, you should consider developing a *double-entry* technique, where you add your questions, reactions, and responses to the content (see Figure 9.2). This summary-analysis process ensures that you move beyond simply reporting on your source and engage with points through critical reflection and response.

As you describe your source's argument in your reading log, use the left column to record aspects of the source to which you might be interested in responding, including claims, examples, illustrations, data sets, subpoints, and quotations.

As you read your source, where are you being invited to enter the conversation?

Quotation	Response
"My Indians, like my princesses, were creatures totally of the imagination, and I did not care to have any real exemplars interfering with what I already knew" (101).	*So she'd rather have her imagination than reality? Is Tompkins saying that Americans are trained to see Indians like this? Has this changed from when Tompkins was a kid (when was that—maybe the 1950s? earlier?), or since she wrote the essay in 1986?*
	It's also an argument that appeals to the ETHOS of her audience, since Tompkins assumes that readers see Indians like she does—even if they haven't seen "real" Indians in the park, they have similar ideas from TV and other shared experiences.
	If people's perceptions haven't changed, then Tompkins's students are going to ask (or at least should be asking) the same kinds of questions she's asking—maybe she's writing for her students? Who's she writing for?
"The phenomena to which these histories testify . . . cry out for judgment. When faced with claims and counterclaims of this magnitude one feels obligated to reach an understanding of what did occur" (115).	*Tompkins is saying that we have to judge—there's no way not to. So the question is, what are we supposed to do with conflicting information that makes easy judgment or conclusions impossible?*
	This means that Tompkins's problem isn't really about how to find out facts or how to find historians' versions of the truth, but what to do when the truth isn't clear.

> Prepare to cite source material in your research papers by always including page numbers in your reading log.

FIGURE 9.2 The double-entry log: Source material/response.

Then, use the right column to begin developing your reactions. You might also use the double-entry log to record the author's rhetorical appeals, and think about responding with your impressions about the effectiveness of the author's strategies.

A writer developed the double-entry log in Figure 9.2 to record key quotations from the text. Identifying the kinds of questions it raised

Quotation	Summary	Response
Rowlandson's captivity narrative, "with its abrupt shifts of focus and peculiar emphases, makes it hard to see her testimony as evidence of anything other than the Puritan point of view" (111–12).	*Although Tompkins initially thinks she'll resolve the problems raised by history scholars, she finds that Rowlandson's testimony actually repeats those problems.*	*Tompkins makes a good move here because she uses both historical scholarship and writing from the time to prepare for her thesis about "perspectivism" in the next section. Very convincing use of evidence, but there must be facts that exist independently of perspective—or are there?*
"[A] better source of evidence might be writings designed simply to tell Englishmen what the American natives were like. These authors could be presumed to be less severely biased . . . because they weren't writing propaganda calculated to prove that God had delivered his chosen people from the hands of Satan's emissaries" (113).	*After finding that captivity narratives cannot resolve the challenges of history scholarship, Tompkins turns to writing by the anthropologists or sociologists of the time.*	*This makes me think about newspaper reporters today who are supposed to be more objective than a talk show host or someone like that. If Tompkins sees that "objective" observers are just as biased as testimony writers, are there examples today that show the same thing?*
"Kupperman performs an ethnographic study of seventeenth-century England in order to explain, from within, what motivated Englishmen's behavior... [L]ike Martin, she reconstructs the worldview that gave the experience of one group its content" (115).	*Kupperman's book explains the English worldview that might have produced their perception of and responses to their encounters with Native Americans.*	*This is interesting, because Tompkins finds a source that doesn't lay blame with one group, but explains how a particular English cultural perspective is "imported" to America. Maybe the problem is that the English don't realize they're someplace different than England? Any examples today that reflect similar encounters?*

FIGURE 9.3   The triple-entry log: Source material/summary/response.

helped the writer follow the argument and show whether or not they were answered later.

Some researchers prefer a *triple-entry* log (see Figure 9.3). Like the double-entry log, the researcher records important passages from their reading in the first column; however, the triple-entry log allows the researcher to divide responses into two separate columns: one that *objectively summarizes* the point or purpose of the passage and one that *critically engages* with it.

It may take only a few minutes a day to keep a reading log, but it will be an essential resource as you get further into your research and the conversation surrounding it.

READING WITH AND AGAINST THE GRAIN

As the previous section shows, the reading log is a good place to record your initial reactions to a text that will ultimately grow into critical responses. Try to read and respond to your text from two different perspectives:

- Read "with the grain" of the text, thinking about ways to *affirm* the author's position. Are there additional examples that would add support to the author's claims? Are there analogous situations, events, or objects that could help explain the thesis in a different way? Do you have personal experiences or knowledge that would help to confirm the author's claims?
- Read "against the grain," thinking about ways to *challenge* the author's position. Are there blind spots in the argument? Can you

---

Student Voice

Glen, whose research projects focus on the meanings and interpretations of "just war" theories, reflects on the advantages of choosing an article he disagreed with:

I first picked my article because I thought it was one that went along with my views of the Iraq war, namely that it is a wrong use of people and resources; but, as I read further I realized that the author's views were very different from my own. This difference turned out for the better because I had a lot of thoughts to express on the subject, which helped me write the response part of my paper.

think of counter-examples or personal experiences that could overturn or complicate the author's claims?

Identifying both kinds of reactions helps you to write balanced, thoughtful responses about your source. Your opinion about what you read is valuable, and your authority as a participant in the conversation increases as you read additional sources in your research area. A detailed and well-documented reading log contains the core evidence you need to recall points of agreement and disagreement with your sources and then develop them in your own words.

As you read, also be sure to record moments where you see the writer's assumptions at work. Whether you agree with those assumptions or not, they provide important points for engagement as you draft your responses.

THE PRESSURE OF ASSUMPTIONS: A CASE STUDY

The following reading excerpts the first five paragraphs in Sherry Linkon's essay "The Reader's Apprentice: Making Critical Cultural Reading Visible."[3] As you read, think about how Linkon's assumptions about the value and purpose of college education shape her argument.

> One of the central goals of undergraduate courses in literature and cultural studies is to help students become skilled readers. Of course, that means more than simply decoding words and phrases. We want students to learn to ask good questions about texts, make inferences and connections, develop interpretations, use research and critical thinking effectively to develop their own answers, and write essays that engage with the critical conversation of the field. These are the central practices of literary study, the elements of what Robert Scholes (2001: 138) calls the "craft of reading." They also reflect the habits of mind that Gerald Graff (2003) suggests define academic culture—questioning and arguing—habits that do not come easily or naturally to many of our students.
>
> Most of the time, we teach these skills and ways of thinking through demonstration. Through a combination of presentation and dialogue with our students, we model the process of critical cultural reading, weaving together inquiry, evidence, and theory. As we discuss a text, we pose questions about it, and we invite students to ask their own questions. We guide the class through the examination of evidence, focused on the text itself.

We use lectures to provide background information, perhaps about the historical context or the literary form or genre. We draw upon our preferred theoretical models to explain the relationship between aesthetics, experience, and society. At best—and I think we often achieve this—witty lectures and discussions that move from explication into more complex analysis make learning exciting and engaging. Yet these same practices, in part because they are funny, smart, and sometimes fast paced, can leave students with the impression that the process of analyzing cultural texts is natural and instinctual. Unintentionally, we hide the effort involved, making textual analysis seem simple and straightforward.

We then ask students to develop their own readings of texts and present them in papers. And all too often, we are disappointed with the results. Students may succeed on the level of explication, but they encounter difficulty when asked to position texts in their cultural or critical context, to apply theory or use critical sources to deepen or complicate their own readings, or to generate their own inquiries. Great lectures and discussions work on many levels, but they do not provide students with sufficient guidance in how to read cultural texts critically and contextually.

I don't want to suggest that we should not give engaging lectures or lead exciting discussions; they are important elements of the learning process, and they're enjoyable for everyone. However, we cannot assume that students will learn the process of critical cultural reading by observing or even participating in these classroom demonstrations (though some will). Nor is it appropriate (though it may be tempting) to blame students for not reading well enough, not trying hard enough, or simply not being smart enough. Graff (2003: 44) suggests that part of the problem is that many students see "standard academic practices" as "bizarre, counterintuitive, or downright nonsensical." Students don't value the process or the outcome, the academic argument about ideas, nor do they know how to use the "conventional formulations that characterize written argument" (168). Yet before they can formulate an argument, students need to develop critical interpretations of texts. However, as educational psychologist and historian Samuel L. Wineburg (2003: n.p.) suggests, we also don't teach this adequately: "Professors may assume that their students are stupid or suffer from a learning disability. Often the truth is much simpler. No one has ever bothered to teach them some basic but powerful skills of interpretation." If we want our students to develop the ability to read, research, and analyze cultural texts, we need to employ more strategic, deliberate methods of teaching.

This goal may sound simple, but like literary analysis, it's harder than it seems. Simply articulating what constitutes good reading is challenging enough, much less identifying clearly the cognitive strategies we use to perform that task. Add to that some misconceptions and bad habits that create difficulties for our students, and "teaching some basic but powerful skills of interpretation" turns out to be extremely difficult. In *The Crafty Reader*, Scholes (2001: 213) invites us to think critically about two questions: "What would it mean to get serious about reading? What would it mean to teach reading seriously?" In this essay, I want to begin to answer those questions by making visible the issues I considered in developing a new course and the pedagogy that I used to try to teach reading seriously. I will define the kind of reading I want students to learn, reflect on the challenges posed by what both students and faculty bring to the learning situation, and offer a model for teaching critical cultural reading that has helped my students make significant progress toward becoming expert readers of cultural texts.

- How does Linkon expose her assumptions early in the essay, and how would you summarize them?
- How does Linkon imagine her students, their skills, and their desires? Are they the same as yours and others' in your class?
- How does Linkon connect her study to key texts in the field? How do you know which texts she is inclined to agree and disagree with?
- Can you describe any assumptions that would oppose Linkon's?
- Do any of Linkon's assumptions contrast with your personal experience?
- How would a shift in Linkon's assumptions affect the claims she makes in her introduction?

Read with the Grain: Agree and Support

In her opening paragraph, Linkon tells us about the set of skills she most wants her students to learn:

to ask good questions about texts, make inferences and connections, develop interpretations, use research and critical thinking effectively to develop their own answers, and write essays that engage with the critical conversation of the field.

Now that you know what Linkon thinks, explain how you react positively to her opening claims. For example:

- Which of Linkon's educational values do you also share, and why?
- Do you think her view is common among all college instructors?
- Is Linkon's view common at least among instructors in her field?
- Can you think of events or examples from your college classes that would support Linkon's position?

Even if you don't agree personally with Linkon's claims and values, imagine how one might support them:

- Does she use strong, persuasive logic in making and supporting her claims?
- Can you imagine why Linkon's colleagues would share her values and goals, whether or not their students do?
- Can you think of examples, or other scholars, to support Linkon's goal of writing as entering a conversation?

Read against the Grain: Disagree and Challenge

If you felt negatively about Linkon's opening claims, explain your reaction. For example:

- Which of Linkon's values challenge your own, and why?
- Would some, or most, college instructors disagree with her claims? Why?
- Why might some of Linkon's colleagues in English challenge her values?
- Can you think of examples and experiences from your classes that contrast with Linkon's position?

Even if you agree personally with Linkon, speculate on the reasons why others might disagree:

- Are there flaws in the logic she uses to make and support her claims?
- Might some of the evidence she uses for support also be used to challenge her claims?

Developing Depth and Nuance through Critical Engagement

As you record moments of reading with and against the grain, you will understand the text in greater depth and express your responses more effectively. With each source you read and critical response you develop, the more you increase your ability to fully participate in an academic conversation.

Regardless of your opinion, try at first to read each source you find with and against the grain. You will probably make a number of important discoveries in this practice:

Reading with the grain:

- First, you can see how an author argues a position on which you already agree, and in the process how she or he provides you with a new perspective or a new way of developing a strong argument.
- Second, you will acquire new examples that allow you to enhance an argument and support the credibility of your position.

Reading against the grain:

- First, in wrestling with a position that you oppose, you will better understand assumptions and arguments behind that position in order to respond as effectively as possible.
- Second, in understanding a position and argument that contrast your own, you will better understand your own assumptions, and thus develop the best articulation and support for your positions.

Practicing with the grain and against the grain responses encourages you to open your mind to being swayed—if only momentarily—by the strength of a claim or position that may challenge your own. As you use your reading log to record quotations and summaries from your source and anticipate your responses, you will be well on the way to doing the critical, engaged thinking that is valued in academic conversations.

DRAFTING AND REVISING YOUR CRITICAL ENGAGEMENT ESSAY

Introduction

Early in your paper, you should introduce the author and title of your text and briefly describe the subject area. As you introduce the author, you may also mention his or her credentials: is the author a professor, an independent researcher, affiliated with an institute or think tank, or a business person? If you chose the text, you might also briefly describe how you found it and what personal, academic, or professional interests led you to working in the field or with this particular author.

Summary Characteristics

The summary should comprise between one-fourth and one-third of the essay's content (for example, about two pages of a six-page essay). After you introduce the source, write a one-sentence description of the thesis to help familiarize readers with the author's main point and purpose and to organize the details that you present in the rest of your summary. In addition to summarizing the content of the source, you might also consider describing the appeals used by the author:

- How does the author appeal to his or her audience?
- How does the author situate the argument?
- How does he or she establish credibility?
- How would you describe the kinds of sources being used?
- Does the author appear to be primarily supporting or challenging peers in the field?

As you describe the author's argument, keep track of the words and phrases you use. Since your goal in this part of the project is to write an objective description of the source, try to avoid value-laden words and phrases. Instead, use value-neutral ones to avoid the appearance of bias.

Reflect on the First Draft

Once you have a working draft, pause before developing your responses and check your summary against the original text. Use this opportunity to revise, so that you can ensure that your responses will be based on an accurate and complete representation of the source.

- Are you describing the source *accurately* and *completely*? Are you describing the source with an eye to *objectivity*?
- Is your summary *concise*? Are there places where you can *consolidate* points or *compress* your descriptions?
- If you include paraphrases or quotations, are they introduced with appropriate attributive tags? Did you include parenthetical citations so that readers can locate quoted passages in the original text?

Attributive tags and parenthetical citations are introduced in Chapter 6.

Before you move on to your own responses, read the source one more time and make sure that you're not misrepresenting the text or the author's position, and that you're not missing any critical pieces of information.

Transition from Summary to Response

Your critical responses will make up the majority (about two thirds to three quarters) of the essay's content, and it's your opportunity to "speak back" to the text, to engage with the author's points and argument, and to participate with the author in an academic conversation.

> *Describe how the source affected you.*

As a way of transitioning between the two parts of the essay, you might consider describing how the source affected you. For example, did it cause you to change your mind about any assumptions you had held, or did it confirm your preconceptions? These initial reactions will help set the tone for the amount of engaged agreement and disagreement you'll develop in detail through your responses.

Consider introducing your responses by reading "with the grain," and transition from your summary by emphasizing and developing a point in the source with which you agree. In choosing this approach, you will acknowledge the author's expertise and credibility; show your ability to develop a point in your own words; and develop your own examples or illustrations to support a claim.

You can also transition by explaining the ways the essay made you think differently or more deeply about an issue. This approach will allow you to emphasize the author's credibility while you add detail or other aspects of the issue; and explain your own positions as you delve into particular points in the essay that made you think more deeply than before.

As you move from summary to response sections of your writing project, consider how certain phrases will prepare your readers for the *kind* of response you plan to develop. In an essay focusing on Linkon's article, for instance, *signal transition phrases* might include:

Phrases Signaling *With the Grain* Analysis

"Before reading Linkon, I had never thought about . . ."

"As I read Linkon's essay, I really began to understand X."

"Reading Linkon made me realize that . . ."

"Linkon was most convincing when she argued . . ."

"Linkon used her sources well, especially when she turned to . . ."

"Linkon's ideas about college students are like . . ."

Phrases Signaling *Against the Grain* Analysis

"While Linkon covers a lot of material, she left out one important aspect: . . ."

"Although Linkon makes a strong point about X, there are issues missing from her argument: . . ."

"Because she published her article in 2005, Linkon was unable to respond to the most recent developments, such as . . ."

"On the one hand, I think Linkon understands X well; on the other hand, though, she should also consider Y."

Now you've reached the point in your draft where you can describe reading with and against the grain of the text. Since you've already introduced certain points from your source in the summary, return to them and describe how effectively they are made. Which details does your source author use well? Which are missing? What has the author overlooked in developing his or her argument?

In crafting your response, you might also find opportunities to interpret and evaluate data presented in the source. Are there places in your source where you might agree with the data or other information presented and yet challenge the author's interpretations and conclusions? Conversely, are you inclined to agree with the author's point, yet able to identify problems in the data that you can imagine solving?

Response Tone

While you had to maintain objectivity toward the source in your summary, you may now shift the tone in your response, moving away from neutral words and phrases to those which reflect your engagement, judgment, and bias as a participant in the conversation.

Audience

Write for an audience of educated readers who may be interested in the source and the field, but who don't share your expertise. Think, for instance, about writing for your classmates, who are beginning their own research journeys in different academic fields or with different focuses. Just as you want them to write about their research in a way that you'll be able to follow as a reader, try to make the same effort when those roles are reversed.

SUMMARY AND CRITICAL ENGAGEMENT
FORMAL PEER REVIEW

Critical Engagement goals: 1) locate a piece of academic writing in the library, through online databases, or through interlibrary loan; 2) summarize the thesis and argument(s) of the piece (approximately 30% of content); 3) engage the text through personal and intellectual reflection (approximately 70% of content).

Peer Reviewers: do not reply to any of the following questions with yes/no answers; instead, make constructive notes on a separate sheet of paper (or type and print out) as you read your partner's draft. Hint: Recall the comments and suggestions that you found helpful when revising the previous paper and try to give your partners the same consideration. If you have time, discuss comments with your partner to clear up any questions.

1. Describe the introduction: do you get a sense of your partner's interest in the topic/question s/he is researching? Is the interest personal? Is it related to your partner's major or anticipated profession?

2. Imagine that you, as the reviewer, are unfamiliar with the summarized source. Does the summary section adequately 1) introduce the thesis of the piece? 2) note the source's academic field (physical sciences, applied sciences, humanities, fine arts, social sciences, etc.)? 3) give you a sense of the construction of the argument (use of examples, references to other sources, definition of key terms, etc.)? What else would you like to know to better understand the piece?

3. Is the tone of the summary as neutral as possible? Identify passages that are overly critical and/or prematurely judgmental, and help your partner move them into response paragraphs.

4. Does your partner incorporate specific passages—quotations—from the source to illustrate a particular argument, or to give readers a sense of its specialized language?

5. Describe the relationship between the summary and response sections. Do the sections flow together well, or do they seem to be two separate papers? How could your partner improve the transition? Could he or she develop a transition sentence—or even a paragraph—to signal the movement between parts?

6. Has the source supported your partner's initial ideas about the topic, or has your partner had to reexamine his/her preconceptions?

7. Has your partner used the source to enter into an academic conversation? Help your partner locate points in the text that can be seen as invitations to participate, to expand on arguments, to add more research, to challenge the thesis, etc.

8. Does your partner acknowledge the source's audience and purpose? How might these two elements provide opportunities for reading with and against the grain?

FIGURE 9.4 Critical Engagement Essay: Formal Peer Review.
(*continued*)

> 9. Does your partner speculate on and present new ideas to support or challenge the source? How might different research, different methods, and/or different qualitative analysis offer new directions? In the paper's conclusion, can your partner begin to pose questions and/or paths for future research that will lead to the proposal and later papers?
> 10. Mark spelling, punctuation, word choice, and other mechanical errors on the paper.

FIGURE 9.4 Critical Engagement Essay: Formal Peer Review. (*continued*)

WRITING SAMPLES

In this section, you can read critical engagement essays written by students like you. Cindy, whose definition of "proximate cause" you read in Chapter 8, continues to work on issues of legal liability with an article from the field of medical law which deals with new approaches to managing malpractice suits and the "liability crisis" in medicine. As you read, note—among other features of the essay—how Cindy organizes the summary, and how she emphasizes certain elements of the article she plans to develop further in her responses.

- How does she transition from the summary to response sections of the essay?
- Does she clearly distinguish the two authorial "roles" she must play in the writing project?
- How does Cindy establish her own credibility as a respondent to Liang and Ren's article?
- If you were her peer reviewer, which elements of the essay would you praise?
- Which elements would you ask her to revise, and why?

Cindy H.
Dr. Richmond
College Writing
21 October 2008

Addressing the Medical Liability Crisis

The article "Medical Liability Insurance and Damage Caps: Getting beyond Band Aids to Substantive Systems Treatment to Improve Quality and Safety in Healthcare" appeared in the *American Journal of Law and Medicine* in

2004. The authors, Bryan A. Liang, Professor of Anesthesiology at the University of California San Diego School of Medicine and Professor at the California Western School of Law, and his research associate, LiLan Ren, discuss the medical liability crisis in the United States and conclude that a new approach to solving the crisis is required. They argue that this new approach must address the deeper root of the liability crisis: medical error. They proceed to rethink our current healthcare systems with a plan designed to reduce medical error.

The authors state that the medical liability crisis is evidenced by the difficulty many doctors and healthcare facilities experience securing affordable medical liability insurance. Hence, healthcare costs rise and availability of healthcare is reduced as doctors cease to practice in high risk areas. This causes some people either to go without care or have to drive up to 100 miles to see a doctor.

The historical way of addressing these problems has been to reform the medical malpractice litigation system so that malpractice insurance premiums need not be so high. In the past, legislators have imposed damage caps on what an injured person can be awarded for non-economic damages (for example, pain and suffering) to try to reign in insurance premiums. Though the authors acknowledge research showing that tort reform has helped control the medical liability crisis, they consider the level of control achieved thus far to be inadequate. Also, there are so many factors at play in the issue that it is impossible to definitively determine cause-and-effect relationships of tort reform on availability of healthcare—especially whether tort reform has actually helped patients receive the medical care they need (521).

However, there is one reliable cause-and-effect relationship that the authors present: reducing medical error will reduce patient injury resulting in fewer patient claims (522). In a complex system such as healthcare delivery, medical errors are rarely the fault of one person; thus, Liang and Ren claim, "one individual is not responsible for the outcome of the entire system" (523). They show how the airline industry, the nuclear energy industry, and the military have reduced error rates by replacing individual "shame and blame" systems with systems that recognize and constructively address human error (524). However, the authors also point out that a similar system is not currently possible within healthcare because of fear of litigation risks; communication of essential information regarding error is often hindered by the possibility of legal consequences.

They propose that the medical and legal communities, along with the general public, need to recognize and accept a new system that will increase safety in healthcare. The authors explain their paradigm for a new approach to address human error within the healthcare system. They believe this approach would be more ethical than the current legal approach and more effective in increasing patient safety, decreasing costs, and, consequently, contributing greatly to solving the medical liability crisis.

The initial target audience for this article is medical professionals and lawyers. The authors did not use overly technical language in any long passages, which enabled professionals from either discipline to understand the article. It can reasonably be construed that this article may become a reference for public policy makers as well. Liang and Ren's goal seems to be to convince others of the importance and validity of implementing their new paradigm for reducing patient error. This paradigm is substantially different from both the current way that medicine is practiced and the legal method of handling malpractice claims. As it is difficult to convince people to make such major changes, the authors must establish that they have a thorough understanding of the healthcare crisis, its causes, and the effect of current and previous methods to address the situation.

Throughout their coverage of studies relating to tort reform's effects on the healthcare crisis, the authors document their research materials well. They include enough references that the reader can obtain the original studies and reports. Thereby, the reader may consult the studies directly if she desires more information or is concerned that perhaps the data or conclusions of any particular study might be misrepresented.

Liang and Ren also achieve credibility by covering studies with differing conclusions. For example, a report by the US General Accounting Office provided different explanations for much of the data discussed in the studies covered earlier in the article. The GAO report's conclusions were so different from the previous studies considered, or at least for very different reasons, that the complexities of conclusively determining cause-and-effect relationships were apparent.

After the review of past attempts to address the medical liability crisis, the authors' offer of a better approach is welcome; their solution strives to solve the crisis from a different angle, that of reducing medical error. Who could argue with reducing medical error as a valuable approach? It would be a winning situation for everyone involved. If the rate of medical injury falls, then malpractice suits would naturally be reduced as well. Fewer malpractice suits allow medical malpractice premiums to decrease, thus removing that obstacle in providing healthcare, particularly in certain specialties. Lives would be saved, and much needless pain and suffering would be eliminated.

Liang's paradigm for reducing medical error is a "patient-provider partnership system" where *cooperation* toward improvement rather than *punishment* toward improvement is the method (533). This systems-based approach would require cooperation among all members of the medical team along with participation by patients and their families. Fundamental to Liang's paradigm is the concept that neither injuries nor positive outcomes in medicine are the result of one single person. Liang and Ren seem to assume that the reader accepts that concept already, but this assumption is not widely held or necessarily correct. Nevertheless, the authors clearly conceptualize a systems-based approach for improving the shortcomings in our complex system of healthcare. After defining error as "an inadvertent occurrence, or an unintended event in a healthcare delivery which may, or may not, result in patient injury" (523), they introduce a "Swiss Cheese Model," where the holes in the cheese represent errors. When the slices of cheese are stacked up—like the levels or stages of medical care—one can visualize that anytime the holes line up so as to go all the way through the stack, an injury will result. This example makes it easy to recognize that if errors were reported at one level or stage, even when no injury has yet occurred, then holes can be eliminated. As holes are permanently eliminated, it becomes increasingly less likely that a series of holes will line up all the way through the stack. Accordingly, if all medical errors are reported in order to be understood and prevented in the future, then the number of medical injuries will also decrease.

Liang and Ren mention that such systems-based approaches to reducing error have been successful in aviation, nuclear power, the military, and anesthesiology. They do not fully explain how those specific successes were achieved. Giving further details about the processes and outcomes in other fields would have provided excellent additional support for the validity of their approach. Only in the footnotes do the authors mention that in anesthesiology error was reduced to less than 1/10th of the previous level (523). Explaining how such an impressive statistic was achieved would have been enlightening and convincing.

The authors want the medical and legal communities, along with the general public, to recognize and accept the "systems concepts" (531) in order to increase safety in medicine. They seem to recognize the importance of appealing to the medical community throughout the article as evidenced by descriptions such as "good, compassionate people with the best intentions" (503) and sympathizing with their plight: "no matter how professional they might be, no matter their care and concern, humans can never outperform the system which bounds and constrains them" (522). The general public is included as well, as essential members of the system and deserving of ethical treatment. While those groups are repeatedly commended by the authors, the legal landscape is only derided, potentially alienating some legal professionals. In order to reach out to the legal community, it may have been productive for the authors to discuss the legal landscape in more diplomatic terms rather than such derogatory descriptions as "rewards the manipulation of fact" (503), "philosophy of punishing the last person to touch the patient" (503), and "lottery like" (519). Changes to the legal system are needed; lawyers are perhaps the most aware of the need for legal reform and could be excellent resources toward achieving common goals.

Litigation reform is essential to the implementation of Liang's systems approach. Medical professionals must have the freedom to speak freely to one another so that they can report, discover, correct, and eliminate errors without the fear of litigation risks created by their efforts. This is a laudable goal and one I believe is well worth the effort to achieve. Whether it is possible or not without sacrificing essential patient opportunities for redress of serious wrongs is questionable. Perhaps the attainment of the goal will require a more socialized approach to medicine, or a no-fault system such as Workman's Compensation, or applying a philosophy of securing the most good for the most people rather than sacrificing the good of the many for the protection of the few.

The United States has a medical liability crisis which is affecting the public's access to safe healthcare. Numerous studies reveal that damage caps and other forms of tort reform may have provided some relief, but not enough. The current medical liability system must be changed and implemented along with a new approach in the medical community for addressing medical error, the root of the crisis. As Liang and Ren show, this is an objective worth the combined efforts of the medical, legal, and general public communities.

WORK CITED

Liang, Bryan A., and LiLan Ren. "Medical Liability Insurance and Damage Caps: Getting beyond Band Aids to Substantive Systems Treatment to Improve Quality and Safety in Healthcare." *American Journal of Law & Medicine* 30 (2004): 501–41. Print.

The second student writer chose an essay from the field of environmental sciences which examines some possible causes for the increasingly rapid spreading and strength of infectious diseases since the late 1970s. Compare Brandon's approaches to Cindy's:

- How does his focus differ, especially the ways he judges the credibility of the article?
- Does he divide his summary and response sections like Cindy does, or take a different approach?
- What questions do you think Brandon and Cindy asked themselves in the process of drafting their papers to make different organizational and argumentative choices for their final drafts?
- Brandon's source text was about seven pages long, while Cindy used a text of about forty pages. How do you think this difference in source length affected each student's decisions about summary and response approaches?

Brandon A.
Ms. Jurgens
College Writing
21 November 2006

Impending Disease Outbreaks: A Number of Human Follies

In his article, "Infectious Disease: The Human Cost of Our Environmental Errors," which appeared in *Environmental Health Perspective* in 2004, Bob Weinhold recognizes how diseases and viruses are rising once again; he claims that humans are doing next to nothing to stop them, and that in many ways humans are fueling powerful microscopic killers. Weinhold begins by explaining how the world as a whole had made a respectable effort at exterminating smallpox during the late seventies, but since then government officials worldwide have turned complacent about disease control and prevention; he argues that the effects of complacency are now surfacing.

Weinhold acknowledges that the world is lax about taking an active role in this fight, and he recognizes many factors that are encouraging infectious diseases to spread. He explains in his article that serious illnesses and disease increase when basic health needs are not met; thus, malnutrition, extensive poverty, and poor public health play important roles in the spread of disease. Another factor he discusses is war: wars destroy public health systems and facilities, and soldiers are likely to bring diseases back to their countries. Adding to the threat of disease, governments and international services are cutting back on vital funding in areas of safe water, sewage treatment, vaccines, research, surveillance, prevention, and emergency response. Other factors Weinhold identifies that encourage infection and spread disease are environmental disturbances, such as deforestation, damming of lakes and rivers, global warming, climate changes, global dust, importing of exotic animal species, and harmful farming techniques. Ultimately, Weinhold argues that humans are in a great deal of trouble. As time passes, diseases and viruses are becoming stronger and are turning into better killers. He admonishes us (Americans) to communicate better internationally and avoid becoming complacent about these microscopic killers.

Although many feel viruses and infectious diseases are being held at bay, Weinhold argues that humans are very vulnerable. His arguments are convincing, and he uses numerous credible sources to back up his claims. He constructs his article intelligently and uses sophisticated language appropriate for the topic and audience. Weinhold's strategy of investigating American and international governments is interesting; but, he misses key issues, such as biologically engineered diseases and the overuse of antibiotics, both of which might solidify his argument about humans' roles in emerging diseases.

Weinhold makes a very good appeal to logic and knows what his academic audience wants to hear. His article is found in the *Environmental Health Perspective*, a peer-reviewed journal aimed at researching and reporting on environmental health issues; their mission statement is as follows: "The mission of *Environmental Health Perspective (EHP)*, the journal of the National Institute of Environmental Health Sciences, is to serve as a forum for the discussion of the interrelationships between the environment and human health by publishing in a balanced and objective manner the best peer-reviewed research and most current and credible news of the field." Because *EHP* has published Weinhold's piece, his work is given a huge amount of credibility. Other than being published by a renowned journal, Weinhold quotes and interjects statistics from nearly thirty outside organizations and authorities on the subject at hand, ranging from the Center for Disease Control (CDC) to the World Health Organization (WHO) to the Institute of Medicine (IOM). This is an article that is clearly aimed at the well educated, most likely doctors and the environmentally knowledgeable. He casually uses medical and biological terms as though the reader is familiar with the topic. This strategy works extremely well, and Weinhold's use of outside organizations, statistics, and other authorities on the matter make his article all the more intellectually appealing and convincing.

Weinhold makes a few appeals to the emotions of the reader, but those appeals do not overshadow his logic. He mentions how diseases not only cost lives and money but also alienate children by leaving them parentless; in turn, diseases and viruses are aiding in the breakdown of social structures (35). I feel, because this is a scholarly, scientific journal, Weinhold mostly avoids emotions and feelings because of the way his audience thinks. He knows how they receive and process information through intellect rather than emotion; thus, a strong appeal to the emotions would be inappropriate and weaken his voice in the argument.

Throughout his article Weinhold discusses political complacency and similar issues. He first mentions complacency in the third paragraph and again in the last paragraph on the same page (34). Later, he returns to the issue of complacency, mentioning the U.S. Department of Agriculture (37), describing treatment of sewage in the U.S. (38), and finally concluding on the risks of slothful attitudes on the last page of the article. I believe Weinhold's objective in discussing government agencies and widespread complacency is not to blame the government for outbreaks of diseases, but he does hold them to a degree of accountability concerning prevention, research, and containment. One phrase stands out in Weinhold's article: "Efforts so far are indeed limited and too disease-specific. . . . There is no master plan" (39). This statement illustrates an underlying theme in the article, Weinhold's disenchantment with the government and its false sense of security. He expects more from political leaders, more assistance, more funding, and more awareness. This message becomes evident, but takes some effort for an average reader to uncover. I think that if Weinhold really wanted to make his voice heard and influence the minds of average readers, he could make his statements more obvious and less complex.

Weinhold develops several outstanding arguments about global warming affecting infectious diseases, pointing out specific discrepancies from international statistics (35). I agree with Weinhold and would also add that global warming has affected not only the spread of infectious diseases, but also weather patterns and violent storms, which further the spread of diseases. For example, this year the Gulf Coast had record tropical storms and hurricanes leaving overwhelming damage. Warm water powers these incredible machines of destruction, and the aftermath leaves thousands of places where disease can fester. With hundreds of human casualties, animal carcasses (both domestic and wild), and the deluge of sewer systems, hospitals, chemical refineries, and government facilities, contamination and disease spread rapidly. Global warming causes some of these drastic weather changes and creates ideal situations for diseases to spawn and spread.

Weinhold also tackles a theory of global dust transferring microbes (especially disease and virus particles) hundreds and thousands of miles from where they originated. Weinhold claims that hundreds of millions of tons of dust float in the Earth's atmosphere, and that humans are in a sense stirring the pot, causing more dust than what is naturally there (36). In this area I agree partly; some microbes may move short distances, but I disagree that massive quantities of harmful microbes are floating to new far away destinations. I would assert that the Earth has a number of natural forces that cause the majority of dust and direct its movement. Volcanoes, for instance, spew millions of particles into the air and disperse them over land and sea. Dust and windstorms in deserts and areas with loose soil can move massive amounts of particles and microbes; even earthquakes can create amounts of dust from land shifting. I would argue in comparison that humans cause a very small fraction of the dust already circling in the atmosphere. One major problem with Weinhold's "dust theory" is the lack of major outbreaks worldwide. For example, if a disease such as Ebola breaks out in Africa, somewhere with desert conditions, Ebola should spread like wildfire to surrounding communities because of the "dust factor." The virus would spread nationally, and then internationally, very quickly. This scenario has yet to occur, which leads me to believe dust and microbes (particles existent from before the age of humans) do not accelerate infection or transport large amounts of harmful microbes.

One topic Weinhold barely mentions is virus mutation and resistance. Viruses specifically have the ability to mutate and change their genetic structure. From a medical standpoint this is alarming because viruses can change an infinite amount of ways and times. This causes difficulty identifying specific viruses and tracking the development of different symptoms in victims; it may require different medications for treatment, or the virus may even develop a resistance to medications. One possible contributor to mutation is the "shotgun antibiotic" used by some physicians. Like the Battleship board game, doctors prescribe a powerful blast of antibiotics, hoping to exterminate the culprit. Sometimes this works, but other times it gives diseases chances to change and even resist medications. This is an important subject overlooked by Weinhold.

Weinhold also misses bioterrorism and engineered viruses, very dangerous possible forms of warfare. Biological agents are engineered by scientists to eliminate the enemy; these killers do not distinguish friends from enemies, so everyone is a possible host for infection. Most countries are completely unprepared for biological warfare and are more vulnerable than they want to admit. Terrorists or other enemies can pollute an entire water reservoir, and by the time the source is identified, thousands or hundreds of thousands might be infected. Weinhold needs to acknowledge this as a serious threat and potential effect humans can have on themselves and the environment.

Bob Weinhold's article covers what he feels are the basic environmental causes of and human impact on new hazardous viruses and diseases. He makes few generalizations and appeals to the logic of his readers through credible sources and through his publisher. Weinhold carries a theme of government complacency throughout the article and argues for increased awareness. Weinhold does omit the two important issues of bioterrorism and the over-prescription of antibiotics, which are definitely related to the spread of infectious diseases and humans' effects on the environment. Nonetheless, Weinhold makes a strong, credible argument that viruses and infectious diseases are again becoming a serious threat to humanity. His concerns: how can government institutions improve current situations; how can they slow or even stop the emergence and spread of infectious diseases; and how have humans negatively affected the environment? Hopefully, Weinhold's warning will be heeded before the time to prepare has expired—or has that time already passed?

WORK CITED

Weinhold, Bob. "Infectious Disease: The Human Cost of Our Environmental Errors." *Environmental Health Perspective* 112.1 (2004): 32–39. Print.

10

Prepare a Research Proposal and Annotated Bibliography

CHAPTER OBJECTIVES

In this chapter, you'll learn how to:

- Pose a research question
- Plan for a research project with multiple sources
- Anticipate the purpose of a future research project
- Compose an annotated bibliography

Academic writers combine their compelling research questions with well-chosen sources to make the research writing process interesting for themselves and their readers. Reading and responding to the work of others helps researchers make connections between academic texts and their ideas and prepares them to make their own contributions to an academic conversation. Effective planning entails preparing a research proposal and annotated bibliography, which are the focus of this chapter.

PLANNING THE PROJECT

The proposal and annotated bibliography help you plan a research project early in the process.

The proposal outlines your goals and purposes, establishing a framework for the final project. It is an opportunity to organize your preliminary thinking and show your instructor that you have:

- An appropriate and manageable research question
- Sources needed to explore the question
- A goal and purpose for your work
- A plan for completing the research project

In courses that require extensive research writing, you will find that the proposal plays an important role in planning your workload for the term. Strong preparation ensures later success because your instructor,

Proposals help research writers in any field plan for success.

who has read many research projects over the years, can assess strengths and weaknesses in your proposal and give suggestions on how to proceed productively.

Proposals Inside and Outside the Academic World

The research proposal has counterparts in many professional and academic fields. Medical and scientific researchers often use a proposal–bibliography approach when they apply for grants to pursue their projects. Businesses and nonprofit organizations use proposals to seek out prospective clients, investors, and contributors for future ventures.

Student Voice

Adil, who wanted to learn more about the social and economic impact of Wal-Mart stores, explains the value of planning the research project ahead of time:

> *Normally, when I start an essay I do massive amounts of research and then never know where or how to begin actually writing. With the proposal I can think about all of that in advance and get a better idea of what I need to do before I start writing.*

Academic researchers write grant proposals similar to those of their counterparts outside of academia. They also write proposals describing projects that they wish to present at academic conferences or are planning to develop into articles and books. Brief sketches, or *abstracts,* allow publishers and peer reviewers the opportunity to see an academic project in a brief, preliminary form, and guide writers toward successful final presentation and publication.

See Chapter 5 for advice on using abstracts early in the research process.

Plan What to Do—and What Not to Do

In the academic and professional worlds, effective proposals speak clearly to the needs of their respective audiences, whether fellow academics or stakeholders such as business partners, clients, and the like. They succinctly explain what their research will accomplish. By clearly framing their projects, researchers are freed from having to cover every aspect of or every possible angle on their topic.

Proposals explain your plan and how you intend to meet your goals.

Budget Time

Researchers can use the proposal to anticipate how long the research and writing will take, and how they plan to succeed within the time they have. Consider incorporating a timeline into your proposal. Take into account, for instance, the requirements of your final project and the weeks or class periods remaining in the term, so that you can stay on course and keep your workload manageable. Consider:

- How many sources do you need?
- Will you have to collect observations, surveys, and other "field" research?

Field research is introduced in Chapter 11.

- Will you have to wait for e-mail or other correspondence?
- Do you have to budget time for group work, such as presentations and peer reviews?
- How does each of these elements affect the time you have to plan and complete your research projects?
- How can you make the best use of time during the research process?

Where Are You Now?

You may have begun the research process with earlier activities and writing projects. If you selected a text for the critical engagement writing project discussed in Chapter 9, you probably chose from a number of options in the library or online databases. If you plan to continue with the same line of research, revisit those sources and incorporate them into your proposal. If your instructor provided texts for earlier writing projects, or assigned texts included in this book, think of ways to develop a research project in a similar field or on a related issue.

Using Your Sources' Bibliographies to Find More Material

Bibliographies summarize a writer's research process by listing all of the sources he or she uses to develop an argument. If you found an engaging source for an earlier writing project, consider retracing that author's research process in building your own body of research. Ask yourself these questions as you review a source's bibliography:

- Does the author reference sources that are fundamental to understanding the context, history, or foundations of a conversation?
- Does the author reference sources that provide further support for your argument or position?
- Does the author reference sources that argue contrary positions? Could you read those sources to better understand multiple sides of a debate or multiple perspectives on an issue?
- Has the author written other articles or books that will help you better understand one researcher's frame of reference or motivations?

As you review the bibliographies of your sources, consider how authors describe building their research projects and assembling their research materials. Which of their techniques could help you succeed in your project?

THE PROPOSAL: FROM REFLECTION TO FORECASTING

While earlier writing projects in this book focused on reflection, the proposal outlines a project based on preliminary research and thinking. This outline anticipates much of the work that you'll be doing over the next few weeks or months.

Consider using some of the work that you've already done in order to get started on the proposal. Think back to when you were reading the text for your critical engagement writing project, and ask yourself some of the following questions to get started:

- Did the text prompt you to ask questions as you read?
- Did you come across issues that you wanted to learn more about?
- Did the author challenge views or beliefs you hold?
- Did you see gaps in the argument that needed to be filled?

If you started to answer these questions in your earlier reading, consider developing the proposal around the answers. Ask yourself:

- How will you develop your own ideas and contribute to the conversation?
- What kinds of sources must you find to further understand the question and to make your contribution?
- Will you work in a single academic field or do you plan to link two or more fields together?

WRITING ASSIGNMENT

I. In the first part of this assignment, explain your research question and your preliminary thinking. Introduce your field of academic research and describe your research to this point. Present a plan for completion of research.

II. In the second part of this assignment, create an annotated bibliography with references to at least three scholarly/peer-reviewed works in an appropriate bibliographic style, each with critical annotations.

A formal peer review form for both aspects of this assignment is presented in Figure 10.1.

The Three-Paragraph Proposal

A three-paragraph proposal is a model that can accommodate a range of possible research questions and approaches.

The first paragraph introduces your subject and research field. You might include a brief anecdote explaining what brought you to your project: Did you develop it from personal interests, base it on an issue important in your academic major, or your anticipated professional field? Your introduction should include an explanation of the significance of your project and how your research will contribute to the larger academic conversation. You should frame your research question as well, showing readers how you plan to keep your project manageable.

The second paragraph describes your preliminary research and reading. Can you find a sufficient amount of research, including the kinds of sources required by your instructor? How did you move from reference works and general audience sources to more scholarly materials? Can you briefly describe each of the sources you found thus far, or group sources together in logical ways? Is there consensus among experts or can you identify points of debate in the conversation?

The third paragraph is where you plan for the completion of research. If you need to include additional sources or find a balance of positions to complete your project, describe your plans here. Will you have to expand your research into other fields in order to get a complete sense of the issue? If so, how do you plan to expand and integrate work in two or more academic conversations? Anticipate the conclusions you expect to reach at the end of your project.

Essential Proposal Elements

Your proposal should include the following elements, regardless of the approach or style you use:

- **A tentative title for your project.** The title should not restate the paper's topic (e.g., "Logging in the Northwest" or "Video Games"). It should suggest your plan to enter the conversation, signal your position in a debate, or in some way give readers a hint of your research purpose.
- **A description of your research question.** How did you get interested in the subject? In what field or academic conversation are you working?
- **A description of your research purpose.** How do you plan to enter the academic conversation? What do you plan to accomplish with your research?
- **An overview of the research you've done so far.** What has your research shown you? What questions have you answered?
- **A plan for completion of the project.** What research must you do to complete your project? Can you complete the research in the time that remains in the term?
- **A working bibliography.** Based either on your research field or your instructor's requirements, write a bibliography using an appropriate style (e.g., MLA, APA, CMS, or CSE).

WRITING ANNOTATIONS

For this chapter's writing assignment, each bibliography entry should include an annotation, an overview of the source and its role in your research project. Your annotations will include both *descriptive* and *evaluative* elements. Consider the following in order to ensure both are present:

- The descriptive annotation (also known as a *précis*) summarizes the source and its argument. Your descriptions may include the author's major points, methods, conclusion, and contribution to the academic conversation.

- The evaluative annotation (also known as a *critical annotation*) comments on the quality of the source. This annotation includes describing the author's credibility, showing the appropriateness and quality of evidence, and assessing the strength of the argument. Evaluative annotations may also describe how each source fits with others in your bibliography.

> *Annotations explain what each source is about and why it is important in your paper.*

Connecting the Strategies

Think about the annotated bibliography as a set of miniature critical engagements, where you are using the same summary–response skills, but in a compressed form. First, you describe the source by:

> *Use summary-response strategies in your annotations.*

- Summarizing the argument
- Explaining its main points
- Describing the methods or structure of the argument

Second, you evaluate the source by:

- Reflecting on its role in your project
- Showing how it adds to your understanding of the research question
- Explaining whether it changes your understanding of the conversation
- Demonstrating how it relates to your other sources and how it might lead to new sources

Student Voice

Anastasia, who planned to argue in favor of open adoption policies in her final research essay, explains how she used the proposal and annotated bibliography:

Writing this paper helped me to analyze my research and to think about what kind of material I have to find to support my argument. The annotated bibliography was helpful because I was able to organize my thoughts on the importance of information in each article.

PROPOSAL/ANNOTATED BIBLIOGRAPHY

FORMAL PEER REVIEW

Proposal/Annotated Bibliography goals: 1) propose the research project that will take you through the rest of the term; 2) write an annotated bibliography listing sources in an appropriate style with brief descriptions and evaluations of each. Since this is a relatively brief essay, take time to discuss comments with your partner to clear up any questions she or he has.

1. Does the writer describe how s/he used personal, professional, or academic interests to develop a research question and project? Help the writer explain the motivations that drew him or her to the project and that could help increase readers' interest.

2. Has the writer done enough preliminary work to convince you that she or he can succeed on the project and complete it in the time remaining in the term? Should the proposal include a timeline?

3. Does the writer describe his or her research purpose? Do you have a good idea of how she or he plans to explore the research question or what s/he plans to do with the research? Help the writer develop strong research goals.

4. Has the writer found the kinds of reference, general, and academic sources required by your instructor? Share your ideas and interests to help the writer find additional materials.

5. Are all the sources used in the proposal cited completely and correctly in the bibliography (see Chapter 7)?

6. Is there an annotation for each bibliography entry? Do the annotations describe and evaluate the sources? Does each annotation give you an idea of how the source relates to other sources the writer plans to use?

7. Help the writer with mechanical concerns that have to be revised before submission. Identify misspelled words, punctuation errors, and run-on and fragment sentences, or mistakes with in-text citations, bibliographic style, or formatting. When you can, help the writer correct mistakes.

FIGURE 10.1   Proposal/Annotated Bibliography: Formal Peer Review.

WRITING SAMPLES

The first student writer uses the three-paragraph approach as she plans a research paper on the effects of caffeine on athletic performance. She includes in her bibliography materials from commercial and academic websites, professional periodicals, and scholarly journals. As you read, note the writer's ability to compress a lot of information and an extensive anticipated project into a brief form.

Maria C.
Dr. Choi
College Writing
6 March 2008

"It Gives You Wings," but Is Caffeine Good for Exercise?

I am interested in researching how caffeine can affect athletic performance, and I plan to focus my research in the field of sports medicine. I used *Academic Search Premier* to search under "caffeine and athletic performance," "caffeine and sports," and "caffeine and exercise" and found good articles in *Sports Medicine*, *Physician and Sports Medicine*, and *Athletic Therapy*. I also found non-scholarly articles on caffeine that have good information. Some of the articles I found had a lot of the same information: for instance, I found that caffeine can affect performance positively and negatively; it helps endurance athletes, but it doesn't help athletes such as sprinters and weightlifters; it keeps the muscles contracting longer, and it turns fat into energy. Caffeine also affects the brain, mainly by preventing physical fatigue. Caffeine doesn't help short, high intensity exercise because it takes at least thirty minutes, and as much as two to three hours, for caffeine to start affecting muscles. These sources also describe some of the risks that caffeine use, and especially caffeine abuse, poses to athletes' bodies. If caffeine is over-used, harmful effects on the body can include tachycardia (a fast heart rate) and high blood pressure. Even with all of the research materials out there, the effects of caffeine are still unpredictable: it may work on some athletes but not others, so it is important to know the possible side effects and proper use of caffeine.

Because it is the most widely used drug in the United States, and perhaps in the entire world, it is important to understand more about caffeine's effects on athletic performance. I always thought caffeine was bad for athletes because it was dehydrating; but now that I've found out about its positive effects and that it may only dehydrate a little, I'm considering using caffeine when I exercise. I am also interested in caffeine in sports because I plan to study nutrition in college and eventually work as a trainer. I need to have accurate and up-to-date information to give proper care to athletes. I think it is important for competing and non-competing athletes to know how caffeine can affect their bodies, if they choose to use it. Finally, where they use it is important as well, because caffeine is banned in college sports but not in Olympic and professional sports.

How much is too much? Especially because high-caffeine "energy drinks" have become really popular, I plan to learn more about caffeine's exact effects on the muscles and how it improves endurance; I also want to learn more about how caffeine helps fatty acids turn into energy. I want to find more case studies of athletes who do take caffeine, so I can understand in more detail how it is used in training, the amounts used and how long before competitions, and the harmful effects caffeine has on the body and how to avoid them, and be able to summarize different expert opinions on caffeine and its use in sports. The sources I have found so far also made me interested in the background of caffeine in sports; I want to find out why caffeine is banned in collegiate sports but not in Olympic or professional sports. I also want to learn more about the rules of and consequences for caffeine use in collegiate sports. I plan on researching the school's library databases for journals such as *Clinical Journal of Sports Medicine, Science and Sports, Medical Science in Sports and Exercise,* and the *Journal of Sports Science and Medicine.* I already searched a little on their websites, and each journal had a lot of material on caffeine. I also plan to search college, athletic training, and Olympic websites for caffeine information and stories.

ANNOTATED BIBLIOGRAPHY

Graham, T.E. "Caffeine and Exercise: Metabolism, Endurance, and

Performance." *Sports Medicine* 31.11 (2001): 785-807. Print.

The main argument is that caffeine allows athletes to train longer and at a greater output and to increase speed and power. The purpose is to show how caffeine affects long- and short-term exercise. The article covers long-term and short-term exercise and how caffeine affects blood flow, ion balance, blood glucose, lactate fluid, electrolyte balance, and caffeine dependency. It describes some case studies that were done with caffeine and different types of athletes, such as cyclists and swimmers.

The article is reliable because it comes from a recent, scholarly sports medicine journal. It is not biased, because its purpose is to inform readers about how caffeine can improve performance and about its side effects. The goal is to give someone in the sports medicine field information about caffeine. I want to read more studies on the effects of caffeine on blood flow, electrolyte balance, and lactate fluid.

Iknoian, Therese. "Caffeine: Performance Aid or Just a Jolt?" *Adventure Sports*

Online. Web. 2 Feb. 2006. <www.adventuresportsonline.com/caffeine.

htm>.

The purpose of this article is to inform the general public about caffeine and exercise. It gives good tips about how much to take and when to take it, and possible side effects.

It is fairly reliable, because the author is an award-winning and internationally published fitness and sports journalist, but the article may not be peer reviewed. The goal is to inform people with general fitness interests about caffeine and provide tips if readers plan to use it for exercise. Most of the information is repeated in the other sources, but it gave helpful tips that I would use if I used caffeine during exercise. I will find other articles with more analysis, but it is a good overview article.

Jenkins, Mark. "Caffeine and the Athlete." Web. 22 Feb. 2006. <www.rice.edu/
~jenky/sports/caffeine.html>.

There isn't a main argument, but the website has good information for athletes about caffeine and its use in sports. It gives background information on caffeine and what happens when it enters the body, health and performance effects, side effects, and recommendations for athletes who choose to use caffeine.

The article may not be scholarly, but I think it is reliable because it was written by a doctor at Rice University and is on the Rice University website. This information is helpful, but it makes me want to find more sources on the physiology of caffeine's effects on the body.

Magkos, Faidon, and Savros A. Kavouras. "Caffeine and Ephedrine:
Physiological, Metabolic, and Performance Enhancing Effects." *Sports
Medicine* 34.13 (2004): 871–89. Print.

The article's main argument is that caffeine can increase time to exhaustion during endurance exercise. The main points are how it increases endurance in long-term exercise but doesn't improve short-distance exercise. Caffeine can also improve speed and power in endurance exercise.

The article is reliable and has good, specific information; Magkos and Kavouras achieve their goal of showing how caffeine can enhance performance. This article is fairly short, so I will find another source with similar information but more depth.

Mangus, Brent C., and Cynthia A. Throwbridge. "Will Caffeine Work as an
Ergogenic Aid? The Latest Research." *Athletic Therapy Today* 10.3 (2005):
57–62. Print.

The purpose of the article is to provide information on caffeine and how it improves athletic performance. The information is directed to athletic trainers to help athletes. The main argument is that caffeine can improve endurance exercise, but not short, high-intensity exercise. The article provides background information on caffeine and covers theories of why caffeine affects exercise as well as possible applications for athletic trainers, including recommended amounts of caffeine, side effects, and ways to provide education for athletes.

This source is reliable because it comes from a scholarly sports medicine journal. It was also very recently published. The authors' goal (which they achieve) is to provide information to athletic trainers, coaches, and athletes about caffeine and how it affects athletic performance. It gives good information for application and it informed me on how caffeine can improve athletic performance.

"Soda Pop: An Athlete's Friend or Foe?" *Physician and Sports Medicine* 30.11
(2002): 17. Print.

This article was a cover story about coaches in Minnesota who weren't allowing their athletes to consume soda pop. The argument is that athletes shouldn't use soda pop for hydration, and the authors focus on the negative effects of soft drinks. The purpose of the article is to look at why soda pop and caffeine affect performance. It focuses on nutrition: soda pop is high in calories and a poor way to hydrate. The authors do admit that caffeine (and caffeinated soda) helps performance in endurance and power events.

It is reliable because it appeared in a scholarly journal. It helped me understand that soda pop is not good for performance. The article contains very little information on caffeine, so I would find more articles with deeper information.

Tarnopolsky, Mark A. "Protein, Caffeine, and Sports." *Physician and Sports Medicine* 21.3 (1993): 140–45. Print.

The purpose of this article is to give information on caffeine and its use in athletic performance. It talks about caffeine's background, issues surrounding its use, performance concerns, mechanisms, and potential benefits.

It comes from a reliable sports medicine journal, but it is not as recent as the other articles I have found. It also has a lot of the same information as the other articles. It is shorter, so I would probably find other articles with more information.

The second student writer plans to examine alternatives to current parole systems and compare their risks and benefits. Unlike the first writer, who used many types of sources, this student begins with newspaper reports of current debates and then turns exclusively to articles in scholarly journals to outline her research project. Consider this student's approach of using recent and older sources to develop a broad understanding of the debate about parole systems. How would you describe the differences between the first and second writers' research purposes?

Natalie B.
Ms. Reyes
College Writing
December 14, 2009

Parole and Probation: Where Can the Systems Go from Here?

Even though federal prisons started granting early release to inmates showing "good behavior" in 1867, it took three years to establish the United States Department of Justice to oversee parole decisions. Then, it took over four decades to get an official parole system in place in the United States. The same parole system has been used since June 25, 1910, when it was officially established as a sentencing option. It is clear to me that the current corrections system has been in need of revision for a long time.

The parole system has had some positive effect on the American judicial system, but it is apparent that new standards need to be set for overseeing this system in order for it to work to its full potential and meet current social needs. Many state governments are now reviewing and revising their probation and parole policies. In recent years, these policy reviews have picked up speed because of the need to address reduced financial and corrections resources. Some suggested revisions include reducing the number of prisons being built, reducing the parole sentences to shorter periods of time, and reducing recidivism rates. Obviously, the parole system directly affects the prison population because it can help control how many inmates use prison facilities and how many may return before their sentences are finished. Changing the parole system and making it more effective will help to reduce prison populations and recidivism rates. There are many possible changes that could be considered, but many states lack the ability to find and implement new approaches and solutions to their problems. Indeed, change is needed, but if no one can make a good suggestion for change (and one that people will accept), the system may be forced to continue to work inefficiently.

I want to look at arguments in favor of keeping the current system and the solutions that have been proposed so far, and compare the arguments supporting and opposing each side. With such arguments taken into consideration, I will probably find that more needs to be done to improve the current system. While many local governments argue that problems with the parole and probation system are difficult to fix, and that few solutions have been found to correct all the flaws that the system has, those simply are not excuses. It is true that the proposed solutions have both pros and cons, but what governmental decision does not? Legislators and governors are there to make decisions, and they can't expect each issue they face to be easy. It is also true that any new legislation or amendments to existing legislation can take a considerable amount of time to put into effect. It is for that very reason that action needs to be taken now so that a prolonging of needed changes doesn't cause more trouble in the long run.

First, I will describe the origin of the parole system and look at both its beneficial elements and its flaws. Then, I will identify the changes the parole system has already undergone. With this strong historical foundation, I hope to show that the parole and probation system is stable and necessary, but can be changed or modified when needed. In researching this topic, I found that some good solutions have been proposed, but so far little action has been taken. I will outline the major concepts or ideas that seem to dominate reform plans in various states. From this information I will demonstrate that the core ideas for change are out there, but due to the nature of politics there is little initiative to push the legislation through that would implement those changes. It is apparent that the current system has a secure foundation and that a few simple modifications can bring the parole and probation systems up to good working order. I will prove that it can be done by making prompt decisions.

ANNOTATED BIBLIOGRAPHY

Evans, Donald G. "Community Engagement: A Challenge for

    Probation/Parole." *Corrections Today* 67.6 (2005): 117–19. Print.

    This article poses a different view from most I have found. It covers how parole affects the people in the community where parolees are released. It describes categories of phases that are used in the proposed system: the protective phase, the preparative phase, and the productive phase. The article concludes with community guidelines. I will use a lot of the information found in this article because it is very different from the other information I found. I am most interested in nationwide community views. It will help me to show that this problem isn't found in just one state but many.

Frase, Richard S. "State Sentencing Guidelines: Diversity, Consensus, and

    Unresolved Policy Issues." *Columbia Law Review* 105 (2005): 1190–1232.

    Print.

    This long article goes over different state policies in the United States. One of the larger challenges is in unresolved policy issues from state to state. Frase covers major conflicts that have been taking place in larger states where the parole system has a higher usage rate and need. One of the unresolved policy challenges is how to maintain balance in monitoring those on parole and probation. This article could be helpful in my research, though it is not one of the most important sources I intend to use. I enjoy having knowledge about the sentencing process, and I will probably use the article for some statistics it offers.

Geerken, Michael R., and Hennessey D. Hayes. "Probation and Parole: Public Risk and the Future of Incarceration Alternatives." *Criminology* 31.4 (1993): 549–64. Print.

Geerken and Hayes address increased population in the jail system, and they focus on options to replace incarceration. The two options they cover are probation and parole, and they argue that probation and parole systems are more effective than many people (especially politicians) think. Their work will help me to argue the validity of the parole system. This article is also older, so it will help me create a timeline of the parole system through the years.

Lurigio, Arthur J., Angie Rollins, and John Fallon. "The Effects of Serious Mental Illness on Offender Reentry." *Federal Probation* 68.2 (2004): 45–52. Print.

This article is probably one of the most intriguing articles that I came across in my research. It presented the variable of mental illness in relation to prison reentry rates. Because my original idea came from a situation of parole and mental illness, I found this to be an especially relevant article. Lurigio and others describe ways that mental health professionals have now been brought into the criminal justice system at all stages of crime. They now play a major role in cases that have been impacted by mental illness. However, health professionals and people in the traditional criminal justice system (like prosecutors and judges) tend to see things differently; the authors argue that if the two sides find a way to work together, they will have immediate good effects on the system. Because my research focuses on what needs to change to have a positive impact, this article will play an important role.

Ward, Mike. "Probation Reforms Flounder at Capitol: Opponents Say Bills Would Create More Prisoners, not Fewer." *Austin American Statesman* 1 May 2005: A1. Web. 16 April 2007.

This article reports on proceedings held by the Texas State Senate to reform current parole and probation systems. Ward gives a few statistics based on the current system and the new system that will be put into place, a comparison I hope to use in my paper. He outlines several reasons for the necessary changes and quotes several senators on their opinions as well. Ward explains that jail building costs need to decrease, so any new system put in place will aim toward reducing the recidivism rate, which will take more involvement from the judicial system. Ward suggests that it is still unclear what will be done with the current parole and probation system. This is helpful research because it validates my opinion on the need for change. From this article, I will cite information concerning prison costs because this article gave more details on this issue than others.

11

The Exploratory Research Essay: En Route to a Thesis

CHAPTER OBJECTIVES

In this chapter, you'll learn how to:

- Write a first-person narrative of your research process
- Bring material together from multiple sources
- Explore possible organizational strategies
- Describe how the research process affects your thinking
- Develop your own voice in the academic conversation
- Incorporate field research

Strong research writing develops from an ongoing process of engagement with ideas and sources. Success requires exploration and reflection; it requires writers who think critically and are willing to be swayed by the strength of others' arguments. This chapter's goal is to help you explore a research question and reflect on the process of gathering and integrating materials from your sources with your own reflections and responses. The exploratory writing project helps you to join an academic conversation like any other discussion—by first listening to what others have to say, then building your own

The exploratory essay tells the story of your research process.

strength as a participant in the discussion, and finally speculating on a response to the question that initially motivated your research.

Your exploratory essay will be a first-person narrative that tells the story of your research process. To develop a compelling research narrative, you will:

- Begin with a challenge or problem that motivates your research
- Critically examine the range of ideas and arguments you find through research
- Describe how the research process affected your thinking (Were you compelled to change your mind about an issue, or come to consider a question in a more complex light than you had originally?)

The exploratory essay works as an intermediate stage between your research proposal and formal research essay.

Rhetorician Kenneth Burke imagined entering an academic conversation as drama about ideas, where people come together to share their views about an issue of common interest. Beginning with a question rather than a thesis, the exploratory essay gives you an opportunity to find those people in your field, listen to their individual voices, then begin to weave them together and add your own voice to the discussion.

Enter a conversation with each source as you explore a research problem.

The exploratory approach to ideas has a long history in the sciences, the humanities, and many other disciplines. Ancient philosophers such as Socrates used an exploratory form, by beginning with apparently simple questions, and then through discussion and dialogue, developing more complex questions and often reaching only tentative conclusions.

WRITING ASSIGNMENT

Write a first-person narrative that describes your exploration of a subject or question through academic research. You don't have to come up with an answer or conclusion. Instead, focus on what you've learned about the ways an issue is discussed within an academic conversation. The paper should include references to your research materials (quotations, paraphrases, and summaries) and a bibliography, which will include sufficiently scholarly sources.

Use the formal peer review in Figure 11.1 to assess your exploratory research essay.

Exploratory goals are important, because they seek to understand the complexity of problems before—or even instead of—attempting to solve them once and for all. After all, as Burke tells us, these conversations were already underway before any of us entered them, and they will continue long after we have left. What we *can* do is explain and narrate for readers our unique encounter with a problem and the ways in which we have turned to research to better understand the problem, if not solve it. Use the questions below to guide your exploration:

- Why is the issue worth considering?
- Who is interested in exploring or debating the issue?
- How did you choose your sources?
- How do your sources make claims and take positions?
- Why should readers see you as a credible researcher and participant in the conversation?

In the process of answering these questions, you can develop a compelling dialogue between you and your sources. Ultimately, you'll have something valuable to say to your audience at the end of the essay, showing that you've learned about the debate and can contribute to the academic conversation, even if you haven't been able to solve the problem you started with.

The exploratory essay uses skills you have already practiced and helps you develop them further. For example, you have practiced key techniques of active reading and critical engagement with sources. Those same techniques help you to weave together and respond to multiple sources in a single paper.

Critical engagement strategies are described in Chapter 9.

The research proposal and annotated bibliography that you produced in the previous chapter called for brief summaries and responses to some of your sources. Use these annotations to develop further detail:

- Find key passages from each source to incorporate into your essay through quotation, paraphrase, and summary
- Respond to each source and connect it to your research question
- Anticipate ways to connect sources to each other by showing how they work together or differ

Quotation, paraphrase, and summary strategies are described in Chapter 6.

- Find additional sources to fill in gaps or incorporate new perspectives
- Formulate your conclusion based on your reading, exploration, and critical thinking

As you gather sources for your essay, consider the role each will play in the conversation, including:

Context

- Does the source provide information and background on your research?
- Does the source show the history of an academic issue or debate?
- Does the source introduce the major players—authors, institutions, groups, and so on—in the debate?

Support

- Does the source make arguments that support your position?
- Does the source make compelling arguments that you're inclined to agree with?
- Does the source add new details that help you make a convincing argument?
- Does the source help you take a position within a debate?

Refutation

- Does the source present a view that opposes yours?
- Does the source conflict with other sources that you find credible?
- Does the source make a strong argument that makes you reevaluate your position or see a new perspective?
- Does the source introduce new details that take the debate in an unexpected direction?

ORGANIZATION

The exploratory essay should begin with an introduction that describes how you got interested in the topic and how you chose and developed your research question. For example:

- What personal, professional, or academic interests lead you to the topic?
- How did you narrow your interests?

Consider opening moves that appeal to your audience and draw them into your exploration:

- Would a personal anecdote help prepare readers for your research question?
- What images, events, or people will your audience relate to?
- How can you begin your paper by building common ground with your reader?

As you read, look for additional opening moves in your sources:

- What techniques do your sources use to draw readers in?
- How do academic writers get an audience interested in exploring a complex issue or argument?
- How might you incorporate techniques from your sources in your own opening?

The bodies of exploratory research essays are usually organized chronologically, but you can also consider using alternative organizational patterns, such as a thematic organization, or a position organization.

Chronological Organization

Using a chronological structure, introduce and discuss each of your sources in the order in which you found them. Chronological organization offers a number of advantages over other patterns, especially by allowing you to draft much of your essay as you read. Because your purpose is to document the research process, your readers will not expect you to know, when you write about one source, your conclusion or even what ideas will emerge when you reach the next source. Think about answering some of the following questions about your sources:

- Why did you choose the first source you read?
- How did each source lead to the next?
- What patterns or themes do you see as you gather multiple sources?
- How did each new source help you reflect on previous sources?
- When did you decide you knew enough to take a position on the question?
- Did your reading cause you to revise your initial question or develop a new one altogether?

Thematic Organization

Think of logical ways to group your sources together. Unlike chronological structure, which allows you to narrate your reflections in the moment, a thematic structure demands that you organize your responses *retrospectively*, after gathering many, if not all, of your sources. If you choose a thematic structure for your exploratory essay, consider the following questions:

- How can you group sources according to their positions?
- Do any of your sources use similar examples or develop ideas along the same lines?
- Is there a historical trend you can show through grouping sources by date?
- Are there particular schools of thought on an issue, or distinct approaches to a debate, that you can group together?

Student Voice

Andrew describes how he began connecting sources thematically for his exploratory research project:

This paper was challenging because I had so much information that I had to manage. It was helpful for me to keep a log of the themes in each article and note page numbers where those themes were.

Student Voice

Toni also used thematic organization in her exploratory essay because it helped her manage the issues and information she found in her sources:

While reading my sources for this paper I found it easier to pick out important themes from each one. Previously I felt like I had to write down anything mentioned in the article, which was time consuming and left me with a surplus of information. This time I spent more time logging information that analyzed the topic I intended to focus on, getting rid of a lot of stuff in between and leaving more time for the information I needed to know for my paper.

Position Organization

If you already have a position you intend to take, a solution you plan to propose, or a claim you plan to make, in your final research project, you can organize your sources to support your case. Consider these questions:

- How would readers be affected by first seeing all the information and arguments that support your position?
- How would placing supporting evidence later in the essay help to strengthen your position?
- How could you integrate strong and weak sources to build evidence for your position?

Regardless of the organizational structure you choose, your essay should focus on the research process and how your thinking evolves with each source or set of sources that you read. Because the emphasis is on your thinking, you should be fairly conservative in the amount of quotations and paraphrases you plan to incorporate. Don't let your voice become drowned out by your sources.

Host your sources: emphasize your voice while incorporating sources into your essay.

Descriptions of the research process should show how you select and move from one source to the next, and how they guide your thinking. You should avoid giving your readers a blow-by-blow description of how you found your sources ("first I got some coffee, then I went to the library, then I turned on my computer . . ."), unless that description will help readers understand your thinking about the issue.

TESTING STRUCTURE—A CASE STUDY

The editors of the psychoanalysis journal *Ethics and Behavior* posed a problem about reality television to their readers and then printed selected responses. Read the question and the four responses below and then consider how you might structure an exploratory essay using the responses as your sources.

- How would you make an argument using a *chronological* structure, moving in order from the first essay to the last?
- How might you group the four essays *thematically* using their positions, their examples, or their conclusions on the ethical problem?
- Finally, if you already have an *opinion* about the ethics of reality television, how might you organize the sources to best support your claims?

Case Vignette: Media Consultation—Reality TV and Professional Ethics

Robin Goodley, a licensed psychologist in part-time private practice and a university professor, received a telephone call from Max Mogul, producer of a string of a reality TV shows known for attracting a significant market share of viewers. Mr. Mogul invited Dr. Goodley to provide consultative services for his next "blockbuster project," to be titled *Who's Crazy Now!* The show will place contestants in a series of progressively more intense series of stressful and embarrassing activities (i.e., involving public nudity, ingesting a variety of nontoxic but unpalatable items, close contact with unpleasant animals, and an assortment of competitive demeaning tasks).

Mr. Mogul wants Dr. Goodley to conduct a self-selected personality assessment, including interviews with each potential contestant, to determine their "sanity" and opine as to whether the candidates might pose a threat to themselves or others in the course of their participation on the show. Dr. Goodley will be allowed up to five hours to meet with all 16 of the potential contestants either as a group, individually, or in some combination. Executives at the major national network and multinational corporation sponsoring the program assure Dr. Goodley that all candidates will sign a waiver of liability that holds harmless any employee of, or professional connected with, the enterprise. The consultant is offered a fee of $2,500 per candidate for a total compensation $40,000.

Discussion Questions

What ethical challenges associated with this offer confront Dr. Goodley? How would you advise Dr. Goodley regarding this interesting well-compensated opportunity?

Discussants

The idea for this vignette was proposed by Dr. Lawrence Rubin, Associate Professor of Counselor Education and coordinator of the Mental Health Counseling Program at St. Thomas University in Miami. He teaches courses on legal and ethical issues in counseling and treats children and families in private practice. Laura S. Brown, PhD, is Professor of Psychology at the Washington School of Professional Psychology at Argosy University in Seattle. She has also maintained an independent practice of psychotherapy, consultation, and forensic evaluation since 1979. In 2000, she served as a consulting psychologist for a popular reality TV show. Andrew Sikula Sr., PhD, is Associate Dean within the Elizabeth McDowell Lewis College of Business at Marshall University, where he directs all of the graduate business academic programs. Lorraine P. Anderson, PhD, is Associate Dean within the Elizabeth McDowell Lewis College of Business at Marshall University, where she coordinates all undergraduate business academic programs. Walter M. Robinson, MD, MPH, is Assistant Professor of Pediatrics and Social Medicine at Harvard Medical School, where he is the Associate Director of the Division of Medical Ethics.

Reality Ethics: Psychology in the Center Ring

Lawrence C. Rubin, Ph.D.

"What an incredible career-altering opportunity this is," Dr. Goodley whispered to himself, making sure no one was within earshot. "This is what I've been waiting for!"

He was tired of the academic rat race, with its ceaseless social politics, and equally burdened with the ever-increasing financial and legal challenges of private practice. This could be his golden moment, the opportunity to expand his competencies into a fascinating new domain, to bring the benefit of his knowledge to the media marketplace—and, oh yes, to make more money in half a day than in half year. And where might this lead? "The new Dr. Phil," he mused, or perhaps "the name" producers thought of when considering a consultant for their new reality TV show. While his mind spun with the possibilities, he decided to think it through, albeit quickly—because, after all, time and Hollywood wait for no psychologist.

The show's producer had made it quite clear that a decision was needed within 24 hours, so that in the event Dr. Goodley declined the offer, another psychologist could be obtained. Feeling quite pressured, he nevertheless recalled the lessons of his graduate ethics instructor who reminded fledgling clinicians to "never react to a client's crisis as if it was one's own," because doing so was a sure way to make a mistake. Therefore, Dr. Goodley decided to quickly yet systematically review the issues before him. He would consider the general practice issues, followed by the primary and secondary ethical issues, or those directly affecting the consumer and general public, respectively.

Regarding general practice issues, Dr. Goodley had been following the fascinating controversy surrounding the burgeoning relationship between psychology and the media. He was keenly aware of both sides of the argument. He understood that the public image of psychology and psychologists had been tarnished by a number of circumstances. These included the inferior quality of information available to the public about the profession, trivialization and distortion of its research in the media, false generalization of that research in high-profile cases, and the blending of the profession with other groups in the public eye (Koocher & Keith-Spiegel, 1998). However, Dr. Goodley was also quite aware that colleagues has already entered the breach as advisors to network scriptwriters, talk show experts and news commentators, and yes, even as consultants to reality TV shows (Brown, personal communication, April 13, 2003). If he didn't grab the opportunity, surely someone else would.

Dr. Goodley also realized that many people view psychologists' involvement with the media as the selling and selling out of psychology. However, he was also quite cognizant of the fact that "psychology with its understanding of the human condition, and the media with its power to reach people" made the match a natural (Pita, 1999). Furthermore, he acknowledged that in an era of misunderstanding psychology, "to improve the credibility of the discipline of psychology, psychologists need[ed] to invest more time in popularizing its accomplishments" (Bertenthal, 2002). It seemed not so much a matter of whether psychologists (and, more specifically, he) should enter into the center ring but how to do so with credibility, care, and conscience. He turned his thoughts to the ethical issues.

"Sixteen contestants, psychological evaluations, danger to themselves or others, sanity . . ." he pondered. The very structure of his involvement seemed to defy the core aspirations set forth in the American Psychological Association's (2002) Ethical Principles and Code of Conduct. How could he competently and reasonably, not to mention quickly, perform such a seemingly unwise process such as this, all the while assuring beneficence and avoiding maleficence? After all, these were contestants on a high-risk, high-payoff reality TV show, not your everyday, conservative, run-of-the-mill folk who look before they leap! How could he structure his involvement so as to avoid harming these people, knowing full well that an accurate assessment, let alone one that sufficiently addressed these referral questions under these conditions, was not likely?

Rolling up his sleeves and laying out the new American Psychological Association ethics code, Dr. Goodley confidently announced, "I'll start with a highly articulated 'Informed and Voluntary Consent' addressing every possible contingency (ES: 3.01)."[1]

He had obtained a copy of the network's waiver of liability, which appeared to include and protect him. However, just to be safe, his document would be more specific to the risks and potential harm from such a limited evaluation as could be done in 20 minutes (the time he figured he would have with each contestant). "Get real, Goodley, these people might not be fully capable of giving consent. The promise of high media exposure and monetary payoff precluded that possibility!"

Dr. Goodley had seen one too many clinical colleague attempt cloaking incompetent, unethical and potentially illegal practice beneath mind-numbing consent forms, and although assessment was well within his clinical competencies (ES: 2.01), and he would certainly take extra precautions in constructing his assessment, this was one of those emerging areas where there was no standard or standardized set of questions or tasks that would adequately address the referral question. Even if he could quickly scour related research and whip up a reasonable protocol, could he possibly justify the far-reaching opinions sought by the network that would also be in accord with his ethical obligations as an evaluator (ES: 9.01)? He was most concerned that even though the ethical code addressed "media presentations" (ES: 5.04), reality TV was so new, and psychology's involvement in it so limited thus far, that prevailing standards would offer neither sufficient guidance nor direction. Beyond the seeming impossibility of constructing an adequate assessment protocol, he would essentially be on his own in interpreting its results, and that seemed too great a risk. Furthermore, should he decide to progress, would he mandate that contestants allow him to release the results of his so-called "evaluation" to the network? Were they and/or the network in any reasonable position to appreciate and use those results in accord with his, rather than their, standards (ES: 9.04)? Moving closer to a decision that might bring down the curtain on his quickly tarnishing golden opportunity, Dr. Goodley turned his attention to the "secondary ethical obligations," his responsibility to the broader consuming public.

Dr. Goodley was acquainted with literature that encouraged academic involvement in the media (Fox & Levin, 1993). His credibility as a consultant, and psychology's credibility in general, would certainly be enhanced by his academic background and research experience. Who better than an academic–clinician to construct, implement, and assess the efficacy of an evaluation protocol? However, he worried that because no standards existed for what he was being asked to do that reasonable steps could not quickly be taken to ensure a competent representation of his profession to the public (ES: 2.01). His name, credentials, and university affiliation in the television credits would be misleading, suggesting to the viewers something other than what he could reasonably be expected to provide. At best, his meager involvement would provide lip service to the general principles of "fidelity and responsibility," to society, and to the specific community of viewers of this and other reality TV shows. Even the related principle of integrity, which cautioned against "unwise or unclear commitments," seemed beyond the reach of his involvement on the project.

So, there it was: the answer that he intuitively knew before even undertaking this exercise. "Oh, well," he lamented, again out of earshot. "Nothing ventured, nothing gained."But this case, and considering the seemingly unavoidable risks his involvement posed to the contestants, himself, and the public, nothing ventured, nothing lost!

NOTES

1. ES refers to Ethical Standard from the 2002 Ethical Principles and Code of Conduct.

REFERENCES

American Psychological Association. (2002). Ethical principles of psychologists and code of conduct. *American Psychologist, 57,* 1060–1073.

Bertenthal, B. (2002). Challenges and opportunities in the psychological sciences. *American Psychologist, 57,* 215–221.

Fox, J. A., & Levin, J. (1993). *How to work with the media.* Newbury Park, CA: Sage.

Gardner, S., Briggs, P., & Herbert, H. (2002). The modern media—Avoiding pitfalls, advancing psychology. *The Psychologist, 15,* 342–345.

Koocher, G., & Keith-Spiegel, P. (1998). *Ethics in psychology: Professional standards and cases*. New York: Oxford University Press.

Pita, P. (1999). Familiar myths and the TV media: History, impact and new direction. In L. L. Schwartz (Ed.), *Psychology and the media, a second look* (pp. 25–27). Washington, DC: American Psychological Association.

Not That Crazy

Laura S. Brown

The universe of reality television is a fascinating, sometimes bizarre place. Because many reality shows, including *Survivor, Big Brother,* and *The Amazing Race,* already use psychologists to assist in the screening of contestants, psychologists, including me, have now had 3 years in which to develop consensual norms for practice in this new venue. All of us who have worked in this realm have, and continue to face, ethical challenges, some of which are currently in front of Dr. Goodley.

Mr. Mogul the producer is pennywise and pound foolish, despite his willingness to pay Dr. Goodley large sums of money for her work. He knows that the reason he must hire a psychologist to screen his contestants is that the network on which his show will air (and presumably make megadollars for all concerned) has required him to do so as a means of reducing its liability. Although it's easy for psychologists working in reality TV to delude themselves that they are there to protect the welfare of contestants, in fact their presence is solely for the protection of their clients, who happen to be Mr. Mogul and the network. Well-screened contestants are less dangerous to these clients than are those whose occult psychopathologies charm and beguile the casting staff who have made the decisions about who goes on air.

Mr. Mogul believes, erroneously, that it will be possible for Dr. Goodley to discharge her duties to him within the allotted 5 hours. Even though Mr. Mogul is willing to pay Dr. Goodley a rather extravagant sum to perform this "evaluation lite," he is understandably failing to understand how his parameters have undermined his own interests. Mr. Mogul is willing to spend the money; he simply doesn't know that he must also spend the time.

It is entirely in Mr. Mogul's interest not to be sued by a contestant for emotional distress damages. All liability waivers aside, anyone can sue anyone. Although the contestants are volunteers and presumably have received semi-adequate informed consent to their participation in the risks of the show, without a thorough and careful psychological evaluation of each contestant the risks mount that someone who is unstable, fragile, or has a paranoid style may get on the show, become angry at Mr. Mogul and his crew, and file a lawsuit. Dr. Goodley cannot guarantee that this will not happen, but if she insists on doing her work correctly she can certainly reduce the risks of this unwanted outcome.

The important first step in resolving the ethical dilemma for Dr. Goodley is for her to ask herself whether doing 5 hours of evaluation with 16 people is in her client's best interest. Welfare of the client is a paramount ethical responsibility for all psychologists. I suggest that the unequivocal answer to this question, translated into Hollywoodese, would be "No way!" When screening contestants for a reality show, I and a colleague required all participants to take four psychological tests which, even when administered in supervised groups, required on average 3.5 hours and then to complete individual hour-long interviews.

If we had only given tests, we would have been in the position of making blind interpretations. Even with more than 20 years and thousands of Minnesota Multiphasic Personality Inventories' (MMPI) worth of experience, no blind interpretation is as good as one informed by a face-to-face interview with the test taker. In at least three cases that I can recall, the additional information gathered from the structured in-person interview made the difference between allowing someone to move forward as a contestant and identifying him or her as potentially at risk to themselves; other contestants; or our client, the producer.

Next, Dr. Goodley can ask herself whether she would agree to render substandard care under any circumstances. After all, she might reason, these are adults, and it is only TV, not a social psychology experiment. The answer should, of course, be "no." The rationale that "some evaluation is better than no evaluation" is seductive. An evaluator's ego might be inflated somewhat by the notion that, MMPI—2 results in hand, she can assess anyone in 18 minutes (allowing for 1.5-minute breaks between interviews). In this instance, the pressure of time, the knowledge that one is being extremely well compensated, and the hope that one might be asked back for another round of well-paid work will all be competing with Dr. Goodley for quality of work product. Quality is unlikely to win. No one should be able to pay a psychologist enough to agree to do substandard work.

Dr. Goodley must inform Mr. Mogul of the risks to him inherent in agreeing to accept the task within the current parameters, and she should tell him that she will not agree to the task under those circumstances. If Mr. Mogul, thus informed, realizes that he must offer Dr. Goodley complete autonomy in structuring the interview process, and the two can come to some sort of agreement that respects both the ethics of assessment and Mr. Mogul's needs to get the show on the road, then Dr. Goodley should have no qualms about proceeding.

Many psychologists find reality TV demeaning, exploitative, and not worth watching. However, to those who clamor to become contestants, reality TV is their avenue for attaining the clichéd 15 minutes of fame. On-screen time in reality shows counts toward the minutes necessary to obtain one's membership in the Screen Actor's Guild or the American Federation of Television and Radio Actors; assisting someone to become a reality TV contestant may be empowering them to realize a life's dream of working in Hollywood.

Thus, although many psychologists might find the entire idea of reality TV ethically problematic, I would urge those colleagues to look carefully at their own biases. Ethical, competent psychologists have much to offer to the world of reality TV. My colleague Richard Levak, who is the senior psychological evaluator for all of the most successful network reality shows, has educated producers to take psychological assessment very seriously while developing a rich database of information about test profiles of reality show contestants. As a psychologist who worked for a reality show I was able, with my skills at assessment, to protect some contestants from a show that might have harmed them and my producer clients from some contestants who might have undermined their work or sued them after the show ended. As the psychologist on site during production, I was daily faced with challenges that are familiar to industrial–organizational and consulting psychologists about to whom I owed a duty of care, particularly when individual contestants found themselves struggling with depression or anxiety in the wake of certain on-set experiences. I had to deal with issues of boundaries as I shared living space with contestants and production staff in close quarters for many weeks. Participating in the show per se was not the ethical dilemma.

In summary, who's crazy now? Not Dr. Goodley if she just says no to substandard practice. And not Dr. Goodley if she agrees to do the evaluation with parameters set by her. I wish her well.

Sane Enough to Play Along, Crazy Enough to Make You Watch

Walter M. Robinson

I address two questions brought up by this case: first, what is the social (and psychological) meaning of the "reality show" in which Dr. Goodley is asked to participate as a psychologist? Second, what exactly is Dr. Goodley being asked to do in her capacity as a psychologist?

Naturalism is hardly a new device in television contest shows. The premise of many game shows is that ordinary people are called on to demonstrate their knowledge and be rewarded for it but also potentially be exposed as ignorant. Embarrassment, or at least the potential for it, is part of the show, but until recently the embarrassment was fairly gentle. On many shows, part of the enjoyment was the discordance between the ordinariness of the contestants and the sophisticated wit of the host: Groucho Marx's ribbing of contestants depended on an assumption of a sophistication shared only between the host and the audience. Many of the good-natured smiles hardened into smirks as game shows evolved from gentle embarrassment to a kind of social humiliation, with wit replaced by the winking, giggling use of crude sexual double entendres; *The Match Game* and *The Newlywed Game* are good early examples of this evolution. The anlage of the current reality shows was *Candid Camera*, in which unsuspecting people were placed in confusing or disorienting situations. On *Candid Camera* there were usually overt attempts to embarrass those who were being filmed, although the host of the show always seemed to intervene and reveal the gag if the embarrassment became too acute.

In contrast, on the currently fashionable crop of reality shows the attempt to humiliate is often crude, intentional, and as imaginative as a sixth-grade playground: How much money will it take to get you to eat that? What is unique about some of these shows are the openness and clarity in which they trade in the humiliation of the participants; it is not a by-product of the contest, it is the contest. The contestant must be debased in order to win, because winning is defined as being willing to obey unreasonable and humiliating orders; losing, on the other hand, is constructed as refusal to obey. And the humiliation of the immediate act—eating the cow genitalia for money, or betraying your girlfriend with a prostitute—is simply the first step in the game: The real humiliation occurs months after the animal parts are swallowed, when the scene is replayed in front of 50 million television viewers. It is not enough that you could be made to do anything for money; the whole world has to know about it. But is the intentional humiliation of others an inappropriate subject for entertainment?

Consider the scene in Bartolucci's *The Last Emperor*, in which the child emperor forces his gentle eunuch teacher to drink ink in order to demonstrate to a playmate that the child is indeed the ruler of the world. The tension of the scene is not whether the servant will drink the ink, because we know he has little choice, but whether the child will push his cruelty so far simply in order to lord his power over his playmate (who happens to be his brother). The scene is excruciating to watch. Few viewers will recall it as entertaining: The kind caretaker is reminded of his inescapable debasement, while the cruelty of the child is given free rein.

Contrast this scene to the nightly television offerings of contestants required to sit in pits of rotten meat in order to win money and celebrity. At face value, the tension of the scene is whether the contestant will do what is utterly unreasonable in order to win money. The contestant is pressured from all sides to perform: egged on by the constant reminders of money to be won, coached with fake solidarity by the celebrity "host" of the show, sometimes hounded by the shouts and jeers of a live audience rivaling that in the professional wrestling arenas, and scrutinized by the close-up intrusion of cameras attached to the contestant's body. At face value, these scenes are played to show how "real" people might react to "real" situations.

Yet the reality of reality shows is that the producers are far more like the child emperor than they wish us to see; on these shows, the producers stage contests of "endurance" in order to measure their own power. Despite their moniker, these shows are only marginally a presentation of reality. Instead, the shows are tightly controlled and, if not formally scripted, then edited so that the broadcast product contains events the producers deem likely to increase the percentage of the television audience watching the show. Rather than a demonstration of the fortitude of the contestant, these shows are better seen as a contest among the producers to devise low-cost programs that bring in the largest audience share and thus the largest advertising revenue. The fortitude of the contestant is not the point: The point is to generate greater revenues by attracting greater audiences. That the contestants, like the eunuch, are debased is the means by which the producers demonstrate their power.

The producers will argue that they are giving the public what the public wishes to see and that the contestants, all adults, have freely agreed to participate. Neither fact immunizes the producers from responsibility. That these shows are popular is no excuse at all—in previous eras, public torture was popular, but its morality was never a function of its ratings. That the contestant agrees to participate is a weak excuse for creating a public spectacle of humiliation. It may well be that there are aspects of these shows that are less pernicious; they do, after all, celebrate a kind of mastery over the body and over fear; we might see them, as some contestants apparently do, as exaggerated displays of bravery or even simply as demonstrations of the ability to cope with a challenging situation. But I think that to laud the contestants for their ability to withstand debasement is to recall the stoic Chinese eunuch, whose forbearance one may value but whose plight is nonetheless tragic. To stage entertaining debasement and then justify it by lauding the fortitude of the debased is perverse; to lure people into the debasement for money is simple exploitation, whether they agree to do it or not. In my view, shows of the type described in the *Who's Crazy Now?* Vignette are not simple extensions of the game show format but are instead unsavory productions that traffic in the humiliation of some for the benefit of powerful commercial interests. They bring to mind the Stanford prison experiments or the Milgram experiments, except in this case the tests of how far someone will go in the face of authority are staged as public spectacles for profit.

What exactly is it that Dr. Goodley being asked to do in her role as a psychologist for *Who's Crazy Now?* We are told that she is to "conduct a self-selected personality assessment, including interviews with each potential contestant, in order to determine their 'sanity' and opine as to whether the candidates might pose a threat to themselves or others in the course of their participation on the show."

First, it should be clear here that Mr. Mogul, not the contestants, is Dr. Goodley's client; Dr. Goodley has a clear obligation to tell the contestants this and make sure they understand it. Second, any competent psychologist should recognize that assessment of "sanity" and dangerousness is a loaded project under the best of circumstances. Given the time constraints of the vignette, Dr. Goodley will have less than 30 minutes with each potential contestant: Is it plausible that she will be able to predict any given contestant's reaction to a set of novel situations? Any such prediction would be unreliable, and a competent psychologist should recognize its unreliability. Third, one has to ask whether Dr. Goodley should take the job description at face value. Given the concerns about the accuracy of any prediction of dangerousness under these circumstances,

Dr. Goodley should strongly consider whether Mr. Mogul is hiring her for another purpose.

I can think of two other possible reasons for Mr. Mogul to hire a psychologist, the first pedestrian and the second more fanciful. The pedestrian reason is to obtain a clumsy form of risk management. Mr. Mogul may want the "cover" generated by the professional assessment if something goes wrong during the show or later, when the show is aired. When something goes wrong, Mr. Mogul wants to point to Dr. Goodley, and say "But the psychologist cleared these folks!" Dr. Goodley should be suspicious when Mr. Mogul outlines the waiver form to her, and she should be wary of the efficacy of such a waiver. It might protect her from legal consequences, but will it protect her from ethical review by her professional organization or the state licensing board? If Dr. Goodley agrees to perform services that she knows no competent psychologist could reliably perform, she sets herself up for such a review.

Allow me to spin out a second, and admittedly more fanciful, reason Mr. Mogul might want a psychological evaluation: He is less interested in weeding out those who might be harmed by participation than in identifying participants whose psychological makeup will allow them to act in the right sort of way for the camera. The producers want contestants who will obey orders, do anything for attention, and play up the tension and competition but ultimately capitulate by eating the bull testicles. What the producers do not want is a contestant who sees the producer as the author of the humiliation. Mr. Mogul might want explicitly to weed out anyone like the Arnold Schwarzenegger character in *The Running Man*, who recognized his real enemy in the deadly game show not as the other contestants but as the show's host/producer; Arnold's return to exact his vengeance for exploitation is likely the stuff of Mr. Mogul's nightmares.

Dr. Goodley is certainly not being asked to help choose ordinary people in order to gauge the ordinary person's reaction to the stresses dreamed up by the producers. The contestants on these shows are far from ordinary: they are almost always young, slender, employed, and portrayed as highly sexual. Real "ordinary people" are tall, short, fat, thin; they may have big noses or bad haircuts; they may or may not think about sex 24 hours a day. But television has trouble depicting ordinary people and so presents only fabricated and extreme caricatures—either they are the uneducated, incestuous, inarticulate trailer-inhabiting loudmouths of Jerry Springer' talk show or they are the college-educated, slender, sexualized, tan models of *Fear Factor*. In both instances, viewers are treated to the spectacle of ritualized humiliation: The slender and handsome are lowered into pits of vipers, and the overweight and toothless are told that their partners are transsexuals. That the humiliation is completely staged is evident in both cases: The producers seek individuals who can convincingly depict the caricatures. Perhaps Dr. Goodley's work will be used to screen for participants who will behave in these caricaturized and presumably entertaining ways, and this may be quite different from screening for overall mental health or "sanity."

So, given my reading of the psychological and social meaning of *Who's Crazy Now?*, and my concerns that the work risks crossing important ethical and professional boundaries, should Dr. Goodley take this consulting job? She'd have to be crazy!

"Unreality TV"

Andrew Sikula, Sr. and Lorraine P. Anderson

"Reality TV"—never has an oxymoron been so contradictory. Never have two words joined together been so incompatible and undescriptive of the real world. In fact, most reality TV programming is just about as far from reality as we can get. In truth, reality TV as today presented is actually fantasy viewing and, unfortunately, usually fantasy of the worst kind.

We have always known that television shows were not real life, but we watched them nonetheless, granting license and latitude under the rationale of entertainment. For awhile, some of this entertainment was healthy and wholesome—but often, not anymore. Using the U.S. Constitution and the First Amendment respectively as a shield and sword, entertainment executives have subjected American and worldwide audiences to an almost unbelievable array of filth, horror, and sometimes near-pornography. It seems as if each new show tries to outdo its viewing competition and predecessor, stooping to newer and ever downward-spiraling lows in decency, taste, and morality. Trying to achieve shock value, nothing is too gross or gruesome to bring into the family home over TV airways. Degenerate studio producers ridiculously defend their right to offend us by stating that we can always turn the TV off or on to another channel, knowing full well that working parents can not constantly control the TV viewing practices of latchkey children or unsupervised teenagers.

Extremely disappointing are the various company advertisers who sponsor these morbid monitors. There was a time when corporate sponsors carefully selected television programs that were associated with their products and services. Sadly, today market share, prime time, Nielsen ratings, and economic factors dominate TV marketing and advertising decisions.

However, the biggest disappointment of all is the size of the viewing audiences for unreality TV. Cultural values, societal norms, and personal morality have become so low that we today find huge numbers of viewing fans for shows that feature human beings at their worst. The basic depravity and original sinful nature of humankind are evidenced in the popularity of trash TV. Dishonesty, cheating, lying, and lust are constant themes throughout shows like *Jerry Springer, Anna Nicole, Fear Factor, Joe Millionaire, Survivor, Big Brother, The Bachelorette, The Real World,* and *Worst Case Scenario*. And believe it or not, to add insult to injury, and to demonstrate just how ridiculous Hollywood has become, and how gullible the public today is, Fox television network producers have just concluded a short-run new reality TV series called *Mr. Personality*, which featured masked suitors hosted by none other than the internationally known immoralist icon Monica Lewinsky!

Regarding the case in point and the tentative programming of *Who's Crazy Now?*, this proposed new show is just more of the same. Putting people in embarrassing activities involving public nudity, eating worms or whatever, and other demeaning behavior violates the basic values and ethics of human respect and dignity. Regardless of the economic incentives involved, it is time for us to put a stop to such madness individually and collectively. Courts need to curb individual First Amendment rights when they offend the majority and hurt society and culture as a whole.

The commercial challenge today is for business to produce goods and services—including mass media print, books, records, CDs, DVDs, films, and television programs—that are inspiring, not degrading. We need to build people and societies up, not tear them down. Reality TV needs to get real. If it insists on dealing with fantasy rather than truth, the fantasies ought to be constructive and godly, not destructive and devilish in nature, purpose, content, and result. So-called "reality TV" needs to be reborn or regenerated in the future so that the human condition and spirit can be enlightened and uplifted rather than being continually debased and destroyed, which is the current state of affairs.

In regard to the specific dilemma presented in this case vignette, Dr. Goodley is confronted with a situation that all leaders and most businesspeople find themselves in at one time or another: whether to act in a manner that is completely legal, but morally wrong. On the one hand, Dr. Goodley can assuage his fears with the knowledge that he is merely responding to what the public wants. Throughout history, mankind has developed grotesque forms of entertainment. In the days of Caesar, gladiator fights to the death filled the coliseum amid the cheers of the audience. Dogfights, cockfights, and lewd exotic dancing are also types of entertainment that appeal to the base side of man. In addition, Dr. Goodley can tell himself that reality TV is legal. The participants are not coerced or forced to be on the shows. Moreover, reality TV has gained such popularity that discussions are underway for the creation of a reality TV network. Finally, Dr. Goodley likely believes in the free enterprise system and feels it would be his good fortune to be chosen to participate as a consultant for $40,000. Yet, the case is not as simple as it may seem.

One would presume that Dr. Goodley pursued a career in psychology because of his desire to help people who wrestle with mental health issues. How can he be part of an effort that he knows holds the strong likelihood of causing mental duress to the participants? Even worse, what happens if Dr. Goodley fails to see the potential for violence in a participant prior to the show and that person does bodily harm to him- or herself or to others? When stressed to their maximum limits, people do things they would never do under normal circumstances. Talk show participants have sometimes committed felonies based upon the embarrassing position they find themselves in following the show and the true confessions revealed on camera. The absurd scenarios played out on reality TV are far from normal circumstances. Dr. Goodley should take heed and listen to his conscious. He needs to now pass up this alleged consulting opportunity of a lifetime so he can look and face himself squarely in the mirror in the future.

Some reality TV shows do not cross the bounds of human decency. Shows such as *American Idol, The Amazing Race*, and *Trading Spaces* have amassed huge audiences because of good programming. During the *American Idol* season the public has seen regular people transformed into music industry celebrities. Each week, we watch them struggle, and we cheered as we see them hit the difficult notes and songs. A recent episode resulted in more than 24 million viewer votes being cast for the show's top two performers to determine who would win the title of American Idol. Admittedly, halfway through the season, there was a scandal: A contestant was kicked off the show for failing to report an arrest. There were also moments of embarrassment for those who couldn't carry a tune, but the show was not centered on depravity and what happens to people in the worst situations. American Idol rejoices in the success of regular people. Other reality shows should look to these examples as models of how to succeed without losing one's moral compass.

Activity 1: Selecting Details

- If you planned to use the four responses to Dr. Goodley's dilemma as your sources, which details would you want to include in your exploratory essay?
- As you read the responses, which claims were you inclined to agree or disagree with?
- How does each author make a unique contribution to the question?
- Which of the passages stood out to you on the first reading because of their clarity or difficulty?
- Which passages would you plan to incorporate into your own essay as quotations, paraphrases, or summaries?

AS YOU WRITE:

✓ Tell the story of your research project by hosting your sources.

✓ Choose how to organize your exploration: through chronology, theme, or position.

✓ Use each source purposefully.

✓ Describe your research process to invite readers into the conversation.

FIELD RESEARCH

If you have ever been the subject of a telephone survey, filled out a customer satisfaction form that came with a product you bought, or kept a viewing log for a media study, you have been involved in *field research*. Field research includes any activity, investigation, or study that takes you from text-based investigations and into the "field," into close contact with the objects and subjects of your research. Here, we explore some of the ways that you might incorporate field research into your writing projects. In many academic disciplines, strong research writing requires some field work conducted according to shared standards and conventions. For example:

- Psychoanalysts use case studies to explore theories about the human mind and develop new treatments for their patients.
- Anthropologists study cultural rituals—such as eating practices, religious ceremonies, and treatments of death and dying—through close observation.
- Archaeologists study the lives of earlier people—such as ancient Persians or migrant workers in 1930s California—by exploring the places they once lived, and the artifacts and records they left behind.
- Sociologists develop surveys, questionnaires, and observation techniques to study group behavior.

Based on your reading, is field research important to the academic conversation you plan to enter? How might you participate in the conversation through performing your own field research?

You may have already done some preliminary field work in developing your research question and research plan:

- Did you visit a professor to learn about issues important to scholars in the discipline?
- Did you contact someone working in a profession that interests you to find a topic for your research project?
- Did you ask your friends, family members, and roommates for help in finding a research issue, or developing a particular question?
- Did your observations around campus lead you to a research project or area of interest?

Results of your field research have to be collected and analyzed. Whenever you plan to conduct interviews, administer surveys or questionnaires, or perform observational research, you must ensure that you budget enough time for processing your data and effectively weaving it into your essay.

Also, if you plan to conduct any kind of field research, and especially if you plan to conduct research on fellow students, shoppers at the local mall, or other "human subjects," ask your instructor to help you find out about the *human subject protocols* on your campus. Depending on the kind of study you plan, you may need to ask the permission of people you observe, or even have them (or their guardians in the case of minors) sign consent forms. The field research you conduct for papers in this course isn't likely to cross legal or ethical boundaries, but it's good to be sure.

Now that you have a sense of the academic conversation surrounding your research topic, consider doing some field research to supplement your work with academic texts. Think about the following ways you might make practical, "real-world" contributions to the conversation.

Interviews and Personal Correspondence

Interviews and correspondence with experts on a subject can help you discover unexplored aspects of a research question, or understand practical applications to issues discussed in your sources.

For example, after reading fiction by Peter Bacho, a student became interested in experiences of Filipino migrant workers during the 1940s and 1950s. The student began his investigation by researching the similarities and differences between Filipino immigrants and white homesteaders in the American West. Feeling unsatisfied with information found in the campus library, the student eventually contacted Bacho, who engaged him in a conversation that evolved over a number of email exchanges. As you can imagine, the student not only learned a lot about Filipino-American experiences from the author (himself the child of migrant workers), but, more importantly, gained a sense of personal satisfaction from pursuing a question in ways that were not possible through textual research alone.

Here are some ways to incorporate interviews or correspondence into your research:

- **Contact an author you have read for help in further understanding aspects of his or her work.** Are you interested in learning more about the personal or professional motivations behind a certain book or article? Many of your sources, scholarly articles especially, will note the author's institutional affiliation (a university, organization, or agency where he or she works), and sometimes even include an e-mail address.
- **Speak with a professor on campus who works in your research field.** Might he or she be able to provide you with examples to

understand difficult concepts, or help you draw connections between two or more issues in the field? Is he or she personally involved in the discipline's newest innovations? You might begin your search on the website of a campus department and find professors whose areas of specialization are close to your interests.

- **Find a business professional in your area who can help you understand practical or commercial aspects of your research project.** How can you extend academic issues into the business or professional world? For example, can a local doctor help you understand the practical impact of a medical issue you've read about, or could a bank manager help you see an economic theory at work in the community?

An interview can enliven your work on just about any research topic. Imagine that you are researching the impact of "English-only" instruction on elementary students. With a bit of searching in the campus directory or on the department website, you could find a professor in your school's education program who can describe his or her experiences in teaching English Language Learning (ELL) students. If the professor has taught for a decade or more, he or she has probably seen a variety of teaching strategies come and go. Given the professor's practical experience, are strategies becoming increasingly effective? How have English-only policies affected teachers? Do teachers in the classroom feel their experiences are being incorporated or ignored by researchers?

Field work can enliven your textual research.

If your subjects are willing to speak with you or respond to your e-mails, assume that they are happy to help you with your research. Nonetheless, you must keep the value of their time in mind: Arrive on time and be prepared for an interview with questions that clearly relate to your subject's expertise and the ways he or she can be of particular help to your project. Avoid going too far afield of your stated purpose for the interview, unless the subject invites such departures. As you prepare, plan for discussions that could go in either very structured or very loose ways, and have both specific and open-ended questions written down when you go into the interview.

Surveys and Questionnaires

Your reading may spark questions or ideas that you wish to test on a nearby population. For example, the writer who interviews one professor of education on approaches to ELL students may develop questions to explore through further field research, including:

- Is the professor's view shared by all, some, or none of her colleagues? The student could interview other professors in the department, or education professors at another university, and compare responses.
- Are classroom practices ahead of, in line with, or behind, the recommendations of scholars in the field? The student could compare practices described by the professor with classroom observations or surveys of local teachers.

Objectivity of the Study and Significance of the Findings

Once you come up with an idea for a survey, you have to maintain objectivity in formulating and asking questions. Avoid asking questions that presume a "right" answer or that otherwise unfairly pressure participants. For example, compare the following two versions of a question about campus alcohol policies:

Version 1

Do you think the absurd policies regarding alcohol consumption on campus are fair or not?

Version 2

Do you believe campus alcohol policies are fair or unfair, or do you have no opinion?

The first question assumes a right answer—if the policies are irrational, then they must be unfair—while the second version of the question is more neutral, and lets respondents answer without undue pressure. Even if the writer believes the policies are unfair, the survey should not presuppose or unfairly guide respondents to that conclusion.

You should also be careful about estimating the significance of the data you collect, including:

- Are you surveying an appropriate group for the question you're researching?
- Are you surveying enough people so that you can fairly apply the data to a larger population?

Make Appropriate Survey Limitations

Field researchers must ensure the relevance of their results. One of the ways they do this is by using a sample population that accurately reflects the purpose of the study. Field researchers carefully consider what kinds of background—or *sample*—information they have to collect as they gather responses to survey questions. They consider ways that personal characteristics, such as age, gender, year in school, profession, and marital status, will help them to understand the people responding to their questions, or to draw certain correlations between their responses.

As you prepare surveys and questionnaires, you need to think similarly about finding an appropriate, relevant population for your research. You should also think about the kinds of responses that will help you the most. Do you want to limit your subjects to yes/no answers, or to choosing from a multiple-choice set of answers; or, do you want to ask open-ended questions that allow for more latitude in written or oral responses?

A writer who wants to investigate classmates' feelings about campus alcohol policies might pose the question in different ways to receive different kinds of responses:

Do you believe campus alcohol policies are fair or unfair, or do you have no opinion?

Please rate campus alcohol policies according to their fairness: 1) very fair; 2) somewhat fair; 3) somewhat unfair; 4) very unfair, or 5) you don't know.

How would you describe campus alcohol policies?

The first version is the most restrictive, since it limits respondents to two opinions; the second, which is organized on a "Likert scale," allows for more variety, but still limits possible answers; the third allows for the widest range of answers because it doesn't even presume that respondents will describe policies in terms of fairness/unfairness.

Observational Research

Sometimes less obtrusive methods of field research are desirable. Direct observation of behavior provides researchers with valuable first-person experiences and data they can add to their work.

For example, researchers at the Southern Poverty Law Center observed the differences in ways white and African American consumers were treated in department stores. The researchers wanted to understand preferential treatment based on ethnic difference, but they knew that bias can be practiced and even experienced unconsciously. Researchers also knew that perpetrators and victims of racism wouldn't be good questionnaire or survey subjects because they might be reluctant to share experiences with socially unacceptable behavior. The researchers chose one location in the store (a jewelry counter) and observed each customer's treatment by employees to build a database of interactions that they could later organize and analyze according to ethnicity.

Opportunities for Observation and Analysis

Direct observation of people and places can often yield more valuable information than interviewing or surveying alone. Imagine, for instance, that you are interested in comparing Americans' concerns about soda and snack vending machines in junior high or middle schools with students' actual behaviors. You could survey students on their snacking habits, but they may be unable to objectively assess their own habits or inclined, for various reasons, to misrepresent them. In this case, your observations of a central vending area (or, with the assistance of colleagues, all of the vending machines on a campus) will produce information that you can use on its own, or perhaps in combination with self-assessments by students.

A different kind of observation could be a comparative study of business practices within a certain market. If you live in a college town, or if your campus is surrounded by a business district that caters to students, spend time at each coffee shop, bar, or nightclub in the district in order to understand how businesses of the same kind use different strategies to appeal to potential consumers. Use the following questions to organize your observations:

- What kind of décor does the business use? Does it adopt a specific sport, art, or cultural atmosphere?
- Do the employees appear to fit a certain type? Are they roughly the same age? Do they wear uniforms? Do they speak more than one language?
- Does the business cater to specialties—such as drinks, food, or music—that would increase the likelihood of drawing a particular kind of customer (international students, country music lovers, chess players, and so on)?

Your comparisons would provide real world examples for applying business or marketing theories, or even for understanding sociological theories of group formation.

Consider the Impact of an Observer's Presence

As you conduct observational research, be aware of the ways that your presence might affect the situation that you're observing. As in the development of surveys and questionnaires, you have to be conscious of the ways your own preconceptions or biases can influence your results and interpretation of data.

EXPLORATORY RESEARCH ESSAY

FORMAL PEER REVIEW

Exploratory Writing Project goals: Incorporate strategies from earlier writing projects to 1) identify and develop a researchable, problematic subject or question; 2) acknowledge multiple points of view, theories, positions, and counterarguments through scholarly research; 3) present a first-person narrative of the research process; 4) use quotations, paraphrases, and summaries with attributive tags and in-text citations, and prepare a bibliography or works cited page. If you have time, discuss comments with your partner to clear up any questions she or he has.

1. Do you feel that the writer did an adequate job of researching his or her question? Are the author's opinions, claims, and discoveries supported with specific evidence from his or her sources? Do you think the sources are sufficiently "academic" in nature? If so, what features demonstrate the quality of the writer's research? If additional work needs to be done, ask the writer some questions that will direct him/her on a return trip to the library before the paper is due.

2. Which organizational structure did the writer use? Is the essay organized chronologically, thematically, or otherwise? Describe your reaction to the paper's organization. Which "moves" were effective? Which ones didn't fit? Give the writer some concrete suggestions for improving the paper's organization.

3. Does the writer use source material (in the form of quotations, paraphrases, and summaries) to describe and illustrate multiple positions on or responses to the research question? Are there strong transitions between sources or themes? Does the paper rely too much on sources and lack development by the writer (specifically, does the writer over-quote)? What additional work needs to be done, either in explaining and developing sources, or in developing transitions? Make suggestions.

4. Does the writer effectively evaluate evidence from sources? Assist the writer in developing his/her research role. How can s/he better mediate between positions presented in the research? How can the writer enter into the academic conversation more effectively?

5. Are sources adequately cited in the text with parenthetical references? Do you have everything you need (such as page number, author, and title of work) to track down the source in the Works Cited page?

6. Identify "free-standing" quotations. Help the writer introduce, contextualize, and/or modify the quotations in his/her own words (see various examples in Chapter 6).

7. Are all the sources used in the paper—whether quoted, paraphrased, or summarized—entered completely and correctly in the Works Cited section (see Chapter 7)?

FIGURE 11.1 Exploratory research essay: Formal peer review. (*continued*)

8. Help the writer identify mechanical problems that have to be fixed before submission. Consider sentence-level problems: fragments, run-ons, or awkward syntax or phrasing; word-level problems: misspellings, missing words, or misuse of words; and problems with in-text citations, bibliographic style, or overall formatting.

FIGURE 11.1   Exploratory research essay: Formal peer review. (*continued*)

WRITING SAMPLES

Andrea wrote her exploratory essay in preparation for the formal research project described in Chapter 12. The exploratory essay was a chance for her to bring together her first set of research materials and test some ways she might expand the original focus of her study. As you read, think about Andrea's approach to organizing her sources:

See "Embed the Thesis Statement in Purpose and Genre" in Chapter 12.

- How does she link sources together and use them as possible jumping-off points for further research?
- What kinds of sources must she find to complete her research?
- What purpose do you believe she will choose when she develops a thesis for the formal research project?

Andrea M.
Professor Gutiérrez
College Writing
19 November 2008

Youth Involvement in Community Development

I have always wanted to join the Peace Corps, and in researching different opportunities I could pursue, youth development and mentoring really piqued my interest. My initial research into mentoring programs seemed promising, but I quickly ran into a dead end and had to re-evaluate the goal of my research. I went back to my Peace Corps material and noticed an interesting connection that had slipped past me before. Youth development and community development, two issues that had at first seemed completely separate suddenly clicked together in my mind. I began to look for material and found a few articles right away that were exactly what I was hoping for. Although I started off by researching mentoring programs, I found several articles with lots of good information that led me to develop my interest in both young people and the communities they live in, and to explore the mutual benefits of combining youth development and community building.

The first article I encountered, "The Meshing of Youth Development and Community Building" by Joel Nitzberg of Cambridge College, was a good starting place for my research because it explains the theory behind bringing community building and youth development together. Nitzberg first describes youth development as "the ongoing growth process whereby youth engage in meeting their own basic personal and social needs" (7), and then explains that "community building strengthens the capacity of neighborhood residents, associations, and organizations to work individually and collectively to foster and sustain positive neighborhood change" (8). Each concept helps Nitzberg to look at four examples of different practices for community building by various organizations, and to develop five goals that connect youth development and community building together. By giving youth a sense of belonging to the community, responding to youths' needs, developing useful skills for the present and future, creating good opportunities for youth involvement, and community protection of youth, Nitzberg demonstrates the key ways of incorporating young people into community development. He expresses his desire to help youth grow into mature adults with all of the necessary skills to be successful adults and with the ability and desire to help the community in which they reside.

Nitzberg's opinion is apparent from the very first paragraph of his article. It becomes clear very quickly that, in his view, young people need to be at the center of community development. Though I don't know that I completely agree with him, from the perspective of helping the youth, involvement in the community is one way to make a huge difference in building skills that will be able to help them grow in all aspects of their lives. I do not see any problems with his proposed goals and I think that it could be very useful when implemented into a real program.

I then looked for a case study of a program integrating youth involvement and community development, and "Young People and Social Action: Youth Participation in the United Kingdom and United States" was the perfect find. Starting with the United Nations Convention on the Rights of the Child, stating that children have the right "to be represented and participate in decisions affecting their lives" (81), Joan Arches from the University of Massachusetts and Jennie Fleming, the director of the Centre for Social Action at De Montfort University in Leicester, UK, described two examples of integrated programs in action. The first study followed a youth project in the United Kingdom which involved fifty young people, ages eight to fifteen, who lived in a low-income community. The project workers led the young people through a four-part process, to describe life as they knew it, to figure out problems they recognized, to list specific things to change within their community, and to present their ideas to peers in their community. The purpose of this project was to involve youth in helping decide where money should go in a new government program called New Deal for Communities. Although there were many reports of youth describing how participation in the project changed them for the better, there was no mention as to whether or not any of the young people's ideas were actually implemented; however, Archers and Fleming report that the New Deal program did not involve young people after they presented their findings. This seems like a huge blind spot, as half of the purpose of combining youth and community development is actual community development. The youth seemed to have benefited from this project, but did the community? And, if the young people do not see any effects of their input, what happens to their sense of accomplishment? It is not promising to me that although a great deal of effort went into involving youth in a program that would hopefully lead to government-sponsored change in the community, there was no follow-up beyond how the youth liked the program and how it seemed to change them for the better. This study showed that the youth involvement program was off to a good start, but was still severely lacking in solid results, whether positive or negative.

The second study in "Young People and Social Action" describes a low-income community in Boston, Massachusetts. Here, young people, ages nine to seventeen, participated in a three-year project directed by the Healthy Initiative Collaborative: Community University Partnership (HIC CUP), which had the same basic idea as that in the United Kingdom but with a few critical adjustments. Participants first described life in their community, identified problems, talked to peers, and then took action. In this case, they focused on working for the creation of a basketball court. They got signatures for a petition, raised money from the community, got publicity for their cause, and even created a logo for their group. Together, these community activities put all of what they were learning to direct and immediate use so that participants learned through action.

However, just like the first project, this one presented its own shortcomings for Archer's and Fleming's analysis. As Archer and Fleming admit, "[n]either of these case studies depicts an unbridled success" (89). The second study was left incomplete not because it was abandoned, but because it is still in the process of being implemented. Even so, I see this case as a success because it is an ongoing example of youth participation in social action (or at least ongoing when the article was written in 2006); these young people seemed optimistic about skills they learned through the experience and participants were all generally happy with what they had accomplished and were glad to have been part of the program. The key difference between these two studies is that, unlike the United Kingdom study, the Massachusetts study had the long-term goal of connecting youth development to practical community building. As youth get older and grow into adults, more children are growing into youth. There are always improvements to be made in the community, and there will always be youth to involve in the process. This is a huge disappointment with the United Kingdom study, because although it is important that the youth felt a difference after the project was finished, the lack of real effect it had in its community is a huge gap in the completion of the case study itself.

The next source I turned to, "Youth Using Research: Learning through Social Practice, Community Building, and Social Change" is about Boston's University High School, an alternative school for students who have failed out of the public school system. Alexander Lynn, the author of the article, and his associates applied teaching techniques of "liberation pedagogy" (39) that see social change as the primary goal of the learning experience for the students. Lynn boldly opens his article with the claim, "[a]ll human knowledge comes from social change" (39), because he strongly believes that using community development to teach young people is the best way to improve both the youth and the community in which they live. He cites several projects his school is involved in, including teaching recovering drug-addicted youth to read with addiction recovery materials and staging a sit-in on the research department of the Boston Public School District to get them to release information that would connect class and income, and not just race, to standardized test scores (43–44). These projects all work to "develop an educational philosophy and practice that is predicated on serving the community" (40).

While I agree with his goals, the main problem I see with Lynn's presentation of his school's "community action project-based learning" approach is that he only speaks of the improvements the students see in themselves and he sees in his students. There is still a lack of evidence of a real difference made in the community—the same lack I saw in the United Kingdom case study. Lynn's students are learning how to make a difference, but so far the difference is more in themselves than in their community. I think Lynn assumes that University High School students will naturally make real changes because of the community-based learning strategies, since he claims the "self-knowledge of the population under consideration is at the center of their ability to affect the changes they seek" (46). I wish he had shown at least one example of real change. Although his focus on the students' learning is important, the article does not help my main focus on differences made in both the community and the youth.

The next source I came across was a good find for me because it looked at community building and youth development in the opposite direction as I had seen previously. "Recreation and the Glenview Neighborhood: Implications for Youth and Community Development" focused more on changes that the community could make by helping the youth, as opposed to looking at the difference the youth could make on the community. The purpose of this article was to research why an attempt at creating a recreation program for the youth in the low-income Glenview community failed within months of its implementation. The article focuses on researching how to successfully apply a working recreation program that will involve all those in the community and ultimately help the youth, concentrating on the question, "what socially based ingredients need to be in place for communities to ultimately defend a local interest and carry it through with success?" (269). Recreation programs would help the youth to have somewhere to go to be active and away from harmful environments.

What I liked about this article is that, in researching this question, parents, prominent community members such as recreation and park administrators, police officers, and even the elementary school principal were all interviewed. The study incorporated the entire community directly and personally, but from the adult perspective, with the ultimate goal of building the community through helping the youth. In order to be successful, Autry and Anderson show that community needs are a lot like the needs of youth in the other articles I read, because when they work together, adult "individuals in low-resource neighborhoods who have traditionally felt disempowered become more empowered by involving them in the process of decision making and facilitating a variety of networking opportunities with open and long-term goals for communication. The residents of a community need to have their voices heard" (282). Adults, just like young people in low-income communities, can't just be told what to do by outsiders; instead, they have to be part of the problem-solving and decision-making process, and their opinions and input need to be valued.

The last source I will touch on is a brief article entitled "Building a Successful Mentoring Program." In it, Robert McCauley, a corporate communications manager for the world's largest specialized staffing firm, Robert Half International, talks about building a mentoring program in a work setting to assist in new employee integration. Although it doesn't directly relate to youth and community development, I like this article because it is a simple step-by-step guide to creating a mentoring program that I believe can work in many settings. For example, just as Autry and Anderson show how people who feel alienated are empowered by taking part in decision-making processes in their communities, McCauley shows how mentoring helps new employees feel like they are part of a workplace community (17). In relating this to youth development programs, mentoring is one way that can both help youth in becoming more successful adults, and build the community by encouraging adults to come together as mentors who support young people.

These articles all show how a direct connection can be made between helping foster community building and youth development. Arches, Fleming, and Lynn all show the benefits for youth in working for their communities, though in some cases there is a lack of solid evidence to show the real difference made for the community by the youth. Autry and Anderson look at the issue from the other direction, showing how community building can lead to youth development. Finally, McCauley provides a concise, step-by-step guide that shows how successful community building works in business situations. In my future research and my research paper, I would like to see what makes these programs successful specifically, including the resources used and the time needed for program development and completion. If possible, I would like to explore what might be required to start a new program that could be implemented in an environment as foreign as an underdeveloped country in need of both youth development and community building. This is an incredibly interesting topic for me and one that I will hopefully be able to use in my future with the Peace Corps.

WORKS CITED

Arches, Joan, and Jennie Fleming. "Young People and Social Action: Youth Participation in the United Kingdom and United States." *New Directions for Youth Development* 111 (2006): 81–90. Print.

Autry, Cari E., and Stephen C. Anderson. "Recreation and the Glenview Neighborhood: Implications for Youth and Community Development." *Leisure Sciences* 29 (2007): 267–85. Print.

Lynn, Alexander. "Youth Using Research: Learning Through Social Practice, Community Building, and Social Change." *New Directions for Youth Development* 106 (2005): 39–48. Print.

McCauley, Robert. "Building a Successful Mentoring Program." *Journal for Quality & Participation* 30.2 (2007): 17–19. Print.

Nitzberg, Joel. "The Meshing of Youth Development and Community Building." *New Directions for Youth Development* 106 (2005): 7–16. Print.

Building on her papers "Understanding Proximate Cause" and "Addressing the Medical Liability Crisis," which you read in Chapters 8 and 9 respectively, Cindy continues her work on understanding and preventing cases of medical error. As you read, compare her use of sources with Andrea's above:

- Do they take similar or different approaches to identifying and understanding debates among researchers?
- How does each writer begin to take a position within the academic conversation?
- How much emphasis do they place on their personal experiences, and which approaches might you incorporate in your own exploratory writing project?

Cindy H.
Dr. Richmond
College Writing
13 November 2008

Full Disclosure and Apology in Medicine:
Is the Risk Worth Taking?

There is a growing effort within the United States to address medical error since the Institute of Medicine's 1999 report, "To Err Is Human: Building a Safer Healthcare System," revealed that as many as 98,000 people die in US hospitals every year due to avoidable medical errors. The Patient Safety and Quality Improvement Act of 2005 made great strides toward improving healthcare in the United States. The act provides anonymity to healthcare professionals which allows them to report error without fear of personal repercussions. While the act will facilitate some improvements in healthcare, what about addressing safety in cases where maintaining anonymity is difficult or impossible? "Full disclosure," explaining adverse medical outcomes to patients and families, poses additional challenges, because it is difficult for healthcare providers to protect anonymity while exposing their errors. Even though full disclosure is encouraged by the American Medical Association, it is unlikely to really take hold unless healthcare providers believe that the benefits outweigh the risks and know how to do it well.

Full disclosure means informing a patient of what went wrong when there has been some harm due to a medical error; it also can include an apology for harm caused by medical error. Of course, doctors are hesitant to provide full disclosure and especially express apology because of the potential for malpractice accusations. I got interested in the challenges of disclosure and apology in a law class, where the instructor, Jane Greenly, explained the process of litigation and stated that the vast majority of personal injury cases are settled through mediation rather than litigation. Mediation is a practical alternative to litigation that saves time and money. But Greenly, who has worked for years as a mediator, said people are really satisfied with mediation because they receive an apology, "Which is often what they really wanted all along." It seems that the expression of apology matters, perhaps to both patient and physician. What would be the benefits of full disclosure and the expression of apology in medicine, and is the risk worth taking?

In "Medical Liability Insurance and Damage Caps," Bryan A. Liang, professor of anesthesiology and health law, describes a way that disclosure could reduce medical error and improve healthcare (531). He proposes a systems approach, where individuals are not singled out as the cause of harm; he describes healthcare as a complex system and emphasizes the fact that "one individual is not responsible for the outcome of the entire system" (523). Building upon the systems approach, he recommends a partnership where "each member of the healthcare team assumes an even greater role as compared to an individually-oriented system" (532). He includes the patient and family in the partnership, realizing that patients have an important perspective on their own cases and hence have valuable input to offer.

I found the concept of a systems approach to healthcare very hard to accept at first. My experience with medicine has usually been with one doctor or nurse at a time and so to me it seems like healthcare delivery is a function of individuals, not a system. Then I considered that medical professionals have to receive their training somewhere, that updates on advancements occur, and that "best practices" are published; medical professionals depend on others for training, information, and often implementation of services. These thoughts caused me to reconsider my understanding of medical error and malpractice. While malpractice is defined as substandard care, errors can occur because of the profession's current educational approaches and practices, because the system has inherent errors in it.

Liang proposes a specific approach for handling medical errors resulting in injury. Special teams are created for discovery, disclosure, recordkeeping, continued communication, and mediation. Mediation is valued because it promotes discussion with the following benefits: settlement costs in money, time, and emotional turmoil are reduced; and the patient and family have input that can lead to improved patient safety. Mediation also allows many solution possibilities, while litigation only allows monetary solutions. In Liang's approach, mediation can also include apology if it remains inadmissible as evidence of guilt; system representatives may always express sympathy, but sometimes they may not apologize.

Liang's idea of using the "system" to disclose error to patients sounds problematic to me in actual practice and possibly even undesirable in one respect. First, a very elaborate combination of teams is required that would not be available to a private practitioner in a small office. Second, even in a large system such as a hospital or HMO it might be difficult for administrators to justify the expenditures of money, human resources, and time required to implement such an approach. Third, I think Liang's specific requirement that a system representative be the one to express sympathy avoids the healing potentially available when physicians interact personally with their patients.

In "Apology in Medical Practice: An Emerging Clinical Skill," Dr. Aaron Lazare, Chancellor and Dean of the Massachusetts Medical School, defines apology as "an acknowledgment of responsibility for an offense coupled with an expression of remorse. An offense refers to a physical or psychological harm caused by an individual or group that could or should have been avoided by ordinary standards of behavior" (1401). Thus, Lazare makes a distinction between the appropriateness of apology when there has been a reasonably avoidable error and the inappropriateness of apology when a poor outcome unavoidably occurred. In the latter case, an expression of sympathy is sufficient and correct. He states that the components of an apology are acknowledgement of the offense, explanation, humble remorse with commitment not to repeat the offense, and reparation. The components he outlines as part of a true and complete apology are probably more than what comes to most people's minds when they hear the word. Apology, by Lazare's standards, includes much more than an expression of sorrow and fault. I think this reflects the ethics of the writer. How could an individual of integrity acknowledge responsibility for someone's harm without making efforts to prevent future harm and make amends to the one offended? According to Lazare's ethics, and my own, a true apology has not been offered unless amends are offered as well.

Lazare describes the many ways apologies can heal: by restoring a patient's dignity and sense of being cared about; giving patients a sense of control over their situations; validating suffering; relieving unnecessary fears; restoring doctor-patient relationships; providing needed assistance; and addressing the hierarchy of power. I appreciate Lazare's addressing the power hierarchy that exists in medicine. Certainly, patients experience the imbalance of power when they put themselves in the hands of a surgeon or simply seek a needed prescription. In my view, imbalance of power makes the lack of apology after an injury all the more offensive; however, Lazare also describes the views of physicians, who may resist apologizing because of the fear of consequences and a need to maintain an image of detached perfectionism, even unto themselves.

Perhaps physicians most need adequate support when they divulge information to patients. Lazare explains that apology is actually a negotiation process, "an exchange . . . a back-and-forth between two parties over how much the physician is willing to offer and how much the patient needs . . . who is in the room and the timing of the apology . . . [each] is a unique event" (1403). I suspect he was speaking from experience or observation, because the process sounds far more difficult than a simple strategy or checklist approach. I am concerned that some physicians do not have the personality, even with training, that would enable them to make good apologies after medical error; an apology gone wrong causes further harm. Perhaps physicians could turn to mediators or other third parties to assist them in apologizing; the physician, just like the patient, is under stress and could benefit from assistance. This may be the concern that Liang was addressing by not having the erring provider involved initially, but I believe a better approach is to have the erring provider offer the apology with assistance. In the case of a complex error that might occur in a hospital, then an apology from a system representative would be reasonable.

Lee Taft is an ethicist with 20 years of experience as a former plaintiff attorney in malpractice cases, who agrees with Lazare on the apology process, and that an apology must be offered by the erring provider. Taft distinguishes between authentic apologies and empathetic disclosures, which provide information and sympathy but no admission of error. Because empathic disclosure indirectly denies error, and may prove more offensive than soothing to patients, Taft argues that it may be better to disclose without sympathy. Taft also describes current legislative trends to prevent apologies from being used as evidence of admission of guilt in a court of law. Unlike Liang, he believes such legislation will effectively change the benefits of an expression of apology, because an authentic apology must include risk. If a "protected apology" does not carry any risk of consequence, it is no longer an apology; the healing powers of apology are lost because "it is the taking of the risk that . . . restores one's integrity with the party harmed, with one's self, and with the community" (71). If, however, a protected apology is expressed and followed by all the other components of a true apology, then the patient will know that the expression of remorse was genuine and experience the healing effects of apology. I find Taft's comments on legislation convincing from a theoretical perspective. In practice, though, I see only the benefits that come from simply making apology inadmissible as evidence in court. However, as Taft explains, some legislatures are enacting much broader laws of inadmissibility which would unfairly hinder legitimate malpractice claims (80). I think that is the real danger.

After reading perspectives from experts in ethics, law, and medicine, I wanted to find data from actual studies. In "What We Know and Don't Know about the Role of Apologies in Resolving Healthcare Disputes," Jennifer Robbennolt, renowned scholar in psychology, law, and dispute resolution, discusses data from surveys, experiments, and a case study. Survey data reveals a "basic disconnect" between patient and physician views and "a correlation between dissatisfaction with the interaction between the patient and physician in the aftermath of the adverse event and the likelihood of running to an attorney for assistance" (1018; 1017). For their parts, patients desire every detail with an expression of apology, without having to ask for more information, while physicians may want to apologize, but fear of legal consequences pressures them to explain with carefully chosen words and expect that the patient will ask for more information. Robbennolt also studied patients' and doctors' reactions to hypothetical care situations. When asked what they would want after a medical error, 88% of respondents wanted the doctor to say he was sincerely sorry. In my view, the most interesting statistic Robbennolt provided was that 99% of people wanted to know something was going to be done so that the mistake didn't happen to someone else. Liang also discusses this point, but from the angle of reducing error overall rather than from the viewpoint of a patient who just experienced error. Lazare and Taft include it as a key component of true apology, but perhaps they do not give it the full weight it deserves.

Robbenholt also includes a case study from the Veterans Affairs Medical Center in Lexington, Virginia. The Center adopted a policy of investigating all injury, fully disclosing all errors resulting in injury, accepting responsibility, expressing apology, and offering reparation. The results have been positive in every respect: even though more settlements have been offered, they have been peacefully settled for lower amounts resulting in a much lower total expenditure; self-reporting of errors has increased, and cases settle quickly. I agree with Robbennolt's concerns that the study may have limited value, because patients in a veteran's hospital are not representative of the general population, and the VA is not subject to punitive damages; nevertheless, the study is very encouraging.

In an effort to discover more study related data, I consulted research done by Thomas Gallagher and colleagues. Using thirteen focus groups and extrapolating common themes from their experiences, these researchers investigated patient and physician attitudes about error disclosure. Some groups were only patients or only physicians, and some were mixed in order to discover more about the actual effects of patient-physician interaction. The researchers agreed with Robbennolt's findings and made some additional findings: patients accept that medical errors are inevitable; disclosure enhanced trust and was reassuring; methods of disclosure "directly affected their emotional experience after the error"; and 100% of patients wanted to know the cause, how it would affect them, and what would be done to prevent it in the future (1005). Physicians were frustrated by the breadth of what patients considered to be errors, including poor service and deficient interpersonal skills; none of the physicians intended to inform patients of steps that would be taken to prevent errors in the future. Physicians described experiencing guilt, feelings of failure, fear of a lawsuit, and fear of harmed reputation, and expressed worry that discussing an error would be inconsiderate of the patient. These focus groups reveal detailed information on the "basic disconnect" described by Robbenholt.

The basic problem I noticed while reading Gallagher's study and findings is that medical professionals do not correctly understand the motivation behind patients' desires for full disclosures and appropriate expressions of apology. After reading Liang, Lazare, Taft, Robbennolt, and Gallagher, I believe that patients want to be able to control their own healthcare; control requires full information and better interpersonal skills by the healthcare system. Patients understand that mistakes happen and they want to know that if a mistake happens to them their suffering will not have been in vain—that the system will learn and improve. Patients are less likely to have the emotional drive to sue if they do not feel that there has been a cover-up. Basic understanding of patient motivations could help create a methodology of disclosure that would better serve physicians' needs, which are generally kept silent but which may well have been expressed by one physician participant in the Gallagher study: "This is one of the few businesses that is around where you have to hit a home run every time . . . and I find that the older I get, the longer I have been at this, the more I worry to the point that this is probably what is going to drive me out of it, is worrying about it" (1005).

After this research, I conclude that the risks involved in full disclosure and expression of apology in medicine are worth taking. The benefits can be extensive but the method used is important to securing those benefits. Liang offered one approach for reducing medical error and described the elements needed. By adding correct and complete understanding of patient needs and motivations, physician needs and fears, and all the factors that drive malpractice litigation, perhaps an ideal model can be constructed—one that would enhance the patient-provider experience in every way. It would outline principles, rather than specifics, so that it could be scaled for large institutions or small offices with all the critical principles addressed. First, however, further research will be needed to address the potential for lawsuits created by greed or misinformation about what actually constitutes medical malpractice.

WORKS CITED

Gallagher, Thomas H., et al. "Patients' and Physicians' Attitudes Regarding the Disclosure of Medical Errors." *The Journal of the American Medical Association* 289 (2003): 1001–1007. Print.

Lazare, Aaron. "Apology in Medical Practice: An Emerging Clinical Skill." *The Journal of the American Medical Association* 296 (2006): 1401–4. Print.

Liang, Bryan A., and LiLan Ren. "Medical Liability Insurance and Damage Caps: Getting Beyond Band Aids to Substantive Systems Treatment to Improve Quality and Safety in Healthcare." *American Journal of Law & Medicine* 30 (2004): 501–41. Print.

Robbennolt, Jennifer K. "What We Know and Don't Know about the Role of Apologies in Resolving Health Care Disputes." *Georgia State University Law Review* 21 (2005): 1009–1027. Print.

Taft, Lee. "Apology and Medical Mistake: Opportunity or Foil?" *Annals of Health Law* 14 (2005): 55–94. Print.

Megan opens her exploratory research essay by summarizing the kinds of "common sense" ideas many people hold about the relationship between video game playing and violent behavior. In order to test those ideas she returns to the earliest academic studies of the violence-video game connection, and then, using a historical development strategy, works her way up to more recent studies.

Megan C.
Ms. Walter
College Writing
28 November 2005

Violent Video Games: The Good, the Bad, and the Ugly

In the early video games of the 1980s, violent content was never serious enough to raise an eyebrow. As a few rounds of Pac-Man or Asteroids show, the plots, the game play, and the characters in older video games were pretty innocent. In recent years though, video game violence has become a serious issue. People are concerned that "first-person shooter" games like Doom and Duke Nukem are to blame for school shootings, increased violence among our children, and a general increase in aggressive behavior by young people. As a video game player myself, I want to find out whether violent video games are actually causing those problems.

At first thought, the answer seems plain and obvious: "Yes." People would be justified to ask: "How could these games *not* be the cause?" After all, our kids are being exposed to graphic images and allowed to take part in gruesome settings for their video game play. They sit and watch—and more importantly, control—their on-screen heroes as they blast away buildings, cars, and human enemies. While there is a lot of violent role playing in today's video games, there are other possible sides to the argument. Of the school shootings that have occurred in the United States, can we say that they have all been triggered by violent video games? There could be dozens of other factors and causes, including problems at home or in the family, stress over school, poor self esteem, relationship problems, and others. Could it actually be helpful to view violence? Maybe dealing destruction to cars and buildings in a fake game world is better than going out to cause such catastrophes in the real world. How do we know which of these positions is right?

Craig Anderson and Brad Bushman of Iowa State University studied one of the most famous cases of school violence, the 1999 Columbine High School shootings. Because Eric Harris and Dylan Kliebold, the teens who committed the crime, were avid video game players, was it possible that the games encouraged, or were responsible for, the crimes? As Anderson and Bushman report, Harris and Kliebold played Doom, a first-person shooting game popular in the 1990s; Harris even "created a customized version of Doom with two shooters, extra weapons, unlimited ammunition, and victims who could not fight back—features that are eerily similar to aspects of the actual shootings" (353). Anderson and Bushman review many reports that study connections between people who view violent or aggressive acts and the increase of aggressive feelings in the viewers. They state that the majority of studies prove this connection exists, and that "the vast research literature on TV and movie violence rests on a firm foundation of three study types" (354). If those studies are right, then perhaps Harris and Kliebold were especially aggressive because of the hours they put into video game play. Their minds were being conditioned as they played Doom, making them less sensitive to images and effects of violence. Anderson and Bushman cite studies showing that if they are less sensitive to images of violence, young gamers, like the shooters at Columbine High, tend to be more violent in everyday situations at school or work (354).

Anderson and Bushman's study is pretty convincing. They made graphs to put together the results of their survey of 35 articles published before 2000 (356), and the graphs show clearly that games caused more aggression (both aggressive thinking and aggressive behavior) and less helping (which they call "prosocial behavior") (357). They conclude by asking if they can show direct effects between gaming and negative actions, why don't video game companies make more games that encourage positive actions? (359). It would be interesting to find articles that study whether it's as easy to encourage positive behavior as Anderson and Bushman claim, because maybe gamers' behavior is more easy to control in one way but not the other.

Instead of focusing on how to rewrite game content, in 2003 Anderson worked with Christine Murphy from St. Louis University to develop their own study that looked at the differences between male and female gamers. They started by stating that females don't seem to be interested in violent video games as much as males are, but what if the females play violent video games with a female main character? They wanted to find out if "controlling a same sex character will increase identification with the character and . . . increase the effect on subsequent behavior" (424). It turned out that getting females to play more violent video games made them feel and act more aggressively, and it didn't matter whether the character in the Street Fighter game was male or female (427). As I was reading, I thought that Anderson and Murphy's study might confuse people who participate in the experiment, because Anderson and Murphy "retaliate" physically on video game players who lose games by "blasting" them with a loud noise (425). By setting up the experiment to connect video game performance and real-world punishment, they might actually encourage more aggressive or violent behavior from the gamers they studied.

Without Anderson and Murphy's confusion, is it true that young gamers can't tell the difference between violence in the game world on the TV screen and violence in the real world? For comparison, I remember my brother, who served in the Marines for eight years, telling me stories about how soldiers would play violent shooting games for several reasons. The first reason was to improve hand-eye coordination. Being able to aim and shoot quicker than your enemy has to be engraved in the soldier's mind, and a shooting game was just the way to accomplish that goal. Second, soldiers need to get used to seeing bodies shot down in front of them so they won't go into shock in a real battle. Third, soldiers get trained in first-person view so that soldiers identify with the character. Although it sounds a little disturbing that these games desensitize players, it creates a huge advantage for the military when soldiers get into real-life situations.

As Chris Suellentrop states in his article "Playing with Our Minds," most of today's soldiers have video game backgrounds that give them less hesitation about using weapons. Suellentrop writes that a "combat engineer interviewed by the [*Washington*] *Post* compared his tour in Iraq to Halo," one of the most popular first-person shooting games, so it was logical for the US Army to develop its own similar video game, called "America's Army." Suellentrop's article is interesting because it starts with the same connections between aggressive games and aggressive behavior made by Anderson and other researchers (and used by the military to encourage aggression), but it ends on a bigger issue. He writes about what David Brooks calls the "Organization Kid," who is produced by hours of video game playing: a "Princeton sociology professor Brooks interviewed could have been describing ideal soldiers when he said of his students, 'They're eager to please, eager to jump through whatever hoops the faculty puts in front of them, eager to conform.'" Of course there are important differences between players who are learning to be more aggressive and violent and players who are learning to be more helpful in society, but what if all gamers are really being taught to be conformists?

To reinforce Suellentrop's report, in "Violent Video Games Recruit America's Youth," Eastern Connecticut University Professor William Lugo explains that today's games are being used not only to train soldiers already in the military like my brother, but also to encourage young people to accept military "conditioning" (14). Lugo claims that people who play America's Army and other military-themed games are taught "company values, techniques, and etiquette" (14). He makes the same arguments made by Anderson and colleagues in their laboratory studies, but now it's the US Army giving gamers free copies of games that make them "ready for combat by the time they finish the last level. And, if all goes as planned, reality and fiction will become so blurred, gamers will not know the difference, nor will they even understand how they ended up in the middle of the desert, fighting an enemy they know nothing about. However, unlike a game, this time there will be women and children walking the streets" (14). Actually, another study at the University of Missouri claims that violent video gaming changes the brain itself, and perhaps permanently ("Violent" 11). What if video game players' brains can't tell or don't care about the difference between soldiers and civilians when they get into real-life situations?

Even though there might be some connection between the hours Eric Harris and Dylan Kliebold spent playing Doom and their actions at Columbine High School, their case seems rare. In fact, as one article in the medical journal *Lancet* claims, there isn't much evidence connecting violent video games to crime (Browne 702). But my brother's experiences and the articles I read about video game use in the military bring up another question: may-be how gamers act depends on how video games are used in society. Maybe all the aggressive feelings and behaviors usually get pushed in directions valued by society, such as serving in the military, and away from negatively valued directions, like crime. If Suellentrop and Lugo are right, then video games do increase violence and aggression, but they also "condition" players to follow orders by authority figures, like military leaders. Whether positive or negative, though, Suellentrop claims that the message in all video games is the same "winner's ideology: Follow orders, and you'll be just fine."

So far, it seems that Anderson and his colleagues are right about the effects of violent video games on players. I still have some questions about the differences between good and bad violence, if such a distinction can be made. I have also found a couple of articles that mention credible research on the other side of the argument, that show how video game playing can have positive results. For instance, an article by Anne Walling in *American Family Physician* describes sources that show "both calming and arousal effects" of video games, even violent ones (1436). I plan to see how researchers justify their position when there's so much evidence on one side. The reading I've done so far has raised a lot of other possible directions to take (such as how aggressive feelings are directed by authority figures), but I'll probably stay with the effects of gaming on violent behavior. When I go back to my research for the final project, I want to find more of the studies that present the other side of the argument before I come to my own conclusion.

WORKS CITED

Anderson, Craig A., and Brad J. Bushman. "Effects of Violent Video Games on Aggressive Behavior, Aggressive Cognition, Aggressive Affect, Physiological Arousal, and Prosocial Behavior." *Psychological Science* 12.5 (2001): 353–59. Print.

Anderson, Craig A., and Christine R. Murphy. "Violent Video Games and Aggressive Behavior in Young Women."*Aggressive Behavior* 29 (2003): 423–29. Print.

Browne, Kevin D., and Catherine Hamilton-Giachritsis. "The Influence of Violent Media on Children andAdolescents: A Public Health Approach." *Lancet* 365 (2005): 702–10. Print.

"Do Violent Video Games Lead to Aggression?" *NEA Today* 24.7 (2006): 11. Print.

Lugo, William. "Violent Video Games Recruit America's Youth." *Reclaiming Children and Youth* 15.1 (2006): 11–14. Print.

Suellentrop, Chris. "Playing with Our Minds." *Wilson Quarterly* 30.3 (2006): 14–21. *Academic Search Premier*. Web. 28 July 2006. <http://search.epnet.com>.

Walling, Anne D. "Do Video Games Lead to Violent Behavior in Children?" *American Family Physician* 65(2002): 1436–37. Print.

12

The Formal Research Essay

CHAPTER OBJECTIVES

In this chapter, you'll learn how to:

- Write a thesis-based research paper using multiple sources
- Establish the context and background needed for your audience
- Explore multiple research purposes and genres
- Practice outlining and other prewriting strategies
- Use the conventions of an academic conversation as a guide for organization and tone

---

This chapter focuses on the formal research essay and provides you with techniques for developing the academic research and inquiry process into a compelling written argument. By adopting approaches that you've experienced in your sources, you will make a claim, present evidence from your research, and persuade readers of the strength of your position. This formal research argument is your opportunity to enter the academic conversation as a full participant. It is an especially important genre to practice because it is the one you're likely to use most often as you advance in your academic major and later in professional writing situations.

Because it is guided by a central *thesis*, or claim, the formal research essay is different than much of the writing that you've done for this course. Here, you'll focus less on the research process that led you to

WRITING ASSIGNMENT

I. Write a formal research essay to support a thesis, take a position, or propose a solution in response to a question that you have developed.

II. Use an academic field's rhetorical, organizational, and bibliographic conventions to guide your formal research writing.

A formal peer review is reproduced in Figure 12.3 in order to assess the essay.

sources and more on developing an issue in ways that will help you make a contribution to the conversation.

ANCHORING YOUR PAPER WITH A THESIS STATEMENT

A thesis is the foundation of a writer's argument.

As you have probably noticed in reading your sources, academic texts are guided by strong theses. The thesis is a claim that anchors a writer's argument, and helps to organize sources, develop points, and ultimately lead readers to a convincing conclusion. A strong thesis will help guide you through many of the important decisions that you'll have to make in the process of drafting and revising your formal research essay.

Consider working with a *tentative* thesis as you begin drafting your project. Your tentative thesis statement describes a claim that you want to make about an issue, a position you want to take in a debate, a solution you want to propose to a problem, or a novel argument that you will make by connecting two or more sources together.

Because it is tentative, this thesis does not trap you into one position or close off possible avenues for your work as it evolves; instead, it is the main point around which you can organize your thoughts and your research. Developed early in the writing process, a tentative thesis will also help ensure that you argue a sufficiently academic claim, because it will evolve alongside your sources while you read and respond to them. As you continue to develop your sources and argue your own position, you can reevaluate your initial thesis and adjust it—either a bit or a lot—as needed.

A tentative thesis may be revised throughout the writing process.

What Is a Strong Thesis?

Your thesis should clearly identify the topic of your project, and the question or issue that motivates your research and argument. Anticipate readers' needs by carefully considering how much prior knowledge they are likely to bring to the subject and academic field. How much background will you have to provide before your claim will make sense to readers, like your instructor and classmates, who may not share your familiarity with the issue? What terms, concepts, and other foundational information are non-specialists likely to need before they can participate in the conversation with you?

Build a foundation of common knowledge.

Your thesis should also be shaped by the length (i.e., a certain number of pages) and scope of research (i.e., a certain number of general and scholarly sources) required by your instructor. Your thesis must be specific enough for you to research the issue, question, or debate in sufficient detail and to make your own contribution to the academic conversation.

Focus your thesis to meet course requirements.

In addition to being clear and focused, an effective thesis should be problematic; it should require you to participate in a debate where there is no obvious right or wrong answer. As you review your sources and read new ones, note how academic writers develop their claims and consider using their approaches as models for your own project. Use your earlier writing projects to pursue research in a field that genuinely interests you and make a claim which you are truly committed to developing and defending. You will be more likely to succeed in the writing project and to maintain your personal interest and energy throughout the process.

Stake out your position within a debate.

STUDENT VOICE

Tony, whose formal research essay, "Video Games: Thinking Outside the XBOX," appears in this chapter, explains the importance of pursuing his own interests through research.

Being able to keep working on a topic of my interest for the formal research essay made researching and writing exponentially easier because I actually cared about what I was learning, and I saw that other people cared about my interest also. I especially like how I was encouraged to give my opinion on the subject matter and add my voice to the discussion in a way that can be understood by others.

Embed the Thesis Statement in Purpose and Organization

As you develop your thesis, consider guiding readers into the essay by describing the *purpose* of your research and outlining the *organization* of your argument.

In the following examples, you can see the ways professional scholars develop their thesis statements by connecting a topic to a purpose. Read the following five excerpts from recent academic articles and consider your own tentative thesis and research goals. Which approach—or combination of approaches—might you consider using as a model?

Purpose 1: Interpret a Text, as in Kylo-Patrick Hart's assessment of the reality TV show Queer Eye for the Straight Guy

---

In this essay, I demonstrate why I find *Queer Eye for the Straight Guy* to offer the most positive representation of gay men in U.S. television history. To do so, I begin by providing a brief overview of representations of gay men on U.S. television over the past four decades. Then I use that essential historical context to show how *Queer Eye for the Straight Guy* is qualitatively distinct from the related kinds of representations of gay men that have preceded it, enabling this reality series to work representational "magic" by consistently communicating, in implicit ways, that gay men are superior—rather than inferior—to heterosexuals.[2]	Hart's claim Hart forecasts the argument's structure—how he will support his claim. Comparison to similar TV programs Hart identifies the "superiority claim" of *QESG*.

How do you think Hart's positive reading of reality TV in Queer Eye might compare to the reality TV case study in Chapter 11?

Hart opens the paragraph with a strong claim about his reaction to the program. He then helps readers anticipate the argument: his analysis will be based on comparisons with other television representations of gay men, and he suggests that there is something about the reality TV genre that allows for *Queer Eye*'s "representational magic."

You can read King's entire essay in Chapter 13.

Here, King foreshadows two claims he will argue in his article: first, contrary to popular perceptions in the United States, the events of September 11, 2001, did not change the world; and, second, historians can add unique critical perspectives to current events.

Purpose 2: Analyze an Event as in Nicholas King's challenge to common beliefs about events on September 11, 2001

Historians can and must shed light on the origins and implications of current events, forcefully elucidating how the world did not change last September. But these events also afford us the opportunity to evaluate our own assumptions and methods, most importantly the manner in which we evaluate continuity and change. Naturally suspicious of the claim to novelty, historians might be excused for seeing only echoes of the past in present events. But the events of the past year also illustrate changes that predate September 11, even though their lineage may be measured in years rather than decades. Forty years ago, Charles Rosenberg observed that cholera epidemics give us a peculiar window into the social and scientific worlds of the mid-nineteenth century. The same is true now. September 11 and its aftermath cast in sharp relief the contours of American anxiety, and the constellations of American institutions and interests, peculiar to the late twentieth and early twenty-first centuries.[3]	King focuses on the field of history. King examines a single event. King describes typical historical research. What might historians bring to the issue? King establishes context—developing from previous studies. King's thesis statement.

Thesis First?

Research writers typically place their theses either in the first paragraph or close to the end of an introductory set of paragraphs. You may want to think about similarly opening your own formal research project with a tentative thesis statement, an introduction to your topic, and a description of your research purpose.

While the most traditional thesis position is at the end of the introduction, you can consider alternative positions as you draft your research project. As you imagine your audience—a professional or academic community you would like to enter, your instructor, or your classmates—how might you *delay* your thesis so that your argument and contribution to the conversation have the most effective impact on readers?

Delay the Thesis

A delayed thesis gives writers some advantages over the traditional thesis-first approach. For example, in his introductory paragraphs

---

Purpose 3: Synthesize and Evaluate Expert Perspectives, as in Jérôme Bourdon's analysis of television's effects on memory

---

The relation of television to memory has usually been the subject of commentaries that propose two contradictory models of television memories: a destructive model, and a hyper-integrative model based on a single program type: media events. In the destructive model television is seen as promoting "forgetting, when it chases after the next 'big story' or inundates us with images of little personal relevance." By contrast, in the integrative, media-event-based model, television is seen as a major instrument in the shaping of collective memory, especially national, and sometimes global. According to Daniel Dayan and Elihu Katz, live television events such as funerals of heads of state, the Olympics or royal weddings have the power of providing "a sense of common past," bridging "between personal and collective history"—"through association with either the traumas to which they are responses or the exceptional nature of the gratifications they provide." In short, in its relation to memory, television appears either as a major "disturber" or "sustainer" of social reality, to use Roger Silverstone's terms, and there seems to be no chance of bridging the gap between those two views or providing other, less radical models of relations between television and memory.[4]

> Bourdon introduces two competing approaches taken by experts.
>
> Bourdon summarizes the two approaches.
>
> He signals the importance of bridging the gap between theories.

Bourdon builds common knowledge by explaining the two ways scholars seek to understand the effect of television viewing on memory. He shows how the two analytic models leave a "gap" that must be bridged by a new model.

Consider delaying the thesis in order to build trust with readers. above, Jérôme Bourdon shows that he will be arguing against the two major theories in his field. Rather than immediately describing his new theory, he instead introduces the work he has to do in order to propose a convincing alternative, which includes a redefinition of memory and field research that supports his theory.

By building their trust and confidence, the delayed thesis invites readers to participate with the writer in reaching a conclusion together. Consider ways you might postpone your thesis, and why a delayed thesis could help you make a convincing argument.

Purpose 4: Report on Field Research, as in Bourdon's interviews, which help him propose a new theory for explaining television's effect on viewer memory

This is precisely my aim: to propose models of the influence of television on memory other than the destructive or hyper-integrative ones. As a prerequisite, I have to specify the meaning I attach to the notion of memory, a still very popular but vague notion in the social sciences, and to clarify what I mean by television memories. I will discuss the results of my fieldwork: a study conducted in France in 1993, based on life stories of television viewers. This will lead me to propose a typology of television memories that requires, beyond generalizations about the medium, an analysis of the way television viewing is embedded in daily life.[5]	Bourdon recalls the two dominant, competing theories of television's effects on memory. Bourdon introduces his field research. Field research leads to a new theory that avoids flaws in the dominant ones.

Even though he focuses on one group of viewers in a specific time and place, Bourdon can help readers understand general forces at work in the television-memory relationship.

Purpose 5: Test a Theory, as in the following passage from Chris Taylor and Annabelle James's examination of closed-circuit video tapes used in police investigations and prosecution

Video evidence is undeniably persuasive, making it a valuable weapon in court, but its use raises issues of collection, retention, disclosure and storage, which can have a critical influence on the conduct of cases. The situation is further complicated by legislation, not least the Criminal Procedure and Investigations Act 1996 (CPIA), which regulates the disclosure of 'unused material' (including videotape) to the defence, the Data Protection Act 1998 and, of course, the Human Rights Act 1998.	Concerns raised by video evidence, related to the pursuit of justice The role of legislation—three key legislative acts Concerns remain after the legislation has gone into effect.
In recent years there has been considerable discussion of issues surrounding video identification evidence. The aim of this article is to examine some additional aspects of video evidence which have proved especially problematic, first in relation to the disclosure of unused video material under CPIA and then in the context of human rights and data protection principles. It will be suggested that although the legislation does, in theory, provide safeguards for those adversely affected by the use of video evidence, in practice these may well be of limited use.[6]	Specific aspects of video evidence to be addressed. James and Taylor plan to explore the relationship between theoretical assumptions and practical applications.

After introducing the subject, Taylor and James foreshadow their purpose: use current case studies to understand the effects of past legislation, and show that theoretical protections of the accused do not always hold true in practical situations.

> *You can read James and Taylor's entire essay in Chapter 13.*

Forecast Argument and Organization

You may have noticed that each thesis in the examples above serves more than one function in the essay. While the thesis presents the writer's claim and purpose, it also provides readers with a sense of how the essay will be organized. For example, Taylor and James *forecast* their organizational plan, introducing aspects of closed circuit video in the order they will appear in the essay. Taylor and James help readers anticipate the six moves they will make to support their claim with the following forecasting techniques:

Video evidence is undeniably persuasive, making it a valuable weapon in court, but its use raises issues of collection, retention, disclosure and storage, which can have a critical influence on the conduct of cases. The situation is further complicated by legislation, not least the Criminal Procedure and Investigations Act 1996 (CPIA), which regulates the disclosure of 'unused material' (including videotape) to the defence, the Data Protection Act 1998 and, of course, the Human Rights Act 1998.

In recent years there has been considerable discussion of issues surrounding video identification evidence. The aim of this article is to examine some additional aspects of video evidence which have proved especially problematic, first in relation to the disclosure of unused video material under CPIA and then in the context of human rights and data protection principles. It will be suggested that although the legislation does, in theory, provide safeguards for those adversely affected by the use of video evidence, in practice these may well be of limited use.

1. Claim that video evidence is persuasive in court cases.

2. Explain how video evidence raises four critical challenges.

3. Describe three key legislative acts related to video evidence.

4. Show who is discussing video evidence and how.

5. Identify "niche" in the conversation.

6. Show that theory doesn't always guide practice.

OUTLINING AND ORGANIZATIONAL STRATEGIES

Once you have a strong tentative thesis statement in place, draft an outline or similar preliminary map of your project. An outline helps you plan the argument and anticipate how to use research materials to support your claim.

A strong outline is composed of complete sentences rather than isolated words or phrases. A sentence works like a thesis, signaling both the subject of a paragraph or section of your essay and the role or purpose it plays in your project. We continue with Taylor and James's article and imagine how they could have planned their argument, first by dividing it into major sections and then by developing subpoints within each section (see Figure 12.1).

Outline with complete sentences.

The Evolving Outline

As they worked on their preliminary drafts, Taylor and James would have been able to add details to their outline and use it as a guide for revisions, helping them to identify redundancies, fill in gaps, and experiment with small adjustments or even radical changes in the essay.

In fact, James and Taylor might have maintained a detailed outline as they worked toward the final draft, so that they could quickly scan their argument and make decisions about organization, determine the need for more evidence, delete less relevant sections, and enhance more relevant sections. Still organized with complete sentences or clear questions, the outline would evolve along with the argument (see Figure 12.2).

ORGANIZATIONAL STRATEGIES

Your instructor may require an outline as an early opportunity to check the strength and clarity of your argument or as part of your final draft. If so, be sure to follow the form he or she requires, even if it differs from the approach illustrated in the previous section.

Use your sources as guides for effective organizational patterns in your own writing projects.

Even if you are not required to write one, an outline may be a good way to compare one or more organizational strategies and decide which best supports your tentative thesis. Your formal research essay can be organized in a number of effective ways, which you might base in part on the patterns used

I. Introduction
   1. Videotape is like computer data, DNA, and other high-tech forms of evidence: they all appear to be objective and accurate. However, these forms of evidence also raise new (or different) challenges to the legal system.

II. Explain uses of video at police stations.
   1. How does police station video raise essential questions about how evidence is created, stored, and used?
   2. Police station video also illustrates the clashes between police and defense lawyers over video evidence.

III. Third-party video evidence (stores, sports events, etc.) presents additional challenges to the legal system.
   1. Introduce the Criminal Procedure and Investigations Act (CPIA) and explain how it's intended to work. How does it protect both prosecution and defense lawyers?
   2. Who exploits CPIA and how?

IV. Analyze precedent-setting cases, and explain what has been done to understand and solve problems of video evidence.
   1. Police must be shown to "act in bad faith," even when they are proven to have destroyed valuable evidence.
   2. How can the legal system resolve the challenges of evidence preservation and still conform to CPIA?

V. Can the Human Rights Act be a solution?
   1. Show how video evidence is directly related to privacy rights.

VI. Conclusion

FIGURE 12.1   Scratch Outline for Taylor and James.

in your sources. As you read, think about which patterns are most effective and consider using them as models for your draft outlines.

The following sections summarize some of the most common organizational patterns for formal research essays. As you anticipate the thesis and purpose of your own project, which strategy—or combination of strategies—might work best?

Problem-Solution: Thesis First

To illustrate two approaches using a problem-solution pattern, let's use a recent student project that examined current concerns about oil production and consumption. The writer gathered sources from economists, geologists, and environmental scientists, first to identify

Section I: Introduction

Section II: "Police Station Video"

1. Police protect themselves by routinely taping suspects, but they don't preserve the tapes for long.
    a. How long is long enough? How long does a case take to work its way through the legal system?
    b. How are decisions made about which tapes to preserve, and who decides?
2. Police and prosecutors have to communicate in order to preserve evidence.

Section III: "Third-Party Video."

1. Video taken by third parties presents particular challenges to police and prosecutors.
    a. Introduce examples (real or hypothetical) to illustrate challenges.
2. Relate police responsibility to existing law (i.e., the 1996 Criminal Procedure and Investigations Act).
    a. In cases of missing and erased video, does CPIA give defense lawyers an unfair advantage over police and prosecutors?
        i. Explain how defense lawyers can exploit missing video evidence.
        ii. Does CPIA maintain a balance between the rights of the accused and the ability of the prosecutor to try the case?
    b. In cases of excessive video evidence, police and prosecutors decide which parts are relevant.
        i. How do they "frame" an event?
        ii. Is there missing context? Who would benefit from more context?

Section IV: "Videotape and Abuse of Process"

1. Both pre- and post-CPIA precedents of cases have been dismissed because of prosecutors hiding video evidence.
    a. Can the precedent be applied to (unintentionally) erased video?
    b. Police are likely to keep tapes that can help the prosecution, and to destroy tapes that will help the defense.
2. Legal opinion suggests that defense should have to prove bad faith by police.
    a. Explain the difficulty of proving bad faith in cases of partial evidence.
    b. Opposing sides argue over police intention: is it "expedience" (prosecutors) or "destruction of evidence" (defense)?
    c. The presence or absence of police malice is directly relevant to the case.
3. Do current solutions really address the challenges of video tape evidence and still conform to CPIA?

FIGURE 12.2 Detailed Outline for Taylor and James. (*continued*)

Section V: "Videotapes and the Right to a Private and Family Life"

  1. Videotaping might also complicate rights to privacy generally.
     a. How does the need to prevent crime intersect with—and per-
        haps undo—privacy rights?
  2. Relate privacy concerns to existing law (i.e., the 1998 Human
     Rights Act).
     a. HRA probably couldn't be used to exclude video evidence.

Section VI: "Video Evidence—The Data Protection Principles"

  1. Is the 1998 Data Protection Act an effective answer to problems
     of video evidence?
     a. Compare the Act's intent to its enforceability.
     b. Most CCTV control rooms get no instruction on existing law
        and how to follow it.
  2. Can even the best control room training ever protect individuals
     against possible abuses of video evidence?

Section VII: Conclusion

  1. Even though additional safeguards are being enacted in law and
     policy, there are many concerns that remain regarding the practice
     of collecting and using video evidence.

FIGURE 12.2   Detailed Outline for Taylor and James. (*continued*)

Develop evaluative criteria to support and refute your sources. problems raised by oil use, and then to show how nonpetroleum fuels could help solve those problems. The writer made four key moves in her argument:

- In the essay's first section, she introduced both the problem and her solution.
- In the following section, she presented and refuted solutions she opposed.
- Through refutation, she introduced *evaluative criteria* (cost effectiveness, environmental soundness, safety, and sustainability) that helped her argue against unfavorable solutions.
- Evaluative criteria were in place to support the favored solution and conclude the argument.

If you write a problem-solution essay, your sources will help identify possible solutions to the problem. Consider drafting a paragraph or brief section for each source or each possible solution you encounter. As you evaluate arguments that support and oppose your position, you will work logically to gather evidence and criteria needed to support your own solution.

Two Thesis-First Approaches

The argument of a thesis-first problem-solution essay will probably take one of two forms:

Option 1

Describe the solutions to be opposed, refute them with appropriate criteria, and finally advocate the solution proposed in the introduction:

I. Thesis: Introduction to problem and solution

II. Possible solutions and related research

III. Refutation of weak solutions

IV. Support of favored solution

V. Conclusion

See Patterns 3a and 3b in Chapter 14 for additional examples of thesis-first organization for problem-solution essays.

Option 2

Describe and refute each unfavorable solution, establish criteria in response to each, and, having exhausted alternatives, return to the solution first proposed:

I. Thesis: Introduction to problem and solution

II. Possible solution #1, related research, and refutation

III. Possible solution #2, related research, and refutation

—Additional possible solutions and refutations, as needed

IV. Return to desired solution with related research as support

V. Conclusion

Problem-Solution: Delayed Thesis

What if our "petroleum" writer believes that she might be addressing a hostile audience, one whose members are not inclined to seriously consider alternatives to oil? In this case, rather than opening with a solution that readers are likely to reject, she could present the problem and simply explain that there are a number of ways to solve it. She could then sketch out the possible solutions—perhaps in a paragraph or section each—and only then introduce evaluative criteria that she will use to favor one solution. At this point, the writer can begin to weigh each of the solutions and show how and why she favors one over the others.

Use the delayed thesis to adopt a neutral stance.

This *delayed thesis* approach can be very effective for writers who anticipate having a skeptical audience, or readers who are unfamiliar with the subject. Using the delayed thesis, the writer opens with a neutral stance toward the problem and its solutions. By gradually working toward the favored solution, the writer increases the likelihood that even skeptical readers will be convinced by the strength of the argument.

Elements of argument are identical to the thesis-first model, but the delayed thesis reorders them in this way:

See Pattern 3c in Chapter 14 for additional examples of delayed-thesis organization for problem-solution essays.

I. Neutral Stance: Introduction to problem and possible solutions

II. All possible solutions developed with related research

III. Introduction of evaluative criteria

IV. Delayed Thesis: Support of favored solution

V. Conclusion

Classification of Parts

As you read your sources, do you see scholars turning to the same examples, analyzing aspects of a problem in similar ways, or making similar arguments? A *classification of parts* approach can help you manage an issue that is especially complex, evolves over a long period of time, or is studied by scholars in many disciplines. Consider organizing your essay according to major divisions, historical breaks, or other distinguishing characteristics. After showing an issue through various angles or perspectives, your contribution to the conversation can come through an original synthesis of the best perspectives, or developing an altogether new perspective from the conversation.

See Pattern 1 in Chapter 14 for additional classification examples.

For example, recall Taylor and James's introduction. As they explain uses of video evidence in court cases, they forecast their classification of the topic in two ways:

1. There are four aspects of video evidence that affect court cases:
   - Collection
   - Retention
   - Disclosure
   - Storage
2. There are three key pieces of legislation that affect uses of video evidence:
   - Criminal Procedure and Investigations Act 1996 (CPIA)
   - Data Protection Act 1998
   - Human Rights Act 1998

If you use the classification approach, begin with an overview that introduces the issue and the number of parts you plan to cover. Each section in the body of the essay uses sources to explain a part in detail, and in the conclusion, you will draw the parts back together in some unique way.

Imagine that you want to describe the paintings of Spanish artist Pablo Picasso, whose work spanned over 70 years and includes many noteworthy examples. You could introduce Picasso and the importance of using classification to organize so many works over so many years. After gathering sources in art criticism and art history, you could identify significant characteristics of each major period in Picasso's work. The purpose of your classification might be to show common threads that run through each period, or to argue that Picasso's work progresses toward a goal as it moves from one period to the next. The basic classification structure might look as follows:

I. Introduction to the history and volume of Picasso's production

II. Blue Period and Rose Period (early 1900s)

III. African Influence and Cubism (pre-World War I)

IV. Surrealism (until World War II)—
    including additional periods as needed

V. Writer develops a claim about the periods (delayed thesis)

Comparison

Rather than using the classification of parts approach to examine Picasso's work, we could use other organizational patterns just as effectively. While our classification approach grouped Picasso's paintings by date of production and the divisions recommended by scholars, we could also organize an essay according to common themes or ideas in the paintings and *comparing* them from one period to another.

After viewing many of Picasso's paintings, we could identify recurring themes, such as "women and love," "war and politics," and "religion and spirituality." Each theme would initiate comparisons of works across periods, so that we could show how Picasso uses different styles to wrestle with an idea, or show how a theme might disappear in one period only to emerge again later. Our sources from art history and art criticism would help to develop academic arguments about these themes.

How do different organizational patterns shift the emphasis of an argument?

In this comparative paper, we would use the same information, and argue the same claim developed in the classification approach. The point/counterpoint approach would shift the *emphasis* of our analysis from the historical periods to issues and ideas common throughout periods (whether during the 1910s, the 1930s, or the 1970s).

A comparative organizational strategy would change the essay to look something like this:

I. Introduction to research question, major issues of debate, and sources

II. Theme 1: Women and Love—compare examples from the Blue Period, Rose Period, Surrealist Period, and so on.

See Pattern 2 in Chapter 14 for additional comparison examples.

III. Theme 2: War and Politics—compare examples from the Blue Period, African Period, Surrealist Period, and so on—including additional issues as needed

IV. Writer develops a claim about the themes across periods

AS YOU WRITE:

✓ Decide what your thesis will be. How does it motivate your argument?

✓ Explain why you are writing. Is your purpose to interpret, analyze, synthesize, conduct field research, or test a theory?

✓ Choose when to introduce your thesis.

✓ Plan how to effectively integrate sources with your thesis. Which pattern will you use to organize your essay?

Activity 1: Organization

Test at least two possible organizational patterns for your formal research essay. Draft a tentative outline anticipating how you will use your sources and develop your own argument. Compare these options so that you can make an informed choice about your approach in the final draft. Consider the following questions:

- Which pattern best matches the conventions of your academic field?
- Which pattern best meets the needs of your anticipated audience members, addressing their prior knowledge and their likely level of skepticism?
- Which pattern helps you make the most effective use of your sources?
- Which pattern helps you effectively present and support your thesis?

TRYING ON A NEW VOICE

In your earlier writing projects, it has been appropriate—and often preferable—to write in the first person, using "I" to describe the process of entering an academic conversation. In contrast, formal research writing often avoids first person voice and works instead in a more neutral, third-person voice. For your own formal research essay, consider adopting an approach used in your sources.

Use sources to guide your choices about voice.

Think about ways academic writers in your research field establish their presence without explicitly discussing themselves:

- How do they provide readers with some insight into their own passion about the subject?
- How do they describe the stakes of the research so that readers can see their interest in understanding or solving the research question?
- How do they uniquely bring sources together in a single project?
- How do they uniquely link the concerns and perspectives of two or more fields?
- How do they demonstrate the originality of their conclusion?

Once you get a sense of expert writers' techniques, you can choose the best to incorporate into your own formal research essay.

Using a formal academic voice means transitioning away from the ways of speaking and writing that you would use among friends

Choose a voice that shows respect for your sources and your audience.

and family, or in a passing conversation in the grocery store or on the subway. You needn't abandon your own personal style or feel as though your contribution is less meaningful. Instead, you will use the language, vocabulary, and style most appropriate for an academic situation—just as, perhaps, conversations among your close friends call for a different language, vocabulary, and style than conversations with your parents or coworkers.

If you began your research process with general audience sources and gradually moved into more academic ones, you have an illustration close at hand of the distinct conventions of the two conversations. Even though you must ultimately incorporate a number of academic sources into your essay, doing so doesn't mean that you have to abandon all of your nonacademic sources. Consider ways that your general audience sources might help you introduce a complex or unfamiliar issue to your readers, who are likely to lack the familiarity you've developed in the course of your research. How can quotations, paraphrases, and summaries of general audience sources bridge the gap between common and specialized knowledge and arguments?

MOVING FROM ANALYSIS TO SYNTHESIS

Analysis

In each of your writing projects, you have been doing *analytic* work with sources. *Analysis* involves breaking an idea, a source, or a concept down into its component parts, details, and aspects. For example, to define an academic concept, you probably found that it's helpful to start with familiar examples and illustrations, and then to explore aspects of its more specialized meanings and uses. Or, to summarize a source, you identified its component parts, including the thesis, important subpoints, and key examples.

Since academic conversations are always complex, it is important to develop techniques for managing that complexity. Your academic reading requires analysis strategies, including:

- Identifying a thesis
- Speculating on an author's assumptions
- Understanding an author's purpose
- Grouping an author's sources
- Understanding examples and illustrations
- Identifying an author's position

The formal research essay requires you to analyze multiple sources, perspectives, and ideas. As you work with each source, you can anticipate connecting them by comparing or classifying their common features:

- What is each author's position?
- What evidence does each author use to argue a claim?
- Which sources (or kinds of sources) does each author use for support?
- How does each author develop examples or make comparisons?
- Which aspects or issues of each essay are unique, and thus show authors' particular contributions to the conversation?

Synthesis

Although you may have begun the process of weaving sources together either in your exploratory essay or in other papers, the formal research essay requires synthesis in addition to analysis. *Synthesis* refers to the practice of combining ideas and building relationships in novel ways. By synthesizing, writers develop ideas identified in the analytic process into meaningful connections which help them to establish and support their own claims, perspectives, and arguments.

As you begin to synthesize material from your sources, consider some of the following approaches:

Show a conversation among experts about an idea, subject, concept, or issue

Compare (and contrast) two or more authors' positions in a debate

Evaluate arguments among experts

Bridge gaps or blind spots between sources

Develop your own position within the conversation

After reading about ethical concerns of psychologists who participate in screening participants for reality TV shows, a writer could synthesize the perspectives of two or more authors to illustrate positions in the conversation. In the following example (drawn from the case study in Chapter 11), authors Brown and Robinson both argue that we need to see the program's producer, rather than potential contestants, as the psychologist's true client. One synthesis could compare Brown and Robinson, *mediating* between the two authors' arguments:

Synthesize to build comparisons between sources.

> Each of the ethics case study articles shows the potential impact of reality programs on contestants, but only Brown and Robinson

describe the importance of the psychologist's relationship with the show's producer. As Brown claims, the psychologist's "presence is solely for the protection of their clients, who happen to be Mr. Mogul and the network" (247). Brown may be correct, but Robinson goes on to explain how Dr. Goodley still has a clear ethical "obligation to tell the contestants this and make sure they understand it" (249). Although Brown and Robinson shift their focus from the psychologist-contestant relationship to the psychologist-producer relationship, they make the move for different reasons. For Brown, once Dr. Goodley recognizes that she is professionally responsible primarily to show producers and the network, she is in a position to convince her clients to "come to some sort of agreement that respects both the ethics of assessment and Mr. Mogul's need to get the show on the road," and thus free herself to participate as a consultant for the program (248). Robinson agrees that, seen this way, the psychologist-producer relationship might shield Dr. Goodley from legal consequences; however, once the psychologist understands the real doctor-client relationship, it becomes impossible for her to participate in the program ethically (250).

Synthesize to compare and evaluate arguments you find in sources.

Another synthesis could use the same two sources, and even many of the same quoted passages, but evaluate them to help the writer *develop a position* within the conversation among experts:

Each of the ethics case study articles shows the potential impact of reality programs on contestants, but only Brown and Robinson describe the importance of the psychologist's relationship with the show's producer. As Brown claims, the psychologist's "presence is solely for the protection of their clients, who happen to be Mr. Mogul and the network" (247). For Brown, once Dr. Goodley recognizes that she is professionally responsible primarily to show producers and the network, she is in a position to convince her clients to "come to some sort of agreement that respects both the ethics of assessment and Mr. Mogul's need to get the show on the road," and thus free herself to participate as a consultant for the program (248). Brown reduces the problem to Goodley's legal liability, thus losing sight of the contestants, who will be harmed by participating in the show. Robinson has a better understanding of the real consequences of participating. Even though the psychologist-producer relationship might shield Dr. Goodley from legal consequences, once the psychologist understands the real doctor-client relationship, it becomes impossible for her to participate in the program ethically (250). In fact, Robinson makes the strongest case against participating when he considers the producer's unscrupulous motivations: using a psychologist to find "contestants who will obey orders, do anything for attention, and play up the tension and competition but ultimately capitulate by eating bull testicles" (250). Unlike Brown, Robinson understands the larger consequences of Goodley's participation in the screening process. She is there to ensure that the "ritualized humiliation" of reality TV works smoothly for producers and viewers, with no regard for the damage done to contestants.

Note how the second example uses *evaluative phrases* in making transitions from Brown's points to Robinson's. Phrases like "Brown reduces the problem," and "Robinson makes the strongest case," signal for readers the writer's preference for one scholar's analysis or solution over the other.

Use evaluative phrases to transition from one source to another.

The examples above are only two possible approaches. Since synthesis is a technique that requires you to explicitly enter into a conversation with your sources, your approaches will be limited only by your own creativity and ability to connect ideas.

ANTICIPATE AND ADDRESS COUNTERARGUMENTS

As you support your claim with evidence from your sources and with strong analysis and synthesis, you should also anticipate challenges readers might make against your claim. Why and how would someone disagree with you, or take an entirely different position in a debate on the issue?

Once you introduce counterarguments you find in your sources or anticipate your readers holding, you can either *refute* them by exposing their weaknesses, or *concede* to them by modifying your argument to acknowledge the validity of alternative positions, solutions, and claims. Your ability to

Refutation, concession, and other elements of argument are explored further in Chapter 14.

include, and then refute or concede to counterarguments will not undermine the strength of your argument. Instead, it will show readers that you are a fair participant in the conversation, someone who can critically consider and evaluate positions other than your own.

AS YOU WRITE:

✓ Analyze each source by identifying thesis, position, evidence, examples, and ideas.

✓ Synthesize two or more sources by comparing, evaluating, and developing connections.

✓ Use evaluative phrases to develop connections between sources in your own words.

✓ Address potential counterarguments by refuting or conceding to them fairly.

STUDENT VOICE

Devin explains how he incorporated multiple perspectives and counterarguments from his sources in his formal research essay.

The formal research essay forced me to look at more than one side of my thesis, weighing all my evidence fairly and honestly considering sources that were both for and against my own position. I joined the side of those whose views support my thesis and who had entered the conversation long before me. I built support for my thesis from their views and brought to the conversation some of my own.

DRAFTING AND REVISING THE FORMAL RESEARCH ESSAY

Writing the Introduction

You have now had opportunities to draft a tentative thesis and to test at least one organizational strategy for your formal research essay. Additionally, you probably have found many of the research materials you plan to use in developing your argument and supporting your claim. At this point, you may want to draft an introduction of one or more paragraphs that summarizes your vision for the essay.

To get started, review introductions of the academic articles you've read. Which are especially effective? How do those authors draw you in and pique your interest in the subject or purpose of the research? How do effective writers convince you to invest the energy required to read and understand complex ideas and arguments? How can you emulate their strategies?

Some of the most common introductions to research essays include, but are not limited to, the following:

- A striking or memorable *quotation* by a major figure related to the research question or purpose
- An *anecdote* that illustrates the personal significance of the project for the writer
- A familiar *event* that illustrates the general significance of the project for the reader
- A brief *sketch of a debate* among experts to be evaluated in detail in the essay
- A summary of the *history* of an issue or debate, and why it's relevant now
- A *rhetorical question* posed to readers
- A *forecasting statement* indicating the organization and main points of the argument
- A *thesis*

If you are just beginning the drafting process, you should see your introduction in the same way as you see the tentative thesis or scratch outline. The draft introduction helps you start the writing process and organize your thoughts early on. Like your tentative thesis and outline, your introduction may (and perhaps *should*) be revised—either a little or a lot—as you draft the rest of the essay. Your tentative introduction is not a trap that locks you into a particular position, purpose, or organizational pattern, but is instead an element of your essay that will evolve along with the rest of the draft.

Writing Transitions between Major Parts

Regardless of the organizational strategy you choose for your research essay, you will connect a number of sources to various aspects of your subject as you explore an issue and support your thesis. In that process, you will develop a complex argument in which you examine multiple positions and perspectives in the conversation. Clear *transitions* will help lead readers through your argument as you move from one source or group of sources to another or one issue to another, and as you build support for your thesis.

Activity 2: Draft an Introduction

I. Draft an introduction for your formal research essay. Your draft introduction should be about one to one and a half pages long and it should incorporate some of the strategies introduced in this chapter and used in your sources. Consider the following:

- Open with an anecdote from your life or a brief story drawn from a source to pique readers' interest in your project.
- State a tentative thesis.
- Forecast the organization of your project.

II. Share your introduction with a fellow student to gauge its appeal to a "live" audience. Reviewers might answer the following questions to help you revise your introduction and plan for drafting the rest of your essay:

- How did the writer choose to introduce the project?
- Does the writer include a thesis statement in the introduction? Whether yes or no, is the decision logical?
- Does the writer forecast the organization and/or major points to be developed in the rest of the essay?
- What else would you like to know as the essay begins?

Transitions with Subheadings

Academic writers often use subheadings to signal transitions between sections. For example, readers of scientific articles expect authors to divide their work into predictable sections, which include an abstract, introduction, methodology, analysis, and conclusion. Those section headings help writers organize their work in conventional ways and indicate to readers each section's content and purpose.

As you draft and revise your essay, identify major themes or turning points in your argument that you could identify with subheadings. How can you signal your movement from one subject, point, or purpose to another? For example, imagine how a writer who analyzes Shakespeare's plays would divide the project by key themes or dramatic forms. To help readers follow the argument, each major section could have a subheading, such as:

Shakespeare's Tragedies
Shakespeare's History Plays
Shakespeare's Comedies

Since there are still many plays, themes, characters, and other aspects to consider in this study, the writer would probably include *second order subheadings* to further help readers anticipate analysis or groupings of particular tragedies, histories, and comedies, such as:

Shakespeare's Tragedies

1. Hamlet
2. Othello
3. King Lear
4. Macbeth

Transitions Using Definition

In the example below, John Gunders uses definition to transition between sections of his argument about public surveillance cameras. Gunders opens his article (included in Chapter 13) with a well known anecdote about a kidnapping captured on shopping center surveillance cameras, then provides an overview of the thousands of cameras used across Australia and Great Britain. In order to help readers move from this introductory section to his analysis of the impact of public surveillance practices, he pauses to explain a concept that plays a crucial role in his argument.

In paragraph 6 of "Thinking outside the XBOX," Tony uses definition to introduce a new problem in his analysis of video games.

A definition transition will be most effective early in an essay, when you explain terms and concepts important to the conversation. Later transitions are more likely to involve some form of *summary* and *forecasting*, where you review the preceding section(s) of the essay and prepare readers for the next section.

Once Gunders defines and illustrates "interpellation," he forecasts his plan to bring together the fact of increasing public surveillance (the topic of the first section) and the philosophical concept of interpellation (the topic of the definition/transition paragraph), thus preparing readers for his contribution to the conversation: an argument that synthesizes the fact and concept in a unique way.

Summary Transition Paragraphs

Consider adding transition paragraphs between major sections of your essay in order to summarize points of debate, significant historical shifts, and your progression from one key source or idea to another. Summary transitions might also work to forecast an upcoming

But as well as these topics, there are theoretical questions concerning the camera and issues of subjectivity. French Marxist theorist Louis Althusser, suggests that every member of society is defined as a "subject" in relation to the ideology of that society, and that the subject apprehends and understands the world through the lens of that ideology (1972:170–71). The subject is brought into compliance with the ideology through the process of "interpellation". Althusser likens this to "hailing" someone in the street: a voice cries out, "hey, you there!" and an individual (usually the one being hailed) turns around, recognising (or at least suspecting) that they are really the one being hailed.

Gunders signals the completion of one section and introduces the next: the "theoretical questions" at stake in the remainder of the essay.

By acknowledging the hail, by realising that they are the one being hailed, the subject is interpellated into the discourse of the hailer (1972:174–75). In other words, the subject, becoming aware of the ideology of their society, recognises themselves as a part of, or in agreement with that ideology. Most often, interpellation is not a conscious process, but operates within the unspoken assumptions of the ideology. An obvious example of this is the way advertising works: advertisements for financial institutions, share trading companies and the like do not specifically ask if the viewer wants to make money-that is assumed.

Gunders defines a philosophical concept unfamiliar to an audience of social workers.

Rather, they portray a Lifestyle that nearly all viewers will immediately accept: "Yes, of course I want financial security and a comfortable existence!" The viewers see themselves in relation to the actors in the commercial, and recognise their own desires and needs. What is not questioned is the underlying assumptions about wealth, its production and distribution. There is one important difference between Althusser's person on the street and my bank ad, and the theory of ideological interpellation: while the examples are sequential, in relation to ideology, the subject is always, already interpellated (1972:172).

Gunders uses another transition to signal his move from definition to application

I wish to extend this concept of interpellation to that of the subject vis-a-vis the surveillance camera by showing that the camera interpellates the subject within an ideological dichotomy of good and bad.[7]

section in the essay, or to summarize a complex issue before you develop it in detail. These transition paragraphs provide readers with breaks in the essay that help them organize and track your argument as it unfolds.

In the following example, literary theorist Jane Tompkins transitions between two sets of research materials about European-Indian relations in the 1600s: from histories published in the 1950s and the 1970s, to eyewitness accounts described in seventeenth-century testimonies:

At this point, dismayed and confused by the wildly divergent views of colonial history the twentieth-century historians had provided, I decided to look at some primary materials.	A transition summarizes the research thus far.
I thought, perhaps, if I looked at some firsthand accounts and at some scholars looking at those accounts, it would be possible to decide which experts were right and which were wrong by comparing their views with evidence. Captivity narratives seemed a good place to begin, since it was logical to suppose that the records left by whites who had been captured by Indians would furnish the sort of firsthand information I wanted.	She introduces the next group of sources and describes what she expects to find. She provides examples of primary sources and forecasts with preliminary evaluation.

This transition paragraph helps move the argument forward in four important ways:

1. Grouping sources together and summarizing responses as they evolve
2. Distinguishing between different types of sources
3. Forecasting the next section of the essay
4. Describing preliminary expectations

Later, as she moves from analyzing research materials to developing a conclusion, Tompkins transitions by inviting her readers to wrestle with the problem alongside her:

> It may well seem to you at this point that, given the tremendous variation among the historical accounts, I had no choice but to end in relativism.

She asks readers, "[W]hat would you have done if you were similarly faced with all of these conflicting research materials?" Her readers may not all agree with her; in fact, they may believe that "to end in relativism" would be a very good choice. The aim is to show readers that she was left adrift in the research process, just as they might be. She then is able to briefly review the evidence she has accumulated and prepare for her contribution to the debate.

Writing the Conclusion

In the conclusion, a writer signals that the time has come to summarize key points and convince readers of the argument's credibility. It is also an opportunity for the writer to reflect on the essay's purpose, helping readers understand the value of the argument. In developing a strong conclusion, writers want to avoid using clichéd words and phrases, such as "in conclusion"; instead, they work hard to find fresh and interesting ways to transition into their closing statements.

While a recap of the major points in your argument can be a useful way of beginning, a strong conclusion typically goes beyond summary. Like the thesis, the conclusion should say something about the purpose, goals, and significance of your work. Make sure that your conclusion gives readers a sense of the impact of your research and thinking. Since they have come this far with you, what now? You might use one or more of the following strategies in your conclusion:

- Demonstrate the broader significance or application of the issue you've addressed.
- Recommend action that should be taken.
- Propose directions for further research.
- Revisit a quotation or anecdote with which you opened the essay.
- Revisit a key example or illustration from the essay.
- If using a delayed thesis approach, state the thesis.

As with other elements of formal research writing, if you get stuck in drafting your conclusion, revisit your sources and consider adopting one or more of the strategies used by experts in your field.

Revising

Once you have a strong working draft of your formal research essay, spend time reviewing and revising each feature of your argument before submitting the essay for peer review or a grade. You should pay particular attention to key features including, but not limited to, **focus, strength of argument, use of sources,** and **clarity.**

Focus

- Are your subject and research question focused specifically enough that you are able to adequately cover them in your essay?
- Would your essay be stronger if you *narrowed the focus* of the research question so that you could get into more detail, explain more positions in a debate, or provide a more detailed history of an issue?
- If you've found yourself simply restating many of the same points, how might you *expand the scope* of your question or the range of your research materials to keep it interesting for your readers?

Strength of Argument

- Did your thesis evolve into a different one than you started with? Should you revise the introductory paragraphs to better reflect your final argument?
- In order to keep the introduction and thesis as they are, should you revise body paragraphs or transitions to better show the evolution of your argument and lead clearly into your conclusion?
- Does each paragraph express a point, and do paragraphs work together in developing a clear and logical argument?

See Chapter 14 for more advice on revising paragraphs for unity and coherence.

- Are you making effective transitions between paragraphs and between major parts of the essay?
- Does your conclusion accurately reflect and develop the claim on which you began?

Use of Sources

- Does every source serve a purpose?
- Should unnecessary or repetitive sources be left out?
- If each source is essential to your argument, can you more effectively incorporate each into the argument?
- Are there any additional places in the essay where your use of source materials is unclear?
- Is every source introduced and contextualized with appropriate attributive tags and then adequately developed?
- Are there any freestanding quotations, and how could you introduce, contextualize, and develop them more effectively?

- Is every source documented with parenthetical citations and in-text references as appropriate for the style you're following?
- If you have included explanatory notes, are they linked accurately to the text with superscript numbers and do they follow your discipline's style correctly?

Clarity

You can read more about jargon and other aspects of conventional academic style in Chapter 14.

- Are your sentences grammatically sound? Is each sentence clear and to the point?
- Are there places where you have used conversational language (such as slang), unnecessary jargon, or awkward sentence structure that you can revise to assist readers?
- Are any sentences too wordy or redundant, and how can you revise for economy?

Try to make every word, phrase, and point strong enough to stand on its own, and only repeat ideas when they genuinely need emphasis.

WRITING SAMPLES

David, our first student writer, combines scholarly journal sources with general audience sources, such as newspapers, commercial and government websites, and trade magazines. Compare this formal research essay with the next student, Tony, who exclusively uses articles from scholarly journals. Compare the amount of references to personal experience by each writer and think about the ways each writer integrates personal information with source material.

- Do you think the writers' choices to work in different fields—the first in physical sciences and engineering, and the second in the humanities and social sciences—affect their approaches to using sources, or to organizing and writing the essays?
- Do the conventions of each field pressure writers to make certain kinds of conclusions, or to make them in certain ways?

FORMAL RESEARCH ESSAY

FORMAL PEER REVIEW

Formal Research Essay goals: 1) argue a thesis through research on a topic, issue, and/or problematic question; 2) develop examples, acknowledge multiple points of view, anticipate counterarguments, and incorporate other conventions of academic argument using scholarly research; 3) use quotations, paraphrases, and summaries appropriately, and prepare a conventional bibliography; 4) use organizational strategies, language, and style appropriate to the research field. If you have time, discuss comments with your partner to clear up any questions s/he has.

1. In one sentence, summarize the writer's thesis and purpose in the essay.
2. Did the writer's introduction draw you into the essay? What elements of the introduction did you find especially effective? What could the writer improve, and how would you suggest s/he revise?
3. Was the argument logically developed? Did the writer use one of the organizational strategies described in this chapter? If so, which strategy best describes the writer's choice? Were there points where the writer's logic seemed to break down? How would you recommend improving the essay's organization?
4. Did the writer make effective transitions between parts of the essay? Did s/he use subheadings, transition paragraphs, chronological signals, and/or definitions to transition from one part to another? Where do you think transitions are missing, and how should the writer develop them?
5. Does the essay include sufficient evidence to support the thesis? Has the writer found enough source material to meet the requirements of the assignment? Where do you think additional sources would strengthen or add depth to the essay?
6. Does the writer use source material (quotations, paraphrases, and summaries) to show multiple perspectives on the central issue or question? Does the writer effectively manage sources with analysis, synthesis, and response?
7. Does the writer rely too much on source material? Does the writer over-quote? What additional work needs to be done to explain and develop source material in the writer's own words? Make suggestions.
8. Are sources adequately cited in the text with parenthetical references or footnotes? Do you have everything you need (such as page number, author, and title of work) to find the source in the bibliography?
9. Has the writer concluded the essay effectively?
10. Help the writer identify mechanical problems that have to be fixed before submission. Consider sentence-level problems: fragments, run-ons, or awkward syntax or phrasing; word-level problems: misspellings, missing words, or misuse of words; and problems with in-text citations, bibliographic style, or overall formatting.

FIGURE 12.3 Formal research essay: Formal peer review.

David C.
Ms. Greenberg
College Writing
14 April 2006

<h2 style="text-align:center">Hope for a Hydrogen Economy</h2>

The turn of the twentieth century saw a lot of excitement about the internal combustion engine, and throughout the century the availability of fossil fuels and oil made it possible for many people to afford and experience a new freedom of mobility. However, as we move into the twenty-first century we can see the dire environmental and economic consequences of the twentieth century's dependence on oil. Problems with global warming, air pollution, depletion of fossil fuels, and even wars have shown us that the world cannot depend on fossil fuels long into the future. For some time, scientists, engineers, and others have worked on solutions to the world's fuel and energy problems. There are a number of options on the table, but the most logical answer is hydrogen power. Hydrogen makes sense from environmental and economic perspectives; and, although renewable resources are preferred for the production of hydrogen, in cases of high demand, nuclear power and coal-fired plants can also be used to meet additional needs.

One of the reasons hydrogen is being considered as a solution to world energy problems is that it is the most abundant substance in the universe, and the third most abundant element on earth. In his book *The Hydrogen World View*, Dr. Roger Billings describes domestic hydrogen sources, like the "[n]aturally-occuring hydrogen [that] has been discovered in vast underground deposits in eastern Kansas" (3). It is unrealistic to think that we can find enough hydrogen in its natural state to give the country a steady fuel supply; fortunately, however, hydrogen is abundant in water, hydrocarbons, and organic matter like cow manure.

Some might laugh at the idea of using water as fuel, but the reality is that people have been using it for years. Billings explains how hydrogen can be produced from water by using electrolysis: when "two metal plates are placed in water in the presence of a catalyst and connected to a source of electricity, water molecules are split into hydrogen and oxygen" (107). Oxygen can be released, while the hydrogen can be compressed and stored to be used later. While hydrogen is easy to produce, hydrogen has a bad reputation because of its past use in bombs and dirigibles like the ill-fated Hindenburg blimp, and people are justifiably skeptical about how safely it can be stored and used. Peter Eisenberger, chairman of a University of Minnesota committee researching hydrogen, explains that once it is generated, the volatile gas still has to be stored, and, in automobiles, for instance, this could have catastrophic consequences (Lortie 12).

To solve problems of storage for stationary and mobile purposes alike, Billings set out with colleagues to perform a number of experiments using metal alloys they hoped would react with hydrogen to make it condense into a metal hydride (comparable to table salt). Their first efforts were disappointing, leaving Billings to ask: "Could the numerous problems associated with a metal hydride storage system be solved?" (66). After additional tests, Billings's team found a formula that successfully turned hydrogen into a hydride that acted like a sponge to soak up large amounts of hydrogen gas, thus allowing it to be stored safely. Later, when the metal hydride storage units were heated, the process was reversed and the hydride dissociated from the hydrogen gas, which could then be used to power a vehicle or generator.

Although it might seem new to people outside the field, the uses for hydrogen as a fuel source for more than bombs and blimps has been around for more than three decades. In fact, at the age of fifteen, in 1963, Billings himself rebuilt the engine on a Briggs and Stratton lawn mower to run on hydrogen (10). Later, in 1975, he built a home that used hydrogen to power everything, from lights to appliances (116). Since those early days, Billings's projects have been repeated by others, including a Minnesota dairy farm that uses biogas from cows to fuel a hydrogen cell that powers the entire farm. The farm was granted $221,000 to continue their research, because it is likely that hydrogen will become a major energy source in the next ten years ("Minnesota" 48). More recently, in 2005, students from the New York Institute of Technology designed a house that was powered by a combination of solar and hydrogen sources. Instead of using batteries to store the power, as was previously done on solar homes, they used the solar electricity to run an electrolysis converter that separated hydrogen from water. The hydrogen could then be stored and used later to produce electricity more efficiently (Tucker 9).

Most importantly, there are many car companies that now realize hydrogen powered cars are going to be the next big thing. The race is on to see which company can come up with the first hydrogen-powered fuel cell vehicle. James Mackintosh interviewed Larry Burns, head of research and planning at GM, for the *Financial Times*. Burns described how GM is under significant pressure to develop a fuel cell car, because other companies, such as Daimler-Chrysler, Toyota, and Honda, have already started putting fuel cell test vehicles on the road and plan to sell them to the general public by 2012 or 2015. Because of industry pressure, GM plans to get their cars on the road by 2010.

Its uses for homes, appliances, and cars make hydrogen appealing because it is a multi-functional gas that burns more cleanly than oil and other major fuel sources. Hydrogen-powered cars are the best example, because their emissions are mainly water vapor, which is obviously far better than the harmful carbon monoxide that cars currently emit. Moreover, carbon monoxide is only one of the many greenhouse gasses emitted from our cars and homes and responsible for climate changes and increasing pollution. Mark Jacobson of Stanford University did a study showing that, by using hydrogen fuel cell technology in our homes and cars, respiratory problems could be prevented in over one million people, including tens of thousands of people who are hospitalized each year with problems from excessive exposure to the nitro dioxide produced by gasoline vehicles (7). Even if we were to use coal gasification to run electrolysis, we could still save thousands of lives each year by switching to hydrogen power for cars (Jacobson, qtd. in J. W. 10).

Following industry lead, the US Department of Energy released a statement in January 2006 supporting the move to hydrogen. The Bush administration has also played an active role in trying to get a hydrogen economy up and running. For instance, in his 2003 State of the Union Address, Bush announced that in an attempt to become less dependent on foreign oil, 1.2 billion dollars were being set aside for the research and development of hydrogen powered automobiles (Lortie 12). However, even with the large amounts of money the government is investing, scientists are skeptical about the methods supported by the President and some government agencies. In his article "Hijacking Hydrogen," Jim Motavalli explains that there is a choice between using "renewables" and oil as hydrogen sources, and Mike Niklas, chairperson for the American Solar Energy Society, warns that even though the Bush administration is publicly supporting hydrogen development through its FreedomCar program, its vision does not support clean energy technologies for hydrogen production:

> "'Clean' in this case means coal, nuclear, and natural gas . . . We're now at the point of making a transition to an entirely new energy paradigm, and we don't need to be continuing the carbon era by other means." (38)

Today, the debate centers on how the electricity that powers electrolysis for hydrogen will be generated. As Motavalli claims, we basically have two choices: using renewable resources or non-renewable resources. Renewable resources include solar power, wind, hydroelectric power, and biogas; when these methods are used for hydrogen collection, they create "green hydrogen." On the other hand, when non-renewable resources, like nuclear power, coal, and natural gas, are used, they create "black hydrogen."

It is my belief that we should do everything in our power to develop and utilize ways of producing green hydrogen. Solar, wind, and hydro/dam power create no emissions, so the power source, like the hydrogen itself, helps in the fight against global warming and continued production of greenhouse gasses. Unfortunately, though, renewable resources may not be able to keep up with demand. Dan Keuter, vice president of nuclear development at the Entergy corporation, claims that it is not practical to think that renewables are "up to the task" of generating all the hydrogen that we will need, which is estimated to be by 2017 about four times what we now use (Lortie 12). However, academic and public researchers still hope that renewables will pull their own weight. Jonas Siegel, for instance, cites a Stanford study which showed that, by strategically placing wind-generating stations around the world, we could potentially generate eight to ten times the electricity currently used by the world. Engineers from a Norwegian energy firm are putting the final touches on floating wind turbines that will capture wind energy at sea. Their goal for the pilot program is to have 200 turbines off the west coast of Norway by 2008 (Hansen 30). In the past, the world couldn't depend on wind power, but hydrogen fuel cells make this form of energy more efficient and reliable. Wind power that was wasted in the past can now be used to produce hydrogen that can be stored for later use; even if the wind didn't blow for several days, the stores of hydrogen can still provide a constant supply of energy.

Even now, we're not doing too badly as far as renewable energy production is concerned. In the 2005 Renewable Energy Industry Review, Michael Eckhart shows that 2005 was the best year for renewables, and 2006 is going to be better. Additionally, the development of renewables, such as biofuels, is having a positive economic effect by creating jobs and investment opportunities. There might be a high overhead to get started with renewables, but, in the long run, they can pay for themselves because they are self-generating. That's more than can be said for fossil fuels, natural gas, and coal; as the US Department of Energy claims, the US uses about 20 million barrels of oil per day, at a cost of 2 billion dollars a week. The cost of oil is only going up, and our consumption of fossil fuels can't last much longer if the sources are limited. Finding new sources of coal might have overhead costs as high as developing renewables; the process involves a lot of time and labor, and even when coal is burned, only thirty percent of its potential energy is utilized. On top of the loss of power, we still have to deal with the pollution that is created and dumped into the air.

The problems associated with finding and using more coal are also associated with other fossil fuels. Too much energy is needed just to find and get to the power sources, which means that the net power produced is very low. If we can use water, wind, and even cow manure to get hydrogen, we have already taken care of the problems of locating and extracting the fuel sources. Recently, researchers at the University of Waterloo in Canada tested eleven "production pathways" to generate and store hydrogen in order to find the one with the least input energy and the greatest output energy. Because the researchers used a "life cycle analysis" process in their comparison, they had to consider the impact on the environment when they evaluated the amount of energy produced in each of the pathways (348). They found that hydrogen produced by hydroelectric power was the best method when compared with oil, nuclear, and natural gas production methods. Unlike coal and oil, which have to be extracted and refined far from where they are used, hydroelectric power can be produced locally in many areas and at reduced overhead costs. Similarly, researchers in Aragon, Spain, showed that when hydrogen is produced locally it cut production cost by 50% over large refineries. After using waste mineral oil to produce hydrogen, which they then used to power a "captive fleet of public vehicles" (6871), the

Spanish researchers showed that "just a very small part of the gas produced (around 2.4%) needs to be burnt to provide the energetic requirements of the process" (6876).

In contrast, while the Spanish study depends on local production and consumption, big companies are investing into hydrogen now in hopes that they will be able to stay in the money and continue to be the ones in charge of production and distribution. Motavalli states:

> Shell established Shell Renewables in 1997 and Shell Hydrogen in 2000, BP/Amoco is investing $500 million in renewables over the next three years, and Chevron Texaco has purchased a 20 percent stake in Energy Conversion Devices, a Detroit-based photovoltaic, battery and fuel cell company. (38)

These companies, along with other large utility companies, want to produce hydrogen by using "clean coal." This means that before combustion they will let the coal react with steam, which will then "sequester" the emissions in liquid carbon dioxide to be stored in deep underground aquifers (Motavalli 38). This method has not been tested and no one knows about its long-term effects.

Nuclear power is also making a big comeback in the hydrogen game. So far, thirty plants have renewed their licenses and plans for new plants, which used to take eighty-four months to be approved, but are now being approved in thirty months. As Dan Keuter stated, "The only practical way to produce large volumes of emission-free hydrogen is from advanced nuclear reactors" (qtd. in Lortie 12). Many countries are following his philosophy; China is planning twenty-five new nuclear plants in the next ten to fifteen years, while Great Britain and India plan to build more new plants as well. Motavalli predicts that nuclear-supplied power will go from twenty to fifty percent in the next thirty years. I believe that the United States should look to other methods of power production, because at some point the problems that come with nuclear power, such as radiation and waste products, are going to catch up with us—maybe only after we have already backed ourselves into an irreversible dependence on nuclear energy.

Even if hydroelectric power isn't available, there are a number of other options for powering hydrogen production locally. In an article she published in *BioCycle*, Angela Crooks looks at ways of using biomass from forests to generate power. Crooks says that it would be possible to fuel around forty-seven percent of our energy needs by using the 368 million dry tons of forest biomass, which is regenerated every year; harvesting biomass could also cut down on fires that burn millions of forest acres every year. As Larry Rohter reports in the *New York Times*, Brazil has been making ethanol from sugar cane since 1975, when they had a major energy crisis. By the 1980s, there were more than 600,000 cars in Brazil that could run on the cane-based ethanol. Thus, rather than depending on large industries, power can be developed from local sources. Otherwise, as Motavalli quoted one environmentalist, "nuclear-generated hydrogen is like a nicotine patch that causes cancer" (39).

With decades of experience, Dr. Billings has become one of the top scientists in the country supporting the development of hydrogen. He claims that we have to move on and get to a point where we are independent of nuclear and coal-burning plants. He also makes it clear that we have the technology to become a "hydrogen society" sooner than many of us think. As other scientists and engineers show, the answer may be in learning how to move from large industries to smaller local production of hydrogen and other renewable fuels. When we depend on nuclear energy or coal for our main power supplies, we are only risking greater long-term problems. If we think ahead and invest in our future, green hydrogen is the best way to go so that we can for once leave the earth in a better condition than we found it.

WORKS CITED

Billings, Roger E. *The Hydrogen World View*. Independence, MO: International Academy of Science, 2000. Print.

Chui, F., A. Elkamel, and M. Fowler. "An Integrated Decision Support Framework for the Assessment and Analysis of Hydrogen Production Pathways." *Energy and Fuels* 20 (2006): 346–52. Print.

Crooks, Angela. "Protecting Forests and Supporting Renewable Energy." *BioCycle* 46.4 (2005): 68–71. Print.

Eckhart, Michael. "Renewable Energy Industry." *Power Engineering* 110.1 (2006): 8. Print.

Hansen, Bret. "Floating Wind Turbines Expand Renewable Energy Possibilities." *Civil Engineering* 76.2 (2006): 30. Print.

J. W. "Healthy Hydrogen." *Mechanical Engineering* 127.10 (2005): 10. Print.

Jacobson, Mark Z. "Towards a Hydrogen Economy?" *Environment* 47 (2005): 7. Print.

Làzaro, María, Isabel Suelves, and Rafael Moliner. "On-Site Production of Hydrogen from Mineral Waste Oils by Thermocatalytic Decomposition: An Aragon Case Study." *American Chemical Society* 39 (2005): 6871–76. Print.

Lortie, Bret. "Bush's Nuclear FreedomCar." *Atomic Scientists* 60.3 (2004): 12. Print.

MacKintosh, James. "GM in the Race to Make Clean Car Investment." *Financial Times* 31 March 2006. Print.

"Minnesota Dairy Runs Hydrogen Fuel Cell on Biogas." *BioCycle Energy* 46.6 (2005): 48. Print.

Motavalli, Jim. "Hijacking Hydrogen." *The Environmental Magazine* 14.1 (2003): 38–39. Print.

Rohter, Larry. "With Big Boosts from Sugar Cane, Brazil Is Satisfying Its Fuel Needs." *New York Times*, 10 April 2006. Web. 22 December 2008.

Siegel, Jonas. "The Mighty Wind." *Atomic Scientists* 61.6 (2005): 13. Print.

Tucker, Patrick. "A Solar-Hydrogen Home." *Futurist* 39.5 (2005): 9. Print.

US Department of Energy. "The Hydrogen Future: Benefits of a Hydrogen Economy." Print.

Tony focuses on the relationship between violence and video games (a topic that you may remember from Megan's paper in Chapter 11). Note that while Tony and Megan use some of the same sources, each ultimately turns in different directions, and into different academic conversations, to further understand the issue. How do their different approaches to researching the importance and impact of violent content in video games affect the arguments they are able to make? How do the writers' uses of research lead, or perhaps even pressure, them to make different conclusions? Note too that Tony begins applying his findings to his own video game play. How could you similarly develop your own experience into a case study to help readers better understand the significance of your findings?

Tony E.
Professor Anderson
College Writing
2 December 2008

Video Games: Thinking Outside
the XBOX?

As I pressed the shift key, a burst of fire erupted forth from the barrel of my semi-automatic rifle, taking the life of my digital opponent. "Sweet!" I thought to myself as the Nazi soldier crumpled to the floor and I stormed past his body to collect the golden treasures he had been guarding.

This was my first experience with a violent video game. I was about 7 years old and the game was Wolfenstein 3D. Now, over a decade later, I have run the gamut of violent video games, playing everything from Doom to Grand Theft Auto, with hundreds in between. My current favorite is Halo 2, where I take on the role of a cybernetically enhanced soldier who defends Earth from wave after wave of alien forces known as the Covenant. My daily indulgence in these games would scare the people who strongly oppose violent game content because of their firm belief that it mentally and emotionally harms young children. Even though fears about violent video games get a lot of media attention, my experiences helped me to begin researching the topic in order to try to prove that the games I enjoy most are not harmful. However, as is often the case with research, I have opened up a new world of possibilities proving to myself, yet again, that I'm never as smart as I think I am.

This paper began with one intent, but through my research I discovered that maybe it's not the violence in video games that we should be concerned with, but the video game medium itself. How does playing video games, violent or otherwise, affect a person's abilities to use problem-solving skills, spatial skills, and hand-eye coordination, and do these games have an overall positive influence on players? How do influences of rules and governance by outside programmers make video game "playspace," the environment created by a video game for the user to play in, different than other playspaces that are defined entirely by users? To put it in other words: do video games support imaginative play or crush it by making players conform to established rules? In essence, I've discovered through my research that violence in video games is something we needn't be overly worried about as a society, but we should be more worried about how video games in general are conditioning us to take orders and conform to rules or limitations established by others, rather than working outside the rules and limitations to truly "think outside the Xbox."

The study of how video games affect players has been going on for more than twenty years, as shown by the article "Personality Differences between High and Low Electronic Video Game Users," published in 1983 by psychologist Gerald T. Gibbs and his colleagues. Their study focused on gamers, those who play video games in general, and did not single out violent games in particular. The authors were looking for the following traits in gamers: "1) self-esteem—self-degradation, 2) social deviancy—social conformity, 3) hostility—kindness, 4) social-withdrawal—gregariousness, 5) obsessive-compulsive, and 6) achievement motivation." (159). The authors concluded: "Within the population sampled, there is no evidence to indicate, as opponents to video games suggest . . .[,] that the games encourage social isolation, anger, anti-social behavior, and compulsivity." (164). This study shows that video games, in fact, do not harm the gamer or cause him/her to behave in a way that would show video games as detrimental for a person. In a paper published in 2001, Craig A. Anderson and Brad J. Bushman concur, claiming, "the fact that some highly publicized school killings were committed by individuals who habitually played violent video games is not strong evidence that violent video games increase aggression" (353). As much as some people want to find a scapegoat for events like the Columbine shootings, violent video games are not the answer. Violent behavior still comes down to the individual's personality; if people desire to do something extreme like killing their classmates, they are going to do it regardless of their taste in video games.

Although Gibb's research found no connection between game play and behavior, it's also important to look at the effects of explicitly violent video games. In their paper "Violent Video Games and Their Effects on State Hostility and Physiological Arousal," Portuguese psychologists Patricia Arriaga, Paula Carniero, and Maria Monteiro study the immediate effects of violent games on their subjects. Arriaga and colleagues published their tests in 2006, well after those performed in 1983 by Gibbs and his colleagues. Arriaga's tests separated male and female gamers, used a virtual reality headset, and focused on Doom, a first-person shooter game released in the early nineties. As a control, two non-violent puzzle-style games were also used in the tests. At the end of their study, Arriaga and her colleagues claim: "The pattern of results obtained suggests that playing violent computer games may have an immediate effect on state hostility, but not on state anxiety" (155). They define "state hostility" as a measurement of a person's level of anger at any given moment, and "state anxiety" as the effect on a person's vital signs, whether they are elevated or not, and how alert a person is; state anxiety is important because it is a precursor for a person's fight or flight response. Arriaga's physiological tests showed that there is little change in male arousal between violent and non-violent games, while females showed more arousal when playing violent video games than when playing non-violent video games (156). This further develops my point that it's not necessarily the level of violence in the video games that most affects a person; additionally, it was shown in the tests that the subject's vital signs were elevated whether participating in a violent game or a non-violent game (156). If gamers' arousal, hostility, and anxiety reactions can be produced by any game, then the main concern here should be simply that they are stimulated by playing video games, regardless of the amount of violence in any one game.

In fact, observing or participating in video game violence isn't the largest potential threat here. In a paper entitled "Playspace Invaders: Huizinga, Baudrillard, and Video Game Violence," Randy Schroeder studies the issue of gamers losing the ability to differentiate between "realspace" and "playspace." Instead of using psychological approaches, Schroeder uses philosopher Jean Baudrillard's theories of the "hyperreal" to argue that the main issue with games is that they blur the line between reality and fantasy. "Hyperreal" is a term Baudrillard uses to describe an environment that takes the place of the real world, such as virtual reality replacing reality itself. When the virtual reality of a video game takes the place of normal reality, the gamer can begin to lose touch with the real world, losing himself in the hyperreal. Schroeder explains the potential problems of virtual reality: "Without direct access to the real and the original, we take the easy way out and claim that they don't exist" (150). When realspace doesn't reassert itself at any given moment, a gamer may run the risk of convincing himself that the virtual reality is truly reality and lose touch with reality itself. The danger, as Schroeder further argues, is that "there is no ethics of the hyperreal . . . video games don't teach the wrong ethics, they teach that ethics are superfluous: only the game counts, and the game can be started over and over again." This conditions a person in a way that they could begin to treat their realspace like playspace. The problem is that, in realspace, there is no reset button.

Some would argue that having the reset button as a best friend is not necessarily a bad thing. From Josh Schollmeyer's "Games Get Serious," I found how more and more organizations are using video games for training and education. Schollmeyer points out how these "serious games" are used by organizations, including the US military, because of "the value of serious games—to allow a user to fail again and again without real world repercussions. . . . It's why the military understands the utility of games so intuitively. The military reasons that if soldiers lose fake lives in simulations it better hones their ability to survive on a real battlefield" (38). I found this point of view fascinating, although I disagree with it. When playing video games, I am aware that the virtual lives of my digital enemies really are meaningless, so I treat them meaninglessly; I try out new ways to kill wantonly and take the life of anything that moves, knowing that if I take someone else's life in the video game playspace it is of little consequence. Later on, after the "war" is over and I've been conditioned through my virtual training and field experience, is it really that hard to condition myself to value human life once again? Then again, perhaps the military thinks of the overall benefit, so that training through video games is more productive and effective for the battlefield, even if the training changes the individual mentally. After the war is won or lost, and after the soldier has served his use, I don't think the military is nearly as concerned about what happens to their little plastic army men.

The US Army has even gone as far as to commission well-known software developing companies to design games, like the popular—and free—America's Army, for their use. In the paper entitled "Playing with Our Minds," Chris Suellentrop examines this game and the military's attempt to "play with our minds." Suellentrop continues the discussion of the emerging genre of "serious games" described by Schollmeyer, where the user plays in order to perform tasks that can really be considered a form of training. I experienced these types of games first hand when the US Air Force demonstrated their flight simulators and allowed students at my high school to try them out. They used a double-wide trailer outfitted for their purpose of creating a new reality (or what Baudrillard would call "hyperreality") through playspace. When I walked through the trailer doors, it was as if I was entering a new world, an effect similar to that of a haunted house. This was the Air Force's obvious attempt at recruitment by making a person believe that joining the Air Force would be as fun as the simulator. The officials running the program made it clear that the simulator I participated in was very similar to the virtual training performed by all their pilots. Through the simulator playspace, they had succeeded in making war fun.

Suellentrop points out that all games, not just military simulators, can teach. He said of "nonserious games" like Grand Theft Auto: "All video games, even the ones that allow you to kill prostitutes, are a form of education or at least edutainment." His reasoning stems from what Will Wright, a well-known game designer and creator of the massively popular game The Sims, had to say. For Wright, Suellentrop explains: "video games teach 'the essence of the scientific method' that 'through trial and error players build a model of the underlying game.'" It would appear that games can teach us how to think, but not just about discovering the model of that one game. Suellentrop takes it a step further and implies that video game play can affect a person's behavioral and reasoning skills. He states:

> Whether you find the content of a video game inoffensive or grotesque, their structure teaches players that their best course of action is always is to accept the system and work to succeed in it. . . . Gamers are famous for coming up with creative approaches to the problems a game presents. But devising a new, unexpected strategy to succeed under the existing rules isn't the same thing as proposing new rules, new systems, new patterns.

It's as if gamers are trapped inside a box that is also inside a box. They can develop new ways of dealing with problems; however, they still have to stay within the set limitations put there by the game designers. In truth, then, gamers are being taught to conform to rules set by other people, the programmers. It's possible that this mental conditioning would then extend to the gamer's realspace and prevent him or her from challenging norms and creating new solutions that make new rules in whatever situations they find themselves. Suellentrop ends his article with this powerful statement: "So don't worry that video games are teaching us to be killers. Worry instead that they are teaching us to salute."

Some may believe the violence portrayed in video games is a problem that needs to be dealt with, but I say that the violence isn't the big issue. Our society has survived violence in every form of the media, from books to radio shows, television, and movies. Violent video games are just another medium to add to the pile. The research shows the real issue here, that video games in general are teaching us as a society to conform to what someone higher up in authority says. While I am a big fan of playing video games and have no plans of stopping, I can now see that if left unchecked the gaming generation could potentially be one of the generations with the lowest aptitude for innovations and creation of new ideas.

WORKS CITED

Anderson, Craig C., and Brad J. Bushman. "Effects of Violent Video Games on Aggressive Behavior, Aggressive Cognition, Aggressive Affect, Physiological Arousal, and Prosocial Behavior." *American Psychological Society* 12 (2001): 353–59. Print.

Arriaga, Patrícia, Francisco Esteves, Paula Carniero, and Maria Benedicta Monteiro. "Violent Video Games and Their Effects on State Hostility and Physiological Arousal." *Aggressive Behavior* 32 (2006): 146–58. Print.

Gibb, Gerald T., James R. Bailey, Thomas T. Lambirth, and William P. Wilson. "Personality Differences between High and Low Electronic Video Game Users." *Journal of Psychology* 114 (1983): 159–65. Print.

Schollmeyer, Josh. "Games Get Serious" *Bulletin of the Atomic Scientists* 62 (2006): 34–39. Print.

Schroeder, Randy. "Playspace Invaders: Huizinga, Baudrillard, and Video Game Violence." *Journal of Popular Culture* 30 (1996): 143-53. *Academic Search Premier*. Web. 12 October 2006.

Suellentrop, Chris. "Playing with Our Minds." *Wilson Quarterly* 30 (2006): 14–21. Print.

13

Research Dossier: Six Readings on Surveillance

T hroughout *Entering the Academic Conversation*, you are encouraged to see critical inquiry, research, and writing as core elements of academic conversations. This chapter brings together a set of readings from a range of professional and academic fields—from police work and criminology to sociology and performance art—all of which deal in some way with the subject of surveillance. Whether you read one or all of these pieces, consider how the authors explain their motivations, their research, and their findings within broader conversations.

Each article is introduced by the writer's personal reflections describing events, conversations, readings, and even television programs that inspired their projects and ultimately led to the publication of their work. The first article is by Darryl McAllister, a police commander for Hayward (California) Police Department. His article discusses the impact of face recognition technologies on traditional police work. He considers the effects of television shows about police, surveillance, and crime-solving technologies on their audiences, especially as they shape assumptions and expectations about how police work actually happens. McAllister examines the difficulties facing police who wish to strike a balance between using new technologies for solving and preventing crime, and guarding the privacy rights of individuals.

John Gunders's article discusses the emergence of surveillance cameras in shopping centers and other public spaces. He looks at the implications of surveillance, showing that even as cameras can aid police in solving crimes, they also affect and shape the behavior of everyone in their sights. How, Gunders asks us, do public surveillance cameras compel people to accept and conform to belief and value systems in their everyday lives? Do the advantages of widespread surveillance systems, particularly in the United Kingdom and Australia, outweigh their risks?

Using public health crises as a focal point, in the third reading, Nick King connects fields of medicine, history, and immunology to explore the relationship between surveillance and social control. As a historian of science, King encourages readers to understand current social concerns in their historical contexts, and he encourages readers to think critically about them instead of jumping to simplistic solutions. Like Gunders, King is interested in understanding the intended, or stated, purposes of public safety programs in relation to their often unintended social effects.

Both a professor of art and a practicing artist, Nancy Nisbet describes a project in which she asks museum goers to become part of her exhibit. As they are tracked by identification badges, Nisbet's audience becomes aware of the manipulating pressures of surveillance technologies. Nisbet's art installations encourage audiences to experience the tension between their support for high-tech approaches to social problems and their resistance to being implicated in an excessively technologized world.

In our fifth reading, law scholars Chris Taylor and Annabelle James focus on the effects of surveillance technologies on legal procedures. They describe the ways in which laws designed to protect people—particularly people accused of crimes—often have difficulty keeping up with the speed of technological developments. Taylor and James show how video evidence poses new challenges to police, prosecutors, and defendants in criminal procedures, because it can be selectively used to "frame" an event and shape perceptions of criminal responsibility.

Finally, sociologist Gary Marx examines the often extreme responses to the new surveillance technologies that have ushered us into a "surveillance society." Although we are probably used to the generalizations made about the state of society, Marx argues that it is more important to wrestle with the complex questions posed by surveillance technologies and their applications rather than jumping to simplistic, and less analytically sound, conclusions.

DARRYL MCALLISTER

For over two decades Darryl McAllister has worked for the Police Department in the City of Hayward, California, where he has commanded its bureaus of inspectors and detectives and crime scene investigations. The article reprinted below, "Law Enforcement Turns to Face-Recognition Technology," was the result of a research project McAllister developed while in a graduate program at the California Command College.

McAllister reflects on the evolution of technology in law enforcement and how he developed a research project that would help him move from common perceptions of face recognition technologies to more complex ones.

> For much of my twenty-five year law enforcement career, I never really was a connoisseur of high-end technological tools for use in catching "bad guys." In earlier years I learned to be very efficient with what we affectionately called good old-fashioned police work—mostly involving a well-trained memory to recall faces and names of criminals, a thick pocket notebook filled with names and descriptions to use as a data reference, and a the power of a hunch to ensure being at the right place and time to be within eyesight of the criminal on the run. Well, with the advancements of image technology over the past decade—particularly video imagery—keeping abreast with their law enforcement applications has been both an intrigue and a paradigm for me.
>
> I decided to delve into face recognition biometrics as the topic of a research project while attending the California Command College—a graduate level futures research program certified by the California Commission on Peace Officer Standards and Training. In deciding a research topic, each student was free to select a relevant social, technological, environmental, economic or political subject matter potentially impacting future law enforcement. Although I knew very little about face recognition biometrics I was intrigued by its depiction in movies and television and thought it would be incredibly interesting to explore all of its implications.

McAllister notes how his Command College experience introduced him to a wide range of research methods and allowed him to choose one approach, the Nominal Group Technique (NGT). He explains that by "marrying the depth of information developed in the NGT to the wide-ranging facts discovered through traditional research of text and online materials, I truly felt uplifted from the entire research experience. I learned more than I ever would have imagined about the subject of face recognition biometrics."

He goes on to describe the experience of writing the article as an opportunity to examine "the public camera aspect of face recognition biometrics and the societal implications of technology as it claws its way into our everyday consciousness." Even though "Law Enforcement and

Face-Recognition Technologies" developed out of McAllister's personal desire to understand and explain the relationship between new technologies and law enforcement practices, he describes the impact of the article on his professional community and on *Information Today*'s broader audience: "I had no idea it would attract the divergent appeal of law enforcement, the general public, and the technology world."

When he was asked to imagine how his experiences as a researcher would relate to some of the challenges facing readers of *Entering the Academic Conversation*, he responded:

> I do have a few words of advice for undergraduate students contemplating research topics to pursue:
>
> 1. Select a topic about which you are truly interested and intrigued. It will make the research process much more enjoyable, and there will be a built-in sense of motivation to keep you moving with your research.
> 2. Select a research methodology that best suits the breadth of your research topic. Some methodologies—although they may eventually ferret out the information you need to adequately answer your thesis—may force you to become mired in processes instead of outcomes. Your methodology should compliment your quest.
> 3. Particularly for controversial topics, be as inviting and accepting of information that contradicts your assertions as you are to information that supports them. It is the divergence of information that makes the research more interesting to you as the finder and thought provoking to others who can share in your experience when they read your work.
> 4. After you have completed your research project, write an article! You never know when your work might end up as a published piece to help others as a point of reference.

For Discussion

McAllister opens his article with set of familiar references, listing the many television programs that feature intersections of law enforcement and technology.

> As he develops his argument, does McAllister suggest that TV programs are best seen as accurate or inaccurate representations of actual law enforcement practices?
>
> How do TV programs work to shape viewers' perceptions and expectations regarding public camera surveillance?

If you already have, or will shortly, read John Gunders's article, "'Here's Lookin' at You,'" compare McAllister's and Gunders's descriptions of face recognition technologies.

> How do McAllister's and Gunders's views compare: where do they agree and how do they contrast? Are there ways in which you could connect each author's research methods or fields to the goals and conclusions of their articles?

Describing itself as the "only newspaper designed to meet the needs of the information professional," *Information Today* appeals to a different audience than most academic journals. *Information Today*'s website describes the publication as "total coverage of late-breaking news and long-term trends in the information industry. Accurate, timely news articles inform the reader of the people, products, services, and events that impact the industry, while hard-hitting, topical articles explain significant developments in the field." As you read McAllister's article, consider the differences between professional and academic research writing in terms of purpose, style, complexity, and any other features that strike you as important.

> How might a researcher use McAllister's article as a jumping off point for further research?

> Which academic fields would you consider turning to if you wanted to develop an argument in support of McAllister's conclusions? Where would you turn to challenge them?

Law Enforcement Turns to Face-recognition Technology

by Darryl McAllister

When the 1950s television hit *Candid Camera* took America by storm, the outlandish situations captivated viewers in living rooms all over the U.S. A hidden camera captured the victim's reactions, and at some point, the prank was revealed with the signature phrase, "Smile, you're on *Candid Camera!*"

In the entertainment world, capturing someone's face on camera has continued to evolve. The intrigue is less about the situational story line and more about technological prowess. From *Mission: Impossible* and *Enemy of the State* to television shows such as *CSI, 24,* and *Las Vegas,* Hollywood generates story lines that often feature face-recognition technologies. The reality is that face-recognition technology— a form of biometrics—is a rapidly growing tool for real-world issues including public safety and security.

Biometrics and Face Recognition

The term "biometric" is a combination of "biology" and "measurement," one of several technologies used to identify individuals by the body's physical characteristics, along with fingerprint readers, iris scanners, voice analyzers, and computer linked cameras that recognize the way people walk. Law enforcement has been learning how to use face recognition and other biometrics for public safety and information security. This controversial technology also raises ethical questions and concerns about law enforcement's use of face recognition in criminal investigations as well as covert operations.

How It Works

A face-recognition biometrics system analyzes the characteristics of a person's face, which is usually captured by a digital video camera. The overall facial structure is measured, including the distance between the eyes, nose, mouth, and jaw edges. These measurements are saved in a database and used for later comparison, if needed.

Face-recognition technology can also be used for surveillance purposes. Unlike iris scans, hand geometry, fingerprint recognition, or voice recognition, face recognition does not require close proximity to the donor for identification. So, face-recognition technology can be used without the subject ever knowing he or she is the focus of such a scan, which opens the door particularly in intelligence and covert operations.

The distinctions for using face-recognition technology are subtle yet compelling. Law enforcement must decide whether it will use the technology for verification versus identification. Verification implies face-recognition biometrics that will be used to answer the question, "Is this that person?" Identification, on the other hand, implies that the technology will be used to answer the question, "Who is this?" by reading a facial sample and comparing that sample against a database.

Historical Perspective

Face-recognition biometrics actually dates from the late 19th century's Bertillon measurement system. In the 1880s, Parisian anthropologist Alphonse Bertillon pioneered the system based on a belief that a person's hone structure remains unchanged after age 20. Bertillon focused much of his work on the shape and breadth of the head and face. Suspected criminals were relegated to physical exams that included having their heads and bodies measured, recorded, and manually compared to Bertillon's elaborate cataloging system.

The manual record filing and checking system was quite fast for its time. Bertillon's system spread worldwide for nearly 2 decades until the system was derailed by inconsistent measurements of the same people, resulting in misidentifications and the jailing of the innocent. The Bertillon system was summarily discredited and abandoned in favor of fingerprinting. Then, computer-vision technology was born in the late 1950s, using rudimentary programming to detect images. Through the 1960s and 1970s, experts increasingly experimented with new ways to enhance the computer's ability to distinguish one image from another, eventually spawning the growth of face-recognition biometrics. The breakthrough came in the late 1980s with the influx of eigenface (statistical analyses of multiple facial images) algorithms in face-recognition computing. Using algorithms, one image of a human face can be mathematically compared to a combination of pictures; a subject's face might compare 10 percent to one picture, 24 percent to another picture, and so on.

Global Recognition

U.S. use of public video surveillance lags far behind Europe, especially in Britain, where public video surveillance is the single-most heavily funded non-criminal justice crime prevention measure. Many British residents live like contestants in a reality TV show each day— a network of public cameras tracks their moves on residential and commercial streets; on buses, trains, and subways; in offices, pubs, and malls; and even in churches and schools. Experts calculate the average commuter in London is filmed 300 times each day, according to "Britain's Big Brother" (Houston Cronicle; www.propagandamatrix.com/ articles/april2004/120404bigbrother.htm).

Canada began using video surveillance on public streets 5 years ago, while recent terrorist activity prompted the French government to permit its police to use electronic surveillance in public places. Spain and Italy have followed suit, identifying the need to increase video surveillance to better monitor public areas and high-profile buildings. Ireland and Russia have been using public surveillance cameras for decades, but they are encouraged to do more surveillance because of advances in face-recognition technology.

Most Americans first heard about face recognition biometrics after the 9/11 terrorist attacks, even though football fans had been scanned en mass at Super Bowl XXXV in Tampa, Fla., months earlier, according to a 2001 article on Wired News online. The concept has since gained support as a potential tool for averting terrorist crimes, but still, the application of face-recognition biometrics for local law enforcement is being debated. Face-recognition technology is far from widespread, with the scales tipped toward federal use for national security issues. This technology has only recently been applied to local law enforcement investigations on a limited basis and remains a virtually untapped resource for the future.

The public has welcomed the technology, especially for post 9/11 immigration and airport security, although the technology has not been proven as accurate and effective to identify terrorists or wanted suspects. Before the 9/11 attacks, the public was skeptical about the notion that public cameras could be used for advanced technologies such as face recognition. Though skepticism has given way to rising fears about terrorism, many people are still wary of its widespread public use. People are most concerned about the risks of identity theft and privacy infringement.

The Advantages

One positive aspect of face-recognition technology is its non-intrusiveness in its methodology to conduct an investigation. Verification or identification can be accomplished from as few as 2 feet away or from a significant distance with appropriate lenses. In situations where cameras are covertly placed, the subject's freedom of mobility is unhindered. Law enforcement could find fugitives and collect vast amounts of information to bolster the quality and expedience of investigations. With well-placed cameras and face-recognition technology as primary tools for investigating local crime, law enforcement's ability to prevent crime could increase because individuals with a criminal history could be identified. At the local level, face-recognition technology could be effective in investigating identity theft—one of the fastest-growing crimes everywhere. Face-recognition applications are an obvious antidote to identity theft by making it more difficult for criminals to impersonate someone else's identity.

Although no verified success stories exist for the effectiveness of this biometric technology, many facial-identification advocates claim that the cameras have not caught any suspects because terrorists and other criminals have been successfully deterred from entering protected areas.

The Challenges

Of all the biometric technologies in use, face recognition is arguably the most-controversial. It can be deployed as pervasive surveillance and can be integrated with other biometric and authentication applications such as smart cards and digital signatures. Civil libertarians and privacy advocates are certainly not comfortable with the emergence of face-recognition technology as a law enforcement investigative tool. According to a 2003 RAND report, many Americans feel the technology facilitates improper, random mass scanning and that law enforcement, bound by the Fourth Amendment, must first have individualized, reasonable suspicion of criminal activity before it can "search" someone's face to see if it matches that of an individual in the database. In the prior ruling ot *United States v. Dionisio* (1973), the U.S. Supreme Court disagreed, citing that a person does not have a reasonable expectation of privacy in those physical characteristics constantly exposed to the public, such as facial characteristics.

Although the non-intrusiveness of face recognition technology can be an advantage to law enforcement, it can also be a drawback for public opinion. Many people are concerned about face-recognition cameras placed inconspicuously around cities to identify passers-by without their consent. Some opponents cite the potential for abuse, since cameras could easily be networked to track individuals from place to place, enabling the government to monitor individuals for social control. Individuals might be less likely to contemplate public activities offensive to powerful interests if they knew their identities would be recorded on video and accessible to opposing interests. People simply fear face recognition technology as a tool for the government to invade privacy.

Advocates of face recognition disagree about privacy issues, arguing that there is no constitutional right to privacy in public. They point to the fact that the U.S. Supreme Court has determined that government action constitutes a "search" when it invades a person's reasonable expectation of privacy. This legal standing, according to proponents, explicitly provides that a person does not have a reasonable expectation of privacy in those physical characteristics that are in the public view, such as facial features, voice, and handwriting. Although the Fourth Amendment requires that a "search" be reasonable, the argument remains that the use of public cameras for face recognition does not constitute a search, and the government is not constrained from employing face-recognition systems in public spaces.

However, face-recognition technology has experienced some recent setbacks. Despite protest by the American Civil Liberties Union, the City of Tampa, Fla., became the first city in the U.S. to install the technology in June 2001 to scan faces in the city's nightlife district and check them against a database of more than 24,000 felons, sexual predators, and runaway children. One police officer remotely monitored video images and could select faces in the crowd to scan and run through a criminal database.

Tampa officials faced strong criticism from residents and public-interest groups objecting to monitoring ordinary citizens in public places. A group of protesters even donned bandanas, masks, and Groucho Marx glasses, taking to the streets of Ybor City District on a busy Saturday night to protest the face-scanning system. During a 2-year period, the system failed to deliver a single match, and city officials couldn't explain why the software wasn't effective (despite successful controlled testing). By August 2003, the Tampa Police Department finally decided to scrap its face-recognition system.

Virginia was the second U.S. state to install a face-recognition system on its public streets in Virginia Beach. In 2002, several closed-circuit cameras were installed to provide a visual canvass of the city's boardwalk. But more than a year later, the system failed to produce a successful identification or arrest. The Virginia Beach system is still operating, and officials, who report the cameras still deter criminal activity, decline to disclose the location of the video cameras and which are equipped with face-recognition software.

But just because face-recognition technology has had a rough start does not mean it will never work. Face-recognition companies are receiving corporate funding in addition to tens of millions of dollars from the Departments of Justice and Defense, respectively, for research and development, according to a report on Homeland Security.

If corporate research and development of face-recognition technologies is enough to spawn its use by law enforcement, though, the same typical barriers remain to innovation. These new technologies include the cost of procurement as well as maintaining and refining the application. In the case of local law enforcement, shouldering those costs depends on taxpayers and their support of the tool. Any community that is wary of facial biometrics may create challenges for local law enforcement that uses it as a tool.

Preparing for the Impact

Although biometric face-recognition applications have the potential to benefit law enforcement's investigative arsenal, future improvements in the technology could also threaten individual privacy rights. Balancing individual privacy against law enforcement's need to investigate is likely to become trickier with this investigative tool. The debate continues, and the accelerated focus to use public cameras for face-recognition bio- ' metrics has been forged by the backdrop of terrorism and other world events. How the technology will proliferate to widespread use in the coming years is uncertain, but world trends are forcing U.S. law enforcement to incorporate a global perspective into its localized view of crime. The potential widespread implementation of face-recognition technology is simply one tool that needs a great deal of work before it becomes a viable tool to investigate crime. The technology is getting better, and its potential is tremendous.

Despite the hoopla in Florida and Virginia, face-recognition technology has gained the requisite momentum. Just as America has accepted face recognition in action-packed movies and television shows, many people agree that real-life acceptance of the technology is simply a matter of time.

According to the San Jose, California-based U.S. National Biometric Test Center, the biometrics market rose from $6.6 million in 1990 to $63 million in 1999 and was expected to jump to $520 million by the end of 2006. This growth speaks to the basic laws of supply and demand. Considering the federal government's keen interest in proliferating face-recognition biometrics as a tool to combat terrorism, local governments are poised to receive help to handle the cost of implementation as the system's cost continues to fall. The Department of Defense already funds more than $50 million for university research to improve the technology, according to figures in the article "Smile, You're On Scan Camera" at find BIOMETRICS.com. Although social opposition may continue, the success of face-recognition systems in the private sector may be the best predictor of future success of public applications of the technology.

Industry insiders rave about the compatibility of face-recognition software with computers and cameras already in use by airports, banks, casinos, and other corporations. The operation of these private systems has become routine, and perhaps the same will be true if public surveillance cameras continue to be used in U.S. cities. The added scrutiny at U.S. airports has become an accepted reality, and the same could be true for public cameras for security and for crime fighting. In the meantime, law enforcement must plan for the continued emergence of this new technology for the future of public safety.

You may now be looking around and wondering whether a camera is recording the details of your face. After all, Airbus, one of the leading manufacturers of commercial aircraft, has already installed hidden security cameras in the light fittings above the seats in many of its planes, according to an online article at NewScientist.com. If you're stopped at a red light in your car, a traffic camera could measure your fWcial image if you decide to run the light. Security cameras such as Mobile Digital Video Recorders have even been widely used in taxis, buses, police cars, and other public vehicles, according to an online article at Security- Camera World.com.

One thing is for sure: The candid cameras of the 1950s pale in comparison to the debate about today's covert cameras, and nobody is laughing anymore. Whether you support or oppose the use of facerecognition biometrics, you may want to smile—wherever you go.

JOHN GUNDERS

John Gunders is currently finishing his PhD in the School of English, Media Studies and Art History at the University of Queensland, Australia, where he works for the Australian Research Council's Cultural Research Network. His article, "Here's Lookin' at You: Video Surveillance and the Interpellated Body," appeared in the journal *Social Alternatives* in 2000. Gunders has also published on the relationship between information theories and literature, and he regularly contributes to the cultural studies blog, *The Memes of Production* (http://thememesofproduction.org).

Gunders describes the origins of "Here's Lookin' at You" as an intersection of his personal and academic interests:

> I can no longer remember which came first: an interest in the sudden proliferation of video surveillance devices, or a fascination with Louis Althusser's theory of interpellation. Certainly, I had been reading Althusser for a graduate course I was doing, and at the same time teaching the concepts in an undergraduate class, but it is hard to separate the two elements when they make such a clear fit. Suffice to say, the theory went a long way towards explaining a phenomenon which was—and remains—an important issue in understanding the way in which our society operates. I believe strongly that theory isn't (or shouldn't be!) a purely intellectual affair that is remote from lived experience, but that used properly it should provide insights into why things are the way they are. Writing "Here's Lookin' at You" was a way of trying out those ideas in

the real world to see if they worked, and to share the results with people who might be interested.

Gunders also reflects on the research process, through which he expanded his thoughts about public camera surveillance into more specialized, academic knowledge. Most importantly, he recalls how he had to combine the work of multiple academic conversations to better understand the significance of increasing surveillance practices in everyday life:

> As it happened, I didn't know a lot about video surveillance aside from what we all read in the newspapers, so my first step was to see if there was enough information available to educate myself about the issues, and to provide a conceptual framework around which to construct an argument. At that time there wasn't a lot of material available, but there was enough to make a start, and soon I could identify the texts that were useful for my purposes. As my goal was to explore the issue of surveillance from a cultural theoretical perspective, I could ignore those articles that focused only on the technical or instrumental aspects of surveillance. One other thing became clear quite quickly: no one had written specifically on surveillance from an Althusserean perspective, so I was confident my article would be original.

Once he knew he had found his niche in the research conversation, Gunders describes the writing process, emphasizing the interrelationship between reading, writing, and revising. He also recalls the importance of peer review and the contribution made by outside readers to an early draft of his article:

> My reading answered a lot of questions and filled a lot of gaps in my own understanding, but I was pleased to find that most of it confirmed my early hypothesis, as well as providing relevant examples to fill out the explanation. I started writing soon after starting the reading: partly because I was writing to a deadline, and partly because it is important to make a start, especially when writing about an unfamiliar topic. When I reached a point in the article where I didn't have the necessary knowledge, I skipped it and moved on to the next section. When writing like this, the revision stage is vitally important in order to iron out any stylistic lumps that might have slipped in, and—more importantly—to ensure that any early misconceptions are corrected. I was lucky that I was writing for a peer-reviewed journal, and both the anonymous reviewer and the editor provided valuable advice that enabled me to clarify certain points.

For Discussion

As you read "Here's Lookin' at You," consider how Gunders brings new readers, such as social workers, into the philosophical conversation that includes the theories of Louis Althusser.

How does Gunders use definition strategies in his argument? Why do you think he chose particular examples to illustrate the concept of "interpellation," and how effectively does he incorporate the concept into the academic conversation around social work?

In paragraph six of the article, Gunders distinguishes between the stated purposes of widespread surveillance cameras and their value for city and provincial governments.

How, in Gunders's view, do public surveillance cameras reinforce certain "social standards" of consumer and public behavior? In your view, would the years between 2000 and now support or challenge Gunders's observations?

Are there significant differences between Gunders's examples, which are drawn from urban Australia, and those you could draw from your own experiences?

Instead of a single answer or proposal, Gunders concludes the article with a series of questions connecting policy needs to concerns raised by increasing public surveillance.

What kinds of practical or policy responses are recommended or implied by Gunders? Do you think his philosophical interests have helped him to see the concerns of social workers in new ways? What additional practical responses does he lead you to consider or would you recommend after reading the article?

"Here's Lookin' at You": Video Surveillance and the Interpellated Body

by John Gunders

The image stared out from hundreds of newspapers around the world: two children and a toddler walking through a shopping mall, one of the older boys holding the toddler's hand. Captured on security video, the boys could have been the toddler's brothers, escorting him back to his guardian, or giving a hassled parent a few minutes respite. But the truth was altogether more chilling: the toddler was two year old Liverpool boy, James Bulger, and the older boys were strangers who lured James away from his mother, abducted him, and ultimately beat him to death. The two boys, then both aged 10, were convicted of abduction and murder (Young 1996: 89).As shocking as this crime was, it is not my intention in this article to discuss the issue of juvenile crime. Instead, I want to look at the technology that was foregrounded during the case: public video surveillance. I will first examine some of the issues that surround the use of this technology, before moving to an analysis of the way the individual is positioned and defined in relation to the video camera.

The conviction of James Bulger's murderers was secured on the basis of confessions and the statements of 32 eye-witnesses, yet it was the blurred video image of James holding the hand of one of his assailants is the best remembered part of the trial. This video image was crucial to the solving of the crime, because its broadcast on television brought most of those witnesses forward. The video surveillance of public places is a contentious issue: it is actively sought by property owners, retailers and policing authorities (Standing Committee 1996: 26); it is decried as invasion of privacy by civil liberty groups and others (Australian Privacy Commissioner cited in Standing Committee 1996: 11); many members of the public see it as making the streets safer (Gibson 1996:59; Standing Committee 1996: 27); yet research suggests that its crime deterrent effect is less than is generally supposed, and even the policing authorities acknowledge that its benefit lies more in the production of evidence following a crime, than in crime prevention (Hillier 1996: 94; Standing Committee 1996:38–39).

Introduced to Australia in the mid 1960s, the surveillance camera has become ubiquitous in public areas in all Australian capitals and many provincial centres since the early nineties. It is found in railway stations, shopping centres, petrol stations, elevators, automatic teller machines, and hotels. Video cameras at both the Melbourne and Sydney cricket grounds allow police and security staff to eject members of the public whose conduct is deemed inappropriate. Britain has the highest concentration of video cameras in the world, with closed circuit TV systems in 250 town centres, including some 1,300 cameras in the City of London, and a further 14,000 throughout the London Underground. In 1996, the central government's budget included $22.5 million to buy a further 10,000 cameras for city centres (Gibson 1996:59). Increasingly, questions are being asked about this level of surveillance, and recommendations have been made that privacy legislation covering the use of video surveillance be enacted; that independent auditors be appointed to oversee the conduct of the surveillance and investigate complaints; that Codes of Practice be developed; that signage indicating the presence of video cameras be erected; and that systems be monitored by properly qualified people (Standing Committee 1996: ix-x). In 1996, the British Local Government Information Unit published a code of practice that banned the use of surveillance video footage for "entertainment purposes" and tried to ensure accountability (Gibson 1996:59), and a similar code exists in New Zealand (Standing Committee 1996:30).

But as well as these topics, there are theoretical questions concerning the camera and issues of subjectivity. French Marxist theorist Louis Althusser, suggests that every member of society is defined as a "subject" in relation to the ideology of that society, and that the subject apprehends and understands the world through the lens of that ideology (1972:170–71). The subject is brought into compliance with the ideology through the process of "interpellation". Althusser likens this to "hailing" someone in the street: a voice cries out, "hey, you there!" and an individual (usually the one being hailed) turns around, recognising (or at least suspecting) that they are really the one being hailed. By acknowledging the hail, by realising that they are the one being hailed, the subject is interpellated into the discourse of the hailer (1972:174–75). In other words, the subject, becoming ware of the ideology of their society, recognises themselves as a part of, or in agreement with that ideology. Most often, interpellation is not a conscious process, but operates within the unspoken assumptions of the ideology. An obvious example of this is the way advertising works: advertisements for financial institutions, share trading companies and the like do not specifically ask if the viewer wants to make money-that is assumed. Rather, they portray a Lifestyle that nearly all viewers will immediately accept: "Yes, of course I want financial security and a comfortable existence!" The viewers see themselves in relation to the actors in the commercial, and recognise their own desires and needs. What is not questioned is the underlying assumptions about wealth, its production and distribution. There is one important difference between Althusser's person on the street and my bank ad, and the theory of ideological interpellation: while the examples are sequential, in relation to ideology, the subject is always, already interpellated (1972:172).

I wish to extend this concept of interpellation to that of the subject vis-a-vis the surveillance camera by showing that the camera interpellates the subject within an ideological dichotomy of good and bad. I say it is the camera that interpellates, rather than the official who monitors the camera, because it is not the image captured on video-tape that is ideological, but the concept of video surveillance: the camera could be unmonitored, turned-off, or even be a dummy, and it would still function as an interpellation device (see Hillier 1996:97).

Throughout this discussion I will call the ideology of the surveillance camera "juridical", although it partakes of other discourses than simply the legal. There are four issues I want to look at, which are raised by this view of surveillance. First, the interpellated subject is positioned by the camera in one of very few available positions: regardless of what they are doing or what their intentions, the subject is seen by the camera as merely a "law-breaker" or a "potential lawbreaker"-the interpellation allows no position of approval, only disapproval. Second, as Althusser points out, the subject is always, already interpellated in the ideology: there is some negotiation over the hailing, but the subject cannot refuse to be interpellated. If a security camera exists, the individual is subject to the values and assumptions of the juridical ideology. This introduces the third point: the juridical ideology is arbitrary and contingent on the assumptions of the ruling class, which are then taken as objective and self-evident truths. Cameras in shopping centres, for instance, are often promoted as protection for the consumer against pick-pockets or physical violence from individuals-a theme that was emphasised in the James Bulger case-yet their main role is to protect shop owners from property crime such as shop-lifting or vandalism. The Walgett Shire Council in New South Wales stated that its goal in installing closed circuit TV in the CBD was to reduce crime and to "encourage businesses to remove bars from shop windows" (cited in Standing Committee 1996:17). For the camera in a shopping precinct, those who are not involved in economic consumption are deviant non-conformists who put at risk the legitimate activities of the consumers (Hillier 1996:99). The juridical ideology is an amalgam of discourses that include the Protestant work-ethic; assumptions about appropriate behaviours in relation to age, gender and occupation; stereotypes concerning race and ethnicity; and specific laws concerning the non-conformance with social standards, such as vagrancy (sanctions against poverty), loitering (sanctions against idleness) and laws of association (sanctions against youth). Finally, there is the body that authorises the surveillance. Althusser states that the precondition for the interpellation of subjects is the existence of a "Unique and Absolute Subject", that entity which is at the heart of the ideology: in religious ideology for instance, the Absolute Subject is God; for legal ideology, it is the Law. Althusser says:

> The Absolute Subject occupies the unique place of the Centre, and interpellates around it the infinity of individuals into subjects in a double mirror-connexion such that it subjects the subjects to the Subject (1972:180).

This is not to say that there is a metaphysical presence at the heart of ideology: rather it is an idealised set of practices against which subjects are defined. A sportsperson, for instance, is defined in relation to the sets of rules, practices and history of their sport. There may never have existed a sprinter with a "perfect" running style, but all athletes are judged as if such an Absolute were possible. The centre of interpellation is a mirror because looking at the Absolute Subject, subjects see only themselves. It both creates subjects and is created by them: "there is no practice except by and in an ideology; there is no ideology except by the subject and for subjects" (1972,170). Individuals are subject to the law, for example, but the law is merely a codex of rules invented and modified by individuals over time. In the same way, subjects are interpellated by an ideology that is largely a set of assumptions, practices, and rules implicitly derived from the values of those subjects. In the case of the juridical ideology that I am describing, the Absolute Subject is a nexus of bodies with differing roles and levels of authority, but which nevertheless form an apparently homogenous ideological body against which the surveilled subject is defined.

First, there is the State, which implicitly or explicitly authorises the use of video cameras; second, there is the controlling body, either the police or a private security company, which monitors the cameras; third, there is the individual who watches the action; fourth, the authority who audits and supervises the logging, recording and storing of the images; fifth, the juridical authority who presents the images as evidence in legal proceedings; and sixth, the organisation or individual who reproduces the images for broadcast in news or current affairs reporting, or as documentary material. There may be other bodies in different situations. Each of these "authorities" has their own set of assumptions and practices, but all work to interpellate the subject into a dichotomy of civil obedience/disobedience, where agency is ignored, and power structures actively place the subject in the position of having to justify their own behaviour in the terms that have already been defined by the juridical ideology.

While the subject cannot refuse interpellation, there is the possibility for a negotiation of response: the camera can be ignored, resisted or subverted. Hillier suggests that "displays of gang warfare, rioting, joyriding or rapping and break dancing might well be as much a response to the camera's attention as to any deeper stimulus" (1996:103). Civil liberty group "Watching Them, Watching Us" declared Christmas eve 1998 "Shoot Back Day", encouraging people to take photographs of public surveillance cameras and have them posted on the internet. However, there is another position in which the subject can be placed by the surveillance camera, one that precedes even the "always, already" of interpellation: that of objectification. Hillier describes how security camera operators in Perth's Burswood Casino compiled a two-hour video of images taken from cameras located in women's toilets, artists changing rooms, and other parts of the interior and exterior of the complex. This voyeuristic video was passed around privately at parties (1996:99-100). Another example is the video Caught in the Act, a 45-minute compilation of excerpts from videos purchased from security firms, retailers and local government authorities. The video includes footage of drug deals, armed robberies, a clandestine sexual encounter in an office stationery closet, and a woman undressing in her bedroom (Gibson 1996:59). This is similar to those "Best of World's Worst Drivers" types of exploitation videos increasingly appearing on commercial television. The individual who is objectified by a hidden camera has no possibility of reacting, because they are unaware of the invasion. This is exploitation that rather than interpellating subjectivity into ideological forms, destroys subjectivity and creates an object of desire or hatred, purely for the use of the observer.

This brief investigation cannot cover all the problems that public surveillance involves. Video cameras, as part of an overall strategy, can have a positive effect on crime prevention or on the ability of police to bring criminals to justice, as the James Bulger case illustrated. On the other hand, videos deal in representations (see Young 1996), and as such, their veracity is never purely straight-forward: take the case of a recent incident in Ipswich Queensland, where four police officers were charged with use of excessive force in making an arrest. The arrest was captured on video, and the same piece of footage was used by the prosecution, claiming brutality, and the defence, claiming it as justification for the force used. There are also questions over the effectiveness of using video to identify individuals. Research in Britain has shown that volunteers' success in matching faces on video stills with portrait photographs can be as low as 61% (Edwards 1999, 27), yet criminal prosecutions often rely on this technology. With the proliferation of video surveillance in our cities, these questions need to be addressed: when will there be legislation, with real penalties, to prevent the misuse of video footage, and the exploitation of those it portrays? When will there be a code of practice governing private security companies, to ensure that issues of privacy and dignity are not ignored? Finally, there needs to be a clear understanding within the public as to the purpose and effectiveness of public surveillance. But even more than this, the individual who is hailed by the camera, who is interpellated into an ideology that they can have little control over, needs to be aware of the issues of subjection and control implied by the technology. Ideology is always invisible from the inside: but a critical and educated analysis will reveal its structures. And once revealed, those structures are open to resistance and opposition.

REFERENCES

Althusser, Louis. 1972. "Ideology and Ideological State Apparatuses (Notes Towards an Investigation)". In Lenin and Philosophy and Other Essays. translated by Ben Brewster. London: New Left Books, pp. 127–86.

Australian Capital Territory. Standing Committee on Legal Affairs. 1996. "The Electronic Eye': Inquiry into the Efficacy of *Surveillance* Cameras. Canberra: Legislative Assembly for the Australian Capital Territory.

Edwards, Rob. 1999, 27 March. "The Camera Lies". New Scientist:27.

Gibson, Helen. 1996, 8 April. "Voyeur on the Corner". Time:59.

Hillier, Jean. 1996. "The Gaze in the City:Video *Surveillance* in Perth". Australian Geographical Studies. 34 (1): 95–105.

Young, Alison. 1996. "In the Frame: Crime and the Limits of Representation". Australian and New Zealand Journal of Criminology 29: 81–101.

NICHOLAS KING

Nicholas King is a professor of biomedical ethics at McGill University in Montreal, Québec, Canada. Before joining the faculty at McGill, King taught at Case Western Reserve University and did postgraduate work at the University of Michigan and at the University of San Francisco, where he wrote the article reprinted below. Professor King received his master's degree in medical anthropology and went on to receive his PhD in the history of science from Harvard University. He has published on the connections between ethics, public health, and infectious diseases in many journals, including the *Journal of the History of Medicine*, in which "The Influence of Anxiety: September 11, Bioterrorism, and American Public Health," appeared in 2003.

Although some of the authors in this chapter, like Marx and Gunders, developed their academic research projects out of compelling personal experiences, King describes his academic research project intersecting with events that unfolded while he wrote. As King explains:

> Academic researchers often work on topics that seem to have little relevance to the lives of people outside the academy, only to find that current events make their research very timely indeed. In late 2001, I was completing a Ph.D. dissertation that critically analyzed the public health campaign around so-called "emerging diseases"—infectious diseases that were novel or whose incidence was on the rise. I had originally become interested in the intense media coverage of small outbreaks of exotic infectious diseases such as Ebola hemorrhagic fever and the West Nile Virus. Why, I wondered, were Americans so apparently obsessed with diseases that presented a relatively small threat to their health?

King continues, recalling how his research helped him explain "the role of journalists and scientists in the formation of public opinion around health threats." He then began to draw connections between historical public health crises and their counterparts in the late 1990s, when "many of the scientists sounding the alarm about emerging diseases had begun turning their attention towards a new threat: biological terrorism. I asked the same question of this new campaign: Why were prominent scientists and security experts so worried about a threat which, though horrifying to contemplate, seemed extremely low? What was the historical background to contemporary concerns about bioterrorism?" As he asked and explored these questions, King notes:

> Only a few weeks later, the topic that I had long considered from the vantage of academic abstraction became a chilling reality. On September 18, 2001, five letters containing processed anthrax spores were sent to news media offices in New York and Florida; three weeks later, two more letters were sent to the offices of U.S. Senators Tom Daschle and Patrick Leahy. Five people died and at least 17 others were infected as a result of exposure to the anthrax in these letters. The effects of the anthrax attacks were immediate and long-lasting: Americans, still reeling from the September 11th hijackings, now worried that terrorists might spread deadly disease through the mail, food, or water supplies.

As fears about a public health crisis became more widespread, King joined researchers working on similar issues in fields including medicine, public policy, biology, political science, and ethics. Within this context, King explains the evolution of his research project, from recognizing the connections between his earlier research and current events, to a conference presentation, and ultimately to the published article:

> A few months after the anthrax attack, a colleague invited me to contribute a paper to a symposium entitled "Reflections on September 11th." I eagerly agreed, as this would give me an opportunity to apply the lessons of my research to an event that I knew would shape the American political and cultural landscape for the foreseeable future. Doing so also forced me to do two difficult things. First, I had to take a step back from the 24-7 media coverage of the September 11th attacks and their aftermath, particularly the consensus that somehow the world had changed completely on that day. Did my research lead me to different interpretations of this event? At the same time, I had to re-assess my research in light of this new event. Should the 2001 anthrax attacks lead me to a different interpretation of my own work?
>
> Ultimately, I concluded that the answer to both of these questions was "yes." The result is the following essay.

For Discussion

Although his article focuses on public health issues after September 11, 2001, King emphasizes the importance of seeing the event in its historical context.

> If, as King claims, "one of the less obvious casualties of the September 11 attacks has been a proper sense of history," what would this sense of history show us about September 11, and how does history help us understand issues of public health?

Like Gunders, King raises some important differences between the stated purposes of epidemic and bioterrorism prevention programs and their effects. For example, both authors stress the ways in which assumptions—about technology and public health for instance—often produce unintended consequences.

> In King's view, how can national decisions about addressing threats to public health actually impede efforts to prevent bioterrorism?

As you read "The Influence of Anxiety," consider how King begins to connect a number of fields, including medicine, history, and immunology.

> How does the concept of surveillance help King tie multiple issues and fields together?

Like Gary Marx, King urges readers toward practices of critical engagement, even in times of crisis. He claims that even though the "kinds of arguments favored among historians of medicine are especially difficult to make under conditions of crisis . . . they are, in fact, our most precious resource in times of 'war.'"

In urging consideration of difficult issues, how does King challenge readers to be especially "courageous"?

Even if critical inquiry is King's goal, does he lead you to imagine practical solutions, projects, or responses to the historical challenges he describes?

The Influence of Anxiety: September 11, Bioterrorism, and American Public Health

by Nicholas King

One of the less obvious casualties of the September 11 attacks has been a proper sense of history. The assumption that this event was sui generis, unfettered by context or precedent, has become an unassailable justification for American foreign and domestic policy. Endlessly repeated, the cliche´ that "the world changed that day" threatens to become consecrated as historical fact. Attempts to counter this sanctification of historical novelty have been decried as inappropriate and unpatriotic.

Did the world really change that day? Historians, now and for the foreseeable future, will have to assess the veracity and the consequences of this truism. It will not be an easy task. Yet we must do so, because understanding the context of and precedents for these events is a necessary component of understanding their causes and consequences. That considerable political and institutional interests are arrayed against this sort of analysis only makes it more vital. We must also do so because the axiom of historical exceptionalism threatens to hijack our understanding of related issues.

One such topic is bioterrorism. Although often conflated with the attacks on the World Trade Center and the Pentagon, the anthrax outbreak in the eastern United States that followed was a separate event, and American responses to it have a considerable historical lineage. Long before last September, American scientists and public health experts were using the threat of novel diseases, both natural and human-created, as a rationale for making changes in public health. On a deeper level, contemporary responses to the threat of bioterrorism occur within an institutional framework, and draw on a repertoire of metaphors, images, and values that have been shaped by historical forces far older and more complicated than this single outbreak.

Historians can and must shed light on the origins and implications of current events, forcefully elucidating how the world did *not* change last September.[1] But these events also afford us the opportunity to evaluate our own assumptions and methods, most importantly the manner in which we evaluate continuity and change. Naturally suspicious of the claim to novelty, historians might be excused for seeing only echoes of the past in present events. But the events of the past year also illustrate changes that predate September 11, even though their lineage may be measured in years rather than decades. Forty years ago, Charles Rosenberg observed that cholera epidemics give us a peculiar window into the social and scientific worlds of the mid nineteenth century.[2] The same is true now. September 11 and its aftermath cast in sharp relief the contours of American anxiety, and the constellations of American institutions and interests, peculiar to the late twentieth and early twenty-first centuries.

Continuities

Bioterrorism—the threat itself, the anxiety that it generates, the responses that it engenders—exemplifies the juxtaposition of historical change and continuity. It is tempting to regard the current fascination with this issue as a direct result of the 2001 anthrax outbreak. But American scientists and policymakers have advocated bioterrorism preparedness for at least a decade, establishing the rhetorical and institutional parameters of the current debate. Beyond that, and most pertinent for historians of medicine and public health, American concerns regarding bioterrorism are part of a longer history of fears about disease more generally. As in earlier eras, American concerns about global social change are refracted through the lens of infectious disease. But the resulting spectrum is notably different from its predecessors.

Biological *weapons* have generated fear for some time. They were first deemed abhorrent in 1925, when forty nations signed the Geneva Protocol prohibiting their initial use.[3] American fears of their development, first by Germany during World War II and then by the Soviet Union during the Cold War, have justified "offensive" and "defensive" research programs since George

---

[1] For examples of engaged scholarship of this sort, see Allan M. Brandt, "AIDS in Historical Perspective: Four Lessons from the History of Sexually Transmitted Diseases," *Am. J. Public Health*, 1988, *78*, 367–71; Nancy Tomes, "The Making of a Germ Panic, Then and Now," *Am. J. Public Health*, 2000, *90*, 191–98.

[2] Charles E. Rosenberg, *The Cholera Years: The United States in 1832, 1849, and 1866* (Chicago: University of Chicago Press, 1962[1987]).

[3] This treaty, negotiated after chemical weapons killed or injured over a million soldiers and civilians in World War I, proscribed the initial use of chemical and biological weapons, but did not prohibit research, development, or stockpiling of these arms, and a number of signatories reserved the right to retaliate in kind. The United States signed but not ratify this treaty until 1975.

Merck became the first director of the secret biological weapons program with the innocuous title of "War Research Service" in 1941.[4] Noted biomedical researchers, including Nobel Laureates MacFarlane Burnet, Rene´ Dubos, and Joshua Lederberg, have joined the public debate over biological weapons since the early postwar era, in some cases advising on or participating in weapons-related research as well.[5]

Bioterrorism also taps into more diffuse but no less powerful social anxieties. From cholera to HIV/AIDS to the West Nile Virus, Americans have long regarded infectious disease with dread, and the bioterrorist resembles two figures familiar to historians of American public health: the carrier and "patient zero." Like Typhoid Mary and Gaetan Dugas before him, he (for the bioterrorist is generally characterized as male) personifies difference, transgression, and contamination.[6] Covertly transporting deadly germs into the United States, this culpable foreigner exposes the increasing permeability of national borders and the vulnerability of American citizens in an increasingly interconnected world.

Proposed responses to bioterrorism have similar historical analogs. In the past, outbreaks of epidemic disease have sometimes led to the curtailment of civil liberties, from compulsory vaccination and treatment to detention and isolation of those deemed threatening to the public's health. As Alan Kraut, Barron Lerner, and Judith Walzer Leavitt have ably demonstrated, the brunt of such restrictions have frequently been borne by the poor and socially marginalized, and protection of public health has often been conflated with attempts to maintain social order and control "difficult" populations.[7] Recent

---

[4]Two informative sources on the early history of the United States BW program are: Barton J. Bernstein, "Origins of the U.S. Biological Warfare Program," in *Preventing a Biological Arms Race*, ed. Susan Wright (Cambridge: MIT Press, 1990); and G. W. Christopher et al., "Biological Warfare: A Historical Perspective," *J. Am. Med. Assoc.*, 1997, *278*, 412–17.

[5]Dubos apparently conducted research on biological weapons during the 1960s; see Gerard J. Fitzgerald, "René Dubos in the Librarywith a Candlestick," *Recent Science Newsletter*, 2000, 2. Burnet includes a lengthy discussion of biological weapons in *Biological Aspects of Infectious Disease* (New York: Macmillan, 1940). Lederberg, deeply concerned about biological weapons for a number of decades, had been active in public debate over international weapons conventions since the nineteen-sixties. Among his recent publications, see Joshua Lederberg, ed., *Biological Weapons: Limiting the Threat* (Cambridge: MIT Press, 1999). I am indebted to Warwick Anderson for the Burnet reference.

[6]Mary Mallon, popularly known as "Typhoid Mary," was an Irish cook incarcerated for more than twenty years in the early twentieth century after repeatedly refusing to cooperate with New York public health authorities. Gaetan Dugas, the archetypal "patient zero," was a Canadian flight attendant whom author Randy Shilts held responsible for spreading the HIV virus across North America during the 1980s. Judith Walzer Leavitt, *Typhoid Mary: Captive to the Public's Health* (Boston: Beacon Press, 1996); Randy Shilts, *And the Band Played On* (New York: Viking, 1988).

[7]Alan M. Kraut, *Silent Travelers: Germs, Genes, and the "Immigrant Menace"* (Baltimore: Johns Hopkins University Press, 1994); Barron H. Lerner, "Tuberculosis in Seattle, 1949–1973: Balancing Public Health and Civil Liberties," *West. J. Med.*, 1999, *171*, 44–49; Leavitt, *Typhoid Mary*.

recommendations have similarly sought to balance civil liberties with public health. One controversial piece of model legislation, prepared for the Centers for Disease Control and Prevention (CDC), expands the state's power to seize hospitals and private property; compel vaccination and treatment of individuals; and quarantine those who refuse medical examination, testing, vaccination, or treatment.[8]

Current recommendations also display a familiar faith that technological fixes will obviate the need for social or political remedies. Since the early 1900s, American public health and national security experts have published recommendations regarding appropriate forms of bioterrorism preparedness.[9] Despite some disagreement over distribution of funds, two assumptions have almost unqualified support: first, that bioterrorism preparedness depends on investment in basic research in the molecular sciences, pharmaceutical development, and epidemiological surveillance networks; second, that the methods and goals of such preparedness and wider public health prevention are synonymous.

For historians, the tone of these recommendations is immediately recognizable. Flush with the promise of the bacteriological revolution, early twentieth-century American public health began to turn its attention and funding from broad preventive measures toward clinical medicine, laboratory science, and the early detection of disease. As a number of historians have argued, the subsequent redirection of funding from public health toward biomedical research contributed to the abandonment of social and structural remedies, and the eventual dismantling of the public health infrastructure in the 1980s under the pressure of Reagan-era budgetary constraints.[10]

---

[8]I refer here to "The Model State Emergency Health Powers Act," prepared by The Center for Law and the Public's Health at Georgetown and Johns Hopkins Universities, and available at http://www.publichealthlaw.net/MSEHPA/MSEHPA.pdf.

[9]The semantic shift—from public health "prevention" to bioterrorism "preparedness"— is noteworthy. These issues are discussed in chapter four of my doctoral dissertation. Nicholas Benjamin King, "Infectious Disease in a World of Goods" (Department of the History of Science, Harvard University, 2001).

[10]There is some controversy over the "narrowing hypothesis" in public health. A number of historians have argued that the bacteriological revolution led public health to narrow its focus to laboratory science and the efficient location, identification, and eradication of germs, while others contend that public health has maintained a broad social focus throughout the century. See, among others, Barbara Rosenkrantz, "'Cart before Horse': Theory, Practice, and Professional Image in American Public Health, 1870–1920," *J. Hist. Med. Allied Sci.*, 1974, *29*, 55–73; Elizabeth Fee, "Public Health and the State: The United States," in *The History of Public Health and the Modern State*, ed. Dorothy Porter (Amsterdam: Editions Rodopi B.V., 1994), 224–75; Georgina D. Feldberg, *Disease and Class: Tuberculosis and the Shaping of Modern North American Society* (New Brunswick, N.J.: Rutgers University Press, 1995); and Nancy Tomes, *The Gospel of Germs: Men, Women, and the Microbe in American Life* (Cambridge: Harvard University Press, 1998).

The rhetorical and institutional equation of national security with public health is also hardly novel.[11] The U.S. Public Health Service's flagship institution, the CDC in Atlanta, Georgia, was established (as the "Malaria Control in War Areas") in 1942 as a "Sentinel for Health" to investigate and control infections among soldiers, and "to keep malaria from spreading to the armed forces from its reservoir in the civilian population."[12] Its Epidemic Intelligence Service (EIS), established in 1951 to "investigate outbreaks of disease in strategic areas," has long served as an invaluable arena for training scientists and epidemiologists.[13] In 1999, one CDC official argued in the journal *Emerging Infectious Diseases* that the creation of the EIS should serve as a model for a "value-added" approach in current public health.[14]

Change

Despite these similarities, the bioterrorist is not just a postmodern Typhoid Mary, nor are post-September 11 responses to the threat of bioterrorism merely a repeat of epidemics past. Bioterrorism presents an historically specific assemblage of risks and responses, illustrating larger changes in the contours of American public health and its place in global society.

First, the archetypal bioterrorist symbolizes something quite different from the infectious bogeymen of the past. His predecessors in the American imaginary were passive carriers, primitive contaminants of modern society identifiable by race, ethnicity, or nationality. The bioterrorist is an active agent, a sophisticated hybrid of primitive and modern who seizes "our" biotechnology—a symbol of American modernity and economic might—and transforms it into a political weapon.[15] He personifies American loss of control over not only its national borders, but also its scientific achievements. On a deeper level, he challenges the moral neutrality of those achievements, exposing what has come to be called the "dual use" dilemma: greater understanding and control over infectious diseases inevitably leads to greater opportunity for transforming those diseases into weapons.

Bioterrorists are also more inscrutable than their historical analogs. American security agencies' extensive racial and ethnic profiling since September 11 aside, bioterrorists are generally assumed to be "nonstate actors," difficult to

---

[11]Nicholas B. King, "Security, Disease, Commerce: Ideologies of Post-Colonial Global Health," *Soc. Stud. Sci.*, 2002, *32*, 763–89.

[12]Elizabeth W. Etheridge, *Sentinel for Health: A History of the Centers for Disease Control* (Berkeley: University of California Press, 1992), p. 2; Fee, "Public Health and the State," pp. 241–49.

[13]A. D. Langmuir and J. M. Andrews, "Biological Warfare Defense 2: The Epidemic Intelligence Service of the Communicable Disease Center," *Am. J. Public Health*, 1952, *42*, 235–38.

[14]J. E. McDade, "Addressing the Potential Threat of Bioterrorism: Value Added to an Improved Public Health Infrastructure," *Emerg. Infect. Dis.*, 1999, *5*, 591–98.

[15]Nicholas King, "Dangerous Fragments," *Grey Room*, 2002, *7*, 72–81.

track and impossible to identify by superficial characteristics alone.[16] Unlike the immigrants of the late nineteenth and early twentieth centuries, they have no particular ethnic or national affiliation. Unlike nation-states, they cannot be negotiated with, bound to international conventions, or forced to undergo routine surveillance.

Bioterrorism is a focal point of American anxieties about globalization, demonstrating the difficulty of maintaining security amidst global transportation and information networks. How does the prospective bioterrorist learn how to weaponize pathogens? He hires a Russian biologist, studies microbiology in an American university on a student visa, or simply surfs the World Wide Web. How does he get the raw materials and tools necessary for weaponization? He buys them—from Russia, or Germany, or (most frequently) the United States. How does he distribute his weapons? He boards a plane and flies across the globe; or he slips them into the millions of tons of international commerce traversing the planet daily; or he simply drops them in the mail. Maintaining the sanctity of national and corporeal boundaries in a globalizing world seems all but impossible.

With regard to responses, American faith in (bio)technological fixes remains as strong as ever, but the specific technologies that we idealize have changed. The Progressives celebrated bacteriology, which promised to identify the pathogens that caused and the vectors that transmitted infectious disease, and to engineer pharmaceuticals to combat it or vaccines to prevent it. Americans now romanticize the molecular sciences, which promise to identify the genetic structure and evolutionary mechanisms of pathogenic organisms; biotechnology, which promises to develop new drugs and vaccines with unparalleled speed and efficiency; and information technology, which could allow us to identify outbreaks and track global patterns of disease with unprecedented accuracy. Earlier Americans marveled at the feats of microbe hunters and the wonder drugs that they produced, exemplars of laboratory science and inductive reasoning. Eighty years later, Americans celebrate the feats of swashbuckling virus hunters, but also fetishize the promise of automated global surveillance networks and mass distribution of pharmaceuticals.

The scale and scope of proposed surveillance regimes is the final area of novelty that historians might productively examine. Epidemiology has been a science of information collection at least since John Snow, François Melier, and George Buchanan's pioneering investigations of cholera and yellow fever 150 years ago. In contrast to this reactive, "shoe-leather" approach, contemporary recommendations favor a form of routinized, computerized global surveillance.

---

[16]As this essay was submitted, the American government had confirmed that the anthrax used in the October attacks was the product of an American weapons laboratory, and public speculation on the attacker's identity focused on American scientists and laboratory workers—belying initial assumptions, prompted by the contents of some of the letters, that an Arab or Islamic group was responsible.

This surveillance would be heavily reliant on new information technologies, databases, and molecular epidemiology, and depend on close partnerships between public health institutions, national security agencies, and private industry. Current proposals, arguing that uninterrupted global surveillance is the backbone of public health effectiveness, emphasize the unity of American national security concerns with global health.[17]

A Place for History

Historians of medicine are in a unique position to assess current responses to the threat of bioterrorism. We are peculiarly attuned to the long-term ramifications of decisions made during real and imagined crises, and we understand that short-term responses can develop into long-lived structures.[18] We also understand both the positive and negative power of analogical reasoning.

We might therefore ask a series of questions largely absent in public discussions of bioterrorism. How much are fears of bioterrorism driven by a reasonable assessment of the risk and consequences of an attack, and how much by the displacement of other anxieties onto the nefarious figure of the (bio)terrorist? Given our historical knowledge that those least willing or able to comply with medical examination and testing are often the most disadvantaged, who would likely bear the brunt of the restrictive measures now proposed to deal with an attack? How might stigmatization and social prejudice drive political decisions under the conditions of extreme uncertainty that would certainly accompany a bioterrorist attack? Given the previous controversies over collection of epidemiological surveillance data, what might be some unintended consequences of routine surveillance and information-sharing between federal public health and national security agencies?[19] Will the current focus on biodefense divert funding and attention from other public health problems, in and outside of the United States?[20] Finally, what long-term fiscal,

---

[17]For discussions of the development of global surveillance programs, see the February and August 1992 editions of the journal *Politics and the Life Sciences*; and Christopher F. Chyba, *Biological Terrorism, Emerging Diseases, and National Security* (New York: Rockefeller Brothers Fund, Inc., 1998).

[18]See, for example, Elizabeth Fee and Theodore M. Brown, "Preemptive Biopreparedness: Can We Learn Anything from History?," *Am. J. Public Health*, 2001, 91, 721–26; as well as the response by one of the leading advocates of bioterrorism preparedness, D. A. Henderson, "Biopreparedness and Public Health," *Am. J. Public Health*, 2001, 91, 1917–18.

[19]Gerald M. Oppenheimer, "Causes, Cases, and Cohorts: The Role of Epidemiology in the Historical Construction of AIDS," in *AIDS: The Making of A Chronic Disease*, ed. Elizabeth Fee and Daniel M. Fox (Berkeley: University of California Press, 1992).

[20]One recent survey of 539 local health departments found that, during the first phase of the smallpox vaccination program, about half had "deferred, delayed, or cancelled" other projects, such as prenatal care, HIV/AIDS prevention,water testing, and tuberculosis tracking. Ceci Connolly, "Smallpox Campaign Taxing Other Health Resources," *Washington Post*, 10 March 2003, p. A4.

political, and institutional consequences could the equation of American bioterrorism preparedness and global public health have? Will the fascination with biodefense be short-lived, or could it fundamentally reshape the relationship between the institutions of American public health, biomedical research, and the private sector?[21]

I should say a final word on doing history in the immediate post-September 11 era. I counsel caution, but I urge engagement. The kinds of arguments favored among historians of medicine are especially difficult to make under conditions of crisis. Constructionist or contextualist claims are often seen as the luxury of peace; but they are, in fact, our most precious resource in times of "war." Biodefense initiatives have the potential to reshape the future of American, and indeed global, public health. We cannot predict every outcome, nor can we prevent every mistake. But we can learn from the distant and immediate past, and we can understand the subterranean contours of contemporary discussions.

As I have indicated, reaching such an understanding necessitates the use of our historical tools; it also necessitates a reconsideration of the utility of those tools. Finally, and most importantly, it demands not only critical insight, but also something more uncommon and far more valuable: courage.

NANCY NISBET

Nancy Nisbet is a professor of Art History and Visual Art at the University of British Columbia, in Vancouver, BC, Canada, where she teaches courses in digital, interactive, and visual arts. She is also a practicing artist, whose recent work includes *Exchange 2006* (www. exchangeproject.ca), a traveling exhibit that explores the effects of Radio Frequency Identification (RFID) technologies. Visitors to the commercial shipping container which houses the exhibit are invited to exchange a personal item of their own for one in the exhibit to explore what Nisbet calls the "blurring and multiplication of identity through the exchange of personal belongings."

---

[21]In his January 2003 State of the Union address, President Bush proposed "Project Bioshield," which would establish a permanent fund of up to $6 billion over ten years to develop and produce vaccines and therapeutics for Ebola, plague, and other biological agents. To provide an incentive for pharmaceutical companies and biotechnology firms, the program guaranteed a market for resulting biodefense products, even if never used. In response, pharmaceutical industry representatives demanded higher guaranteed profits, fewer restrictions on spending, and protection from liability in case of adverse effects. Michael Barbaro, "Biodefense Plan Greeted with Caution; Drug Firms Want Better Guarantees," *Washington Post*, 2 May 2003, p. E1.

Nisbet's article, "Resisting Surveillance: Identity and Implantable Microchips," appeared in the art studies journal, *Leonardo*, in 2004. "Resisting Surveillance" describes *Pop! Goes the Weasel*, an art installation in which Nisbet asks the audience to explore technology and surveillance in their own lives. Although her article focuses on the intersections of performance art and philosophy, Nisbet recalls how her project emerged from a conversation with scholars in a number of academic disciplines:

> The research topic of my paper emerged directly from a casual conversation. A few friends, mostly graduate students, had gathered for dinner and the conversation inevitably turned to our respective research areas. One grad student was in zoology and studied fish and their patterns of location within streams. In her project, RFID microchips were implanted under the skin of fish. Multiple antennae laid on the streambed picked up the specific swimming patterns of individual fish. My immediate response to the use of RFID in this project was: "Wow! What if this was done to people?"
>
> Over the next few weeks I couldn't get the idea of RFID and human surveillance out of my mind. Questions kept circling around: What if humans were implanted? What information would be tracked? Who would track it? Why would this information be tracked? What political and social conditions might enable the acceptance of human microchip implantation? Could such acceptance ever arise? I not only considered these questions but also wondered how I might engage with the issues of this type of surveillance within my artistic research and practice. My immediate consideration to actually implant an RFID microchip into my body was restrained by my need to understand the technological, political and critical implications and meaning of such an invasive action. I needed to do research and come to a better understanding of my potential place or role in the conversation.

Nisbet also describes the process of making her unique contribution to academic conversations about surveillance:

> It was about two years later when the tastes of the individual ideas finally coalesced into the complex flavor that I recognized as my "aha" moment. The background and indirect reflections on the questions and issues I identified long before gradually developed into an interesting critical approach. The most important discovery was the method by which my actions could directly challenge the

underlying assumptions of the technological system itself: that identifying technologies rely on the singularity and uniqueness of the thing being identified. My inspiration was to implant TWO microchips into my ONE body: I would become multiple in the 'eyes' of the system.

Following up on my visceral reaction to and intellectual curiosity about RFID eventually evolved into the foundation of my research and artistic practice. More than just a dinner party, that casual conversation among friends was really a crucial catalyst. I had found my entrance into the debate.

For Discussion

Nisbet opens her article with a quotation from the French philosopher Michel Foucault, whose academic work often explored the history of surveillance and its effects. The quotation Nisbet has chosen, however, has to do with the relationship between knowledge and power relations.

How does the relationship posed by Foucault set the tone for Nisbet's own experiment with RFID implants?

How does she develop Foucault's ideas to make them her own and give them a purposeful role in her argument?

As Nisbet notes, visitors to *Pop! Goes the Weasel* wear their own RFID badges in the gallery. Her observations of people interacting with the exhibit provide her with field research which she then incorporates into her study of the effects of surveillance.

How are visitors affected by becoming part of the exhibit, and how in your view does the exhibit "allow visitors to practice intervening in and avoiding surveillance as possible forms of resistance"?

Nisbet concludes by arguing that, given all the popular support for high-tech surveillance in our everyday lives, it "may be too late to prevent such pervasive and invasive technical developments, but it is not too late to demand protection for individual privacy and freedom" (214).

How might another researcher respond to Nisbet's challenge with a project of his or her own? Which academic fields might be brought into the conversation to add to, or even challenge, Nisbet's intersecting fields of philosophy and performance art?

Resisting Surveillance: Identity and Implantable Microchips

by Nancy Nisbet

There is no power relation without the correlative constitution of a field of knowledge, nor any knowledge that does not presuppose and constitute at the same time power relations.

—*Michel Foucault*[1]

Although surveillance of human behavior is not new, technological developments and heightened concern over public security are increasingly facilitating, and arguably justifying, ubiquitous surveillance. Leading contenders in contemporary social surveillance systems include: the establishment of national ID cards, the use of biometric identifiers and, potentially, the implantation of identifying microchips. Perhaps the most serious risk to personal privacy and freedom that any of these systems pose is through the possible development of an involuntary centralized or interconnected database. The implementation, control of access, and restrictions of use of such information repositories have many privacy advocates concerned [2,3]. The trend toward the convergence of diverse databases of collected information in North America and elsewhere recalls Bentham's Panopticon[4] and the specter of coercion that emerges in Foucault's analysis of power and knowledge in a disciplinary society.

My concern with the limits and risks of the explosion of surveillance technologies prompted me to undertake an artistic exploration of a particularly threatening system, that of implanted radio-frequency identification microchips. *Pop! Goes the Weasel*, an interactive art installation first presented at the Inter-Society for Electronic Art (ISEA) symposium in Nagoya, Japan, in October 2002, is the first of several artworks that I have undertaken to this end.

2001–2002: I have two microchips implanted in my body—one in the back of each hand. The first was injected in October 2001 and the second in February 2002[5].

---

[1]M. Foucault, *Discipline and Punish: The Birth of the Prison*, Alan Sheridan, trans. (New York: Pantheon, 1977) p. 27 (orig.: *Surveiller et Punir: Naissance de la prison* [Paris: Gallimard, 1975]).

[2]Elaine M. Ramesh, "Time Enough? Consequences of Human Microchip Implantation," <http://www.fplc.edu/risk/vol8/fall/ramesh.htm>.

[3]C.W. Crews, "Human Bar Code Monitoring Biometric Technologies in a Free Society," *Cato Institute Policy Analysis* No. 452, 1–20 (17 September 2002).

[4]Jeremy Bentham, "Panopticon Papers," in Mary Peter Mack, ed., *A Bentham Reader* (New York: Pegasus, 1969) pp. 194–208. Bentham's Panopticon is a circular architectural model designed in 1791. The essence of its power is that it allows seeing without being seen.

[5]J. Scheeres, "New Body Art: Chip Implants," <http://www.wired.com/news/culture/0,1284,50769,00. html>, 11 March 2002.

Radio Frequency Identification Technology

Since the 1980s, Radio Frequency Identification Technology (RFID)[6] has developed to the point that today it is widely used in tracking and access applications. It is a wireless system commonly used for livestock and pet identification as well as automated vehicle identification systems such as toll roads and parking garages. RFID technology has the potential to drastically alter human surveillance. As microchips get smaller and power supply issues[7] are resolved, forms of human surveillance that invade the body will increase. Some human bioengineering research in the United Kingdom already uses implanted RFID technology[8]. In October 2002, the United States Federal Drug Administration's apparent[9] decision that RFID microchips used for nonmedical applications do not need FDA approval for implantation into humans[10] significantly bolstered corporate interest. Applied Digital Solutions, Inc. (ADS) is marketing external[11] human tracking devices such as the wristwatch-like Digital Angel and the internal VeriChip for "a variety of security, financial, emergency identification and healthcare applications"[12].

---

[6]An RFID system is composed of three parts: an antenna, a reader (transceiver) and a unique radio frequency microchip (transponder or RF tag). The reader sends a pulse to the antenna that emits radio signals of a specific frequency (134 kHz, in this case) to activate a microchip. Power generated from the transceiver allows the passive microchip to relay its ID information back to the reader and positively identify the object or individual. See <http://www.aimglobal.org/technologies/rfid/what_is_rfid.htm>.

[7]Currently, RFID microchips used in animals, and in a few people, are passive (have no power supply), and reading of the ID number can only occur at a maximum distance of about 5 feet. If these microchips could be powered and still remain small enough for implantation, it would enable tracking over larger distances.

[8]Kevin Warwick of the Cybernetic Intelligence Research Group at the University of Reading in the U.K. has used microchip implants in his bioengineering research on interfacing with the nervous system via RFID; <http://www.rdg.ac.uk/KevinWarwick/html/project_cyborg_1_0.html>.

[9]It is noteworthy that subsequent to the ADS press release, the FDA issued a warning letter to ADS Inc. on 8 November 2002, indicating that in marketing the chip for medical benefit, "the VeriChip is adulterated . . . or misbranded" under the Federal Food, Drug, and Cosmetic Act"; <http://www.fda.gov/foi/warning_letters/g3668d.htm>. This points to conflicting statements issued by ADS to the media and to the FDA—one wonders why ADS feels this "misbranding" is necessary. One must also question the FDA's evident lack of concern over the implantation of such a device into humans for any reason.

[10]ADSX Press Release, 22 October 2002, announcing the FDA's permission to use implanted microchips for "security, financial and personal identification or safety applications": <http://www.adsx.com/news/2002/102202.html>.

[11]"The Digital Angel Safety and Location Systems surpass ordinary location-enabled devices. Only Digital Angel alerts you to the exact location of people, pets and objects in real time"; <http://www.digitalangel.net>.

[12]ADSX Press Release, 31 October 2002, announcing the use of VeriChip for the above-mentioned (see Ref. [10]) purposes, including "healthcare applications"; <http://www.adsx.com/news/2002/103102.html>.

2001: I approached four surgeons and a veterinarian and asked whether or not they would agree to perform the microchip implantation for artistic research purposes. The vet agreed to supply me with the microchip but refused to inject it into me. One surgeon did not reply to my message. The second declined. The third agreed on condition that the Canadian Medical Association sanctioned the procedure. The fourth simply agreed

Identity and Microchip Implantation

For any surveillance or tracking data to be meaningful it must be associated with a particular person, location or thing being observed; ultimately, it is a process that relies on some form of identification. The dystopic futures of much science fiction are only too replete with the tracking and controlling of humans through surveillance implants. Such fictions are becoming science, and the future is imminent[13,14].

Deciphering and altering the underlying assumptions of a system can enable disruption of that system. Some of the assumptions of identity upon which surveillance relies are: that a person's identity is singular, that one's identity is constant and unchanging, that identity has a fundamental connection to the body and, finally, that identity is ascertainable.

I had two chips implanted into my body because of the assumption that each surveyed person has one unique ID number—not two: one chip, one person and one unique code. Surveillance relies on minimizing confusion and keeping one's boundaries clear. I implanted only two chips because it takes only two to create a binary system—like the zeros and ones of computer code. With exactly two chips I am able to "code for" an infinite number of identities just through the sequence in which they are scanned.

2000: Wanting to push beyond the spectacle of the implantation of a microchip, I struggled to come to a point of departure—to make a bold and playful entrance into a resistance to corporate- or government-sanctioned surveillance.

Pop! Goes the Weasel—Installation Details

There are four main components of this installation: access gates, photographs, video projection and the RFID scanning system. The viewer first encounters one of two RFID-controlled gates that allow passage into and out of the installation space. Those viewers choosing to wear an RFID microchip badge will be able to

---

[13]J. Wilson, "Girl to Get Tracker Implant to Ease Parents' Fears," 3 September 2002; <http://www.guardian.co.uk/uk_news/story/0,3604,785071,00.html>.

[14]"Fla. Family Takes Computer Chip Trip," 10 May 2002; <http://www.cbsnews.com/stories/2002/05/10/tech/main508641.shtml>.

"unlock" the gates, while those without a badge will be locked out. Five black circular pedestals, each topped with a transparent, backlit photograph of a hand against a background of surgical green silk, are interspersed in the installation. The five hands (Color Plate A No. 2) resemble those of an elderly woman, a gentleman, a patient, an elegant woman and a workman (article frontispiece). Projected on one wall is a short video loop documenting the surgical implantation of a microchip into my hand inter-cut with images of the five hands described above. The background audio of the video is an almost unrecognizably warped interpretation of the nursery rhyme "Pop! Goes the Weasel" alternating with a medical sounding beep. The final and crucial underlying component of this installation is the RFID scanning system. The installation houses eight RFID antennae, one hidden under each photograph, one visible at each gate, and the last one in a smaller sixth pedestal that exposes the wiring and scanner of the RFID system. The scanner at this last location is programmed to display, in real time, the viewer's badge ID number at the bottom of the video projection. As someone with a RFID badge approaches the gates or any of the pedestals, the antenna will detect the badge's unique ID number and store viewer-tracking data (ID number, date, time and location) in a database.[15] The presence of an RFID badge at one of the photograph pedestals will also activate a light in the bottom of the pedestal to illuminate the image.

> *1997: At a dinner party with friends, I was introduced to the use of microchips to track fish. The disturbing thought of using such microchips for human surveillance took root in my mind.*

Pop! Goes the Weasel—Objectives

The installation presents issues of surveillance as they relate to identity and the body. It is a site of experimentation with surveillance resistance strategies involving possible avoidance, intervention and subversion of the system.

> *When no one was looking, a gentleman crawled under the gate.*

Avoidance: Although the gates suggest restricted access, they are actually "leaky" and allow motivated visitors to discover ways to circumvent the access control.

> *A workman hurried over to the photograph before the light went out.*

---

[15]The functioning of the installation occurs primarily behind the scenes. The surveillance system designed for this installation consists of eight antennae, two RFID readers and many RFID microchip badges. Five of the antennae are contained within the photograph pedestals; two are visible at the gates, and the eighth antenna is visible through the transparent top of a sixth, shorter, pedestal located beside the computer and RFID system box (Fig. 2).

Intervention: A forthcoming component of future installations will enable the viewer to effect direct intervention in the surveillance database itself. The small pedestal where the electronics are visible will be the site where the visitor may alter some of the collected information. Each microchip badge is pre-programmed with a unique ID number. This number is associated with a database record that contains other information, such as name, occupation and country of residence. After scanning the badge to open the associated data record, visitors may change the name, occupation and country of residence associated with "their" card. This information remains linked to the card until another visitor adopts the card and changes the associated "identity" yet again.

After the others left the installation, an elderly woman quietly altered the database.

Subversion: In the constant change in "whom" the data belongs to, identity is blurred (the data is associated with multiple people but with one ID badge), and the collected information becomes meaningless.

A lady covertly passed off her badge to another.

This installation aims to remind participants of the ubiquity of surveillance structures, encourage visceral responses to potential future modes of surveillance and allow visitors to practice intervening in and avoiding surveillance as possible forms of resistance. Already significantly conditioned to surveillance and authentication interfaces, visitors routinely placed their own hands upon the photographs. This connection is a form of selfimplication. The hand that reaches out is also the hand surveyed. Whose hand is it? Is this person someone you know? Is it someone like you? Could it be you?

Further Work

I am interested in the interface between the body and interactive informational technologies. Subjection of my body to the cultural coding and technical invasion of implanted microchips is fundamentally different from wearing them as an accessory like a watch or tattooing numbers on my body. I am interested in embodiment versus adornment. These chips are permanent, nontransferable and hidden, and they "talk" to certain machines.

In future work I will use my implanted microchips to interface with my computer and to track my identities as I travel in both physical and cyber spaces. I will use an RFID reader attached to my computer to scan the chips in my hands, depending on my perception of the nature of how I am using my computer at that moment. The scanning will initiate the collection of data for my own private database.[16] I have arbitrarily associated the chip in my left hand with my identity at play, while the chip in my right hand is associated with my identity at work.[17] I am interested in juxtaposing *where* "I" go inside my computer and cyberspace with *which* "I" is going there and *what* "I" am doing there. While collecting this "virtual" data, I will also record "real world" observations. Using a GPS (global positioning system) unit, I will record my geographical coordinates; with a web cam I will document my physical surroundings. Where am I (is my body) when I go *"there"* in cyberspace? I want to explore the connections of my physical body and associated identity(ies) to my computer and my virtual identities. I will investigate the nature of these identities and how my perceptions of identity/self may be shifting.

Exploration and experimentation with the RFID human computer interface will have significant impact on the project. What is the experience of tracking my every computer encounter? How do I negotiate the conscious decisions to identify with one or another identity (as represented by chip ID number)? How does the performative aspect of using my system in public spaces such as cyber cafés, libraries, etc., influence the project—my notion of self, my awareness of self?

As a more public aspect of this work I plan to develop a scanner "detector." As RFID technologies become more widely used, I may not be able to determine when my implanted chips are responding to hidden scanners. The scanner detector will ensure that I remain aware of my microchips' "conversations" with public surveillance devices: The detector will allow me to resist accordingly and play with the performative potential of such knowledge.

Conclusion

Tracking and identification systems are rapidly being developed: RFID technology is one of the forerunners of ubiquitous surveillance. I am interested in provoking questions about these authentication systems: How is identity ascertained/ maintained? What are the hidden risks? Will chipping become mandatory? How will these systems be implemented? Who will have or control access to the information? What are the weaknesses that resistance can explore? *Pop! Goes the Weasel* aims to encourage resistance to surveillance structures by blurring viewer identities, by avoiding access control mechanisms, and by intervening directly in the database. My ongoing work will closely examine my

---

[16]In this project I am not becoming a passive subject of others, but remain empowered and pro-active in the representation and interpretation of my identity(ies).

[17]Rather than affirming a dualistic approach to understanding identity, the choice of assigning the microchips with "work" and "play" was made in recognition of widespread familiarity with shifts in one's identity(ies) between that expressed in workplace environments and that predominating when engaging in play. The tracking project is not limited to these two versions of my identities but will expand over time to track several identities.

personal microchip interface with the computer and playfully consider the resulting data with respect to my body and my perception of self.

Current concern for national security around the world reflects international political tensions and is one factor that has done much to bolster support
for increased human surveillance and has brought such identification technologies to the forefront of discussion. It may be too late to prevent such pervasive and invasive technical developments, but it is not too late to demand protection for individual privacy and freedom. For all the benefits that may emerge
from the digital "angels" being developed, there is the very real risk of their becoming the 21st century's all-too-watchful Big Brothers.

CHRIS TAYLOR AND ANNABELLE JAMES

Chris Taylor, senior lecturer in Law at Bradford University in
West Yorkshire, UK, teaches courses in constitutional and administra-
tive law, the law of evidence, and business law. As a specialist in pre-
trial disclosure law, Taylor studies the United Kingdom's 1996 Criminal
Procedure and Investigations Act (CPIA), which plays an important
role in the following article, "Video Games: Some Pitfalls of Video Evidence," from the *Journal of Criminal Law*, 2005. Coauthor Annabelle
James is principle lecturer in Business and Law at Leeds Metropolitan
University, Leeds, UK, where she teaches courses in criminal justice,
criminal law, and human rights.

Taylor recalls how "Video Games" built on an earlier research
project, where he examined the challenges surveillance camera evidence posed to criminal justice professionals in the United Kingdom.
Here, he describes the role of field research, such as conversational interviews, in sparking a new project:

> My interest in the treatment of CCTV evidence stemmed from my
> previous research into pre-trial disclosure/discovery and the col-
> lection and disclosure of evidence by UK detectives. This is a prob-
> lematic area of UK criminal procedure and has produced many
> miscarriages of justice. In the course of the study, I had interviewed
> a large number of police officers and the difficulties posed by
> CCTV evidence had arisen in a number of these conversations. Al-
> though this was beyond the scope of the original study, it became
> clear that this was an issue which was causing widespread diffi-
> culty for police and lawyers and, as such, presented a ready topic
> for a subsequent paper. Regular discussions with professionals,
> such as police officers or judges is always an excellent way of iden-
> tifying areas for research as their practical perspective serves to
> highlight the shortcomings in legislation.

Taylor also describes the ways he begins gathering material and putting sources together, highlighting online research databases; he then goes on to explain how he and James came to work together on this project:

> In the case of a paper, I begin the process with a directed information gathering exercise, drawing together all of the available material in the field under a number of different headings depending on the specific topic. This sort of exercise is now much more efficient due to the increased availability of online resources. For example, in the case of the CCTV paper, there are no statutory provisions which apply solely to such material, which is merely an aspect of the wider disclosure/discovery procedures. Therefore, rather than conduct a search of online databases around a statutory provision, a search was conducted around key terms such as 'CCTV' and 'abuse of process' (which is the ground on which the defective treatment of such material is challenged in court). This produced a list of recent decisions where the courts had grappled with the subject. I also compiled a list of 'interested parties', such as the Home Office, Crown Prosecution Service and Courts Service which would be expected to have a view on the subject, and a search of their published reports and Codes of Practice revealed additional material from their various perspectives. From here, a detailed consideration of the law reports was conducted to identify key areas of difficulty for the courts and the decision making process which was employed. This produced the key findings of the paper which were then discussed with serving police officers to assess whether the theoretical findings equated with their operational experience (which they did).
>
> At this point, I realised that a paper on the subject really needed to consider the application of the European Convention on Human Rights to the evidential process, which is not within my field of expertise. This represented an opportunity to involve my colleague Annabelle James, who contributed this section of the paper.

For her part, James recalls how the "Video Games" project meshed with her existing interests in related cultural and legal issues:

> I have always been interested in the issues surrounding the protection of an individual's civil liberties and human rights and had previously published comments on case law following the coming into force of the Human Rights Act 1998. At the time of writing the article, I was also involved in the teaching of Intellectual Property Law with specific regard to data protection principles and therefore the co-authoring of this article tied in with both my research and teaching interests at the time.

While Taylor's approach to research involves a detailed, comprehensive information gathering process, James describes her process as one that combines research and writing, along with an evolving outline:

> My approach to starting the 'research process' has changed. I used to collect everything I could on the area and read and research thoroughly before committing pen to paper. The difficulty I had with this approach is that I would often be approaching deadlines with many ideas but very little actually written down. I now approach the task by undertaking preliminary research to ensure that the area has not been covered in depth elsewhere, to get an outline of the key areas and themes and to compile a list of possible sources. I then write a basic outline of the piece and go back over each section, adding detail and checking for accuracy as and when I have done the research.

Although they have different approaches to the research process, Taylor and James reflect similarly on knowing when they felt ready to present their work to a wider audience. James focuses on validity, noting that "the question of whether you have read or researched enough to make a contribution to a debate is an entirely subjective one and is dependent on the readership of the journal in question or the audience you are presenting to. Whilst errors can be made in the accurate reporting of legislative provisions or the interpretation of case judgments, academic and legal arguments and opinions are valid so long as they can be backed up by reference to other sources." For Taylor, there

> is no "magic badge" that tells you that you have the right to contribute—you contribute when you feel you have something to say. Every researcher has to start somewhere and there is always the first paper or the first conference where you are unknown and you wonder whether anyone will be interested in what you have to say. The key is to be familiar with your subject because if you know the topic well and you find a debate interesting, then the chances are that others in the field will as well and remember, the worst that can happen is that the journal says "no"—and there is always another journal.
>
> In terms of "when is enough," this is more difficult to answer but, in reading around a subject, you soon reach the point where the issues start to sounds familiar and you have the sense of having read this before. This is the point at which you have familiarised yourself with the key areas and if, having reached this point, you still believe that something remains to be said, then congratulations!—that is *your* contribution.

Finally, Taylor emphasizes the importance of writers pursuing their interests in, and instincts about, a question or issue, since:

> At the start of this project I was not entirely convinced that there was enough material to produce a paper for a refereed journal and it was only as the project took shape, that I grew to appreciate the depth of the debate. Because of those initial doubts, the paper was very nearly not written at all; yet, since its publication, I have been contacted by research students, police officers and both the UK Home Office and the Parliament of New South Wales Australia who have all cited this paper as the reason they considered me to be the person to speak to. The message is, if your instinct tells you that there is a question to be asked then ask it—you never know where it will lead you.

For Discussion

As you read Taylor's and James's article, note how they open by distinguishing between the theory and practice of data protection in criminal procedures.

> How do James and Taylor, as scholars of law, perform critical academic research without losing sight of the practical implications of legal theory?

In section IV, "Videotape and the Abuse of Process," Taylor and James focus on the problematic applications of data disclosure requirements.

> How do they negotiate their way through competing explanations for failures in data disclosure? Do they fairly present each position explaining those failures, and how effectively do they propose their own explanation within the conversation?
>
> How do Taylor and James take and support their position on data disclosure based on their field research?

The legal scholarship practiced by Taylor and James develops through a conversation between competing legal principles, statutes, and provisions.

> How do Taylor and James choose a position within this legal conversation, and how do they demonstrate the legitimacy of one principle, statute, or provision over others?

Video Games: Some Pitfalls of Video Evidence

*by Chris Taylor** and Annabelle James**

Although the courts are increasingly faced with sophisticated forms of evidence, from computer data to DNA, it is the everyday videotape which continues to present some of the greatest difficulties for investigators, prosecutors and defendants. Criminal trials regularly involve consideration of video evidence, partly due to the growing popularity of urban surveillance systems[1] and also the proliferation of CCTV within private businesses, such as shops and petrol stations. Video evidence is undeniably persuasive, making it a valuable weapon in court, but its use raises issues of collection, retention, disclosure and storage, which can have a critical influence on the conduct of cases.[2] The situation is further complicated by legislation, not least the Criminal Procedure and Investigations Act 1996 (CPIA), which regulates the disclosure of 'unused material' (including videotape) to the defence, the Data Protection Act 1998 and, of course, the Human Rights Act 1998.

In recent years there has been considerable discussion of issues surrounding video identification evidence[3]. The aim of this article is to examine some additional aspects of video evidence which have proved especially problematic, first in relation to the disclosure of unused video material under CPIA and then in the context of human rights and data protection principles. It will

---

*Principal Lecturer in Law, Leeds Metropolitan University; e-mail: A.N.James@leedsmet.ac.uk.

**Senior Lecturer in Law, Leeds Metropolitan University; e-mail: C.W.Taylor@leedsmet.ac.uk.

[1]Under the government's Crime Reduction Programme CCTV Initiative alone, around £170 million has been spent on 684 CCTV schemes across England and Wales. House of Commons, Written Answer 16 Septmber 2003, col. 675W.

[2]For an examination of the broader issues arising from the use of CCTV see K. Williams and C. Johnstone, 'The Politics of the Selective Gaze: Closed Circuit Television and the Policing of Public Space' (2000) 34 *Crime, Law and Social Change* 183–210; M. Constant and P. Ridgeon, *The Principles and Practice of CCTV*, 2nd edn (Miller Freeman UK Ltd: 2000); B. Brown, 'CCTV in Town Centres: Three Case Studies', Police Research Group, Crime Detection and Prevention Series Paper No. 68 (HMSO: London, 1995); Scarman Centre National CCTV Evaluation Team, *National Evaluation of CCTV: Early Findings on Scheme Implementation—Effective Practice Guide*, Home Office Statistical Bulletin 5/03, April 2003 (available at www.crimereduction.gov.uk/cctv32.htm, accessed 23 March 2005); House of Lords Select Committee on Science and Technology (1998) Eighth Report. HL 121; N. Taylor, 'You've Been Framed: the Regulation of CCTV Surveillance' (2002) 7(2) J Civ Lib 83–107.

[3]This area has raised a number of issues, not least following the introduction of the Video Identification Parade Electronic Recording (VIPER), discussed in S. Nicholls, 'Police Station Practice: Video Identification' (2003) 7(3) *Magistrates' Courts Practice* 1–2. For further aspects of video identification, see *Attorney-General's Reference (No. 2 of 2002)* [2002] EWCA Crim 2373, *The Times* (17 October 2002), (2003) 67 JCL 91.

be suggested that although the legislation does, in theory, provide safeguards for those adversely affected by the use of video evidence, in practice these may well be of limited use.

Police station video

At many police stations CCTV is routinely employed to record dealings at the front inquiry desk and, more importantly, within the station custody area to record the processing of suspects. Such tapes may be used to counter any allegations of police misconduct and, therefore, can be seen as providing protection for officers and suspects alike, notwithstanding that, in the vast majority of cases, they record little or nothing of interest to either side. For this reason, together with issues of storage and cost, it is usual for tapes to be recycled on a rolling basis after a period of time has elapsed; however this is a policy which leaves the police vulnerable to later requests from the defence for disclosure of the tapes as unused material. If the initial circumstances of the inquiry have not indicated that the custody video might be significant it is quite possible that a defence request for copies might arrive after the tape concerned had been re-recorded, thereby erasing any evidence which it contained. It therefore falls to the individual officer in the case to assess not only whether the custody tape might contain potentially contentious material but also whether there is any reason to suspect that the accused may make a false allegation. In both cases the tape must be retrieved and secured before it is reused.

It is important to realise that the implications of a failure to safeguard the tape adequately in such circumstances extend beyond the potential loss of evidence as it is not unknown for officers to include the custody video on the MG6C schedule of non-sensitive unused material which is submitted to the defence and which forms the basis for subsequent defence requests for additional prosecution disclosure. Including a custody video in the schedule when the tape itself is no longer in existence could have serious consequences should the defence later request sight of the tape, as such an omission will, inevitably, raise doubts over the accuracy of the disclosure schedules as a whole.[4]

---

[4]There is now a considerable body or research on the failings of the disclosure regime including, Law Society, *CPIA 1996 Disclosure Provisions Survey* (1999); British Academy of Forensic Sciences and the Criminal Bar Association, *Survey of the Practising Independent Bar into the Operation in Practice of the Criminal Procedure and Investigations Act 1996 Disclosure Provisions* (1999); Crown Prosecution Service Inspectorate, *Report on the Thematic Review of the Disclosure of Unused Material*, 2/2000 (March, 2000); J. Poltnikoff and R. Woolfson, *A Fair Balance? Evaluation of the Operation of Disclosure Law* (HMSO: London, 2001); Auld LJ, *A Review of the Criminal Courts in England and Wales, Final Report* (HMSO: London, 2001); Butterfield J, *Review of Criminal Investigations and Prosecutions Conducted by HM Customs and Excise* (HMSO: London, 2003). For an overview of the disclosure regime in general, see D. Ormerod, 'Improving the Disclosure Regime' (2003) 7 E & P 102–29; M. Redmayne, 'Criminal Justice Act 2003: (1) Disclosure and its Discontents' [2004] Crim LR 441; C. W. Taylor, 'Advance Disclosure: Reflections on the Criminal Procedure and Investigations Act 1996' (2001) 40(2) *Howard Journal of Criminal Justice* 114.

Third-party video

If the procedures for handling police videos places undue emphasis on the foresight of the individual officer then the position in relation to third party material is even more hazardous. With the increasing use of urban CCTV systems it is inevitable that many street crimes, public order offences and commercial thefts may entail consideration of video evidence which is rarely, if ever, under the direct control of the police. The potential destruction of material by third parties raises additional difficulties in that, whereas the third party may be summoned to present the evidence in court,[5] there exists no general prosecution duty to preserve the evidence beyond a requirement to make the third party aware of the existence of the investigation and to make the prosecutor aware of the existence of the third-party material.[6] This creates problems for the investigator in the conduct of the initial investigation which are both chronological and geographical in nature, as illustrated by the following (fictional) examples.

Case 1

A charge under s. 18 of the Offences Against the Person Act 1861[7] is supported by pub CCTV showing the defendant striking the alleged victim in the face with a beer glass. The defence of self-defence is based on the allegation that there had been an altercation between the two men in the same pub the previous week which led the defendant to believe that he was in imminent danger of attack by the alleged victim. Whereas the tape from the evening of the assault had been seized, the tapes from the previous week had not and they have subsequently been lost.

Case 2

A charge of theft from a shop is supported by a poor-quality CCTV tape from the store in question, raising the question of the identity of the accused. The defendant claims that, at the time of the alleged theft, he was in a shop some distance away but which also has CCTV facilities. As there was nothing initially to suggest that the other shop was involved in the investigation, their CCTV tapes had not been seized.

In each case it is possible to conclude that the missing tapes should have been secured by the police as part of the investigation and CPIA and the associated Codes of Practice state that the police are under a duty to:

> pursue all reasonable lines of enquiry, whether these point towards or away from the suspect.[8]

---

[5]*Re Barlow Clowes Gilt Managers Ltd* [1992] Ch 208.
[6]Codes of Practice, para. 3.5.
[7]Grievous bodily harm with intent.
[8]Codes of Practice, para. 3.4.

Yet, equally, it is clear that in both cases the significance of the missing tape has only become apparent once the proposed defence has become known, which presents the defence with a tactical advantage. Under CPIA the defence is required, after primary disclosure has been made by the prosecution, to reveal the scope of the proposed defence by means of the defence statement,[9] submitted with the objective of:

a setting out in general terms the nature of the accused's defence,
b indicating the matters on which he takes issue with the prosecution, and
c setting out, in the case of each such matter, the reason why he takes issue with the prosecution.[10]

Receipt of a defence statement compels the prosecution to revisit their initial assessment of the unused material in the case by means of 'secondary' disclosure.[11] The aim is to provide additional protection for the accused, without reverting to the pre-CPIA regime, which often required the police to undertake the time-consuming exercise of copying all the material in their possession for the defence. However, in the majority of cases the defence statement contains nothing more than a simple denial of the charge[12] and so provides little justification for the police to secure additional material such as that featured in the above cases. Even where the defence statement is more expansive, research[13] has indicated that there is frequently a significant delay in the submission of the defence statement, making it probable that the third party will have disposed of tapes which were not initially identified as potentially relevant to the investigation in the period before the defence statement is received.[14] The result is a situation where the defence are able to ascertain what video evidence is in the possession of the police before seeking to draw attention to an otherwise unrelated video in order to undermine the prosecution case and where the prosecution, and in particular the investigating officer in the case, is largely powerless to preserve the video

---

[9]C. W. Taylor, 'Stating the Obvious: the Misuse of Defence Statements under the Criminal Procedure and Investigations Act 1996' (2001) 74 *Police Journal* 155.

[10]CPIA s. 5(6). For an overview of the provisions of CPIA, see J. Sprack, 'The Criminal Procedure and Investigations Act 1996: the Duty of Disclosure' [1997] Crim LR 308; R. Ede and E. Shepherd, *Active Defence* (Law Society: London, 2000); J. A. Epp, *Building on the Decade of Disclosure in Criminal Procedure* (Cavendish: London, 2001); J. Niblett, *Disclosure in Criminal Proceedings* (Blackstone: London, 1997).

[11]CPIA s. 7.

[12]For an overview of the area, see Taylor, above n. 9.

[13]See Crown Prosecution Service Inspectorate, above n. 4; Plotnikoff and Woolfson, above n. 4.

[14]For an illustration of the operational difficulties this presents, see *R v Dobson* [2001] EWCA Crim 1606.

evidence held by the third party unless this has been identified as potentially significant at an early stage in the investigation.[15]

The critical point is that, even though the tape in question may have little
or no evidential value, the very fact that the police are unable to produce a copy
for the defence may, itself, be sufficient to generate doubt in the minds of the
jury.

Paradoxically, the situation is little better when there is too much, rather
than too little, video evidence to be considered and the police will frequently
find themselves in the possession of a quantity of videotape far in excess of that
required for evidential purposes. Such a situation may arise following continuous video surveillance of a given area by a single camera over a period of hours
or even days. Alternatively, many commercial premises and city centre CCTV
systems operate 'multiplex' systems on which the tape displays the images from
a number of cameras simultaneously. The common factor in each case is that the
investigator is left with a wealth of tape of which only a small proportion is
likely to be of relevance to the case, and this raises important questions over how
the remaining portions of the video are handled. Clearly the primary evidential
issue is identification of the pertinent segments of the tape and their assembly
for use in court, however, of equal importance is what happens to the remainder
of the tape, by virtue of its status as unused material in the case. The significance
of this is to be found in the 1996 Act which requires the prosecution to:

(a) disclose to the accused any prosecution material which has not
previously been disclosed to the accused and which in the prosecutor's opinion might undermine the case for the prosecution
against the accused, or

(b) give to the accused a written statement that there is no
material of a description mentioned in paragraph (a).[16]

In this way it falls to individual officers, in their capacity as 'disclosure officer' in the case, to assess the extent to which the remaining tape might con-
ceivably undermine the prosecution case and to ensure disclosure to the defence accordingly.

Videotape and abuse of process

The court may halt a prosecution *inter alia* where:

The prosecution have manipulated or misused the process of the
court so as to deprive the defendant of a protection provided by
law or to take unfair advantage of a technicality ... the ultimate

---

[15]In the case of *R* v *Sadhev* [2002] EWCA Crim 1064, the defence waited a full year
after the alleged offence before raising the question of CCTV at the scene.

[16]CPIA s. 3(1).

objective of this discretionary power is to ensure that there should be a fair trial according to law, which involves fairness both to the defendant and the prosecution.[17]

There have been a number of attempts to employ this principle in relation to lost or destroyed evidence,[18] based on defence assertions that the absence of the item in question renders the trial unfair, and there is clearly a potential application of this principle where there have been errors in the handling of video evidence. As has been shown, the identification of the relevant sections of any video evidence lies solely in the hands of the investigator and the danger for the prosecution is that a police failure to retain and disclose unused video material will later be judged sufficient to justify a stay of proceedings on the grounds of abuse of process. This has led to instances, both under CPIA and the previous Attorney-General's Guidelines,[19] where the defence have sought to argue abuse of process in order to capitalise on the mishandling of videotape by the police or prosecution. Consideration of a number of recent decisions illustrates some of the factors influencing the court in such cases.

Perhaps the most straightforward grounds for an application arise where there has been a total failure by the police to disclose video evidence to the defence, as in *R v Birmingham and Others*.[20] Here the videotape in question recorded events immediately preceding and during a fracas outside a nightclub, as a result of which seven defendants faced charges of violent disorder and assaulting police officers. At the start of the trial it emerged that although the tapes had been viewed by the police in the immediate aftermath of the incident, they had not been retained and their existence had not been revealed by the police to the CPS or the defence, even after there had been a number of requests for access to any remaining unused material including specific requests for copies of any videotapes. Against this background, and having visited the scene, the judge concluded that the tape would have been valuable in relation to the alibis asserted by some of the defendants and, consequently, that to allow the trial to continue would constitute an abuse of process.

In reaching this conclusion, the court in *Birmingham* was influenced not only by the actions taken by the police (in concealing the existence of the tapes from both the defence and the CPS) but also by the fact that the officer in the

---

[17]*R v Derby County Council, ex p. Brooks* (1985) 80 Cr App R 164. See also *R v Latif (Khalid)* [1996] 1 WLR 104.

[18]See *R v Howell and Howell* [2001] EWCA Crim 3009 and *R v Parker* [2003] EWCA Crim 390.

[19]*Attorney-General's Guidelines for the Disclosure of 'Unused Material' to the Defence* (1982) 74 Cr App R 302. For a discussion of some of the issues raised see *DPP v S* (2003) 67 JCL 87.

[20][1992] Crim LR 117 (albeit before the implementation of the Criminal Procedure and Investigations Act 1996).

case justified his actions on the basis that he had viewed the tapes and was 'satisfied that they were of no evidential value to our case'. This clearly ignored the potential value of the tapes to the defence, but served to illustrate the tendency of investigating officers to seek to minimise the significance of material which does not support the prosecution case. This can be contrasted with the later case of *R v Swingler*[21] where the police had acted on the erroneous assurance that a video surveillance system was not operational at the relevant time and had, consequently, not seized the tape before it became lost. In dismissing an application for a stay on grounds of abuse of process in this case, Rougier J noted:

> before there can be any successful allegation of an abuse of process based prosecution authorities before an application can possibly succeed. That was the situation in the case of *Birmingham* ..., if it were otherwise every time a significant piece of evidence by accident were not available, a defendant facing a serious charge, which might be supported by other cogent evidence, would effectively be able to avoid it on this somewhat technical ground.[22]

Such cases established the enduring principle that *mala fides* or egregious fault on the part of the investigator was the essential prerequisite for a successful stay and, whereas, this may be relatively simple to ascertain in cases of total non-disclosure, such as *Birmingham* and *Swingler*, the position is considerably less clear in those cases involving the selective compilation of tapes. Here the question of what material has been omitted by the police may be central to the defence and the consequences of this process may be illustrated by the decision in *R v Stallard*,[23] where the Court of Appeal considered the impact of such a compilation tape made from an in-store multiplex system operating at the time of the theft of a customer's purse. Following the incident the police viewed the entire tape and arranged for the portions they judged to be relevant to be assembled for evidential purposes although it was clear from the outset that this final compilation showed only a limited portion of the events surrounding the theft.[24] The routine destruction of the original tapes before the case came to trial meant that there was no opportunity for the defence to examine the segments discarded by the police but, rather than immediately applying for a stay, the defence waited until the victim had stated in her evidence that she could not confirm that no one but the accused had been in the vicinity of the theft, thereby raising the question of whether the missing tapes might show another person to have been responsible.

---

[21]Unreported, 10 July 1998.
[22]Unreported, 10 July 1998 at 6F.
[23]Unreported, 13 April 2000, Transcript No. 199904391/X3, 199905674/X3.
[24]See also *R v Stephen* [2001] EWCA Crim 2561.

This left the question of whether to continue the trial in the absence of the missing portions of the tape was sufficient to constitute an abuse of process and here the prosecution sought to justify the police actions by reference to para. 4.2 of the Codes of Practice under CPIA which states:

> where it is not practicable to retain the initial record of information because it forms part of a larger record which is to be destroyed, its contents should be transferred to a durable and more easily stored form before that happens.

The court declined to explore this interpretation of the Codes of Practice, although it is debatable whether this provision was ever really aimed at the selective copying of video evidence, which does not entail transfer to a more 'durable' medium but simply replicates portions of one videotape on to another. In dismissing the appeal the central issue for the court appeared not to be whether the police had faithfully transferred all of the relevant material contained in the original tape to the compilation provided to the defence, but rather the question of good faith as highlighted in *Swingler*. Notwithstanding some criticism of the police actions in relation to the tape, the court saw no evidence of bad faith, a conclusion based largely on the evidence of the officer in the case that the missing portions of the store tape did not show anyone else in the vicinity of the theft. Clarke LJ saw no reason to doubt this, stating that it 'would have been quite clear [to the officer]' if another potential suspect had been identified on the tape.[25] Similarly, in *R v Medway*,[26] although CCTV tape from the scene had been seized and examined by the police, it was not retained as the investigator concluded it contained nothing of interest and, as a consequence, the tape was later destroyed. The Court of Appeal concluded that this was insufficient to render trial unfair. Again the issue of whether the police had acted in good faith in discarding the tape was seen as central to any possible stay on grounds of abuse of process. Although the purpose of such an order, if granted, was to prevent an unfair trial, not to punish the investigator, it was held that the presence or absence of malice on the part of the police was of direct relevance.

This generous acceptance of the investigator's assessment of the evidence is in keeping with the earlier decision in *R v Beckford*[27] and appears to reflect the settled view of the court in all but the most extreme cases where evidence is lost or destroyed before trial, yet this approach must be contrasted with the view of the court in the earlier case of *DPP v Chipping*, where it was concluded that:

---

[25]A similar approach was taken in the pre-CPIA case *R v Reid (Hainsley)*, unreported, 10 March 1997, Transcript No. 9605572/Y3.

[26][2000] Crim LR 415.

[27][1996] 1 Cr App R 94, concerning the destruction of the defendant's car by the police before it could be examined by a defence expert.

it was not good enough in this case, any more than it was good enough in the *Birmingham* case, for the Crown to rely upon the simple assertion of a police officer that the video did not reveal anything of relevance or assistance.[28]

This raises the question of whether a police officer's assertion that only the unimportant sections of a tape have been discarded, as in *Stallard*,[29] in any way differs from an assurance that a tape *in its entirety* contains nothing of relevance, as in *Birmingham*, and the result is a degree of uncertainty over the extent to which any tape can safely be edited without the risk of a later challenge from the defence. Clearly one solution would be to copy for the defence *all* videotape in the possession of the prosecution as a matter of procedure, however the logistical implications of such a policy would be daunting, particularly as this would, inevitably, require the defence to be provided with tapes in a format which they could view. In the case of a tape from a 'multiplex' system this could entail the production of a separate tape for each of the four or more cameras recorded on each tape. Multiply this by the number of defendants, if they are represented separately, and the scale of the problem soon becomes apparent.[30]

In many cases the only solution has been a system of informal disclosure between the police and solicitors, whereby the defence are not provided with copies of the unused tapes (on the basis that nothing else of relevance is present) but, instead, are invited to visit the police station to examine the unedited tapes if they so wish. For the police this undoubtedly saves the time and expense of arranging for additional copies to be made, however what is less clear is whether it addresses the spirit of CPIA in relation to disclosure. The aim of the Act was to confine prosecution disclosure to circumstances where the prosecution had, either of its own volition or as a result of representations from the defence, identified material as capable of undermining the prosecution case or assisting the defence. However, the widespread use of such informal disclosure replaces this with a system based on expediency and an acceptance that a strict application of the disclosure provisions is simply not worth the effort. The potential danger in such an approach is either that potentially valuable evidence will be missed as it is clear that where such informal disclosure operates, the offer to inspect video material is seldom taken up by the defence, thereby leaving the prosecution compilation as the definitive version of events.

Inevitably, it falls to the courts to assess the degree to which the defendant's due process rights have been infringed by defective prosecution treatment of

---

[28]Unreported, 11 January 1999.

[29]See also *Omar* v *Chief Constable of Bedfordshire* [2002] EWHC 3060.

[30]Such difficulties were illustrated in *R* v *Calderdale Magistrates' Court, ex p. Donahue and Cutler*, unreported, 18 October 2000, Transcript No. CO/1508/2000.

video evidence and it has been suggested that, in considering alleged abuse of process, the courts should move away from their hitherto, somewhat technical, approach and instead consider cases by reference to more general equitable principles.[31] However, in the recent decisions of *R v Feltham Magistrates Court, ex p. Ebrahim; Mouat v DPP*[32] the Divisional Court reiterated that the basis for any claim lay in the prosecution duty to retain the video evidence in question and concluded:

> If in all the circumstances there was no duty to obtain and/or retain that videotape evidence before the defence first sought its retention then there could be no question of the subsequent trial being unfair on that ground.

Similarly, where the prosecution had breached their duty to retain the video evidence then the test remains one of bad faith or serious fault. The problem with this approach is that it risks penalising the defence for the operational and logistical difficulties of dealing with the large quantities of videotape as outlined above due to the amorphous nature of the prosecution duty under CPIA.

Videotapes and the right to a private and family life

Although it is clearly possible to challenge the misuse of CCTV as part of the broader issue of non-disclosure under Article 6,[33] this is not the only Convention right potentially engaged by the use of videotape evidence. Article 8 provides for, *inter alia*, the right to a private life in that 'Everyone has the right to respect for his private and family life, his home and his correspondence'. This is not an absolute right but cannot be subject to 'interference by a public authority' unless that interference is not only 'in accordance with the law' but also falls into one of the listed categories, the relevant one for the purposes of this discussion being for the 'prevention of disorder or crime'.

Covert surveillance has in the past been found to violate Article 8 in the absence of legal authority.[34] However, while the use of CCTV developed in the virtual absence of any legal regulation,[35] its installation and replacement is permitted under the Town and Country Planning (General Permitted Development) Order 1995 (SI 1995 No. 418) and its use encouraged by s. 163 of the Criminal Justice and Public Order Act 1994. A statutory basis for legal control of surveillance over public areas was established in March 2000 when the Data

---

[31]J. A. Epp, 'Destroyed or Lost Evidence and Abuse of Process' (1999) 3 E & P 165.
[32][2001] EWHC Admin 130, [2001] 1 WLR 1293 at [H2].
[33]Following the principle in *Jespers v Belgium* (1981) 27 DR 61, that the accused should have 'at his disposal ... all relevant elements that have been or could be collected'.
[34]See, e.g. *Khan* v *United Kingdom* (2001) 31 EHRR 45 applied in *R v Sargent* [2002] 1 All ER 161 and *PG* v *United Kingdom* [2002] Crim LR 308, (2002) 66 JCL 246.
[35]Taylor, above n. 2.

Protection Act 1998 came into force. The applicability of the data protection principles in relation to videotaped material will be discussed in more detail later.

Any interference with an individual's private life would also have to be seen as being necessary for the prevention of crime. Difficulties arise at the outset as to the definition of the privacy sought to be protected and these are well rehearsed.[36] While the concept of privacy could be argued to exist under domestic law, at least in the context of breach of confidence,[37] the problems with its applicability to CCTV footage relate to the fact that videotaped footage is bound to have been recorded in public, whereas Article 8 privacy rights are only invoked in this situation when private acts are performed in public.[38]

While it has been argued[39] that Article 8, as given greater effect by the Human Rights Act 1998, could extend current thinking and shape it more to suit a modern society, it is submitted that, even if this were to be the case, Article 8 would be of little use for anyone wishing to challenge the admissibility of or non-disclosure of video evidence although perhaps the effect of Article 8 could be argued to be to instill more ethical treatment of CCTV evidence by CCTV operators rather than a direct impact upon the trial. The actual taking of video footage will always be justifiable under the derogations contained within Article 8(2) relating to the prevention of crime so long as the action taken is not disproportionate to the harm sought to be prevented. The failure to disclose the footage is, within the human rights context, more obviously an Article 6 issue as discussed above. Even if an Article 8 action were to be taken and a violation to be found, it is unlikely to affect the outcome of a criminal trial or appeal.[40]

Video evidence—the data protection principles

The Data Protection Act 1998 came into force on 1 March 2000 as a result of the UK's obligations under Community law in enacting Directive 95/46/EC (the Data Protection Directive). Accompanying the Act is a CCTV Code of Practice,[41] issued by the Data Protection Officer under 51(3)(b) of the 1998 Act and

---

[36]See, e.g. Taylor, above n. 2; D. Feldman, *Civil Liberties and Human Rights in England and Wales*, 2nd edn (Oxford University Press: Oxford, 2001) 511.

[37]*Douglas and Others* v *Hello!* [2003] EWHC 786; cf. *Kaye* v *Robertson and Another*, *The Times* (21 March 1990). See also *Peck* v *United Kingdom* (App. No. 00044647/98).

[38]See *Peck* v *United Kingdom* (App. No. 00044647/98); *Herbecq* v *Belgium* (App. No. 32200/96) and *von Hanover* v *Germany* (App. No. 59320/00, 24 June 2004).

[39]Taylor, above n. 2.

[40]See, e.g. D. Ormerod, 'ECHR and the Exclusion of Evidence: Trial Remedies for Article 8 Breaches' [2003] Crim LR 61 at 67 where it is suggested that the lack of coherent guidance for trial judges in such issues leads to the courts routinely admitting covert surveillance evidence 'despite acknowledged breaches of Article 8'. See also, B. Fitzpatrick and N. Taylor, 'Human Rights and the Discretionary Exclusion of Evidence' (2001) 65 JCL 349.

[41]Available from www.dataprotection.gov.uk, accessed 23 March 2005.

is intended to provide 'guidance as to good practice' for users of surveillance equipment such as CCTV. Contained within the 1998 Act are the data protection principles[42] which state that data must be fairly and lawfully processed for limited purposes.[43] Data must be accurate, adequate, relevant and proportionate to the aim for which the information is obtained.[44] The data must not be kept for longer than necessary,[45] processed in accordance with individuals' rights,[46] kept securely[47] and should not be transferred to countries where adequate protection measures do not exist.[48]

While, if adhered to, these principles could be said to provide for a basic minimum standard of care to be taken with data and thus help in dealing with at least some of the pitfalls of video evidence, it would appear that they have little to offer an individual who wishes to contest the retention or lack of disclosure of videotaped material to him. Presumably, CCTV footage used by the police, for example, would be processed fairly and lawfully for a specific lawful purpose, i.e. the detection and prevention of crime. Indeed, most security cameras set up by companies would be covered although the status of private security cameras handed over for the purposes of criminal investigation could be a little more problematic. There is little else covered by the principles to help an individual aggrieved by the fact that some of his activities may have been captured on videotape. Accuracy is obviously of paramount importance so any inaccurate time or date details could be challenged as could the inaccuracy of any automatic facial recognition systems used. Various issues could be contested provided that, first, the defendant is aware that the footage exists in the first place (see above regarding the difficulties in ensuring full disclosure is given) and, secondly, that the defendant is aware of his data protection rights.

There is more awareness of the principles enshrined in the 1998 Act than those of its predecessor, the Data Protection Act 1984.[49] Those who work in professions involving data collection and retention will, with adequate training, hopefully be aware of the issues pertaining to their particular areas as will those who have to deal with s. 7 subject access rights on a regular basis. If CCTV operators are unaware of their DPA obligations, it is of little surprise that the DPA is not as influential as it could be. A recent Home Office study found that levels of knowledge and instruction varied and were more often a result of 'shared

---

[42]The data protection principles are contained within Sched. 1, Part 1 to the 1998 Act.
[43]Data protection principles, para. 2.
[44]Ibid, paras 3 and 4.
[45]Ibid. para. 5.
[46]Ibid. para. 6.
[47]Ibid. para. 7.
[48]Ibid. para. 8.
[49]In any event, the 1984 Act was more limited in its scope in that it only applied to data stored on computers.

wisdom' amongst operators rather than formal training.[50] Indeed, of the 13 control rooms dealt with as part of the study, only one provided its operators with specific data protection guidance in the form of a booklet. The study concludes that guidance should be given as part of the Codes of Practice, accompanied by advice on interpretation as it was felt that interpretation of the principles varies from operator to operator. Clearly, CCTV operators need to be aware of not only 'best practice' when dealing with the capturing and retention of images but need also to be aware of the ethical considerations which undoubtedly should be taken into account. The influence of the data protection regime is a regulatory one and therefore its potential influence on culture and existing practice should not be underestimated. Only through proper training could the regime eventually contribute to the reduction of the hazards associated with video evidence. Those responsible for the operation of CCTV equipment can, in an ideal world at least, be expected to have at least some knowledge of the data protection principles governing the operation of the equipment. But as far as those on the receiving end of the CCTV operation are concerned, what awareness does the type of individual have who happens to get captured performing some kind of dubious activity by a CCTV camera? And even if he is aware of the data protection principles, is there even any use that he could make of them? Following breaches of the data protection principles and the Codes of Practice, the Data Protection Commissioner can issue an Enforcement Notice under s. 40. However, breaches of the principles in themselves surely will not make the obtaining, processing and sharing of the evidence unlawful and therefore inadmissible in a court of law.

Conclusion

As has been shown, the treatment of CCTV evidence (most notably by the police) will continue to cause concern, given the ease with which it can be lost and distorted by means of selective compilation. A more positive application of the courts' powers regarding abuse of process may, ultimately, lead to a more equitable stance towards cases of missing video evidence but, unless or until this occurs, the courts will continue to risk confusion and unfairness in the treatment of this particularly compelling form of evidence. The difficulty is that the third party who initially produces the video in question is largely beyond the scope of the law of disclosure for, as with other forms of evidential material, it falls to the Office of the Information Commissioner to retain any CCTV material which might, ultimately, prove relevant to the investigation. For this reason it is suggested that a

---

[50]M. Gill, A. Spriggs, J. Allen, M. Hemming, P. Jessiman, D. Kara, J. Kilworth, R. Little, D. Swain, 'Control Room Operation: Findings from Control Room Observations', Home Office Online Report 14/05 (24 February 2005) 25, available at www.crimereduction.gov.uk/cctv42.htm, accessed 23 March 2005. This report presents the findings of a large-scale study of the operation of 13 control rooms in order to assess the practical impact of various factors on the overall effectiveness of CCTV systems.

more rigorous application of the doctrine of abuse of process represents the most practical and expedient mechanism by which investigators can be compelled to adopt a more rigorous approach to the treatment of CCTV material in order to prevent the loss/ destruction of potentially valuable material.

Similarly, although an individual may, in theory, be able to contest the collection and retention of material against him under the human rights or data protection principles, it would seem that avenues of redress are, in practice, limited and, notwithstanding that the collection of video material relating to an individual might, *prima facie*, appear to be a breach of Article 8 privacy rights, this will almost always be justified under the Article 8(2) derogations in order to prevent or detect crime. The use of data protection principles raises similar issues because, although redress may be available (if the individual concerned is even aware of the principles) this will be of little practical use. It is evident that CCTV will continue to play a vital role in a growing number of cases, however the danger is that the desire to utilise this compelling form of evidence will, ultimately, have deleterious consequences for the due process rights of the accused.

GARY T. MARX

Gary T. Marx, professor emeritus at the Massachusetts Institute of Technology, received his PhD in Sociology from the University of California–Berkeley and has taught at some of the most prestigious universities in the United States and the world. Marx's first book, *Protest and Prejudice: a Study of Belief in the Black Community* (1967), was one of the earliest sociological studies to challenge many widely held stereotypes about African Americans and their communities.

"What's New about the 'New Surveillance'," appeared in the journal, *Knowledge, Technology, and Policy*, in 2004. Here, Marx updates and develops work on the effects of surveillance from his earlier books such as *Undercover: Police Surveillance in America* (1985) and *Undercover: Police Surveillance in Comparative Perspective* (1995). Showing how "scholarly papers can begin at home," Marx describes his interest in surveillance growing "out of contradictions in personal experience," as a child during the 1950s and as a student during the 1960s:

> I had an early respect for authority as a result of seeing cowboy hero movies at the Hitching Post theater on Hollywood Boulevard (where you had to check your cap guns at the door) and being in a Boy Scout troop sponsored by the Los Angeles Police Department. At that time the police, as archetypical boy scouts wearing the white hats, were role models.
>
> Some years later as a student at Berkeley, I encountered police in a different role. I was active in CORE (the Congress of Racial Equality), an organization dedicated at that time to integration

through nonviolence. After a major fund raising effort, an event occurred that severely damaged the group—our treasurer disappeared with the money. It turned out she was a police agent, as were several other disruptive members.

These contradictory experiences lead Marx to conclude that surveillance isn't always or necessarily negative. He writes:

> I have always been drawn to dualities and seeming paradoxes. For example, societies need both liberty and order; group life is impossible without normative boundaries, yet rule-breaking can be creative and a factor in positive social change; our sense of self is defined by our ability to control personal information, yet fundamental to a democratic society is openness and the idea that accountability is produced through visibility. These concerns have helped frame a broad, decades-long research agenda involving surveillance in which I can assimilate a great many theoretical questions, social issues, and empirical inquiries.
>
> With respect to my article classifying characteristics of surveillance means, I was also responding to the tendency of so many people to "shoot from the lip." That is, to make sweeping empirical and ethical generalizations about social issues that suggest that the changes we see are "revolutionary" and "qualitative" in their nature or in contrast that "there is nothing new here." Or consider claims about dystopia and utopia. The former suggest that the sky is falling and that we are already far beyond the horrors Orwell envisioned in 1984. The latter welcomes control through technology as not only necessary in terrible times, but as far superior to control by humans.

For Marx then, scholarly approaches to current issues can help us go beyond simplistic and uncritical ways of thinking. After all, he explains:

> Rhetorical excesses are expected, and perhaps to be tolerated, from politicians and activists, single mindedly pursuing a goal. However, the scholar must go beyond this in seeking greater precision and qualification, for example by not treating a topic such as surveillance as if it was a single, simple entity. Rather, general concepts must be broken into components and these need to be empirically assessed before scientific, evaluative or policy conclusions are reached. Having separated what most people see to be connected, the scholar can then suggest new forms of connection. Society would not necessarily be better off with more analysis and less action, but it would certainly be better off with more analysis before action is taken.

For Discussion

As you read "What's New about the 'New Surveillance'," consider how Marx pursues his goals of "precision and qualification," as he identifies new aspects of, and develops new definitions for, key concepts which we might otherwise think of as obvious.

How does a new definition change the ways Marx examines surveillance?

Also, consider why, for Marx, it is important to distinguish between "new" and "traditional" surveillance.

How do new technologies ease surveillance and speed the collection and possible connections between bits of information? Why are features of speed and ease so important to understanding the new surveillance?

Think, too, about Marx's conclusion, "Surveillance Slack." He claims that "even with an empirical pattern that lends itself to conclusions, the issues of moral evaluation are far from simple," when it comes to knowing "whether the control of personal information has increased or decreased."

Has Marx offered readers enough analysis to imagine possible actions, or policies regarding the new surveillance? If so, what kinds of actions should be taken? If not, what kinds of additional analysis would help guide actions and policies?

What's New About the "New Surveillance"?: Classifying for Change and Continuity
by Gary T. Marx

We are at any moment those who separate the connected or connect the separate.

—*Georg Simmel*

In an interview with the individual responsible for an all-purpose student ID access card used for building entrance, the library, meals and purchases at a large Southern university, I encountered the following case:

> The registrar came into his office and discovered an arson effort that failed. A long burn mark on the carpet led to a Gatorade bottle full of flammable liquid in a closet. In an adjacent building police found the area where the bomb was assembled. They requested card access records for that building. A review of the logs found some early

408   Part Three | A Research Dossier

morning card swipes which looked suspicious. They also checked the lot number on the Gatorade bottle that was holding the liquid and determined it had been delivered to a campus convenience store. Upon matching the records of purchasers of Gatorade with those entering the building where the bomb making materials were found, the police got a hit. They confronted the suspect and he confessed to arson. His motive was to burn up his academic records, as he was failing several classes and didn't want to disappoint his parents.

This high tech discovery of human spoors needs only to be bolstered by a video camera, DNA matching and thermal lie detection to serve as a paradigmatic case of the "new surveillance" (Marx, 1988). New technologies for collecting personal information that transcend the physical, liberty enhancing limitations of the old means are constantly appearing. These probe more deeply, widely, and softly than traditional methods, transcending natural (distance, darkness, skin, time, and microscopic size) and constructed (walls, sealed envelopes) barriers that historically protected personal information.

The social causes and consequences of this are profound and only beginning to be understood. These involve broad changes in economic and social organization, culture and conceptions of freedom and constraint. The last half of the twentieth century has seen a significant increase in the use of technology for the discovery of personal information. Examples include video and audio surveillance, heat, light, motion, sound and olfactory sensors, night vision goggles, electronic tagging, biometric access devices, drug testing, DNA analysis, computer monitoring including email and web usage and the use of computer techniques such as expert systems, matching and profiling, data mining, mapping, network analysis, and simulation. Control technologies have become available that previously existed only in the dystopic imaginations of science fiction writers. We are a surveillance society. As Yiannis Gabriel (2004) suggests Weber's iron cage is being displaced by a flexible glass cage.

Three common responses to changes in contemporary surveillance technology can be noted. One general historical and functional view holds that there is nothing really new here. All societies have certain functional prerequisites, which must be met if they are to exist. These include means for protecting and discovering personal information and protecting social borders. Any changes are merely of degree, not of kind.

An opposing, less general view is that we live in a time of revolutionary change with respect to the crossing of personal and social borders. There are two variants of this. One is that the sky is indeed falling and, "you never had it so bad." Some journalists and popular writers claim "privacy is dead."

A related view holds that while the technologies are revolutionary, the way they are used reflects social and cultural factors. In that regard the forces of modernity operate to extend individual control. The trend on balance, whether through countertechnologies or changing customs, policy, or law, is for protection of personal information to become stronger as new threats appear, although given the piecemeal approach to privacy legislation in the United States (in contrast to that in much of Europe in which protections are based on a broad principle such as "respect for human dignity"), there is usually a lag.

Yet simple sweeping assertions about such a complex, dynamic, and varied topic are not very helpful. Broad concepts may in Neil Smelser's (1959: 2) words "shroud a galaxy of connotations." However useful as an intellectual shorthand, ideal types such as "developed vs. undeveloped nations" or "traditional vs. the new surveillance" must be considered in light of the multiple dimensions which usually run through them.

The academic literature on particular surveillance technologies is gradually expanding.[1]

In contrast this article offers a minimalist rendering of the most basic dimensions which cut across and can be used to characterize any surveillance activity.[2]

It is at the middle range, situated (and offering a bridge) between more abstract theoretical explanations and empirical description.

As a prelude to specifying dimensions let us note some shortcomings of popular definition.

A Deficient Definition

One indicator of rapid change is the failure of dictionary definitions to capture current understandings of surveillance. For example in the *Concise Oxford Dictionary* surveillance is defined as *"close observation, especially of a suspected person."* Yet today many of the new surveillance technologies are not *"especially"* applied to *"a suspected person."* They are commonly applied *categorically*. In broadening the range of suspects the term "a suspected person" takes on a different meaning. In a striking innovation, surveillance is also applied to contexts (geographical places and spaces, particular time periods, networks, systems, and categories of person), not just to a particular person whose identity is known beforehand.

The dictionary definition also implies a clear distinction between the object of surveillance and the person carrying it out. In an age of servants listening behind closed doors, binoculars, and telegraphic interceptions, that separation made sense. It was easy to separate the watcher from the person watched. Yet self-monitoring has emerged as an important theme, independent of the surveilling of another. In the hope of creating self-restraint, threats of social control (i.e., the possibility of getting caught) are well-publicized with mass media techniques. A general ethos of self-surveillance is also encouraged by the availability of home products such as those that test for alcohol level, pregnancy, menopause and AIDS. Self-surveillance merges the line between the surveilled and the surveillant. In some cases we see parallel or co-monitoring, involving the subject and an external agent.[3] The differentiation of surveillance into ever more specialized roles is sometimes matched by a rarely studied de-differentiation or generalization of surveillance to non-specialized roles. For example regardless of their job, retail store employees are trained to identify shoplifters and outdoor utility workers are trained to looked for signs of drug manufacturing.

The term *"close observation"* also fails to capture contemporary practices. Surveillance may be carried out from afar, as with satellite images or the remote monitoring of communications and work. Nor need it be *close* as in detailed— much initial surveillance involves superficial scans looking for patterns of interest to be pursued later in greater detail.

The dated nature of the definition is further illustrated in its seeming restriction to visual means as implied in *"observation."* The eyes do contain the vast majority of the body's sense receptors and the visual is a master metaphor for the other senses (e.g., saying "I see" for understanding or being able to "see through people").[4] Indeed "seeing through" is a convenient short hand for the new surveillance.

To be sure the visual is usually an element of surveillance, even when it is not the primary means of data collection (e.g., written accounts of observations, events and conversations, or the conversion to text or images of measurements from heat, sound or movement). Yet to "observe" a text or a printout is in many ways different from a detective or supervisor directly observing behavior. The eye as the major means of direct surveillance is increasingly joined or replaced by hearing, touching, and smelling.[5] The use of multiple senses and sources of data is an important characteristic of much of the new surveillance.

A better definition of the new surveillance is *the use of technical means to extract or create personal data.* This may be taken from individuals or contexts. In this definition the use of "technical means" to extract and create the information implies the ability to go beyond what is offered to the unaided senses or voluntarily reported. Many of the examples extend the senses by using material artifacts or software of some kind, but the technical means for rooting out can also be deception, as with informers and undercover police. The use of "contexts" along with "individuals" recognizes that much modern surveillance also looks at settings and patterns of relationships. Meaning may reside in cross-classifying discrete sources of data (as with computer matching and profiling) that in and of themselves are not of revealing. Systems as well as persons are of interest.

This definition of the new surveillance excludes the routine, non-technological surveillance that is a part of everyday life such as looking before crossing the street or seeking the source of a sudden noise or of smoke, as well as the routine attentiveness to others that is fundamental to being a social being and to interaction central to the symbolic interaction tradition. An observer on a nude beach or police interrogating a cooperative suspect would also be excluded, because in these cases the information is volunteered and the unaided senses are sufficient.[6]

I do not include a verb such as "observe" in the definition because the nature of the means (or the senses involved) suggests subtypes and issues for analysis and ought not to be foreclosed by a definition, (e.g., how do visual, auditory, text, and other forms of surveillance compare with respect to factors such as intrusiveness or validity?). If such a verb is needed I prefer "attend to" or "to regard" rather than observe with its tilt toward the visual.

While the above definition captures some common elements among new surveillance means, contemporary tactics are enormously varied and would include: a parent monitoring a baby on closed circuit television during commercials or through a day-care center webcast.

- a database for employers containing the names of persons who have filed workman compensation claims.
- a video monitor in a department store scanning customers and matching their images to those of suspected shoplifters.
- a supervisor monitoring employee's e-mail and phone communication.
- a badge signaling where an employee is at all times.
- a hidden camera in an ATM machine.
- a computer program that monitors the number of keystrokes or looks for key words or patterns.
- a thermal imaging device aimed at the exterior of a house from across the street analyzing hair to determine drug use.
- a self-test for level of alcohol in one's system.
- a scanner that picks up cellular and cordless phone communication.
- mandatory provision of a DNA sample.
- the polygraph or monitoring of brain waves to determine truthfulness.
- Caller ID.
- computer matching, data merging, and mining.

Dimensions of Surveillance

To note that the above are examples of new forms of surveillance tells us rather little, even if such laundry lists drive journalistic engines. Nor is the most commonly used form of classification based on the type of technology (e.g., electronic location monitoring) very helpful. Such general terms can mask differences found within the same family of technologies. This also does not help us see elements that may be shared or absent across technologies—whether traditional or new. Descriptive terms are often emotionally laden (e.g., persons have strong feelings of support or aversion to terms such as drug testing or video surveillance) and that can distort analysis. The social analyst needs frameworks for locating variation which go beyond popular language, even if some call it jargon.

Let us move from these descriptive terms to some more abstract and analytic concepts. There is need for a conceptual language that brings some parsimony and unity to the vast array of both old and new surveillance activities. The logic of explanation proceeds best when it accounts for systematic variation.

Table 1 suggests a number of dimensions for categorizing aspects of surveillance. Of course Occam's razor must be applied deftly. The proliferation of categories must have an end other than itself. One must avoid the danger of

TABLE 1   Surveillance Dimensions

Dimension	Traditional Surveillance	The New Surveillance
senses:	unaided senses	extends senses
visibility:	visible (the actual collection who does it, where, on whose behalf)	less or invisible
consent:	lower proportion involuntary	higher proportion involuntary
cost:	expensive per unit of data	inexpensive per unit of data
location of data collectors/ analyzers:	on scene	remote
ethos:	harder (more coercive)	softer (less coercive)
integration:	data collection as separate activity	data collection folded into routine activity
data collector:	human, animal	machine (wholly or partly automated)
data resides:	with the collector, stays local	with third parties, often migrates
timing:	single point or intermittent	continuous, (omnipresent)
time period:	present	past, present, future
data availability:	frequent time lags	real time availability
availability of technology:	disproportionately available to elites	more democratized, some forms widely available
object of data collection:	individual	individual, categories of interest
comprehensiveness:	single measure	multiple measures
context:	contextual	acontextual
depth:	less intensive	more intensive
breadth:	less extensive	more extensive
ratio of self to surveillant:	higher (what the surveillant knows the subject probably knows as well)	lower (surveillant knows things that the subject does not)
emphasis on:	individuals	individual, networks, systems
realism:	direct representation	direct and simulation

TABLE 1   *(Continued)*

form:	single media (likely narrative or numerical)	multiple media (including video and/or audio)
who collects data:	specialists	specialists, role dispersal, self-monitoring
data analysis:	more difficult to organize, store, retrieve, analyze	easier to organize, store, retrieve, analyze
data merging:	discrete, non-combinable data (whether because of different format or location)	easy to combine visual, auditory, text, num. data)
data communication:	more difficult to send, retrieve	easier to send, receive

making distinctions that only a social scientist could love. But what is life without risk?

A good classification scheme should capture the major differences the researcher thinks are important and be broad enough to encompass all examples (an inclusive general dimension can always be further divided into sub-types). Its application to a given case across observers should be clear. Classification schemes are to be judged by whether or not they are useful given the goals of the researcher.[7] We also hold apart the empirical question of whether or not (or under what conditions) the surveillance tactic actually works as claimed.

My goals in classification are to organize the empirical patterns in order to:

1. more systematically contrast surveillance technologies.
2. elaborate on the profound changes in contemporary technologies for collecting and analyzing personal information.
3. specify the variation across time periods, settings and methods that theory needs to account for.
4. offer a more logical grounding for ethical and policy judgments about particular tactics and practices.

The dimensions draw from the characteristics of the technology, the data collection process and the nature of the data. Taken together these variables offer a way of classifying and comparing surveillance. Table 1 highlights differences between the new and traditional surveillance. Table 2 suggests criteria that are relevant to surveillance but which I am hesitant to see as being more characteristic of the new or traditional forms. By reducing the size of the angels or increasing the size of the pin, categories can further proliferate. But these distinctions capture major sources of variation relevant to many social, ethical, and policy considerations.

TABLE 2   Surveillance Dimensions Not Showing a Clear Historical Trend

Dimension		
resistance:	easier to neutralize	more difficult to neutralize
specificity:	laser-like focus on specific person or attribute	sponge-like absorbency, non-differentiated
invasiveness:	less invasive	more invasive
reliability and validity:	lower	higher
honesty:	deceptive	non-deceptive
knowledge that tactic is used:	more likely to be known	less likely to be known
specific knowledge regarding where and when used:	more likely to be known	less likely to be known

For simplicity I have arranged this largely in a series of discrete either/or possibilities (e.g., visible or invisible, gathered by a human or a machine). But there may be continuous gradations between the extreme values (e.g. between visible and invisible). Some dimensions involve mutually exclusive values (e.g., single vs. multiple measures) but many do not (e.g., the hybrid case of a guard dog wearing a tiny video camera).

In some cases classification reflects an inherent property of the technology (e.g., infrared and sound transmission devices go beyond the unaided senses). In other cases where a means is classified depends on how it is used. A technology may seem to lend itself well to a value (e.g., a video lens can be used invisibly relative to the traditional bulky 35mm camera), but a policy announcing that a video camera is in use would lead to its being classified as visible.[8]

The differences between traditional and new surveillance can be approached in terms of the categories in Table 1. Traditional surveillance tends to be characterized by the left side of the table. The traditional means have certainly not disappeared. They have however been supplemented by the new forms which tend to fall on the right side of the table.

I don't claim that the values on the right side of the table cleanly and fully characterize every instance of contemporary surveillance that has appeared since the development of the microchip and advances in microbiology, artificial intelligence, electronics, communications, and geographic information systems. Nor do the values on the left side perfectly apply to every instance of the old surveillance prior to this. Social life is much too messy for that. There is some crossing over of values (e.g., informers, a traditional form, have low visibility; drug testing, a new form, is discontinuous). These are after all ideal types whose virtue of breadth often comes with the vice of combining elements that show significant variation at a less abstract level. But if the categories are useful in analyzing big variation (or more useful than the descriptive *ad hoc* naming we presently have), they will have done their job.

The broader project from which this article is drawn is drenched in empirical examples. For limitations of space, here I offer only a summary of the new and traditional surveillance in the abstract terms of Table 1. The dimensions emphasize elements that I think have changed. I thus exclude other very important dimensions useful for comparing types of surveillance apart from the issue of changes. These include the extent of deception and ease or difficulty of neutralizing a technique, factors which appear not to have changed significantly over the last century. I also exclude others such as degree of invasiveness and validity about which the evidence of change is mixed.

The new surveillance relative to traditional surveillance extends the senses and has low visibility or is invisible. It is more likely to be involuntary. Data collection is often integrated into routine activity. It is more likely to involve manipulation than direct coercion. Data collection is more likely to be automated involving machines rather than (or in addition to) involving humans. It is relatively inexpensive per unit of data collected. Data collection is often mediated through remote means rather than on scene and the data often resides with third parties. Data is available in real time and data collection can be continuous and offer information on the past, present, and future (a là statistical predictions). The subject of data collection goes beyond the individual suspect to categories of interest. The individual as a subject of data collection may also become the object of an intervention. There may be only a short interval between the discovery of the information and the taking of action.

The new surveillance is more comprehensive, often involving multiple measures. But since it is often mediated by physical and social distance (being more likely to be acontextual) it is not necessarily more valid. It is more intensive and extensive. The ratio of what the individual knows about him or herself relative to what the surveilling person knows is lower than in the past, even if objectively much more is known. Relative to the past the objects of surveillance are more likely to be an anonymous individual, a mass, or an aggregate. The emphasis is expanded beyond the individual to systems and networks. The data often goes beyond direct representation to simulation and from narrative or numerical form to also include video and audio records. The monitoring of specialists is often accompanied (or even replaced) by self-monitoring. It is easy to combine visual, auditory, text, and numerical data and to send and receive it. It is relatively easier to organize, store, retrieve, and analyze data. Traditional surveillance is the reverse of the above.

Table 2 lists factors which appear not to have changed significantly over the last century, such as the extent of deception and the ease or difficulty of neutralizing a technique. It also lists factors where the case for a change might be made, but so might its opposite. For example the new surveillance is both more and less invasive. Absent the specification of indicators and measurement it is difficult to say. While the greater invasiveness of many tactics is obvious, as we note in the social process chapter, one trend is toward less invasive techniques (e.g., drug testing from a strand of hair, rather than from a urine sample). Also given the potential for sophisticated neutralization it is less clear whether the techniques are more valid, or whether given room for adversaries to maneuver, we have a moving equilibrium. Do we have an ever expanding monolith or even some increased equality, as surveillance becomes more democratized?

The Talmud states, "for instance is not proof." In contrasting traditional and new forms of surveillance in light of these categories I am convinced that significant change has occured. Yet given the breadth of the net cast and limited resources, this has been argued by illustration. A next step is to operationalize concepts and collect quantitative measurements.

Given the nature of perception, lists imply an egalitarianism among terms that is often unwarranted. The dimensions in Table 1 are hardly of equal significance. They can be clustered or ranked in various ways. Among those on the new surveillance side with the clearest social implications are extending the senses, low visibility, involuntary nature, remoteness, and lesser cost. These create a potential for a very different kind of society and call for stringent vigilance. In extending the senses (the ability to see in the dark, into bodies, through walls and over vast distances, etc.) they challenge fundamental assumptions about personal and social borders (these, after all, have been maintained not only by values and norms and social organization but by the limits of technology to cross them). Low visibility and the involuntary and remote nature of much contemporary surveillance may mean more secrecy and lessened accountability, less need for consent and less possibility of reciprocity. Lesser costs create a temptation to both widen the net and thin the mesh of surveillance. For example what if brain scan technology lives up to the claims of its advocates to identify what people feel, know or are thinking? (*The New York Times*, 9 December 2001). In the interest of preventing terrible things from happening (which after all it would be irresponsible not to do, not to mention legal liability), the sacred value traditionally placed on interior life would be eroded.

Commonalties across Societies and Time Periods?

Of course whether one sees difference or similarity, rupture or continuity, qualitative or merely quantitative change is conditioned by the level of abstraction. Viewed very abstractly, qualitative changes are rare given the constants (both common needs and resource restrictions) and the influence of tradition in human societies. Generally the more fine-grained the analysis, the easier it is to see differences, or in this case, changes.

Societies show a significant degree of cultural continuity as the past informs the present and the present must work with the basic and largely unchanging elements of natural, social and biological systems.[9] Regardless of the society, time period, or institutional area, there will be parallels and functional equivalents.

Information boundaries and contests are found in all societies and beyond that in all living systems (Beniger, 1986). Humans are curious and to survive individuals and groups must engage in surveillance and protect their borders. A degree of information protection and technology-enhanced (whether science or magic based) efforts to go beyond sensory impressions likely characterizes all societies. But such a vapid assertion cannot capture the profound emotional experience of change (and often affront and invasion) many individuals feel in the face of the new surveillance, nor does it help in understanding variation across contexts.

Means matter and are not simply reactive. Function or need is not the same thing as structure or means. Granted there are some common needs, yet these can be met in very different ways with different consequences. I don't think we gain a great deal by noting that trial by ordeal, torture, the polygraph, and DNA analysis are all means of gathering information and assessing truth claims. Nor are we helped much by seeing that at some level intercepting a cellular telephone message is equivalent to one group reading another's smoke signals. If one wishes to understand a given form in its context and its relation to the culture and social structure in question, to reach moral conclusions and to seek answers via analyzing variation across settings, such commonalties are thin gruel indeed.

Many needs are hardly cast in bronze. Changes in physical conditions such as climate or social conditions—the rise of urban and later industrial societies, may generate new needs and new means to obtain them. For example a mass society with national borders needs to identify and determine the reputation of strangers and validate claims to identity and competence, as well as eligibility for government services.

New means, beyond meeting old needs and appearing in response to new needs, may play an independent role. In considering questions of invention, whether social or material, new means may generate new needs and in a seldom-recognized process may even determine ends, apart from strains originating elsewhere. The push from possibility may lead to a redefinition of or re-prioritizing of need. This can be aided by the advocacy of entrepreneurs and activists stressing the benefits of applying a favored technology. For example with respect to both health and crime control, the new goal of prevention or risk avoidance has become increasingly important as scientific means have developed, making early identification possible, particularly on a broad aggregate basis. The efficiency and relatively low cost of categorical mass data collection seems to be eroding the value of individualized suspicion, although not without struggle.

Even if surveillance by definition always involves the quest for information, considered concretely, the way it is gathered and the specific goal and content vary enormously within and across societies. Apart from the new mechanisms, the content and predominant forms of surveillance have significantly changed over the last five centuries.

Changes in Content and Form

In the fifteenth century religious surveillance was a powerful and dominant form. This involved the search for heretics, devils, and witches, as well as the more routine policing of religious consciousness, ritual and religiously based rules such as those involving adultery and wedlock and keeping basic records of births, marriages, baptisms, and deaths. While this continued for several more centuries, its significance has gradually declined.

In the sixteenth and seventeenth centuries, with the appearance and growth of the embryonic nation-state which had both new needs and a heightened capacity to gather and use information, political surveillance became increasingly important relative to religious surveillance. The slow spread of a scientific world-view and protections for religious dissent weakened the latter.[10]

Over the next several centuries there was a gradual move to a broadly "policed" society in which agents of the state, industry and commerce came to exercise control over ever-wider social and geographical areas (Silver, 1969; Shils, 1975; Foucault, 1977; Fogelson, 1977; Nisbet, 1977; Fijnaut and Marx, 1995; Ericson and Haggerty, 1997; Deflem, 2000).[11]

We see the gradual and continuing expansion, systematization, and scientification of police (and more generally state and market) observation and detection. For the state beyond enhanced informing and infiltration, this involved the creation of specialized units and an expanded census, improved record keeping, police registers and dossiers, identity documents (including those based on biometrics), and inspections. These forms blurred the line between direct political surveillance and in some ways a more modern and benign, or at least neutral, governance or administration. Personal information came to be collected not only for taxation, conscription, law enforcement and border control (both immigration and emigration), but also to determine citizenship, eligibility for democratic participation, and in social planning.

In the nineteenth and twentieth centuries, with the growth of bureaucracy and the regulated and welfare states, the content of surveillance expanded yet again to detailed personal information in order to determine conformity with an ever-increasing number of laws and regulations and eligibility for various welfare and intervention programs—from social security to the protection of children and animals. A state bureaucratically organized around the certification of identity, experience, and competence is dependent on the collection of personal information. Risk assessment, prediction, prevention, and rational planning also require such information. Government uses in turn have been supplemented (and on any quantitative scale likely overtaken) by contemporary work, market place, and medical surveillance. The contemporary commercial state is inconceivable without the massive collection of personal data.

The historical summary above documents changes noted by those of the most diverse ideological perspectives from Foucault to Nisbet. What is likely to be disputed is what it means and if it is desirable or undesirable. I will briefly explore one strand of this in looking at changes in telecommunications.

Empowerment, Disempowerment, or "Both"?

It is not easy to reach a conclusion about what the changes in surveillance technology imply for western democratic conceptions of individualism, as expressed in the issue of control over personal information. This recalls a story about a young couple who are very excited bout taking the train for the first time. They arrive at the station and ask the conductor, "will the train be on time?" He takes out a schedule, studies it for a long time and says, "that depends." They then ask, "what does it depend on?" He then looks at another schedule, looks up and down the track, pauses in deep thought and finally replies, "well, that depends too." Below I offer a brief history with respect to efforts to intercept and protect telecommunications. Any conclusion as to whether things are getting better or worse with respect to the protection of personal information depends. The scholars' task is to indicate what it depends on.

Looked at broadly across time periods has the ability to protect forms of electronic communication been increasing or decreasing? It is difficult to say. Almost as soon as the telegraph appeared so did wiretapping and the same holds for efforts to intercept every new form of communication. The absolute amount of intercepted telecommunications has increased as the telephone has become nearly universal and as population and the various forms for communication have increased.

However, we do not have adequate information to reach strong conclusions about whether the interception of telecommunications has increased in a relative, as well as an absolute sense, declined or remained roughly constant. An assessment of this would require determining the number of involuntary interceptions as a percentage of all telecommunications. It would be ideal to have this broken down by type–interceptions by domestic law enforcement, by NSA and other domestic and foreign intelligence agencies, by telephone company employees, by employers and by private citizens and by factors such as number of, and length of interceptions and number of persons intercepted. Beyond the use of technical means, it would as well be ideal to have interception data for other forms such as the extent of uninvited listening in on a party-line (when they were in existence) or on an extension or speaker phone.

With recent developments estimates should also include overhearing cordless and cellular conversations and intercepting fax, e-mail, and webcam communications. Those making loud use of their cell phones in public also have their conversations partially intercepted (although this is not quite the same since it is more voluntary). The appearance and gradual disappearance of phone booths would also be of interest.

We would also want measures for other aspects of interception beyond direct listening and recording such as for call and trap devices that can be used by law enforcement without a warrant to identify when and what number was dialed. The extent of the use of newer techniques that permit identifying networks of communication beyond the traditional one line to another is also of interest. When a communication has been intercepted whether the content stays secret (as is often the case with intelligence agencies) or becomes public (as is often the case with journalistic snooping on film stars and politicians) would ideally also be considered.

Interception issues apart, these means also have implications for *protecting* some aspects of personal information. Telecommunications has traditionally offered freedom from visual observation. In permitting interactions on a vastly expanded scale without the need to travel and physical co-presence, they greatly enhanced the ability to communicate, while increasing control over information such as appearance, body language, facial expressions, exact location, who one is with and even who the communicator was.[12] Contrast this with a conversation visible to a third party overheard in a public place such as a restaurant.

Over time, elements of the telephone's intrusive potential were curtailed even as other intrusive potentials appeared. Claims must be time, as well as component, specific. For example the eavesdropping potential present when all calls had to be made through an operator (the classic telephone operator of Lily Tomlin) disappeared as automatic switching spread, starting in the 1930s. Greater affluence and technical changes have led to the almost complete disappearance of the party line in which several households shared a phone line and conversations could easily be overheard by just picking up the phone. Initially the service monitoring of phone lines required an operator to listen to conversations, that need can now generally be served by merely checking electronic signals.

While it took almost a century, non-court approved wiretapping eventually was prohibited with the Katz decision (*Katz v. United States*, 389 U.S. 347 (1967)) which found that there is a right to privacy even in a "public" phone booth. The Court held that the Fourth Amendment applied to persons not to places and to electronic, as well as physical searches. Title III of the 1968 Omnibus Crime Control and Safe Streets Act made unauthorized wiretapping a felony. To judge from impressionistic accounts, the amount of wiretapping without a warrant appeared to have declined after that.

Cordless and cell phone communication, appearing in the 1980s, which rely on radio transmissions were technically easy to legally intercept with scanners and even some UHF television channels. But 1986 legislation made their interception without a warrant illegal. Greater technical protection also came to be built into the phones.

Starting in the 1980s, as analog voice communications carried over copper wires began to be replaced by digital based technologies and services carried on fiber optic wires, interception in principle became easier. Messages whether by phone, fax, or e-mail routinely arrived with identifying details that were much more difficult to locate with the analog system. Phone numbers could be automatically linked to reverse directories for additional information. In addition, communication content could be tapped directly through remote computer entries, rather than having to go through the risky procedure of directly tapping into the line at the location of interest. However, without appropriate design of the system, locating the actual transmission carrying a message was apparently more difficult. The controversial Digital Telephony Act of 1994 is intended to change that by requiring communications manufacturers to engineer systems that make remote wire tapping via computer easy.

However, no matter how much more communication there is to intercept, or how much easier it becomes to do, this can be thwarted, or at least inhibited by use of encryption. While it took almost a century, public encryption of telecommunications is now widely available, offering an unprecedented level of communications privacy. On the other hand there are technical efforts via remotely (or directly) planted sniffers to get to a message before it can be encrypted.

The silent recording capability now built into many answering machines makes it easier to secretly record conversations and the marketing to the public of telecommunications surveillance equipment once available only to police may also have increased the interception of communication. However this is matched by the marketing of equipment for protecting communications.

E-mail could be legally intercepted until the passage of the Privacy Protection Act of 1986. The sending of junk fax and automated phone dialing was prohibited not long after.

Until the appearance of Caller ID in 1988, the caller was not required to reveal his or her phone number. Then by technological fiat all callers, even those who were unlisted, had their number delivered. This reversed the previous advantage for callers of anonymity and the ability to intrude at will. Caller ID as initially offered increased the control of the caller, while decreasing control of the person called, since his or her phone number and other information could be involuntarily delivered (and by implication all the other information this can be automatically related to through data bases). Yet several years later a public outcry over Caller ID led to a blocking option, restoring some of the status quo.

Other forms are more difficult to label as involving an increase or decrease in control. What should we make of the ability to record conversations? On the one hand if this is done secretly and/or against the will of one of the parties, their control is weakened. But if done with their consent, it may increase control by offering a means of validating claims as to what was communicated. This cuts against the natural tilt toward favoring the claims of the more privileged and those of higher status.

Developments such as video phones, internet web transmissions, use of phone technology to transmit biometric data and the merging of the cell phone and still camera further illustrate the dynamic nature of the situation and the mixture of empowering and controlling elements. A central question of course is just who is being empowered or controlled, and for what ends? In the case of Caller ID is this the caller or recipient of a call, or both relative to third parties? Since all of us play a variety of roles the technology both empowers and lessens power, although hardly to the same degree across roles, institutions and broad contexts.

Within any measure of the amount of personal information collected is the tricky question of the ratio of involuntarily to voluntarily provided information.

The new surveillance is of social concern partly because of its ability to gather information secretly and involuntarily. For many observers, if the ratio stays constant or even moves toward an increase in voluntarily provided information, that is progress. As a formal matter, there has never been more informed consent in our society and the amount seems to be increasing. Consider the ratio of voluntarily recorded phone conversations vs. those from wiretaps. Most recorded phone conversations are formally consensual, as with the millions of service calls each day in which persons are told their conversation is being recorded. In most work settings it is also now standard practice to inform employees of the kind of communications monitoring (phone, e-mail, etc.) they face.

Yet we must also ask just how "voluntary" such recording is. In principle the individual can always hang up or choose not to work for a super-surveilling employer. Sometimes there is a choice and a request not to record a phone call will be honored. But usually such consent is specious since one needs the service, information or job and just saying "no" denies these. The role of manipulation and deception in obtaining consent also need to be considered, as does the relative ease of consenting (note the contrast between "opt in" and "opt out" systems). Still in general a principle of consent is to be preferred to secrecy and non-consent.

Surveillance Slack

Some aspects of the new surveillance lend support to claims regarding the extension of individualism and the ennoblement of human affairs associated with modernism. Thus the techniques can contribute to restrained and enlightened social control, helping to create a society orderly enough to enjoy its freedoms. The usual social class implications may even be reversed—those most subject to many forms of the new surveillance are the more privileged who rely so extensively on credit cards, cell phones, and computers.

Through offering high quality documentary evidence and audit trails, the new surveillance may enhance due process, fairness, and legitimacy. It may contribute to the political pluralism central to democracy by making the tools of surveillance widely available so that citizens and competing groups can use them against each other, as well government, to enhance accountability.[13] In the United States, unlike in many societies, surveillance technology is widely available to the public (even satellite imagery). A common transmission process is from military to law enforcement to industry to the public at large (e.g., night vision technology, drug testing, the internet). The surveillance may move from being a one-way mirror to being a window.

Another general indicator of progress can be seen in considering the extent of *surveillance slack*. With sensationalist and often unrepresentative examples, the media talk of the death of privacy with implicit reference to a supposed utopian past and privacy advocates are constantly documenting new risks. In contrast entrepreneurs too often discuss hypothetical benefits of new technologies as if they were fact. In the rhetorical excesses, which shape public awareness, there is a failure to differentiate the potential of a tactic from its actual use. This suggests the need for a broad comparative measure of *surveillance slack* which considers the extent to which a technology is applied, rather than the absolute amount of surveillance.

We can envision settings in which technology is relatively weak and in which there are few restraints on its application as in Europe in the Middle Ages. Conversely there are situations in which technology is very powerful, yet there are significant restraints, as with wiretapping in the United States. This contrasts with situations in contemporary authoritarian societies in which the technology is strong and the restraints on it applications are few.

In the United States from the end of the nineteenth century to the present, the individual's formal rights to, in principle at least,[14] control personal information have increased through legislation and judicial rulings with the greater institutionalization of civil liberties and privacy. Organizational policies and counter-technologies have also brought protections.

The ratio between what could be known, given the means for discovering personal information, and what is actually known was probably much smaller in the nineteenth century than is the case today and was much smaller still in the Middle Ages and throughout most of recorded human history. The weakness of the technology was matched by the fact that there was much less to be known about behavior.

In absolute terms, given ways of living and comparing pre-industrial, industrializing and contemporary societies, the amount of personal information that is potentially knowable would seem to have increased markedly over time as societal scale, density, differentiation and formal record keeping increased (e.g, remote communications, the number of people interacted with, geographical mobility, etc.).

In the nineteenth century there was also less physical privacy, given smaller living quarters, and larger families. The notion of the stifling, fish-bowl environment of the small town is a truism, having been well publicized by escapees to the more anonymous city. The idea of citizenship, labor, consumer and privacy rights were less developed and the borders between work and home or the home and the state were weaker (note the company town and unrestrained police searches). While the technology was weak, there were fewer restraints on its use and fewer means of neutralizing it.

The surveillance slack measure may be too relativistic for many observers.[15] A lesser evil is still evil and a greater good is not the best. For those in the Biblical tradition of the prophets, or believing in the inevitable cascading of slippery slopes, the only standard is the absolute ideal. To make judgments based on empirical data is irrelevant when the principle is the standard.

In summary, even with just one technology such as telecommunications, no simple empirical conclusion can be drawn about whether the control of personal information has increased or decreased. Holding apart crisis periods such as wartime, the pattern is neither consistent over time, nor equivalent across *different* kinds of personal information or border crossings.[16] How much more difficult then to draw conclusions about improvement across all means of surveillance, particularly in the absence of broad empirical research. Even with an empirical pattern that lends itself to conclusions, the issues of moral evaluation are far from simple.

It is also necessary to consider technologies in relation to each other and *in toto*. Functional alternatives in which if one way of meeting a goal or need is blocked another will be found, must also be considered. Thus restrictions on wiretapping may result in an increase in the use of informers or undercover operations which are alternative, less restricted means of obtaining information. Or these may increase together as informers' tips are used to justify obtaining wiretaps.[17] Efforts to successfully limit the application of the polygraph through legislation (Regan, 1995) resulted in a decline in its use but were accompanied by a significant increase in other, even less validated, forms such as paper and pencil honesty tests.

In democratic free market societies, along with more powerful technologies may come counter-technologies and the strengthening of individual rights to protect personal data. Nor are individuals (or groups) simply passive reeds in a technological hurricane. They have resources to fight back (Marx, 2003). A dialectical process can often be seen in which changes in behavior patterns and the development of extractive technologies lead to new rules and technologies for limiting their application. Technologies are both determined and determining. They do not enter a neutral culture, but one with informal and formal protections for personal information, as well one with value and organizational supports for collecting such information. Yet having appeared, their distinctive attributes may have independent and unanticipated impacts.

In the United States, within very broad boundaries over the last century there is something of a moving equilibrium—as the ability to technically cross personal informational borders has increased over time, so has the ability to legally and technically protect personal information.[18] But the road is broad and elastic indeed with respect to both form and time period and the multi-dimensional lines are jagged rather than straight. It is important to appreciate complexity and to be very clear about the frames of reference applied when making either empirical (new or not new, more or less control) or moral (good or bad) claims regarding surveillance developments.

Finally, in spite of the social analyst's predilection for noting the constraining elements of social systems, the past needn't be a guide to the future. Powerful forces work against any easy assumption that a decent society is self-perpetuating or that once set in motion, progress must continue. The masthead of a black civil rights newspaper in Sun Flower County, Mississippi reads, "Freedom Is a Constant Struggle." This heralds an important truth. There are no permanent victories in the liberties business. Liberty and individualism are fragile and historically the exception rather than the rule. There is no guarantee that hard won rights will stay won or be extended, in the face of continual social and technical challenges. But vigilance, knowledge, and wisdom are likely to help.

NOTES

1. See for example Gilliom, 2001; Cole, 2001; Caplan and Torpey, 2001; Nippert-Eng, 1997; Nelkin and Tancredi, 1994; Smith, 1994; Gilliom, 1994; Gandy, 1993; Laudon, 1986; Marx and Reichman, 1984; Rule, 1973. Also the general treatments by Gutwirth, 2002; Garfinkle, 2000; Rosen, 2000; Smith, 2000; Froomkin, 2000; Etzioni, 1999; Brin, 1998; Ericson and Haggerty, 1997; Staples, 1997; Allen, 1988; Bogard, 1996; Lyon and Zureik, 1996; Bogard, 1996; Lyon and Zureik, 1996; Lyon, 1994; Allen, 1988.

2. This article draws from *Windows into the Soul: Surveillance and Society in an Age of High Technology*, University of Chicago, forthcoming based on the Jensen Lectures for Duke University and the American Sociological Association. Additional articles are at www.garymarx.net. An earlier version appeared in the online journal *Surveillance and Society*, vol. 1, no.1 (surveillance- and-society.org).

3. The self-restraint and voluntary compliance favored in liberal democratic theory receives a new dimension here. The line between the public and the private order maintenance becomes hazier. The border may be blurred in the sense that there can be a continuous transmission link between sender and receiver as with brain waves or scents. Other broken and reconstructed borders are discussed in Marx, 1997. Consider also a federally funded "Watch Your Car" program found in 11 states in 2001. In this program vehicle owners attach a decal to their car inviting police to pull them over late at night to be sure the car is not stolen. To the extent that this "co-production" of social order becomes established it is easy to imagine individuals wearing miniature video, audio, location, and biological monitors sending data outward to protective sources. New borders and forms of neutralization will of course appear, but it will be a new senses-transcending ball game and we will become more aware of the extent to which the limits of the physical world shape cognition and norms.

4. William Holden nicely captures this in his self-analysis in the film *Picnic*," *What's the use, baby? I'm a bum. She saw through me like an x-ray machine.*"

5. Taste is the most under-utilized of the senses for surveillance. Drug agents sometimes taste a suspect substance. Historically the tasters who sampled the food and drink of elites to see if they were poisoned are another example. Evaluating the performance of a chef by tasting the product, a chef's self-monitoring by sampling a dish before serving and a baking contest in which there is a taste test are other examples.

6. However applying a polygraph to an uncooperative subject or for verification purposes, or using a telephoto lens to capture and record an image from far away would fall within the definition. The exposure (if that is the term) volunteered by those at the nude beach is presumably intended to be available only momentarily to the unaided senses of others in the immediate vicinity. To record images or observe from far away introduces considerations of the new surveillance.

7. If one's goal involves the physical or technical elements rather than the social, different factors than those in these would be emphasized e.g., the type

of technology such as optical-imaging, sensor, radiating or nonradiating communications devices, whether or not (and what types) of computer chips are involved, what the energy sources are, ease of manufacturing and impact on the environment. Or if the concern were with a particular goal such as testing for drugs, one would contrast the variety of techniques for doing this. These of course may have social implications (e.g., batteries need to be recharged, sensing chips can be easily hidden, living surveillors give off heat). David Lyon (2001) deals with some related themes in classifying surveillance (e.g., coercive vs. seductive forms).

8. However in this example a general announcement need not necessarily indicate where the camera is. The situation is similar to employers announcing that they use "secret shoppers" to test employees.

9. Technology of course may push these limits redefining the meaning of life, overcoming gravity, and permitting us to see in the dark. A part of genius as well as insanity is in not "accepting" supposedly inherent limits.

10. To be sure religious surveillance in the west has not disappeared. Within sects surrounded by a hostile and tempting world, such surveillance (in the form of inquisitions, self-policing, group confessionals) remains strong—whether involving groups such as the Amish, new age cults, or rigidly fundamentalist groups. Theocratic states such as Iran and Afghanistan during the 1990s experienced a resurgence and merging of religious and political surveillance.

11. This of course extended the values of the center outward. But since conduits carry flows in both directions, this has had mixed consequences and represents much more than a monolithic cultural, social, and political imperialism.

12. However using surveillance to serve the citizenship rights and welfare needs of citizens may serve the political interests of elites by enhancing legitimacy.

13. However this may change to the extent that video phones become widespread and manners (or technology) mandate their use. In principle one would be free to choose whether or not to have this and then whether or not to turn it on. Yet subtle and not so subtle social pressures may tilt toward continual use. Lack of reciprocity on an individual's part (failure to use it) may lead the other party to a communication to wonder what the individual is hiding. There is some parallel to expectations about not wearing a mask in face-to-face interactions.

14. Of course an insecure society in which individuals need to be constantly watching over their shoulder is hardly ideal.

15. The empirical analyst concerned with these issues as a citizen faces a dilemma in that the kind of scholarly analysis suggested here can create undue complacency in the face of potential dangers to liberty. Yet in the long run honesty is a better ally than rhetoric.

16. In an article that suggests a framework for drawing ethical conclusions I suggest that when violations of personal borders occur this is likely to involve one of four conditions (Marx, 1998). For example this may involve a breaching "natural" border presumed to be protective of personal information such as clothes, inner thoughts and feelings, doors, spatial distance, darkness, skin or bodily orifices, and directed communication. It can

involve a social border where there is an expectation of confidentiality or a spatial or temporal border separating information from various periods or aspects of one's life. It may also involve breaching the tacit assumption that interaction and communication are ephemeral and transitory and not to be captured and preserved through covert means.

17. This raises an issue of when one technology displaces another, rather than serving to simply pile on what is already there. Gillom (2001) for example notes that the appearance of an elaborate computerized monitoring system for those on welfare has supplemented rather than displaced the traditional system of "rat calls" as a means of information on violations.

18. There are of course profound conflicts here over the meaning of privacy and the multiple meanings of the terms public and the private. In stressing one rather than another meaning, individuals often talk past each other. Note for example public and private places as geographically defined, public and private information access, customary expectations and manners, the accessibility or inaccessibility of information to the unaided senses, the actual state of information as being publicly known or unknown and social status and roles with differential access to information (Marx, 2001).

REFERENCES

Allen, A. (1988). *Uneasy Access: Privacy for Women in a Free Society*. Totowa, NJ: Rowman and Littlefield.

Beniger, J. (1986). *The Control Revolution: The Technological and Economic Origins of the Information Society*. Cambridge, MA: Harvard University Press.

Bogard, B. (1996). *The Simulation of Surveillance: Hyper Control in Telematic Societies*. New York: Cambridge University Press.

Brin, D. (1998). *The Transparent Society*. Reading, MA: Perseus Books.

Byrne, J., et al. (1992). *Smart Sentencing: The Rise of Intermediate Sanctions*. Beverly Hills: Sage.

Caplan, J. and Torpey, J. (2001). *Documenting Individual Identity*. Princeton, NJ: Princeton University Press.

Cole, S. (2001). *Suspect Identities*. Cambridge, MA: Harvard University Press.

Deflem, M. (2000). "Bureaucratization and Social Control: Historical Foundations of International Police Cooperation," in *Law and Society Review*, 34(3): 601–640.

Ericson, R. and Haggerty, K. (1997). *Policing the Risk Society*. Toronto: University of Toronto Press.

Etzioni, A. (1999). *The Limits of Privacy*. New York: Basic Books.

Fijnaut C. and Marx, G. (1995). "The Normalization of Undercover Policing in the West: Historical and Contemporary Perspectives," in Fijnaut and Marx (eds.) *Undercover Police Surveillance in Comparative Perspective*. The Hague: Kluwer Law International.

Fogelson, R. (1977). *Big-City Police*. Cambridge, MA: Harvard University Press.

Foucault, M. (1977). *Discipline and Punish: The Birth of the Prison*. New York: Pantheon.

Froomkin, M. (2000). "The Death of Privacy?" in *Stanford Law Review*, 52(5).

Gabriel Y., (2004). "The Glass Cage: Flexible Work, Fragmented Consumption, Fragile Selves," in J. Alexander, G. Marx, and C. Williams (eds.), *Self, Social Structure, and Beliefs: Essays in Honor of Neil Smelser*, University of California Press, forthcoming.

Gandy, O. (1993). *The Panoptic Sort: A Political Economy of Personal Information.* Boulder, CO: Westview.

Garfinkel, S. (2000). *Database Nation.* Sebastopol, CA: O'Reilly.

Gillom, J. (1994). *Surveillance, Privacy, and the Law: Employee Drug Testing and the Politics of Social Control.* Ann Arbor: University of Michigan Press.

Gillom, J. (2001). *Overseers of the Poor.* Chicago: University of Chicago Press.

Laudon, K. (1986). *The Dossier Society.* New York: Columbia University Press.

Lyon, D. (1994). *The Electronic Eye.* Cambridge: The Polity Press.

Lyon, D. (2001). *Surveillance Society: Monitoring Everyday Life.* Buckingham: Open University Press.

Marx, G.T. (1988). *Undercover: Police Surveillance in America.* Berkeley: University of California Press.

Marx, G.T. (1997). "The Declining Significance of Traditional Borders (and the Appearance of New Borders) in an Age of High Technology," in P. Droege (ed.) *Intelligent Environments.* Amsterdam: Elsevier.

Marx, G.T. (1998). "An Ethics for the New Surveillance" in *The Information Society*, 14(3): 171–185.

Marx, G.T. (2001). "Murky Conceptual Waters: The Public and the Private," in *Ethics and Information Technology*, 3(3): 157–169.

Marx, G.T. (2003). "A Tack in the Shoe: Neutralizing and Resisting the New Surveillance," in *Journal of Social Issues.* (Special issues on technology and privacy), 59(2): 369–390.

Marx, G.T. and Reichman, N. (1984). "Routinizing the Discovery of Secrets: Computers as Informants," in *American Behavioral Scientist*, 27(4).

Nelkin, D. and Tancredi, L. (1994). *Dangerous Diagnostics: The Social Power of Biological Information.* Chicago: University of Chicago Press.

Nippert-Eng, C. (1997). *Home and Work: Negotiating Boundaries Through Everyday Life.* Chicago: University of Chicago Press.

Nisbet, R. (1977). *Twilight of Authority.* New York: Random House.

Regan, P. (1995). *Legislating Privacy: Technology, Social Values, and Public Policy.* Chapel Hill: University of North Carolina.

Rosen, J. (2000). *The Unwanted Gaze.* New York: Random House.

Shils, E. (1975). *Center and Periphery: Essays in Macro Sociology.* Chicago: University of Chicago Press.

Silver, A. (1969). "The Demand for Order in Civil Society: A Review of Some Themes in the History of Urban Crime, Police, and Riots," in D. Bordua (ed.) *The Police.* New York: Wiley.

Smelser, N. (1959). *Social Change in the Industrial Revolution.* Chicago: University of Chicago Press.

Smelser, N. (1997). *The Problematics of Sociology: The Georg Simmel Lectures.* Berkeley: University of California Press.

Smith, H. J. (1994). *Managing Privacy: Information, Technology, and the Corporation.* Chapel Hill: University of North Carolina Press.

Smith, R.E. (2000). "Ben Franklin's Web Site." Providence, RI: *Privacy Journal.*

Staples. W. (1997). *The Culture of Surveillance.* New York: St. Martin's Press.

14

Designing, Organizing, and Editing Your Research Writing Projects

This guide collects information you will find useful when you work on the writing projects described in Part 2 of *Entering the Academic Conversation*. Based on your needs and the recommendations of your instructor, these sections can be read and reviewed at any point in your writing course.

We'll start with the basics: *formatting* your writing projects according to the conventions of each major style guide. Conventionally formatting your papers includes margins and spacing, where to place information about yourself and your course, and special formatting for long quotations. These features will ensure the right "look" for your writing project and enhance readability for your audience.

Next, we'll explore aspects of *argument, purpose,* and *organization* especially relevant to your research writing projects. The concepts, techniques, and examples in this section will help you become more conscious about ways you can organize a paper and present an argument. You'll also see some ways of incorporating visual features (such as graphs, figures, and images) and design features (such as boxes, shading, and color) into your research projects.

Then, we'll review *usage* and *style* to help you ensure that you develop and express your ideas as clearly and conventionally as possible. We'll look at paragraphs, sentences, and word choice as important parts of writing projects that work together to ensure clarity and increase the impact of your work on your audience.

This chapter is a condensed overview of issues and strategies that tend to be the most important and relevant to beginning college research writers. To build on this information, you should consider buying a full-length handbook, which will provide you with more detailed explanations and examples, and will cover a wider range of writing issues. If you already know your major, consider purchasing the style guide preferred by scholars in your academic field. Along with detailed explanations of format, citation, and bibliographic conventions, style guides like the *Modern Language Association Handbook* and *The Chicago Manual of Style* include general guidelines for writers in the field.

FORMATTING

Just as each major style guide (MLA, APA, CMS, and CSE) uses unique approaches to in-text citations and bibliographies (see Chapter 7), each also has particular requirements for the appearance, or the *format*, of the paper.

General Conventions of Document Design

Some features are common to all the major styles, including the following:

- **Margins** With the exception of the running header, which is ½ inch from the top (see Figure 14.2), your margins will be one inch all around.
- **Size and Font** Ensure that your paper will be readable and avoid using distracting typefaces. Fonts such as Times New Roman, Bookman, and Helvetica, used in eleven to twelve point sizes, are clear and readable. Do not use creative typefaces, like Old English script or cursive-style fonts.
- **Spacing** Your paper will be double-spaced throughout, including titles running over one line, bibliography entries, and quotations.

The problems associated with finding and using more coal are also associated with other fossil fuels. Too much energy is needed just to find and get to the power sources, which means that the net power produced is very low. If we can use water, wind, and even cow manure to get hydrogen, we have already taken care of the problems of locating and extracting the fuel sources. Recently, researchers at the University of Waterloo in Canada tested eleven "production pathways" to generate and store hydrogen in order to find the one with the least input energy and the greatest output energy.	The problems associated with finding and using more coal are also associated with other fossil fuels. Too much energy is needed just to find and get to the power sources, which means that the net power produced is very low. If we can use water, wind, and even cow manure to get hydrogen, we have already taken care of the problems of locating and extracting the fuel sources. Recently, researchers at the University of Waterloo in Canada tested eleven "production pathways" to generate and store hydrogen in order to find the one with the least input energy and the greatest output energy.

FIGURE 14. 1 A right ragged edge (left) creates more readable text than a justified right edge (right). MLA First Page

- **Alignment** Justify the left side of the paper so that text runs in a straight line down the left margin, other than indentations for paragraph breaks and block quotations. Do not justify on the right. This prevents text from being stretched in hard-to-read ways (see Figure 14.1).

While these are generally accepted conventions, be sure to follow your instructor's requirements for formatting and design.

MLA-formatted papers include the following information on the first page:

Last Name 1

Your Name

Instructor's Name

Course

Date

Full Disclosure and Apology in Medicine: Is the
Risk Worth Taking?

There is a growing effort within the United States to address medical error since the Institute of Medicine's 1999 report, "To Err Is Human: Building a Safer Healthcare System," revealed that as many as 98,000 people die in US hospitals every year due to avoidable medical errors. The Patient Safety and Quality Improvement Act of 2005 made great strides toward improving healthcare in the United States. The act provides anonymity to healthcare professionals, which allows them to report error without fear of personal repercussions. While the act will facilitate some improvements in healthcare, what about addressing safety in cases where maintaining anonymity is difficult or impossible? "Full disclosure," explaining adverse medical outcomes to patients and families, poses additional challenges, because it is difficult for healthcare providers to protect anonymity while exposing their errors. Even though full disclosure is encouraged by the American Medical Association, it is unlikely to really take hold unless healthcare providers believe that the benefits outweigh the risks and know how to do it well.

No additional style is needed for your paper title, so avoid using bold or italic type, underlining, or otherwise enhancing the title.

APA Cover Page

APA-formatted papers use a separate title page that includes personal and course information, and the title of your paper. Your paper title is centered horizontally and vertically, and followed by your name and the name of your institution:

Full Disclosure 1

Full Disclosure and Apology in Medicine: Is the
Risk Worth Taking?

Your Name

Your Institution

CMS and CSE Cover Pages

Both CMS- and CSE-formatted papers use separate title pages, which include your paper title, your name, the course, your instructor's name, and the date.

Full Disclosure and Apology in Medicine: Is the
Risk Worth Taking?

Your Name

Course
Instructor's Name
Date

Making a Running Header

MLA- and APA-formatted papers repeat certain information in the upper right corner of each page. Your paper will have this kind of *running head,* which you can make by using the "header" tool in your word-processing program:

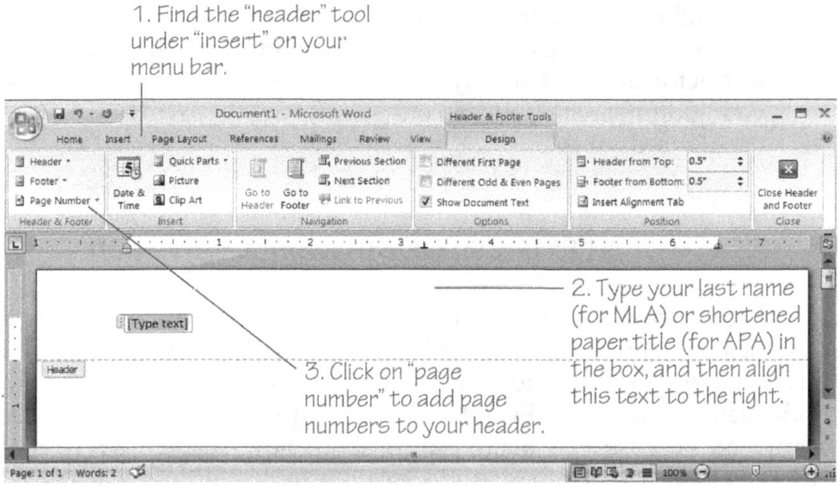

1. Find the "header" tool under "insert" on your menu bar.

2. Type your last name (for MLA) or shortened paper title (for APA) in the box, and then align this text to the right.

3. Click on "page number" to add page numbers to your header.

FIGURE 14.2   "Header" tool in Microsoft Word.

The header appears on the first page of an MLA paper and on the title page of an APA paper; in CMS and CSE papers it appears on the first page of main text. Even though no page number appears on the CMS and CSE title page, it is still "counted," so the first page of main text is page 2.

OFFSET QUOTATIONS

See Chapter 6 for more information on using quotations.

Offset (or "block") quotations are used when you plan to include a lengthy excerpt from a source. Because offset quotations are separated from the main text of your essay, no quotation marks are used. Following is how each major style guide treats offset quotations:

- *MLA:* Quotations of more than *four lines* are offset, and parenthetical citations for offset quotations appear outside the end punctuation.
- *APA:* Quotations of more than *forty words* are offset.
- *CMS: The Chicago Manual of Style* doesn't impose the number of words or lines at which to make a break, but recommends that quotations of *similar length* should be treated alike. For example, if you decide to offset one quotation of five lines, you should offset all other quotations of five or more lines in your paper.

- *CSE:* Like *CMS*, *Scientific Style and Format* does not specify a particular length to distinguish short from long quotations. If your instructor does not specify when to apply block quotations, use your judgment and remain consistent once you decide on a number of words or lines.

ELEMENTS OF ARGUMENT

Each of your research projects requires you to make an argument of some kind. Among many possible goals, your projects may argue a position, offer a solution to a problem, or seek to explain new ways of understanding an issue. Even the definition project in Chapter 8 uses argument, because you make claims about how academic reference works help you understand and explain a term within a specialized conversation.

Since academic writers work in conversation with each other, their arguments are not debates between two sides of an issue in which one side wins and the other loses (as in a political debate on a TV program or between presidential candidates). Instead, arguments in the academic sense are critical discussions, in which multiple points of view, claims, hypotheses, or possible solutions are considered by readers with shared interests. Unlike a debate, where participants consider an issue closed when one side wins, an academic argument works like a "parlor conversation" (described in Chapter 1), where many participants come and go, listen in, and contribute to an ongoing discussion.

Classical appeals—ethos, logos, and pathos (see Chapter 9)—are important tools for understanding the kinds of arguments you're likely to encounter in your research. The *elements of argument* developed by philosopher Stephen Toulmin help writers craft effective claims that use strong logic and appeal to readers. The following terms—*claim, reason, warrant, ground and backing, conditions of rebuttal, refuting and conceding*—are used by Toulmin to name essential elements of strong argument.

Making a Claim

The thesis, or *claim*, of an argument is a simple statement summarizing a writer's position on the research question or issue. For example, consider our student writers from Chapter 12, where David claims of hydrogen fuel:

> There are a number of options on the table, but the most logical answer is hydrogen power.

... and Tony claims of video games:

> Video games in general are teaching us as a society to conform to what someone higher up in authority says.

Stating Reasons

Reasons are the evidence used to support your claim. Claims and reasons are connected, either explicitly or implicitly, by a "because" clause. For example, David develops his claim as follows:

> Hydrogen makes sense from environmental and economic perspectives; and, although renewable resources are preferred for the production of hydrogen, in cases of high demand, nuclear power and coal-fired plants can also be used to meet additional needs.

David anticipates how he will support his claim, and at the same time forecasts his argument's structure:

Reasons are connected to claims with explicit or implicit "because" clauses.

- His solution is both environmentally and economically sound
- There are multiple ways to produce hydrogen that can replace or supplement fossil fuels

David uses an *implicit* "because" clause to argue:

> Hydrogen is the most logical solution to our fuel needs **because** it makes sense from environmental and economic perspectives, and **because** there are both renewable and non-renewable sources for hydrogen power.

Acknowledging Warrants

Warrants are used to connect claims and reasons to assumptions, values, and beliefs. We can see how David's reasons for advocating hydrogen fuel are supported by warrants. When he writes that "Hydrogen makes sense from environmental and economic perspectives," and "renewable resources are preferred for the production of hydrogen," he expresses two warrants:

What assumptions and values underlie your claims and reasons?

The fuel sources we use should be environmentally sound and renewable.

Establishing Grounds and Backing

The *grounds* of an argument include all the evidence (facts, statistics, observations, data, and examples) a writer uses to support reasons. Just as reasons support a claim, grounds support reasons. Your arguments may use many kinds of supporting evidence, but your most effective grounds will come from your research.

For instance, to show that local availability of energy resources supports using hydrogen fuel, David provides evidence from three sources:

> Even if hydroelectric power isn't available, there are a number of other options for powering hydrogen production locally. In an article she published in *BioCycle*, Angela Crooks looks at ways of using biomass from forests to generate power. Crooks says that it would be possible to fuel around forty-seven percent of our energy needs by using the 368 million dry tons of forest biomass, which is regenerated every year; harvesting biomass could also cut down on fires that burn millions of forest acres every year. As Larry Rohter reports in the *New York Times*, Brazil has been making ethanol from sugarcane since 1975, when they had a major energy crisis. By the 1980s, there were more than 600,000 cars in Brazil that could run on the cane-based ethanol. Thus, rather than depending on large industries, power can be developed from local sources. Otherwise, as Motavalli quoted one environmentalist, "nuclear-generated hydrogen is like a nicotine patch that causes cancer" (39).

He cites Crooks's study of forest biomass and Rohter's report on Brazil's use of sugarcane because they illustrate two ways of using local resources:

- Crooks describes the portion of total energy needs satisfied by forest biomass
- Rohter shows sugarcane's application to power cars

The final quote from Motavalli provides readers with an easily understood metaphor that illustrates the value of renewables over nuclear power sources.

These grounds also allow David to provide support, or *backing*, for his warrants. For example, if forest biomass studied by Crooks is "regenerated every year," David recalls his warrant that fuels should be environmentally sound. Crooks's study provides further

Grounds support reasons, while backing supports warrants.

backing for this warrant by showing that harvesting biomass produces renewable fuel and reduces the risk of forest fire.

Anticipating Counterarguments: "Conditions of Rebuttal"

Anticipate how readers might challenge your reasons and warrants.

Besides making and supporting claims, strong arguments must also anticipate *conditions of rebuttal*, the grounds of possible counterarguments. By anticipating how skeptical readers might challenge an argument, writers appeal to readers who may be inclined to disagree with them. Always consider the ways readers could object either to the reasons or the warrants supporting your claim.

For example, while literary theorist Jane Tompkins claims that our understanding of historical events is shaped by value judgments, she also anticipates alternative claims. In the following passage, she anticipates a challenge to her *reason* that evidence requires us to make judgments:

> It may well seem to you at this point that, given the tremendous variation among the historical accounts, I had no choice but to end in relativism.

Continuing, shs shows that this conclusion may appear logical and reasonable, but is misleading, because:

> The historian can never escape the limitations of his or her own position in history and so inevitably gives an account that is an extension of the circumstances from which it springs. But it seems to me that when one is confronted with this particular succession of stories, cultural and historical relativism is not a position that one can comfortably assume.

In a later paragraph, Tompkins anticipates challenges to her *warrant* that a "poststructuralist" position leads to a credible claim about European-Indian encounters:

> Someone else, confronted with the same materials, could have decided that one of these historical accounts was correct. Still another person might have decided that more evidence was needed in order to decide among them. Why did I conclude that none of the accounts was accurate because they were all produced from some particular angle of vision?

Responding to Counterarguments: Refuting and Conceding

Your responses to counterarguments depend on how strongly you want to advocate your claim and the strength of challenges you anticipate.

In *refuting* counterarguments, you strengthen a claim by exposing the weakness of alternatives. If you plan to refute counterarguments, show how objections to your reasons or grounds are inaccurate, implausible, incomplete, or otherwise lack the strength of your own claim.

For example, philosopher John Gunders anticipates a generally held warrant regarding public surveillance cameras, and refutes it with evidence from his research. Gunders's refutation helps him introduce a new warrant that further supports his claim:

> Cameras in shopping centres, for instance, are often promoted as protection for the consumer against pick-pockets or physical violence from individuals—a theme that was emphasised in the James Bulger case—yet their main role is to protect shop owners from property crime such as shop-lifting or vandalism. The Walgett Shire Council in New South Wales stated that its goal in installing closed circuit TV in the CBD was to reduce crime and to "encourage businesses to remove bars from shop windows" (cited in Standing Committee 1996:17).

This refutation allows Gunders to develop a point about the coercive effects of public surveillance cameras:

> For the camera in a shopping precinct, those who are not involved in economic consumption are deviant non-conformists who put at risk the legitimate activities of the consumers (Hillier 1996:99). The juridical ideology is an amalgam of discourses that include the Protestant work-ethic; assumptions about appropriate behaviours in relation to age, gender and occupation; stereotypes concerning race and ethnicity; and specific laws concerning the non-conformance with social standards, such as vagrancy (sanctions against poverty), loitering (sanctions against idleness) and laws of association (sanctions against youth).

Alternately, in *conceding* counterarguments, you acknowledge the credibility of multiple positions and responses to an issue. Concession can have a positive effect on your readers, because they will see you as a critical thinker who is willing to fairly consider other possible views, reasons, and warrants even as you argue your own claim.

Cindy's entire essay appears in Chapter 11.

For example, in her exploratory research essay Cindy responds to Bryan Liang's claim that medical care works as a system. She first disagrees based on personal experiences, but then concedes to Liang. Concession leads her to a new understanding of medical error, which strengthens her support for apology and mediation approaches:

> I found the concept of a systems approach to healthcare very hard to accept at first. My experience with medicine has usually been with one doctor or nurse at a time and so to me it seems like healthcare delivery is a function of individuals, not a system. Then I considered that medical professionals have to receive their training somewhere, that updates on advancements occur, and that "best practices" are published; medical professionals depend on others for training, information, and often implementation of services. These thoughts caused me to reconsider my understanding of medical error and malpractice. While malpractice is defined as substandard care, errors can occur because of the profession's current educational approaches and practices, because the system has inherent errors in it.

Concession is a valuable technique to use in your argument, because it can often help you transition to new grounds, reasons, and warrants, which demonstrate the strength of your thinking to readers.

DEVELOPING ROGERIAN ARGUMENTS

Anticipating and responding to counterarguments shows how participation in academic conversations requires us to work with the ideas of others. Although we would like to assume that our audience is neutral and always willing to weigh every side of an argument fairly, we often write for audiences whose ideas are based on deeply held values and convictions, whose members may feel threatened by critical engagement. In these cases, elements of argument can be organized to engage empathetically with an audience and help guide them toward your claims. *Rogerian argument*, named for psychologist Carl Rogers, focuses on approaches writers can use to listen carefully to the views of others and build common ground with their audience.

The delayed thesis argument is one way to elicit support from your readers, because it opens with a neutral stance on an issue or problem. This stance allows you to introduce multiple perspectives on an issue or possible solutions to a problem without favoring one over the others. As you introduce perspectives you can focus on points of connection and agreement, showing how shared values and convictions among different positions can be used to reach a compromise. By maintaining respect for others, you will:

Delayed-thesis arguments are further described in Chapter 12 and in organizational pattern 3c, below.

- Appeal to readers who hold multiple perspectives and values
- Acknowledge the validity of multiple perspectives and values
- Build connections and compromise between perspectives and values as you argue your claim

PURPOSE

Why are you writing this paper, and what do you hope to do with it? Your answers to these questions comprise your statement of *purpose*. If you remain aware of your *goals* for a project and the *contribution* you want to make to the academic conversation you're entering, you'll be able to ensure either that you have successfully achieved your purpose, or that you can revise to meet a new purpose.

As you consider ways to develop your argument, keep your purpose in mind, using some of the following questions:

- How do you want to impact your reader—intellectually, emotionally, or both?
- Is your argument likely to support or challenge preconceptions and values held by your readers?
- How can you appeal to readers to help you achieve your goals?
- Do you want to give readers a new understanding of, or solution to a problem?
- Do you plan to advocate a position in a debate?
- What organizational pattern will best support the type of argument you want to make and purpose you wish to have?
- What kinds of evidence will appeal to your audience and help you achieve your purpose?

As you think about organization, keep in mind the ways you plan to appeal to your audience (see Chapter 9). Which patterns are the most logical? Which resemble the patterns used in your sources?

Since many of this book's writing projects are process-oriented it's often appropriate to let your purpose emerge as you research and write a paper. Nonetheless, the sooner you have at least a tentative purpose in mind, the easier it will be to:

- Choose and organize your sources logically
- Select the best material for quotations, paraphrases, and summaries
- Develop your argument to support your purpose

ORGANIZATION

Organization refers to the ways in which ideas are meaningfully and purposefully connected together. Although there is no one way to organize your ideas, academic arguments tend to fall into a number of patterns you can use in your writing projects. Strong organization helps ensure that readers will follow the progression of your ideas in a logical, coherent way and ultimately arrive with you at a convincing conclusion.

You may already have read about some basic organizational patterns in Chapter 12. This section reviews those patterns and offers additional strategies to consider as you shape your research writing projects to best support your arguments.

Pattern 1: Classification of Parts

Because academic conversations value complex thinking, we can often feel overwhelmed by new issues and ideas, or by seeing familiar subjects examined in new ways. *Classification of parts* is an effective way to organize an idea by examining it in its various aspects.

The analytic strategies covered in Chapter 12 play an especially important role in the classification pattern, because writers faced with multiple sources, perspectives, and interpretations must first be able to break them down into significant parts, and then identify and develop meaningful connections between them. Analytic skills allow a writer to select important aspects of a complex issue and to represent them in a clear and coherent way for readers. The purpose of classification will likely be to:

1. Explain a debate among experts on an issue
2. Show the complexity of an issue readers may believe they already understand
3. Prepare the foundation for development into a position or other claim

For example, a writer who wants to analyze hip-hop culture might divide the study into related aspects of the whole, by describing major regional differences (for example, in New York, Los Angeles,

Atlanta, and Oakland) or national characteristics (as in the United States, Colombia, and France); by defining elements of hip-hop culture (DJ-ing, graffiti, MC-ing, and dancing); or by exploring the hip-hop community's stance in relation to American popular culture (oppositional or integrational, underground or mainstream). A classification approach begins with a claim, such as

> Contrary to what people outside the scene may think, hip-hop is about more than music. Truly understanding hip-hop means knowing about the many aspects that make up the culture.

Following the introduction, each characteristic or part is described in detail. Those details are later *reintegrated*, allowing the writer to make a point or pursue a purpose based on the analysis.

Pattern 2: Comparison

Comparison adds a strategy to the classification pattern. In this pattern, writers build on analysis by evaluating similarities and differences between aspects of an idea or issue.

If we stay with the analysis of hip-hop culture from Pattern 1 above, a writer could compare and contrast among the characteristics identified in the classification. For example, if there are distinct regional characteristics of Atlanta and Oakland hip-hop scenes, how can they be compared? In which ways are they similar, and in which ways are they different? Again, the classification of parts (music, clothes and style, lyric content, staying underground or going mainstream, and so on) plays a role, but the writer's purpose is to develop meaningful comparisons between the parts. Additional comparisons could be built from the first, because a writer could then show how, despite their differences, Atlanta and Oakland are more similar when compared to scenes abroad, such as in Havana or Montréal.

We could organize a comparative argument in one of two ways. Once we know the locations to be compared (Atlanta and Oakland) and the aspects of comparison (music, clothes and style, etc.), we can then anticipate how the two patterns would follow a single thesis claim, such as:

> Although urban hip-hop scenes share a number of characteristics, those characteristics are practiced in unique ways in different locations. For example, there are four main differences between Atlanta's and Oakland's hip-hop scenes.

2a: Part-by-part comparison

There are four main differences between Atlanta's and Oakland's hip-hop scenes.

I. Atlanta
   1. Music
   2. Clothes and Style
   3. Lyric Content
   4. Staying underground vs. going Mainstream

II. Oakland
   1. Music
   2. Clothes and Style
   3. Lyric Content
   4. Staying underground vs. going Mainstream

2b: Point-by-point comparison

There are four main differences between Atlanta's and Oakland's hip-hop scenes.

I. Music
   1. Atlanta
   2. Oakland

II. Clothes and Style
   1. Atlanta
   2. Oakland

III. Lyric Content
   1. Atlanta
   2. Oakland

IV. Staying Underground vs. Going Mainstream
   1. Atlanta
   2. Oakland

Pattern 3: Problem/Solution

There are a number of ways to organize a problem/solution argument, but each includes the same essential parts:

1. A clear **statement of the problem**, such as the threatened extinction of grizzly bears;
2. A number of **possible solutions**, such as limiting suburban sprawl, more restrictions on hunting, public education to increase knowledge about bears, and so on;
3. A set of **evaluative criteria**, such as cost effectiveness, long-term benefits, environmental impact, and so on;
4. An **argument** for the best solution, based on clear evaluation and comparison to alternatives.

Once a writer has the basic parts, the problem/solution argument is usually organized into one of three patterns. If we stay with the problem of grizzly bear extinction, these patterns might be developed in the following ways:

3a: Thesis first

This pattern begins with an introduction to the problem and identification of favored solution. In the body of the essay, the writer describes all possible solutions, introduces evaluative criteria to compare the solutions, and finally shows in the conclusion why the favored solution is best. For example:

I. Introduction: explanation of problem and introduction of favored solution:

> Although there are a number of ways to prevent grizzly bears' continued slide toward extinction, the best solution is to limit suburban sprawl into their habitat.

II. Possible solutions and related research

After explaining the problem, the writer introduces a number of possible solutions:

> Limiting suburban sprawl is only one of the possible solutions, which include limiting or eliminating bear hunting and increasing public awareness about the importance of grizzly bear survival.

III. Introduction of evaluative criteria

After describing possible solutions, the writer adds evaluative criteria and weighs each solution:

Evaluative criteria include the reasons and warrants that help you compare possible solutions.

> While each solution has certain advantages, which one has the best chance of helping bears survive over the longest period of time (and/or other evaluative criteria)?

IV. Support of favored solution

After showing the weaknesses of less-favored solutions, the writer emphasizes the favored solution:

> Only limitations on suburban sprawl will have immediate impact on grizzly survival and preserve grizzly habitat for years to come.

3b: Thesis first with point-by-point evaluation

Like pattern 3a, this pattern begins with the writer introducing the problem and identifying the favored solution. Next though, each possible solution is individually evaluated with appropriate criteria, so that the writer concludes by supporting the solution that has stood the test of the criteria:

I. Introduction: explanation of problem and statement of favored solution

> Although there are a number of ways to prevent grizzly bears' continued slide toward extinction, the best solution is to limit suburban sprawl into their habitat.

II. Description and refutation of possible solution #1

The writer introduces a possible solution and explains its shortcomings. In the process, evaluative criteria are introduced:

> While it's true that increased public education will have a positive impact on people's attitudes toward bears over time, my research shows that too little time remains before the bears become extinct. Even though changing attitudes is a good long-term goal, how can grizzlies be protected in the meantime?

III. Description and refutation of other solutions

The writer introduces and evaluates additional solutions as necessary:

> Obviously, hunting and poaching have a significant impact on the total number of grizzly bears; however, while stopping hunting and poaching will preserve the number of bears, it does nothing to preserve the habitat needed for their survival and reproduction.

IV. Return to favored solution

Having refuted alternative solutions and introduced evaluative criteria in the process, the writer argues for the favored solution:

In the conclusion, this writer recalls each of the evaluative criteria used throughout the essay.

> Only limitations on suburban sprawl will have immediate impact on grizzly survival and preserve grizzly habitat for years to come.

3c: Delayed thesis: using a neutral stance

This approach can be especially effective for writers who are exploring a controversial problem, or whose solution is likely to meet resistance from readers. Like other patterns, this argument opens by clearly identifying the problem; here though, the writer introduces possible solutions without favoring one among them. Only after introducing evaluative criteria and weighing each solution does the author then conclude with the favored solution, which is supported logically and without apparent bias or prejudgment:

> *A delayed thesis can prevent the perception of bias.*

I. Introduction: explanation of problem

The writer describes the problem and focuses on the importance of solving it, not on a particular solution:

> Studies by conservation biologists and other scientists have raised concerns about the threatened extinction of grizzly bears. And, although these bears haven't received as much media attention as whales, bees, and even kangaroo rats, they still play as important a role in North American ecosystems as those better known animals. If it is important to protect grizzly bears and the larger ecosystem of which they are a part, what is the best way to ensure their survival?

II. Description of possible solutions

The writer describes each possible solution, showing the merits and credibility of each:

> One of the easiest ways to address the slide to extinction is to prevent the deliberate killing of bears by hunters and poachers. Researchers have shown that deliberate killing accounts for up to ten percent loss of bear populations nationwide. Although it may seem like a small percentage, that loss has long-term impact, because each bear killed by hunters and poachers is then prevented from reproducing and contributing to population growth.

III. Introduction of evaluative criteria

Once all solutions have been introduced and described, the writer introduces criteria used to evaluate solutions and arrive at the best one:

> Which solution protects both bears and their habitat? Which one is the most cost-effective? Which solution has the clearest long-term impact on preserving bear populations?

IV. Elimination of alternatives and identification of favored solution

Evaluative criteria are applied to each solution, emphasizing the merits of the favored solution:

> While each possible solution has certain advantages, only limitations on suburban sprawl will have immediate impact on grizzly survival and preserve grizzly habitat for years to come.

Pattern 4: Time

Writers use *temporal* (or time-based) organization to explain issues and ideas as they are connected historically or chronologically.

For example, to analyze the effects of online social organizations (such as *Facebook* and *MySpace*), a writer might open with the earliest examples of online communities (MUDs and newsgroups), then examine their evolution to the present. How have technological changes (Internet speed, wireless Internet connections), social changes (increased personal access to computers), and economic changes (lowering cost of personal computers) affected online communities and their values over time? Are there other social changes (fragmenting families, geographically divided friends, and so on) that, while not directly related to online communities, are nonetheless affected by them?

INTEGRATING VISUAL ELEMENTS INTO AN ARGUMENT

When appropriate, consider incorporating *visual elements* into your argument. These include tables and graphs; diagrams, charts, and figures; and photographs and drawings. Visual elements also include boxes, highlighting, shading, strategic use of white space on the page, colored text, and other design features.

For example, Marcus wrote his final research project on digital photography, but knew that many readers, including his instructor, would not be familiar with important techniques and their history. In the passage below, Marcus integrates argument and illustrations to support his claim that digital photography is a credible art form:

Photographs were being manipulated long before technology for digital media was available. Examples of pre-digital manipulation can be seen in works such as Oscar G. Rejlander's *The Two Ways of Life*, which was done in 1857 and composed of many models being photographed individually and then merged together for one grand scene, and the famous surrealistic landscapes of Jerry Uelsmann, which were all cleverly pieced together from negatives in a dark room in the 1960s.

FIGURE 1 Jerry Uelsmann, *Untitled,* 1969.

FIGURE 2 Jerry Uelsmann, *Untitled,* 1975.

Thinking of this and the examples of altered film photographs listed previously, Bardis agrees with Pedro Meyer, a once traditional photographer who now works exclusively with digital, when he said: "Now with a heightened awareness with what digital photography can accomplish, we are beginning to discover what photography was all along: the very act of deception" (Bardis 217).

Marcus clearly illustrates his point with concrete examples of "manipulated" photographs. As with any source material, he integrates relevant visual texts into his argument by:

> *Visual elements must be integrated through effective introduction, contextualization, and development.*

- Introducing the concept of photographic manipulation
- Describing an early instance of manipulation
- Providing examples from Uelsmann's work
- Connecting historical manipulations to today's digital photographers
- Including a quotation that reinforces his argument from an academic perspective

ENSURING CLARITY: PARAGRAPHS AND SENTENCES

You want to ensure that your writing reflects strong critical thinking. Effective elements of argument, organization, and development are your paper's most important aspects, its "higher order concerns."

You must also ensure that mechanical aspects, "lower order concerns," have been addressed before you submit a writing project. Clear, purposeful paragraphs and sentences, well chosen words, and effective punctuation will guide readers through your argument and ideas.

"Higher order" concerns include:
- *Purpose*
- *Claim*
- *Organization*
- *Development*

"Lower order" concerns include:
- *Word choice*
- *Grammar*
- *Punctuation*

Paragraphs

A paragraph is a set of sentences that together describe and develop a main idea. Often, the main idea is stated in a topic sentence, with other sentences in the paragraph relating clearly and logically to the topic. Strong paragraphs express both *unity* and *coherence*:

Unity means keeping sentences focused on the larger point of each paragraph, and paragraphs focused on the larger point of the entire essay. A unified paragraph develops, explains, and illustrates a point, using relevant support. A unified paper is one in which each part—individual paragraphs and groups of paragraphs—contributes to the thesis and purpose.

Be conscious of your paragraph's purpose: do you intend to

1. *summarize* a source's argument?
2. *define* a key term or concept?
3. *provide background* on an issue?
4. *synthesize* multiple approaches to an issue or question?
5. *evaluate or take a position* in a debate?
6. *transition* from one subtopic to another?

As you review your draft, consider whether readers will understand each paragraph's purpose.

- Will readers be able to connect each paragraph to your thesis?
- Should you break or join paragraphs in your draft? Is there a part—a sentence, an example, or a quotation—that doesn't fit

with the paragraph point? If so, consider deleting irrelevant elements, developing awkward parts into a new paragraph, or incorporating parts into an existing paragraph.

- Can you identify two or more paragraphs in your draft that, together, might make a more effective point? If so, consider combining them.

Coherence means ensuring that each sentence in a paragraph flows logically to the next, and is clearly connected to the sentences around it. A coherent essay follows a logical organizational pattern with paragraphs that develop from point to point, connected to each other with clear transitions.

- Does each sentence develop the paragraph point? Consider using transitional words to show the logical flow of sentences in a paragraph, such as those showing:

  - *cause and effect* (therefore, in turn, consequently)
  - *example* (for instance, for example, specifically)
  - *similarity* (likewise, similarly, also)
  - *contrast* (however, on the contrary, yet)
  - *emphasis* (in fact, indeed, moreover)

- Do sentences in your paragraph move from broad to specific claims? See the hourglass approach for writing coherent paragraphs in Chapter 6.
- Are examples clearly introduced and explained?
- Are quotations and paraphrases introduced and contextualized?
- Do you develop sources with your own ideas?

Sentences

A complete sentence links a *subject*, a person or thing that performs an action, with a *predicate*, a verb or verb phrase that expresses action:

Natalie read.

subject-verb (performer and action)

Natalie read the article.

subject-verb-direct object (this sentence includes the object of the action)

Simple sentences can be modified by adding words and phrases that further describe an event or situation:

> Preparing for class, Natalie read Tompkins's article from *Critical Inquiry*.

> As Tompkins found, historical researchers shifted their approaches between the 1960s and 1970s, when they began to reevaluate the relationship of Europeans to Native Americans.

Combining Short Sentences

When possible, combine two or more short sentences around a common idea, or into a single process.

Two sentences discussing a common idea:

> Up until this point I understood that "cognition" means mental processes. That seemed too basic.

These two sentences could be combined by developing the idea of "understanding":

> Up until this point I understood that "cognition" means mental processes, but that seemed too basic.

Two sentences describing a process:

> At the beginning of the paragraph, Tompkins compares essays by Hudson and Martin. She talks about how they take very different approaches to explaining Indian hunting practices.

These two sentences could be combined by describing the process Tompkins uses to compare and evaluate the essays:

> At the beginning of the paragraph, Tompkins compares essays by Hudson and Martin, showing how they take very different approaches to explaining Indian hunting practices.

Completing Fragment Sentences

Sentences missing either the subject or predicate are incomplete, and should be fully developed:

> For instance, Linkon's essay.
> *a subject (Linkon's essay) but no verb*
> Wrote the article on college students' expectations.
> *a verb (wrote) but no subject*

Such as addiction and habit, were used interchangeably throughout the article.

*even though there are a number of nouns here, the sentence still lacks a
subject*

In order to avoid incomplete (*fragment*) sentences:

- Ensure that each sentence has a subject and predicate.
- Identify and correct misplaced periods.

Add a verb: what does Linkon's essay *do*?

For instance, Linkon's essay describes important shifts in students'
expectations.

Add a subject: *who* wrote the article?

Sherry Linkon wrote the article on college students' expectations.

Add a subject: *who* used these terms interchangeably?

The authors introduced terms such as addiction and habit, which
they used interchangeably throughout the article.

A complete sentence may start with any word, but fragment sentences often begin with a *subordinate clause* (words like *because, when,
although,* and *while*) and are not completely developed.

Defining the elements and structure of mentoring programs was a
very important step toward establishing common ground for researchers to study programs' effectiveness. Although Karcher's
study only scratches the surface for research that could be done in
the future.

Karcher and colleagues define types of relationships well, showing
how mentors and mentees are matched based on social and economic status, age, race, and sometimes gender. Matching is also
determined by the type of program and the type of mentoring it is
designed to pursue. Which brings me to another question: where
do mentors come from?

To correct these fragments, either connect the subordinate clause
to an independent clause (one that can stand alone as a sentence), or revise the fragment into an independent clause that can stand on its own.

Defining the elements and structure of mentoring programs was a
very important step toward establishing common ground for
researchers to study programs' effectiveness, although Karcher's

study only scratches the surface for research that could be done in the future.

Karcher and colleagues define types of relationships well, showing how mentors and mentees are matched based on social and economic status, age, race, and sometimes gender. Matching is also determined by the type of program and the type of mentoring it is designed to pursue. After reading Karcher's essay, I still have one question: where do mentors come from?

Correcting Run-on Sentences

Sentences that incorrectly connect two independent clauses are *run-on*, and should be separated into two or more complete sentences.

Several experiments were performed removing food believed to aggravate hyperactive behavior, the results indicated positive outcomes.

Schnoll and colleagues reveal that "children presently consume between 40 and 50 teaspoons of sugar per day" in comparison previous studies used miniscule amounts of sucrose, most likely too small to have any notable effect on children's behavior (69).

In order to correct run-on sentences:

- Break the run-on into two complete sentences.
- Add a comma and conjunction (*and, but, or, nor*, etc.).

Several experiments were performed removing food believed to aggravate hyperactive behavior. In each case, the results indicated positive outcomes.

Several experiments were performed removing food believed to aggravate hyperactive behavior, and the results indicated positive outcomes.

Schnoll and colleagues reveal that "children presently consume between 40 and 50 teaspoons of sugar per day" (69). This high amount calls into question previous studies which used miniscule amounts of sucrose, most likely too small to have any notable effect on children's behavior.

Schnoll and colleagues challenge previous studies, which used miniscule amounts of sucrose, most likely too small to have any notable effect on children's behavior, when they reveal that "children presently consume between 40 and 50 teaspoons of sugar per day" (69).

Expressing Action, Time, and Emphasis with Verbs

Verbs are words that describe action. They also convey information to readers about time (*tense*), and whether a sentence's emphasis is placed on the subject or object (*voice*).

Tense

Your research writing projects will use some standard tenses to express the time in which action takes place:

Present	*Past*	*Future*
She finds useful material in each source.	She found five new sources.	She will find the most important passages to cite in her paper.
Popper describes the evolution of knowledge.	Popper described his experiences in Austria during the 1930s.	Popper will describe scientific progress between 1920 and 1950.
He observes the students at work.	He observed teacher behavior.	He will observe teacher-student interactions.

Research writers often describe the arguments and points in their sources as being made in the present, as in the student work below:

Tompkins **looks** at the parts of the captivity experience Rowlandson focuses on in her narrative, especially the role of Indians. Tompkins **points** out here that Rowlandson's views were really limited and did not describe the whole picture.

Past tense means that the action of the sentence happened and was completed in the past, as in this student writer's reflection:

When I first **saw** the Tompkins essay, I **thought** her point was unclear.

Voice

A verb's *voice* may be either active or passive. A sentence in the active voice places emphasis on the subject, or the doer of an action, while a sentence in the passive voice emphasizes the object of an action. For a simple distinction, consider the following active and passive versions of a sentence:

> Bill caught the ball.

> The ball was caught by Bill.

Active voice tends to be more direct and keeps the sentence focused on the people who or things that instigate action. There's nothing inherently wrong with passive voice, but passive sentences can seem vague and give readers the impression that actions simply happen without clear causes, or describe actions without people. In the following example, for instance, something "unscrupulous" is happening, but the people doing it appear incidental to the action:

> In online communities like *MySpace*, anonymity can be used by unscrupulous community members to disguise or hide important personal information, such as age and gender, from other members.

A writer who wants readers to understand how some *MySpace* members behave in unscrupulous ways might revise the passive sentence into an active one, thus emphasizing the doers of the action:

> In online communities like *MySpace*, unscrupulous members use anonymity to disguise or hide important personal information, such as age and gender, from other members.

Passive voice can be used to evade taking responsibility for an action, as in the following examples:

> A number of mistakes were made.

> The rest of the cake was eaten last night.

Active versions of these sentences might be:

> I made a number of mistakes.

> Julie ate the rest of the cake last night.

Shifting Emphasis with Passive Voice

The passive voice is often used in science writing, especially when writers want to emphasize the results of a study rather than researchers' efforts. For example, in a study of converting waste oil into auto fuel, engineers use the passive voice to describe their procedures:

> Primary decomposition was carried out in a tubular reactor (25 mm diameter and 500 mm long) filled with adsorbent (approximately 30 g) and externally heated by an electrical oven. The oil sample (around 13 g during each 1h run) was fed from a graduated glass column and injected into the reactor by the upper side using a pump.

This use of passive voice ensures that readers will focus on the experimental process rather than the researchers.

Pronouns and Pronoun Reference

Pronouns are generic nouns that stand in for other, more specific nouns, such as *she* for "Jane Tompkins," *they* for "Karcher and colleagues," or *it* for "Linkon's article." Because they are used as replacements, every pronoun must always clearly refer to a specific noun.

Pronouns help writers make statements more economically and avoid using the same noun repeatedly. Thus, a sentence like

> When Jane Tompkins read *Errand into the Wilderness*, Jane Tompkins began to develop Jane Tompkins's consideration of perspective in studying the history of European-Indian contact.

can be rewritten as

> When Jane Tompkins read *Errand into the Wilderness*, **she** began to develop **her** consideration of perspective in studying the history of European-Indian contact.

Even though the author replaced the noun with pronouns, the meaning remains clear. Sometimes, however, writers will use pronouns that do not clearly refer to a particular noun, as in this case:

> Although many parents have moved children into charter schools from public schools in the past few years, they rarely perform any better.

This is an example of *unclear pronoun reference*, because "they" could logically refer to either "children," who may not perform better in a different kind of school, or to "charter schools," which may not perform better than public schools. Depending on what the author means to compare, the sentence could be revised in two ways, by identifying either children or charter schools:

> Although many parents have moved children into charter schools from public schools in the past few years, children rarely perform any better.

> Although many parents have moved children into charter schools from public schools in the past few years, charter schools rarely perform any better than their public counterparts.

As you read and revise your papers or as you comment on a partner's draft, look especially for appearances of *it*, *that*, *this*, and *they*, common vaguely used pronouns. Ensure that a reader will know to what noun (or nouns) those pronouns refer. If you feel the pronoun reference may be vague, consider ways a sentence could be revised to make noun-pronoun reference as clear as possible.

"You" as a Generic Pronoun

Another example of vague pronoun use involves using "you" as a generic pronoun, as in the following examples:

> In my apartment you will often hear a wide variety of topics being discussed and debated.

> If you were reading that definition for the first time with no previous knowledge of the word, it would be very confusing.

Most of the time, writers who use "you" in this way are really describing their personal experiences or perceptions. In this case, "you" can be replaced with "I." This use of "you" as a generic pronoun also suggests a writer's assumption that his or her experiences are universal, and that the reader's experiences ought to be the same the same as the writer's. As you can probably imagine, if the writer's assumption is incorrect, it can distract readers or make them resistant to the writer's arguments and points.

The sentences above could be revised to describe individual experiences:

> In my apartment we often discuss and debate a wide variety of topics.

> Because I read that definition for the first time with no previous knowledge of the word, I was very confused.

Alternately, the sentences could be revised to describe a general claim, without assuming a reader's experience:

> Visitors to my apartment often hear a wide variety of topics being discussed and debated.

> Someone who read that definition for the first time with no previous knowledge of the word would probably be very confused.

STYLE

Redundancies and Wordiness

Identify places in early drafts where you are being redundant or are simply using more words than are necessary to express an idea. For instance, the following sentence is redundant because it expresses the same ideas repeatedly and unnecessarily.

> To finish off, the authors conclude by saying that they are trying to bridge the gap between economists' view of addiction and that of the sociological field by showing that the economists' view of repetition can be a precursor to the flow state.

Identify redundant phrases and ideas, such as "To finish off" and "conclude." Choose the best way to express your point and eliminate redundancies. Consider the following:

> The authors conclude by saying that they are trying to bridge the gap between economists' view of addiction and that of the sociological field by showing that the economists' view of repetition can be a precursor to the flow state.

Even though they are not redundant, sometimes a writer simply uses unnecessary words to express a simple idea. For example, the sentence

> There are some researchers who have challenged Finnegan's findings.

could be revised to express the same meaning more efficiently:

> Some researchers have challenged Finnegan's findings.

Note how the wordy connection between studies in the following sentence may confuse readers:

> Boschker and colleagues, as well as an additional outside source, relate with my experience when they state "Cordier, Mendes France, Blon, and Pailhous (1993) claimed that by means of route

finding, expert climbers are capable of 'producing a series of well-formed movements which are linked together into actual "sentences" and serve to structure the climber's motor behavior'" (27).

The author could revise by naming the purpose of the "relation" he finds between the source he read, his own experiences, and Boschker's source, in this way:

> Boschker and colleagues confirmed previous studies showing that "by means of route finding, expert climbers are capable of 'producing a series of well-formed movements which are linked together into actual "sentences" and serve to structure the climber's motor behavior'" (27).

Word Choice: Specialized Language or Jargon?

Academic writers use specialized language to describe the world. Sociologist Jonathan Kozol noticed among education specialists "a peculiar tendency to use a polysyllabic synonym for almost any plain and ordinary word: 'implement' for do, 'initiate' for start, 'utilize' for use" and so on. It's not that big or technical terms are wrong, but in Kozol's view, "big words that say nothing more than little words could say sometimes have the added benefit of making a circular statement sound like a real idea."

As you write, keep in mind that your readers may not share your familiarity with a particular academic conversation. You can appeal to your audience by avoiding unnecessary uses of *jargon*, a field's technical terms, when common words work just as well. Consider the following, a paraphrase from *Dora: An Analysis of a Case of Hysteria* by Sigmund Freud:

> Freud observed that the patient suffered from a tussis nervosa precipitated by a common catarrh.

Because Freud's Latin terms are unnecessary, the writer could just as easily substitute more common words which express the same meaning:

> Freud observed that the patient suffered from a cough caused by a runny nose.

Conversational Language

Avoid conversational language and development, as in the following example:

> The *Oxford Dictionary of Psychology* builds on the definition by stating that automatism "may be motor or verbal, and ranges from simple repetitive acts, such as lip smacking or repeatedly using the

same phrase (e.g., as it were), to complex activities, such as sleep-walking and automatic writing." So my initial, naïve understanding of automatism was that it was just simple bodily functions, but the academic definition explains that it can go far beyond that.

Here, the writer transitions from one sentence to another as he would in speaking. The second sentence should be rewritten using a more conventional transition:

> The *Oxford Dictionary of Psychology* builds on the definition by stating that automatism "may be motor or verbal, and ranges from simple repetitive acts, such as lip smacking or repeatedly using the same phrase (e.g., as it were), to complex activities, such as sleep-walking and automatic writing." While my initial, naïve understanding of automatism was that it was just simple bodily functions, the academic definition explains that it can go far beyond that.

SUBJECT-VERB AGREEMENT

Subject-verb agreement means ensuring that the sentence's subject and verb agree in *number* and *person*. "Number" describes whether a noun refers to one person or object (singular in number) or multiple people or objects (plural in number). "Person" describes the subject of the sentence as either first person (the person who is speaking), second person (the person spoken to), or third person (the person spoken about). The two concepts work together like this:

	Singular	*Plural*
First person	I	we
Second person	you	you
Third person	he/she/it	they

Agreement

Agreement means that the verb form used in a phrase or sentence is the correct one for the subject:

Singular:	He is a first grade teacher.
Plural:	They are first grade teachers.

Singular subject

Miller's book, *Errand into the Wilderness*, is the first source Tompkins reads.

(the book is)

Plural subject

Tompkins expected her primary sources to express a more unified perspective than the historians she studied.

(sources express)

Singular indefinite subject

Each source in Tompkins's essay illustrates a different perspective on many of the same facts.

(each illustrates)

Plural indefinite subject

All of the article's sources work together to prompt Tompkins's perspectivist conclusion.

(all work)

Parallel Construction

In a sentence that includes a list or compares items, similar grammatical forms and structures have to be used for each element and item. If the first item or phrase in a series or list uses a particular verb form, such as *–ing* or *to* with an infinitive verb, the other items or phrases will use the same form, as in:

Good decision-making abilities are important for apparently disconnected activities, such as driving a car, climbing a rock face, or choosing an apartment.

Tompkins found herself "not only unable to decide among conflicting versions of events but also unable to believe that any such decision could, in principle, be made."

Similarly, lists must be parallel:

After reading the articles, students will be able to

- identify a thesis
- form an opinion
- propose a solution to the problem

Techniques of academic research include the following:

1. Using local catalogue systems
2. Searching online databases
3. Selecting relevant sources
4. Understanding complex arguments

Comparisons also require parallel construction:

In the beginning of the research process, some students find navigating online databases easier than learning libraries' catalogue systems.

PUNCTUATION

Commas

Commas are used following a sentence's introductory words, phrases, and clauses, when they come before the main clause, as in these examples:

Introductory word

Generally, much was made of the Indian presence in Manhattan.

Introductory phrase

In simpler language, it concerns the difference that point of view makes when people are giving accounts of events, whether first or second hand.

Introductory clause

While explaining how he came to write his history of the New England mind, Miller writes a sentence that stopped me dead.

Commas are also used to separate elements in lists and processes.

Elements in a list

According to Kupperman, what concerned these writers most when they described the Indians were the insignia of social class, rank, and of prestige.

Elements in a process (here, an if-then relationship)

But if you are convinced that the alternative does not exist, that there are really no facts except as they are embedded in some particular way of seeing the world, then the argument that a set of facts derives from some particular worldview is no longer an argument against that set of facts.

This sentence describes a three-part process and concludes with a list:

It starts with trumped-up charges, is carried on through a series of increasingly bloody reprisals, and ends in massacres of scores of men, women, and children.

Apostrophes

Apostrophes are used to indicate *possession* (ownership) and *contraction* (combining two words into one).

Possessive nouns signify ownership.

Singular possession

The girl's dog caught the ball.

(one dog belonging to one girl)

The car's engine failed to start.

(one engine belonging to one car)

Plural possession

The girls' dog caught the ball.

(one dog belonging to two or more girls)

The cars' engines failed to start.

(engines belonging to two or more cars)

Possessives without apostrophes

his	ours
hers	yours
its	theirs

Apostrophes are never used to indicate plural nouns, unless they are also possessive.

She eventually took two months' vacation.

They started shopping by comparing many stores' prices.

Contractions are two words combined by an apostrophe:

Don't   (do + not)
It's   (it + is)
Won't   (will + not)

Since some people avoid contractions in written English, ask your instructor about his or her preference.

SPELLING: HOMOPHONES AND IDIOMS

Often, words are misspelled because writers attempt to spell them as they sound in speech:

I was able to put it into perceptive.

Rather than:

I was able to put it into perspective.

Use, but don't depend on, your spell-check program.

A word processor's spell check tool will not catch these kinds of misspellings because "perceptive" is a properly spelled word. It's likely, however, that you or a classmate would catch the mistake if the sentence were read out loud.

Commonly used phrases can pose particular problems. Because we hear them more often than we read them, they are easily misspelled. For example:

I should of gone to the store today.

I could of started writing last week.

In these instances, the author has written the phrases as they typically sound. However, in these and similar cases (phrases using *modal* verbs like *could*, *should*, and *must*), the correct expression is "have":

I should have gone to the store today.

I could have started writing last week.

A similar confusion is this:

I could care less about what they think.

Here, the meaning of the phrase is actually the opposite of the one intended by the author. The author has represented the phrase as it often sounds in speech; however, as used here, it implies that the author

---

Accept—to receive or agree, as in "He accepted the gift with grace," or "She accepted the judge's ruling."
Except—other than, as in "I like all colors except blue."

Affect—to influence, as in "Vertigo affects people differently."
Effect—a result, or to accomplish, as in "The effects of vertigo include disorientation," or "Congress finally effected change in minimum wage standards. "

Any more—refers to a number of things, as in "Are there any more places to see?"
Anymore—now, or henceforth, as in "He won't play ball with me anymore. "

Its—possessive form of *it*, as in "The car lost its tire."
It's—contraction of *it is*, as in "It's too late for sorry."

Role—a dramatic character, as in "As Juliet, she played her role to perfection."
Roll—a type of bread, or a verb showing motion, as in "These buttery rolls are delicious," or "The ball rolled down the hill."

Then—showing sequence or chronology, as in "We went to school, and then we went dancing."
Than—comparison, as in "Active sentences usually use fewer words than passive ones."

There—showing location, as in "She prefers to stand over there."
Their—possessive form of *they*, as in "Their train left early."
They're—contraction of *they are*, as in "They're leaving early to catch the train. "

To—showing location or movement, as in "He went from the mall to the post office."
Too—addition or excess, as in "I went there and she went there too," or "That fourth drink was just too much."

Where—showing location, as in "Where should we go Saturday night?"
Were—a verb, as in "They were planning a party for her."

Whose—possessive form of *who*, as in "Whose clothes are in the dryer?"
Who's—contraction of *who is*, as in "Who's planning to come along?"

Your—possessive form of *you*, as in "Are these your clothes in the dryer?"
You're—contraction of *you are*, as in "You're in trouble now!"

FIGURE 14. 3   Commonly misspelled words.

does care about the issue, rather than the meaning the phrase is used to express. Thus, the common phrase correctly written is:

I could not (or couldn't) care less about what they think.

A third confusion, which is known as a *malapropism*, is writing idioms and other commonly used metaphors and figures of speech as they sound, such as:

It's a doggie dog world out there.

He tried repeatedly, but eventually gave up the goat.

CAPITALIZATION

Titles of books, articles, and other texts are typically capitalized. Proper nouns, such as individuals' names and their titles, nationalities and ethnic groups, trade names, historical periods, and events given names are all capitalized:

Names and titles:

Sigmund Freud, Albert Einstein; Doctor Freud, Professor Einstein

Nationalities and ethnic groups

Canadians, South Africans, Asian Americans, Hutus and Tutsis

Trade names

Xerox, Coke

Historical periods and events

China's Three Kingdoms era, the Weimar Republic; the Revolutionary War, the Great Depression

Endnotes

Chapter 1

1. Burke, Kenneth. *The Philosophy of Literary Form*. New York: Vintage, 1957. Print. [pp. 94, 95–96].
2. Friere, Paulo. *Pedagogy of the Oppressed*. New York: Continuum, 1998. Print.
3. Popper, Karl. *The Myth of the Framework*. London: Routledge, 1994. Print. [pp. 100; 140–41].
4. Davis, Robert, and Mark Shadle. "Building a Mystery: Alternative Research Writing and the Academic Act of Seeking." *CCC* 51.3 (2000): 417–46. Print. [pp. 439–40].

Chapter 2

1. Ciment, James, ed. *Colonial America: An Encyclopedia of Social, Political, Cultural, and Economic History*. Armonk NY: Sharpe Reference, 2005. Print. [pp. 954, 1013]
2. Ciment, James, ed. *Colonial America: An Encyclopedia of Social, Political, Cultural, and Economic History*. Armonk NY: Sharpe Reference, 2005. Print. [pp. 954, 1013]
3. Henretta, James A., David Brody, and Lynn Dumenil. *America: A Concise History*. Boston: Bedford/St. Martin's, 2005. [pp. 61–62]
4. Loewen, James. *Lies My Teacher Told Me*. New York: Touchstone, 1995. [pp. 84, 85]
5. Loewen, James. *Lies My Teacher Told Me*. New York: Touchstone, 1995. [pp. 84, 85].
6. Hatton, John, and Paul Plouffe. *Science and its Ways of Knowing*. Upper Saddle River, NJ: Prentice Hall 1997.

Chapter 3

1. Eriksson, Erik. "An Object-Oriented Model of the Writing Process." Web. http://spadassin.ling.umu.se/~erike/papers/conferncepaper/pdf>. [p. 2]
2. Tompkins, Jane. "'Indians': Textualism, Morality, and the Problem of History." *Critical Inquiry* 13.1 (1986): 101–19
3. Gage, John. *The Shape of Reason*. Boston: Allyn and Bacon, 2001. Print. [p. 19]
4. *New Webster's Dictionary*
5. *New Webster's Dictionary*
6. *Wikipedia*
7. Brix, H. James, ed. *The Encyclopedia of Anthropology*. Thousand Oaks, CA: Sage, 2006. [pp. 854–55].

8. American Psychological Association. *Oxford Encyclopedia of Psychology*. Ed. Allan E. Kadzin. New York: Oxford, 2000. [p. 377]

Chapter 4

1. "Surveillance, New York Style." *New York Times* 23 Dec. 2005: A26.

Chapter 5

1. Marie Evans Schmidt and Elizabeth Vanderwater, "Media and Attention, Cognition, and School Achievement," *The Future of Children* 18.1 (2008): 63–85.

Chapter 6

1. Lieberman, Trudy. Homeland Security: What We Don't Know Can Hurt Us." *Columbia Journalism Review* 43.3 (2004): 24–31. Print. [p. 26].
2. Gomez, James. "Dumbing Down Democracy: Trends in Internet Regulation, Surveillance, and Control in Asia." *Pacific Journalism Review* 10.2 (2004): 130–50.
3. Gomez, James. "Dumbing Down Democracy: Trends in Internet Regulation, Surveillance, and Control in Asia." *Pacific Journalism Review* 10.2 (2004): 130–50.
4. Bellia, Patricia L. "Spyware and the Limits of Surveillance Law." *Berkeley Technology Law Journal* 20.3 (2005): 1283–1344.
5. Tuhkanen, Mikko. "Of Blackface and Paranoid Knowledge: Richard Wright, Jacques Lacan, and the Ambivalence of Black Minstrelsy." *Diacritics* 31.2 (2001): 9–34.
6. Linkon, Sherry. "The Reader's Apprentice: Making Critical Cultural Reading Visible." *Pedagogy* 5.2 (2005): 247–73. Print. [pp. 247–49]
7. Baruh, Lemi. "Audience Surveillance and the Right to Anonymous Reading in Interactive Media." *Knowledge, Technology, and Policy* 17.1 (2004)
8. Niedzviecki, Hal. *Hello, I'm Special: How Individuality Became the new Conformity*. San Francisco: City Lights, 2006. Print. [pp. 141–42]
9. Sidney, Philip. "An Apology for Poetry." *Critical Theory Since Plato* Ed. Hazard Adams. New York: Harcourt, 1992. 142–62. Print. [p. 145].

Chapter 8

1. Blum, Virginia L. "Objects of Love: *I Want a Famous Face* and the Illusions of Star Culture." Configurations 15 (2007): 33–53
2. Talbot, Margaret. "Darwin in the Dock." *The New Yorker* (5 December 2005): 66–77. Print. [p. 68]
3. Antolin, Michael F., and Joan M. Herbers. "Evolution's Struggle for Existence in America's Public Schools." *Evolution* 55.12 (2001): 2379–88. Print. [p. 2380]
4. Marx, Gary T. "What's New about the 'New Surveillance'?: Classifying for Change and Continuity." *Knowledge, Technology, & Policy* 17.1 (2004): 18–37.

5. "Theory." *Academic Press Dictionary of Science and Technology*. San Diego, CA: Academic Press, 1996.

Chapter 9

1. Bartholomae, David. *Writing on the Margins*. New York: Bedford-St. Martin's 2005. Print. [pp. 60–61, 67, 194]
2. Flower, Linda. "Preface." In Linda Flower, et al., *Reading to Write: Exploring a Cognitive and Social Process*. New York: Oxford UP, 1990.
3. Linkon, Sherry. "The Reader's Apprentice: Making Critical Cultural Reading Visible." *Pedagogy* 5.2 (2005): 247–73. Print. [pp. 247–49]

Chapter 12

1. Hart, Kylo-Patrick. "We're Here, We're Queer—and We're Better Than You: The Representational Superiority of Gay Men to Heterosexuals on Queer Eye for the Straight Guy." *Journal of Men's Studies* 12.3 (2004): 241–253. Print. [p. 242]
2. Hart, Kylo-Patrick. "We're Here, We're Queer—and We're Better Than You: The Representational Superiority of Gay Men to Heterosexuals on Queer Eye for the Straight Guy." *Journal of Men's Studies* 12.3 (2004): 241–253.
3. King, Nicholas B. "The Influence of Anxiety: September 11, Bioterrorism, and American Public Health." *Journal of the History of Medicine and Allied Sciences* 58.4 (2003)
4. Bourdon, Jérôme. "Some Sense of Time: Remembering Television." *History and Memory* 15.2 (2003): 5–35.
5. Bourdon, Jérôme. "Some Sense of Time: Remembering Television." *History and Memory* 15.2 (2003): 5–35.
6. Taylor, Chris, and Annabelle James. "Video Games: Some Pitfalls of Video Evidence." *Journal of Criminal Law* 69.3 (2005): 264–76
7. Gunders, John. "'Here's Lookin' at You': Video Surveillance and the Interpellated Body." *Social Alternatives* 19.1 (2000): 22–26. Web.

Index

Credits

PHOTO CREDITS

TEXT CREDITS